Time and Commodity Culture

ESSAYS IN CULTURAL THEORY AND POSTMODERNITY

JOHN FROW

CLARENDON PRESS · OXFORD
1997

Oxford University Press, Great Clarendon Street, Oxford OX2 6DP

Oxford New York

Athens Auckland Bangkok Bogota Bombay
Buenos Aires Calcutta Cape Town Dar es Salaam
Delhi Florence Hong Kong Istanbul Karachi
Kuala Lumpur Madras Madrid Melbourne
Mexico City Nairobi Paris Singapore
Taipei Tokyo Toronto
and associated companies in
Berlin Ibadan

Oxford is a trade mark of Oxford University Press

Published in the United States
by Oxford University Press Inc., New York

British Library Cataloguing in Publication Data
Data available

Library of Congress Cataloging in Publication Data
Data available
ISBN 0–19–8159471
ISBN 0–19–815948–X (Pbk)

1 3 5 7 9 10 8 6 4 2

Typeset by Cambrian Typesetters, Frimley, Surrey
Printed in Great Britain on acid-free paper by
Bookcraft Ltd, Midsomer Norton, Somerset

PN
98
1P67
F76
1997

Acknowledgements

I speak in one of these essays of the list as postmodernism's preferred genre for organizing both itself and the universe. The list is partial, potentially infinite, and always arbitrary, and this one certainly has all of those characteristics. But here goes.

Many people have helped in the writing of these essays. I have probably spoken most of what follows, in paraphrase or verbatim, to my classes, which means they have been scrutinized, criticized, puzzled over, and extensively reshaped by my undergraduate and postgraduate students. I have also presented much of this material more formally in seminars and conferences, where a similar process of criticism and reformulation has gone on; I am particularly grateful for an invitation from Rey Chow and Alex Gelley to present the gist of 'Gift and Commodity' to a series of seminars organized by the Critical Theory Emphasis at the University of California, Irvine, in 1995, which allowed me to get a better sense of what that essay was doing. The editors of a number of journals, and publishers' readers of the various stages through which the manuscript of this book passed, have also made substantial contributions to its structure and to the detail of its argument. May I give particular thanks, though, to the following friends who have been particularly generous in the sharing of this work: Tony Bennett, Anne Freadman, Larry Grossberg, Ian Hunter, Noel King, Meaghan Morris, Stephen Muecke, Tim Rowse, Ken Ruthven, Lesley Stern, Nicholas Thomas, Helen Tiffin, and Graeme Turner.

Eleanor Frow and Christine Alavi proved themselves to be excelsior persons.

A previous version of Chapter 1 was published as an occasional paper by Local Consumption Publications. Versions of the other essays have been published in: *October*; *South Atlantic Quarterly*; *UTS Review*; *New Left Review*; *Cardozo Studies in Law and Literature*; Frank Lentricchia (ed.), *Introducing Don DeLillo* (Durham: Duke University Press, 1991); Ian Adams and Helen Tiffin (eds.), *Past the Last Post: Theorizing Postcolonialism and*

Postmodernism (Calgary and Hertfordshire: University of Calgary Press/Harvester Wheatsheaf, 1990); Leigh Dale and Simon Ryan (eds.), *The Body in the Library* (Amsterdam: Rodopi, 1996); Helen Grace (ed.), *Aesthesia and the Economy of the Senses* (Sydney: University of Western Sydney, 1996); and David Perkins (ed.), *Theoretical Issues in Literary History*, Harvard Studies in English Literature (Cambridge, Mass.: Harvard University Press, 1991). I am grateful to the editors for permission to reprint.

Contents

Introduction   1

1. What Was Postmodernism?   13

2. Tourism and the Semiotics of Nostalgia   64

3. Gift and Commodity   102

4. *Toute la mémoire du monde*: Repetition and
   Forgetting   218

Bibliography   247

Index   273

Introduction

'We have never been modern', writes Bruno Latour;[1] meaning that the world has never conformed to the model of a universal rupture which, at a certain moment, would have divided historical time into two great blocs: on the one side the 'hybridizing' societies of the old world, where things and people were interrelated, where words had causal force, where practical knowledge was separate neither from power nor from cosmology; and on the other, the 'purifying' societies of modernity, in which knowledge and power become quite separate domains, words describe the world rather than performing it, and material things are ontologically distinct from the people who make use of them.

There was no rupture; 'modernity has never begun' (p. 47). The logic of Latour's argument is that the institution of modernity (and of its necessary successor, postmodernity) is the effect of a process of back-projection in which the present constructs itself as a unity of all present time by distinguishing itself from a stable and archaic past which has a singular form. The primary work of the concept of modernity is thus not to describe a delimited period containing a particular and homogeneous set of contents, but rather to cut across the knot of heterogeneous strands of time in such a way as to produce the stabilities and unities of a now and a then. What is at stake is not so much the reality of the 'then' as the establishment of a division within the present which is at the same time a geopolitical division: as Naoki Sakai argues, the pairing of the modern and the premodern opposes modernity at once to its own historical past and to the non-West. It thereby produces a synthetic contrast between a West which is quintessentially modern, and a non-West which is quintessentially premodern.[2]

---

[1] Bruno Latour, *We Have Never Been Modern*, trans. Catherine Porter (Hemel Hempstead: Harvester/Wheatsheaf, 1993); hereafter cited in the text.

[2] Naoki Sakai, 'Modernity and its Critique: The Problem of Universalism and Particularism', *South Atlantic Quarterly*, 87: 3 (1988), 476; hereafter cited in the text.

In this process, the 'West' (which of course is not a stable geographical or cultural location but a geopolitical myth) comes to constitute 'the universal point of reference in relation to which others recognize themselves as particularities' (p. 477), and this imaginary point is in turn the condition of possibility for a number of strategies of power: the strategies of primitivization that have regulated the relations of the imperial centre to its others; the strategy of contrasting development with backwardness which organizes the planning of programmes of economic 'modernization' by the international monetary agencies and by Third World governments themselves; but also the strategies of idealization of or lament for a lost past which displace political action to the outbreak of a future in which time will be redeemed.

A classic version of this strategy of cultural description is elaborated in Schiller's *Naive and Sentimental Poetry* (1796).[3] It works like this. First, there is the projection of a 'division in ethical substance'[4] between nature and culture, between the 'naive' immediacy of unselfconscious Being and the alienation from Being of reflexive or 'sentimental' consciousness. Second, this division is laid out in time: the naive is conceived nostalgically, as what is lost (childhood) or as the past within the present ('the customs of country folk and the primitive world') (p. 83); the 'sentimental' poet, by contrast, is always belated, always an aftercomer. The third moment in this strategy then involves playing out the tensions that have been set up in order to bring them to a point of reconciliation—in Schiller's case within a projected and never fully attainable future that 'takes up' at a higher level the original moment of immediacy. Schiller's account is of course a good deal more complex than this, because it quickly turns out that the category of the naive (of immediacy) is necessarily a mediated category: the natural is what is 'taken by us as such' (p. 83), and is thus always internal to a 'sentimental' perspective. Moreover, as the argument progresses, the moral complexity of the balance between the two categories, as well as the logical complexity of the

---

[3] Friedrich von Schiller, *Naive and Sentimental Poetry*, trans. Julius A. Elias (New York: Ungar, 1966); *Über Naive und Sentimentalische Dichtung, Werke in Drei Bänden* (Munich: Hanser, 1966).

[4] Ian Hunter, *Culture and Government: The Emergence of Literary Education* (London: Macmillan, 1988), 6.

mediations between them, increases. Nevertheless, the underlying structure of the strategy is clearly defined and has been exemplary for later accounts of cultural modernity.

Such a periodizing division is not, of course, an illusion. It is an operation; it performs a certain work, it makes certain things possible, including some of the forms of difference from the past (the *various* pasts) that it imagines as given in the order of things. John Law thus argues about the dualistic structures that organize modernity (both temporal dualisms and, for example, the mind/body dualism that organizes metaphors of reflexivity) that to turn away from them

doesn't mean that we should ignore the ordering strains *towards* dualism built into the modern project. Instead, we should seek to treat dualism as a social *project*, a sociological topic, rather than treating it as a resource. Accordingly, the argument is that modernism [i.e. modernity] more or less successfully (though partially and precariously) *generates* and performs a series of such divisions.[5]

It is perfectly valid to talk about the ways in which many contemporary societies differ from many other societies past and present. Nor of course do I want to deny the scope and intensity of the changes that have taken place in the world over the last several centuries. But such changes do not consolidate into the vast binary opposition through which 'modernity' is defined as an essential tranche of historical time. It is a matter, rather, of thinking in terms of continuous shifts and of partial continuities running through multiple strands of time. 'Archaic' societies can then be seen to be no less complex and no less informed by highly abstract systems, 'modern' societies to be no less informed by 'magical' and cosmological modes of thinking, their knowledges no less structured by desire. It is thenceforth possible to abandon the topoi of a state of nature and a fallen world which have formed the basis of the social contract of modernity.

The four essays collected in this book represent an attempt to find a way through a historical situation which I reluctantly call postmodernity, and which (without any originality) I see as an exacerbation of the figure of modernity. My concern is not to 'explain' postmodernity and postmodernism, but rather to analyse

[5] John Law, *Organizing Modernity* (Oxford: Basil Blackwell, 1994), 138.

the process of periodization which constitutes them, and which does so in a way directly homologous to the constitution of modernity through its opposition to a surpassed historical stage. It is the content of this formal structure that interests me: its imagining of time.

At the heart of most theories of the postmodern is an account, in one form or another, of the extension of commodification to many areas of life. In the first of these essays, 'What Was Postmodernism?', I explore the structured anxiety about the commodification of culture that we call 'postmodern theory'; and in the longest of the four essays, 'Gift and Commodity', I analyse two areas in which the speed of commodification has increased markedly in recent years: that of the person, and that of information. I look in particular at such things as the development of markets in human DNA, in human organs, and in the human 'personality'; and at private property rights in information including the codes of the human genome and of plant varieties, and more generally in the commons in information. While I take these to be real processes, embedded in discourses with great social authority and having direct consequences on human lives, it is also important to say that the concept of the commodity is not itself 'real': it is a theoretical fiction which is more or less useful for setting up explanatory metaphors. It has historically been an extremely powerful fiction, and it has been intimately connected to the cultural vision of modernity against which the book is directed.

Let me elaborate briefly on this connection by looking at its development in an influential text, Guy Debord's *The Society of the Spectacle* (1967).

The dissolution of the Situationist International in 1972, writes Peter Wollen, brought to an end 'the epoch of the historic avant-gardes with their typical apparatus of international congress, quarrels, scandals, indictments, expulsions, polemics, group photographs, little magazines, mysterious episodes, provocations, utopian theories and intense desires to transform art, society, the world and the pattern of everyday life'.[6] One of the last splinter groups of the dying Surrealist Movement, the Situationist International was a

---

[6] Peter Wollen, 'Bitter Victory: The Situationist International', in Iwona Blazwick (ed.), *An Endless Adventure . . . An Endless Passion . . . An Endless Banquet: A Situationist Scrapbook* (London: ICA/Verso, n.d.), 10.

small and ultra-sectarian grouping[7] which recruited 'only geniuses' to carry out its avant-gardist task[8] and was productive of innumerable manifestos, 'theses', and 'tendencies', a direct line of influence from Lukács's *History and Class Consciousness* to the Sex Pistols,[9] and a critique of the commodity form which has become a major piece of cult theory.

The Society of the Spectacle is structured as a numbered series of discontinuous theses, aphoristic statements which are neither arguments nor dialogue but authoritative pronouncements. At its core is a critique of representation. The epitaph from Feuerbach speaks of the 'present age' as one 'which prefers the sign to the thing signified, the copy to the original, representation to reality, the appearance to the essence';[10] in Debord's analysis the 'present age' is defined in more precise terms as a set of social relations of production, and the 'sign', 'copy', and so on reappear as the category of the 'spectacle': the fetishized form of the commodity in a system of representation which is in part to be understood as the system of the mass media, including advertising and design; in part more specifically as the social force of television (which can often be directly substituted for the word 'spectacle'); but at times more generally as the visual, or the forms taken by the gaze within a consumer-capitalist society. As Martin Jay notes, Debord's critique of commodity fetishism has strong links to the puritan critique of idolatry.[11]

Thus in the broadest terms the book's argument is that the

---

[7] 'In its fifteen-year history, only seventy people had actually been official members, and because of the frequency of splits and exclusions, never more than twenty belonged at a time'; particularly vicious campaigns were waged against the 'Nashists', the followers of the renegade Jorgen Nash. Martin Jay, *Downcast Eyes: The Denigration of Vision in Twentieth-Century French Thought* (Berkeley: University of California Press, 1993), 430.

[8] Michèle Bernstein, 'The Situationist International', in Blazwick, *An Endless Adventure . . . An Endless Passion . . . An Endless Banquet*, 61.

[9] Greil Marcus traces the line of affinities and influence running (not necessarily just in a forward direction) between punk rock, the Situationist International, and its even more violently sectarian predecessor, the Lettrist International, in *Lipstick Traces: A Secret History of the Twentieth Century* (Cambridge, Mass.: Harvard University Press, 1989).

[10] Ludwig Feuerbach, Preface to the Second Edition of *The Essence of Christianity*, cited in Guy Debord, *The Society of the Spectacle*, trans. Donald Nicholson-Smith (New York: Zone Books, 1995 [1967]), 11. Future citations from Debord are to the thesis numbers rather than page numbers.

[11] Martin Jay, *Downcast Eyes*, 419.

modern world 'presents itself as an immense accumulation of *spectacles*. All that was once directly lived has become mere representation' (1). Detached from the former unity of life, images are rearticulated and made autonomous, in such a way that reality becomes 'a pseudo-world apart' (2). Grounded in the commodity, an 'illusion which is in fact real', the spectacle 'is its most general form' (47), corresponding 'to the historical moment at which the commodity completes its colonization of social life' (42). Standing both as an expressive part of and simultaneously quite separate from the world, the spectacle 'is both the outcome and the goal of the dominant mode of production'; as news or propaganda, advertising or entertainment, it 'epitomizes' social life, is 'the very heart of society's real unreality' (6).

This centrality of the spectacle derives in part from the increasing integration of 'cultural' processes and 'cultural' goods into the system of production—a thesis that anticipates more recent accounts of post-Fordist capitalism. The spectacle is thus at once appearance (*Schein*, packaging, the surface of things);[12] the visual projection of a logic of production; and itself a sector of production (15). If it can be understood as '*capital* accumulated to the point where it becomes image' (34), then the logic of mass culture that it embodies is in no way merely technological: the technical 'apparatus' of the mass media 'answers precisely to the needs of the spectacle's internal dynamics' (24), a dynamics of separation and abstraction.

Abstraction is an operation performed upon the immediacy and unity of 'lived experience' (37): 'The origin of the spectacle lies in the world's loss of unity, and its massive expansion in the modern period demonstrates how total this loss has been: the abstract nature of all individual work, as of production in general, finds perfect expression in the spectacle, whose very *manner of being*

---

[12] The spectacularity of the commodity form becomes entangled, in many later writers, in an implicit gendering of the opposition between depth and surface. Cf. Roberto Finelli, 'Production of Commodities and Production of the Image: Reflections on Modernism and Postmodernism', trans. Lorenzo d'Auria, *Rethinking Marxism*, 5: 1 (1992), 50–1: 'In the postmodernist era, things—mass-consumed commodities—become more and more sheer occasions for capital's realization and less and less the means for satisfying the natural and cultural needs of human beings. Things progressively become less authentic and lose their use qualities; they turn into superficial, rapidly seductive, and consumable commodities.' They turn—in Finelli's sexist imaginary—into women.

concrete is, precisely, abstraction' (29). Ruling over the 'living value' of human labour, the spectacle represents that ghostly animation of dead systems that Hegel spoke of in the *Jenenser Realphilosophie* in describing money as 'the life, moving of itself, of that which is dead', a principle which Debord says 'has now been extended by the spectacle to the entirety of social life' (215).

Time and space now too become entirely abstract categories, the architecture of a world which 'is at once *here* and *elsewhere*' (37). The time of the commodity is irreversible time: the time of things, and of mass production, the opposite at once of an earlier, cyclical time and of 'historical time lived by individuals and groups' (142). Now standardized across the world, it

is an infinite accumulation of equivalent intervals. It is irreversible time made abstract: each segment must demonstrate by the clock its purely quantitative equality with all other segments. This time manifests nothing in its effective reality aside from its *exchangeability*. . . . This is time devalued—the complete inversion of time as 'the sphere of human development'. (147)

In Debord's account of the commodity form become spectacular are to be found many of the constituents of later theories of postmodernity: the replacement of depth by surface and of reality by the simulacrum; the inauthenticity of the subject form; the spatialization of time; the rule of abstraction over everyday life. What his work makes particularly clear is the dependence of such accounts upon an operation of division which opposes representation *as such* to the immediacy and unity of life, and which sets the latter pole within a lost past. 'Many accounts of modernity view the world retrospectively, in sadness':[13] *a fortiori*, many accounts of postmodernity mourn a loss of history and of memory. Debord's 'spectacle' is 'the reigning social organization of a paralysed history, of a paralysed memory, of an abandonment of any history founded in historical time' (158); elsewhere he writes that 'the first priority in the spectacle's domination is to obliterate all knowledge of history', to impose upon us 'a world without memory'.[14] It is a

---

[13] Rey Chow, *Writing Diaspora: Tactics of Intervention in Contemporary Cultural Studies* (Bloomington: Indiana University Press, 1993), 41.

[14] Guy Debord, extract from *Commentaires sur la société du spectacle*, in Blazwick, *An Endless Adventure . . . An Endless Passion . . . An Endless Banquet*, 95.

mode of argument, as Susan Stewart writes, 'whereby a surface is projected so that a profundity can be lost—or perhaps more aptly, so that a profundity can be restored in a utopian and futuristic politics of deferral'.[15]

This is the linkage between history, memory, and the theorization of postmodernity that I try to work through in these essays. In refusing the historicism of Debord's narrative, I refuse as well the generalized denunciation of the commodity form in so far as it works as a historico-philosophical principle; I refuse the critique of representation as abstraction, and I refuse the narrative teleology that relegates real history and the time of lived experience to a time before representation and the mass-mediated spectacle. This is to say that I refuse the epochal coherence assigned to the world by an expressive conception of modernity.

If the world is not to be understood in terms of such an epochal coherence, however, then what other means are available to us for thinking about its temporal organization? Consider a parallel critique of the periodization of 'modernity' in anthropology: Johannes Fabian's *Time and the Other*. Anthropology, Fabian argues, 'is a science of other men in another time',[16] since its founding category of the 'primitive' (or its cognate terms: 'savage', 'tribal', 'traditional', and so on) is essentially a temporal concept derived from a social-evolutionist model: the peoples it studies in the present are assumed to belong, in some sense, to the past. At the same time, however, this temporal distancing involves a simple denial of the fact that 'anthropology's Other is, ultimately, other people who are our contemporaries' (p. 143). This denial of *coevalness* has political as well as intellectual conditions of existence, and makes the discipline of anthropology complicit with a repression or subordination of difference in the name of difference itself.

The relativization of times flows from a relativization of cultures. Fabian accuses cultural relativism (that is, the insistence that each cultural system is self-contained and possesses both its own structure of time and specific regularities of which its members— but not the outside observer—are unaware) of being unable to

---

[15] Susan Stewart, *Crimes of Writing: Problems in the Containment of Representation* (New York: Oxford University Press, 1991), 279.

[16] Johannes Fabian, *Time and the Other: How Anthropology Makes its Object* (New York: Columbia University Press, 1983), 143.

answer the political question of the relation between disparate times, disparate social structures, and disparate modes of knowledge. The concept of coevalness or cotemporality is intended to specify the conditions under which the interests of both 'observed' and 'observer' societies can be put into relation. Coevalness is assumed to be grounded in the shared intersubjective time that precedes all more culturally specific experiences of time, and it is this that opens the way for 'truly dialectical confrontation' (p. 154).

The word coevalness is equivalent to the German *Gleichzeitigkeit*, and is meant to include the senses both of co-occurrence in physical time (synchronicity) and of co-occurrence in typological or epochal time (contemporaneity). The problem with it is that it seems to posit the present as pure presence, as what Kubler calls a 'radial design conferring its meaning upon all the pieces' rather than as 'a mosaic of pieces in different developmental states, and of different ages'.[17] Its counter-concept, *Ungleichzeitigkeit* (non-synchronicity, the uneven layering of times within any historical formation) seems to me in fact to provide a more adequate way of understanding the *unequal* relations that hold within a synchronic framework characterized by uneven development and a global division of labour.[18] 'Not everyone occupies the same Now', is the way Ernst Bloch tersely pre-empts Fabian:[19] it is not necessary to posit a common human experience of time in order to speak of the interlinkage of political and economic destinies.[20]

The end of modernity, or the refusal of the simple division in time that the concept works to achieve, is an end of history and the beginning of many histories. This end is radically different from the closure envisaged by Fukuyama:[21] it is neither the climactic self-

[17] George Kubler, *The Shape of Time* (New Haven: Yale University Press, 1962), 28.

[18] Cf. Siegfried Kracauer, *History: The Last Things before the Last* (New York: Oxford University Press, 1969), esp. 147–55.

[19] Ernst Bloch, 'Ungleichzeitigkeit und Pflicht zu ihrer Dialektik', in *Erbschaft dieser Zeit* (1935; repr. Frankfurt: Suhrkamp, 1962), 104.

[20] Indeed, as Bloch shows in his analysis of the different temporal trajectories occupied by different classes in fascist and pre-fascist Germany, understanding the non-convergence (or rather the *partial* convergence) of times may be the necessary prerequisite to understanding the dynamics of a complex system.

[21] To the contrary: for Fukuyama it is precisely the existence of a rational and teleological process that makes such an end of History possible as its culmination. Francis Fukuyama, *The End of History and the Last Man* (New York: Avon Books, 1992).

recognition of Spirit in free-market capitalism nor the shattering of the global into a myriad of dispersed and local narratives. It is, precisely, a question of the *linkage* of unequal times in the contingent, shifting, and relatively unstable orderings—political, economic, cultural—which make up our entangled world, and which, while organized as goal-seeking structures, drive towards no predetermined end.

This move away from the essential unities and the singular time of historicism, with its 'linear equivalence of event and idea'[22]—a move for which, again, I claim no originality: it is to be found in many areas of contemporary work—offers the chance to open up a number of conceptual fields that had been stabilized and simplified by the concept of modernity. 'The whole apparatus of levels, standards, hierarchies, boundaries, limits, centres and sources needs to be rethought', writes Peter Wollen.[23] The attempt to do so underlies the detailed analyses in this book: the exploration of the commodity form, for example, as a relational structure which, rather than being readable as a constant function, is here understood as possessing different valencies in different contexts. The goal of the essay on gift and commodity exchange is thus to break down an opposition structured along the lines of that of the premodern to the modern, and instead to think about the way aspects of each type of exchange run through both 'traditional' and 'modern' societies; about the particular kinds of benefit or disbenefit wrought by the commodity form in societies of increasing commoditization; and about how such judgements might be made. In the same way, in the chapter on memory the question of Holocaust remembrance is edged away from the question of correct representation (important and necessary as that question continues to be in certain contexts) and towards a positing of the event of the Holocaust as a story that moves through and is put to diverse uses in historical time and space; memory is here understood as a reconstructive process which works against the irreversibility of time.[24]

---

[22] Homi Bhabha, 'Dissemination: Time, Narrative and the Margins of the Modern Nation', *The Location of Culture* (London: Routledge, 1994), 140.

[23] Peter Wollen, 'Ways of Thinking about Music Video (and Post-Modernism)', *Critical Quarterly*, 28: 1–2 (1986), 169.

[24] Jankélévitch is thus only half right in insisting on irreversibility as the defining feature of temporality ('L'irréversible n'est pas un caractère du temps parmi d'autres

My hope in writing these essays has been that these abstruse worries about the organization of time will, eventually, take me to the heart of the questions that confront us in a world torn apart by systemic dysfunction—questions about the destruction of work, about the increasing gap between the very rich and the desperately poor, about the destruction of wilderness, about the power of financial markets over national economies and national polities, about the increasing destruction of a public sphere that would control the prisoner's-dilemma game of private interests undermining the collective good. But I approach these questions obliquely, in a spirit of deep distrust of the realist genres of sociological, economic, and political description. I am by training a literary theorist, and what expertise I possess lies in the study of genres—that is, in the study of the way effects of the real and the authority to speak it are constituted by generic conventions and a generic frame.

Georg Lukács has written that the concern of the essay (a determinedly non-realist genre of writing) is with forms, understood as a central constituent of reality.[25] My writing in this book is essayistic to the extent that its concern is with the analysis of structuring processes rather than with structured substances. This is also, however, a matter of methodological purpose: I take it as axiomatic that cultural things cannot be understood in isolation from economic and political and technological things, and that the analytic objects I construct will be ontologically heterogeneous. The essay is the form in which I feel able to get at some of these complexities of connection, and to do so by groping my way towards a structure of explanation which cannot be defined in advance, rather than by enacting the certainty and the mastery that are inherent in the exhaustive and systematic analysis of a closed

---

caractères, il *est* la temporalité même du temps'). In doing so he reduces time to one of the scales by which it is measured, that of biological duration. Other scales (solar and lunar, and the circadian and ecological rhythms corresponding to them, but also biological duration at the level of the species) are cyclical, and the systems of writing and memory, as I argue in the final chapter, have to do, not with the storage of time, but with its representation and reconstruction, and thus with a temporality which is not inherently linear. Vladimir Jankélévitch, *L'Irréversible et la nostalgie* (Paris: Flammarion, 1974).

[25] Georg Lukács, *Soul and Form*, trans. Anna Bostock (Cambridge, Mass.: MIT Press, 1974), 8.

field. 'Even in the manner of its presentation, the essay may not act as though it had deduced its object and there was nothing left to say about it.'[26] I hope that these essays convey my conviction that there is a great deal more to be said.

[26] Theodor W. Adorno, 'The Essay as Form', *Notes to Literature*, Vol. i, trans. Shierry Weber Nicholsen, ed. Rolf Tiedemann (New York: Columbia University Press, 1991), 16.

I

What Was Postmodernism?

The edges of the earth trembled in a darkish haze. Upon it lay the sun, going down like a ship in a burning sea. Another postmodern sunset, rich in romantic imagery. Why try to describe it? It's enough to say that everything in our field of vision seemed to exist in order to gather the light of this event.[1]

Götterdämmerung. *Why try to describe it? It's been written already, by Conrad (*Youth: *'Between the darkness of earth and heaven she was burning fiercely upon a disk of purple sea shot by the blood-red play of gleams',*[2] *not 'like' but really 'a ship in a burning sea'), for example; postmodern writing comes late, the postmodern sunset is another sunset, an event within a series, never an originating moment but mass-produced as much by the cosmological system as by the system of writing. But the word 'postmodern' here means more than this: the passage from* White Noise *that I have cited refers to an earlier one about the effects of an industrial (or post-industrial) disaster:*

Ever since the airborne toxic event, the sunsets had become almost unbearably beautiful. Not that there was a measurable connection. If the special character of Nyodene Derivative (added to the everyday drift of effluents, pollutants, contaminants and deliriants) had caused this aesthetic leap from already brilliant sunsets to broad towering ruddled visionary skyscapes, tinged with dread, no one had been able to prove it. (p. *170*)

The conditional and the repeated negation convey a pessimistic sense of undecidability, but it seems clear that industrial poison is a crucial component of the postmodern aesthetic, 'rich in romantic imagery'—and vice versa. We could as well say 'another poisonous *sunset', or speak of an 'airborne aesthetic event'. It is not that the*

---

[1] Don DeLillo, *White Noise* (London and New York: Picador and Viking Penguin, 1985), 227.
[2] Joseph Conrad, *Youth* (London: Dent, 1920), 53–4.

postmodern marks the return of aestheticism, a non-ironic deploy-
ment of the full romantic cliché, but rather that it is the site of
conjunction of the beautiful and the toxic, of Turner ('Fire at Sea',
1835, the 'broad towering ruddled visionary skyscapes' of the
decade to 1845) and post-industrial waste. This is thus, in
Lyotard's sense, an aesthetic of the sublime ('with the sublime, the
question of death enters the aesthetic question').[3] *It involves* terror
(the skyscapes are 'tinged with dread') and ineffability, 'the
unpresentable in presentation itself'[4]*—'Why try to describe it?' The*
twist here is that the sense of the inadequacy of representation
comes not because of the transcendental or uncanny nature of the
object but because of the multiplicity of prior representations.
Priority of writing, priority of television, priority of the chain of
metaphors in which the object is constructed. 'We stood there
watching a surge of florid light, like a heart pumping in a
documentary on colour TV' (p. 227).

   Nor is there a lack of irony so much as a kind of self-effacement
before the power of the stories that have gone before. The passage I
quoted at the beginning continues: 'Not that this was one of the
stronger sunsets. There had been more dynamic colours, a deeper
sense of narrative sweep' (p. 227). Far from declining, the great
nineteenth-century narratives continue to infuse the world with
meaning, with a meaningfulness so total that the only possible
response is ambivalence. The skies of this belated world are 'under
a spell, powerful and storied' (p. 325); they take on

content, feeling, an exalted narrative life. The bands of colour reach so
high, seem at times to separate into their constituent parts. There are
turreted skies, light storms, softly falling streamers. It is hard to know how
we should feel about this. Some people are scared by the sunsets, some
determined to be elated, but most of us don't know how to feel, are ready
to go either way. (p. 324)

Malign and beautiful, interpretable not so much to infinity as
within an endless loop between two contradictory poles, this labile

---

[3] Jean-François Lyotard, 'Complexity and the Sublime', *ICA Documents 4
(Postmodernism) and 5* (London: Institute of Contemporary Arts, 1986), 10.
[4] Jean-François Lyotard, 'Answering the Question: What is Postmodernism?',
trans. Régis Durand, in Lyotard, *The Post-Modern Condition: A Report on
Knowledge*, trans. Geoff Bennington and Brian Massumi, Theory and History of
Literature 10 (Minneapolis: University of Minnesota Press, 1984), 81.

postmodern object causes 'awe, it is all awe, it transcends previous categories of awe, but we don't know whether we are watching in wonder or dread' (p. 324). Singular but recurrent, an 'event' (a change, a deviation, a production of newness) within the serial reproduction of sameness, it announces (but how typically modern- ist a gesture) nothing but its own gesture of annunciation: 'There was nothing to do but wait for the next sunset, when the sky would ring like bronze' (p. 321).

But rather than try to unravel the 'meaning' of the concept of postmodernism, let me suggest that the word can be taken as designating nothing more and nothing less than a genre of theoretical writing. To speak or to write the word is to be caught up in a prescriptive network which loosely specifies a limited number of possible moves. You could, for example, begin by describing postmodernism as a spectre haunting Europe (or America, or the world)—as H. R. Jauss and Peter Fuller and Thomas Docherty all do.[5] But your first major gambit must be to predicate the existence or non-existence of the postmodern. The classical structure of this gambit—we can find it in Stanley Aronowitz's essay on 'Post- modernism and Politics', amongst others[6]—is this: first, you assume the existence of a historical shift in sensibility, which you call the postmodern; then you define it by opposition to whatever you take the modern to have been; finally, you seek to give a content to the postmodern in terms of this opposition. The content, that is to say, is deduced logically from the axiom of existence and only then described as historically real.

The function of the opposition between modernism and post- modernism is thus to act as an operator of value (something like Claude Lévi-Strauss's totemic operators), the simple binary structure of which is capable of generating an almost infinite number of

---

[5] Hans Robert Jauss, 'Der literarische Prozeß des Modernismus von Rousseau bis Adorno', in Ludwig von Friedeburg and Jürgen Habermas (eds.), *Adorno-Konferenz 1983* (Frankfurt am Main: Suhrkamp, 1983), 95; Peter Fuller, *Aesthetics after Modernism* (London: Writers and Readers, 1983), 3; Thomas Docherty (who actually speaks of the 'ghostly' or 'ghastly'), 'Postmodernism: An Introduction', in Thomas Docherty (ed.), *Postmodernism: A Reader* (Hemel Hempstead: Harvester Wheatsheaf, 1993), 1.

[6] Stanley Aronowitz, 'Postmodernism and Politics', *Social Text*, 18 (1987), 99–115.

further oppositions.[7] Typically the operator sets up a series of categorical oppositions between, for example, modernity and postmodernity, without ever questioning the status of the opposition itself. Ihab Hassan's synoptic chart can stand for many others:[8]

Modernism	*Postmodernism*
Romanticism/Symbolism	Pataphysics/Dadaism
Form (conjunctive, closed)	Antiform (disjunctive, open)
Purpose	Play
Design	Chance
Hierarchy	Anarchy
Mastery/Logos	Exhaustion/Silence
Art Object/Finished Work	Process/Performance/Happening
Distance	Participation
Creation/Totalization	Decreation/Deconstruction
Synthesis	Antithesis
Presence	Absence
Centering	Dispersal
Genre/Boundary	Text/Intertext
Semantics	Rhetoric
Paradigm	Syntagm
Hypotaxis	Parataxis

[7] Dana Polan speaks of postmodernism as 'a machine for generating discourse', and says of it that 'it is as if the current forms of the postmodernist discussion simultaneously establish a certain number of terms or basic elements and set the procedures by which one can operate with these terms. One is constrained in advance to refer to certain figures, certain key texts—for example, Lyotard versus Habermas; Horkheimer and Adorno on the administered society of modern rationality—and constrained to do no more than take up any one of a number of pre-set positions on them.' Dana Polan, 'Postmodernism and Cultural Analysis Today,' in E. Ann Kaplan (ed.), *Postmodernism and Its Discontents: Theories, Practices* (London: Verso, 1988).

[8] Ihab Hassan, *The Postmodern Turn: Essays in Postmodern Theory and Culture* (n.p.: Ohio State University Press, 1987), 91–92. Steven Connor writes of this table: 'Invisibly but unmistakably, the mark of discredit hovers over the left hand column, while the right hand column reads like a list of all that is obviously desirable. . . . The effect of associating modernism with such drearily authoritarian principles as "form", "hierarchy", "totalization" and "synthesis" is actually to deny the will-to-unmaking in modernism itself about which Hassan has had so much to say. Modernism now becomes the name for the purblind logocentric past, expressive as it is of a totalitarian will to absolute power'; and Hassan is forced to rely upon a 'binary logic to promote the very things that appear to stand against binary logic, the ideas of dispersal, displacement and difference'. Steven Connor, *Postmodernist Culture: An Introduction to Theories of the Contemporary* (Oxford: Basil Blackwell, 1989), 112.

Modernism	Postmodernism
Metaphor	Metonymy
Selection	Combination
Root/Depth	Rhizome/Surface
Interpretation/Reading	Against Interpretation/Misreading
Signified	Signifier
Lisible (Readerly)	*Scriptible* (Writerly)
Narrative/*Grande Histoire*	Anti-narrative/*Petite Histoire*
Master Code	Idiolect
Symptom	Desire
Type	Mutant
Genital/Phallic	Polymorphous/Androgynous
Paranoia	Schizophrenia
Origin/Cause	Difference-Differance/Trace
God the Father	The Holy Ghost
Metaphysics	Irony
Determinacy	Indeterminacy
Transcendence	Immanence

The effect of any such charting of oppositions is to construct an idealist representation of a historical time which proceeds by the epochal succession of spiritual totalities. Binarism works as a mode of historical explanation. This generative activity of the operator is independent of whether or not you accept the reality of the postmodern. Indeed, it is quite characteristic of the genre of the postmodern to deny any reality-value to the concept, or at least to find it highly problematic;[9] and the only thing that is anomalous about this is that the denial goes on being made in an ever-swelling flood of essays and books.

---

[9] 'The term Postmodernism has become a household word even before there was time to establish its meaning', 'Introduction' to Douwe Fokkema and Hans Bertens (eds.), *Approaching Postmodernism* (Amsterdam: John Benjamins, 1986), p. vii; 'Even the most cursory survey of the field of discourse on post-modernism suggests that there is no unified concept or meaning to the term', Blaine McBurney, 'The Post-Modern Transvaluation of Modernist Values', *Thesis 11*, 12 (1985), 95; 'Die Spannweite der Diskussion deutet an, daß wir es mit einer Vielzahl verschiedener Problemkonstellationen zu tun haben', 'Einleitung', in Andreas Huyssen and Klaus R. Scherpe (eds.), *Postmoderne: Zeichen eines kulturellen Wandels*, Rowohlts Enzyklopädie (Reinbek bei Hamburg: Rowohlt, 1986), 7; 'Postmodernism: does it exist at all and, if so, what does it mean? Is it a concept or a practice, a matter of local style or a whole new period or economic phase? What are its forms, effects, place? How are we to mark its advent? Are we truly beyond the modern, truly in (say) a postindustrial age?', Hal Foster, 'Postmodernism: A Preface', in Hal Foster

The values constructed as a result of this productively empty opposition have been extremely diverse.[10] Dick Hebdige writes that the concept of postmodernism designates 'a plethora of incommensurable objects, tendencies, emergencies', including:

the décor of a room, the design of a building, the diegesis of a film, the construction of a record, or a 'scratch' video, a TV commercial, or an arts documentary, or the 'intertextual' relations between them, the layout of a page in a fashion magazine or critical journal, an anti-teleological tendency within epistemology, the attack on the 'metaphysics of presence', a general attenuation of feeling, the collective chagrin and morbid projections of a post-War generation of Baby Boomers confronting disillusioned middle age, the 'predicament' of reflexivity, a group of rhetorical tropes, a proliferation of surfaces, a new phase in commodity fetishism, a fascination for 'images', codes and styles, a process of cultural, political or existential fragmentation and/or crisis, the 'de-centring' of the subject, an 'incredulity towards metanarratives', the replacement of unitary power axes by a pluralism of power/discourse formations, the 'implosion of meaning', the collapse of cultural hierarchies, the dread engendered by the threat of nuclear self-destruction, the decline of the University, the functioning and effects of the new miniaturised technologies, broad societal and economic shifts into a 'media', 'consumer' or 'multinational' phase, a sense (depending on whom you read) of 'placelessness' or the abandonment of placelessness ('critical regionalism') or (even) a generalised substitution of spatial for temporal co-ordinates.[11]

In one account, postmodernism appears as a late mutation within modernism, or as a hyper-modernism: at once speed and swerve, parodic intensity. Many uses of the term, especially within literary studies, correspond to this sense. Linda Hutcheon speaks of postmodernist texts in terms of self-consciousness, paradox, provisionality, the subversion of convention: that is, precisely in

---

(ed.), *The Anti-Aesthetic: Essays on Postmodern Culture* (Port Townsend, Wash.: Bay Press, 1983), 17; 'Postmodernism is now dead as a theoretical concept and, more important, as a way of developing cultural frameworks influencing how we shape theoretical concepts', Charles Altieri, 'What is Living and What is Dead in American Postmodernism: Establishing the Contemporaneity of Some American Poetry', *Critical Inquiry*, 22:4 (1996), 764.

[10] Eco calls it a term *'bon à tout faire'*. Umberto Eco, *Postscript to 'The Name of the Rose'*, trans. W. Weaver (New York: Harcourt Brace Jovanovich, 1983), 65.

[11] Dick Hebdige, 'Postmodernism and "The Other Side"', *Journal of Communication*, 10:2 (1986), 78.

terms of a recognizably *modernist* aesthetic.[12] In this tradition the examples usually cited are the writers of so-called metafiction— Acker, Barthelme, Beckett, Borges, Calvino, Cortazar, Doctorow, Gibson, Powers, Pynchon, Rushdie. . . . Brian McHale works with a similar list, but defines it in terms of a shift from the epistemological uncertainty that characterizes modernism to a predominant concern with questions of ontological relativism.[13] Alternatively, the term can be used in quite the opposite sense to mean the abandonment of modernism, or its irrelevance. The yearning right across the political spectrum for a restoration of the certainties of the unified subject, of a History that would be transcendent of its textual forms, and of a stable domain of cultural values, has led many either to espouse a postmodernism which would call a halt to the moral ambivalence, the élitism, the political pessimism of the art forms of modernity, or to identify the postmodern as precisely the obstacle to such a desire.

In a rather different sense—and following its initial development in relation to architecture—the term refers to a broader cultural domain, and perhaps to a later period of time. It is centred in the realm of the mass media rather than in high culture, and typically it refers to television (soap operas, advertisements, video clips, the 'real world of postmodernism')[14] and to phenomena of style and fashion. Taking music clips as the exemplary postmodernist form, Peter Wollen speaks of a crossover between heterogeneous cultural and subcultural forms and technologies which breaks down the generic distinction between programme and advertisement and makes exemplary use of eclecticism and historicism, such that the characteristic modes of the postmodern 'are those of appropriation, simulation and replication. It plunders the image-bank and the word-hoard for the material of parody, pastiche and, in extreme cases, plagiarism.'[15] Or you could say, with Michael Bérubé, that what is at stake is neither a 'style' nor a breakdown of styles but rather 'a more subtle and elusive cultural shift, in which it's getting

---

[12] Linda Hutcheon, 'The Politics of Postmodernism: Parody and History', *Cultural Critique*, 5 (1986–7), 179–207.

[13] Brian McHale, *Postmodernist Fiction* (London: Methuen, 1987), 9–11.

[14] Arthur Kroker and David Cook, *The Postmodern Scene: Excremental Culture and Hyper-Aesthetics* (London: Macmillan, 1991), 267.

[15] Peter Wollen, 'Ways of Thinking about Music Video (And Post-Modernism)', *Critical Quarterly*, 28: 1–2 (Spring, Summer 1986), 167–8.

harder (and more challenging) to determine what it means for ostensibly "avant-garde" cultural works to be available in so many media instantaneously'.[16] And vice versa. More recently, the emblematic medium has been the Internet, with hypertext, game software, and virtual identity foreshadowing an utter transformation of the social relations of communication and of the nature of textuality itself 'at the close of the mechanical age'.[17] Here the key focus is on the provisionality of electronic selves and social relations, on the open-ended drift of a rhizomatic mode of reading intensely structured by desire and distraction, and on the transformative potential of an emergent technosocial which is then mapped onto and merged with that epochal structure of the postmodern which it at once prefigures, expresses, and produces.

There are, finally, several very diffuse senses of the word which, while lacking all precision, have nevertheless acquired a wide currency, and indeed have become the most widespread forms of its usage: a political sense, indicating something like a prevailing mode of political cynicism or an aesthetically informed quietism; and a pop-philosophical sense which makes the word a synonym for poststructuralist 'theory', thus allowing rapid summation of or allusion to complex and mutually conflicting bodies of work in the absence of any textual engagement with that complexity. It is a mode of reading of the proper name, and like the Hollywood and Mumbai star systems or television's celebrity system, it is both fascinated by and reproductive of its aura. The classic gambit in this usage of the word is what Judith Butler calls 'the fearful conditional': ' "if discourse is all there is . . .", or "if everything is a text . . .", or "if the subject is dead . . .", or "if real bodies do not exist . . ." '. That opening move is then followed by a rigorous and reproving exercise of common sense, in an attempt to establish that any theory and any form of political activity 'needs from the start to presume its subject, the referentiality of language, the integrity of

[16] Michael Bérubé, *Public Access: Literary Theory and American Cultural Politics* (London: Verso, 1994), 120.

[17] Cf., amongst many others, George P. Landow (ed.), *Hyper/text/theory* (Baltimore: Johns Hopkins University Press, 1994); Allucquère Rosanne Stone, *The War of Desire and Technology at the Close of the Mechanical Age* (Cambridge, Mass.: MIT Press, 1995).

the institutional descriptions it provides'.[18] Since I have no interest in engaging in these imaginary battles, I shall make no further reference to this dimension of the genre.

The concept of the postmodern therefore freely gives rise to quite contradictory and, because of its constitutive vagueness, to quite disparate descriptions. It can be taken to mean the ultra-modern or, as Charles Jencks announces, 'to mean the opposite of all this: the end of avant-garde extremism, the partial return to tradition and the central role of communication with the public'.[19] It means the overcoming or the self-recognition of modernism, or else it means 'its old ideological opponent, which then and now assumes the form of a popular front of pre- and antimodernist elements'.[20] You can use it to proclaim an unashamed philistinism or you can think of it as the cutting edge of aesthetic radicalism. Postmodernism can be taken to be the expression of postmodernity, or to be its enemy;[21] both terms can be used either as periodizing or as stylistic concepts.[22] And, once you have granted the existence, or the problematic existence, or the quasi-existence of the concept of postmodernism, the genre allows you to associate it with any political position whatsoever.

Thus Fredric Jameson has constructed a calculus of the positions logically possible within the field constructed by the structural opposition of modernism to postmodernism. It works as in the diagram on p. 22.[23]

The plus and minus signs designate 'progressive' and 'reactionary' orientations (terms themselves taken from a modernist representation of history as sequential flow) within each structural slot. The

---

[18] Judith Butler, 'Contingent Foundations: Feminism and the Question of "Postmodernism" ', in Judith Butler and Joan W. Scott (eds.), *Feminists Theorize the Political* (New York: Routledge, 1992), 3.

[19] Charles Jencks, *The Language of Post-Modern Architecture*, 4th edn. (1977; repr. London: Academy Editions, 1984), 6.

[20] Hal Foster, '(Post)Modern Polemics', *New German Critique*, 33 (1984), 69.

[21] Simon During, 'Postmodernism or Post-colonialism Today', *Textual Practice*, 1: 1 (1987), 32.

[22] ' "Postmodern" is probably a very bad term because it conveys the idea of a historical periodization. "Periodizing," however, is still a "classic" or "modern" ideal. "Postmodern" simply indicates a mood, or better, a state of mind.' Jean-François Lyotard, 'Rules and Paradoxes and Svelte Appendix', *Cultural Critique*, 5 (1986–7), 209.

[23] Fredric Jameson, *Postmodernism, or, The Cultural Logic of Late Capitalism* (Durham, NC: Duke University Press, 1991), 61.

	ANTI-MODERNIST	PRO-MODERNIST
PRO-POSTMODERNIST	+/–	+/–
ANTI-POSTMODERNIST	+/–	+/–

table is the basic organizing format of the genre, and it makes it possible for you to denounce a reactionary or a subversive modernism in the name of a progressive or of a conservative postmodernism, or vice versa; or to celebrate either one against the other, again with any political inflection; or to celebrate or to denounce both modernism and postmodernism, from either side of the political fence.

It begins to look as though the very engagement with the term represents a trap: as though your words, whatever their content, have nothing to do but to roll through the clown's mouth into the groove waiting to receive them. Wouldn't it perhaps be better, in this case, to practise a strategy of avoidance: to dismiss the concept as a non-concept, imprecise, incoherent, contradictory, lacking any real historical reference? It would be a quintessentially *ideological* concept, not designating but attempting to fabricate a reality, and for the most banal purposes of cultural or academic self-aggrandizement.

This opposition between the truth of reference and the falsity of representation would itself, however, be called into question by a postmodern logic. Whether or not you accept this questioning, there are two further reasons working against the strategy of avoidance. The first is that this strategy is still a move *within* the genre of the postmodern; it may indeed even be the most characteristic move, and it is disarmed in advance by the paradox that it works to strengthen the concept's contemporary resonance (any publicity is good publicity). It is for this reason that the many serious and responsible critiques of the concept (with titles like *Against Postmodernism, What's Wrong with Postmodernism, The Truth About Postmodernism, The Poverty of Postmodernism*) will inevitably miss the mark.[24] And the second is that the very

---

[24] Alex Callinicos, *Against Postmodernism: A Marxist Critique* (Cambridge: Polity Press, 1989); Christopher Norris, *What's Wrong with Postmodernism:*

persistence of the word, however irritating this may be, seems to indicate that something is at stake, something that cannot be brushed aside as a theoretical fashion (partly because the temporality of fashion, and its relation to aesthetic production, is no longer a given but is one of the issues at stake). It may be that the term is the index of a real epochal shift (or of the threshold of such a shift); or it may be that it indicates something less well defined, more obscure and more heterogeneous but nevertheless of genuine theoretical and practical interest, in the operation of epochal division itself.

In any case, you can only produce a knowledge of the concept by operating within the rules of the game; any point that seems to be outside it is in practice a false exteriority, blind to its own involvement in the game. But one of the preconditions for knowing something about the concept is that, rather than simply taking up one of those predefined positions and pursuing all its consequences as though you were discovering rather than repeating them, you should devise a way of analysing the logic of the grid itself. This, together with some questioning of the institutional and social necessities to which the concept seems to respond, is what I seek to do in the pages that follow.

The world of White Noise *is a world of primary representations which neither precede nor follow the real but are themselves real— although it is true that they always have the appearance both of preceding another reality (as a model to be followed) and of following it (as copy). But this appearance must itself be taken seriously.*

Consider these two passages about an adult looking at sleeping children: 'I looked for a blanket to adjust, a toy to remove from a child's warm grasp, feeling I'd wandered into a TV moment' (p. 244); and 'These sleeping children were like figures in an ad for the Rosicrucians, drawing a powerful beam of light from somewhere off the page' (p. 154). Both moments are mediated by another moment, a memory or a metaphor which shapes them, endows them with a certain structure; this structure is a part of their reality. It is quite possible to distinguish one reality (the sleeping children) from another (the TV moment, the ad for the

Critical Theory and the Ends of Philosophy (Baltimore: Johns Hopkins University Press, 1990), and *The Truth about Postmodernism* (Oxford: Basil Blackwell, 1993); John O'Neill, *The Poverty of Postmodernism* (London: Routledge, 1995).

Rosicrucians), just as we can in principle distinguish literal from metaphorical language; it is possible for the novel to be ironical about the gap between these two realities. But this distinguishing and this irony are insecure. Real moments and TV moments interpenetrate each other—and it is, in any case, another (novelistic) representation that offers us this reality and this distinction. The world is so saturated with representations that it becomes increasingly difficult to separate primary actions from imitations of actions.

Indeed, it seems that it is only within the realm of representation that it is possible to postulate a realm of primary actions which would be quite distinct from representation. During the evacuation Jack notices groups of refugees:

Out in the open, keeping their children near, carrying what they could, they seemed to be part of some ancient destiny, connected in doom and pain to a whole history of people trekking across wasted landscapes. There was an epic quality about them that made me wonder for the first time at the scope of our predicament. (p. 122)

What he is seeing is of course a movie; and it is precisely because it is cinematic, precisely because of its 'epic quality', that the scene is real and serious to him. 'Epic' here perhaps means something like 'naïve', lacking self-consciousness, and above all lacking any awareness of the cinematic nature of the experience. This paradox is even clearer in the case of Jack's fantasy about the death of Attila the Hun: 'I want to believe he lay in his tent, wrapped in animal skins, as in some internationally financed movie epic, and said brave cruel things to his aides and retainers' (p. 99). The image is again of a heroic lack of self-consciousness, a naïve immediacy to life and death:

No weakening of the spirit. No sense of the irony of human existence . . . He accepted death as an experience that flows naturally from life, a wild ride through the forest, as would befit someone known as the Scourge of God. This is how it ended for him, with his attendants cutting off their hair and disfiguring their own faces in barbarian tribute, as the camera pulls back out of the tent and pans across the night sky of the fifth century A.D., clear and uncontaminated, bright-banded with shimmering worlds. (pp. 99–100)

It is only in the movies, only through cultural mediation, that a vision of non-mediation is possible—and therefore absurd.

The central mediating agency in this world is television; indeed, 'For most people there are only two places in the world. Where they live and their TV set. If a thing happens on television, we have every right to find it fascinating, whatever it is' (p. 66). The major statement is a speech made by Murray. He tells his students, he says, that

they're already too old to figure importantly in the making of society. Minute by minute they're beginning to diverge from each other. 'Even as we sit here,' I tell them, 'you are spinning out from the core, becoming less recognizable as a group, less targetable by advertisers and mass-producers of culture. Kids are a true universal. But you're well beyond that, already beginning to drift, to feel estranged from the products you consume. Who are they designed for? What is your place in the marketing scheme? Once you're out of school, it is only a matter of time before you experience the vast loneliness and dissatisfaction of consumers who have lost their group identity.' (pp. 49–50)

The assumptions are astounding: we know that human worth can't be measured in terms of our relation to consumption—to money and commodities; that the order of things transcends 'the marketing scheme'. But all that Murray is doing is stating the central, the deadly serious principles of a capitalist society. This is really how it is, 'the marketing scheme' really does work, for most purposes, in a capitalist society, as the scheme of things; the whole social organization is geared to this equation. The propositions are monstrous, but only because we find it so hard to believe in the true and central awfulness of capitalism.

Television comes into this because of its crucial role in marketing—and this is to say that its importance lies not in the sheer quantity of representations that it generates, nor even in their content as messages, but in the fact that they are always directly linked to commodity production and the generation of profits, and that in order to serve these ends they work as an integral part of a system for the shaping and reshaping of human identity. Murray's students are thus 'beginning to feel they ought to turn against the medium, exactly as an earlier generation turned against their parents and their country'. When he tells them that 'they have to learn to look as children again. Root out content. Find codes and messages', they reply that 'Television is just another name for junk mail' (p. 50).

But cultural criticism—the moralistic critique of the mass media *that has been the stock in trade of liberal journalism—is of course not an option, certainly not for this novel, which is much more interested, in its own ironic but unconditional way, in, for example, Murray's quasi-mystical experience of television. It is, he says, 'a primal force in the American home. Sealed-off, self-contained, self-referring', television*

offers incredible amounts of psychic data. It opens ancient memories of world birth, it welcomes us into the grid, the network of little buzzing dots that make up the picture pattern. There is light, there is sound. I ask my students, 'What more do you want?' Look at the wealth of data concealed in the grid, in the bright packaging, the jingles, the slice-of-life commercials, the products hurtling out of darkness, the coded messages and endless repetitions, like chants, like mantras. 'Coke is it, Coke is it, Coke is it.' The medium practically overflows with sacred formulas if we can remember how to respond innocently and get past our irritation, weariness and disgust. (p. 51)

A whole aesthetic is elaborated here, although unfortunately it is made up of the dregs of other aesthetic systems. Murray has the quixotic ability to disregard the banal surface of television and, with all the innocence of a formalist semiotician, to discover a cornucopia of aesthetic information in its organization. The key term here is 'data', a meaningless word which suggests that the relevant level at which to decode the television message is that of the physical structure of light on the screen—but in fact the word has the effect of conflating this level with other levels of information. Gestalt and perceptual psychology mingle with genre theory and a mysticism of the proper name in Murray's postcritical celebration of the medium. For his students, however, television is 'worse than junk mail. Television is the death throes of human consciousness, according to them. They're ashamed of their television past. They want to talk about movies' (p. 51). Murray is a postmodernist. His students, wishing to return to the high modernism of cinema, are postpostmodernist.

There are two main reasons why the concept of postmodernism is logically incoherent. The first has to do with the question of exemplification. The literature on postmodernism is notorious for its contradictory assumptions, rarely made explicit, about what is contained in the set of the postmodern. Characteristically it gives almost no examples (the ubiquitous Warhol excepted), or else is so over-inclusive as to blur all boundaries (thus Hassan lists 'Sterne, Sade, Blake, Lautréamont, Rimbaud, Jarry, Hofmannsthal, Stein, Joyce, Pound, Duchamp, Artaud, Roussel, Bataille, Queneau, Kafka'[25] amongst its antecedents—his lists, like his definitional categories, rarely make a good distinction between postmodernism and modernism). The result of this is that much of the polemic around the concept is shadow-boxing. If I think postmodernism means Olson and Heissenbüttel and Pynchon and catastrophe theory, and you think it means MTV, fashion advertisements, political sound-bites, and the excremental vision, and someone else thinks it's hypertext, trompe-l'œil façades, 'Oprah', and Blue Velvet, then we're probably talking right past each other, since the definition of the concept shifts with the objects taken to exemplify it. This is to say that the concept cannot be thought as the representation of a given field of cultural production, or of a tendency within this field; it is rather the embattled attempt to construct the unity of such a field or tendency. This need not be taken as a criticism if we can agree that all discourse in fact works at the construction rather than the discovery of its truths (and works according to domain-specific criteria of verification and validity)—and we know, too, that other periodizing concepts like baroque and romanticism are similarly difficult to define with any rigour. Nevertheless, some minimal agreement on an identifiable field of reference, however shifting and multi-layered, is surely a precondition for a productive use of the concept.

What replaces any rigorous practice of exemplification is the list, which is characterized by arbitrariness and eclecticism. Meaghan Morris writes of the Baudrillardian theory of simulation that its fascination lies in its offering 'a universe, an inexhaustible, infinite world of examples, exemplary matter, for the citing of the theory itself'.[26] Todd Gitlin, to take another example, both thematizes and practises the list (as I indirectly do too, both ironizing and incorporating it through another postmodern trope, the quotation that comes unanchored from its surrounding text):

One post-modernist trope is the list, as if culture were a garage sale, so it is appropriate to evoke post-modernism by offering a list of examples, for

---

[25] Ihab Hassan, The Right Promethean Fire: Imagination, Science, and Cultural Change (Urbana: University of Illinois Press, 1980), 108.

[26] Meaghan Morris, 'Room 101 Or A Few Worst Things in the World', The Pirate's Fiancée: Feminism, Reading, Postmodernism (London: Verso, 1988), 208.

better and for worse: Michael Graves's Portland Building, Philip Johnson's AT&T, and hundreds of more or less skillful derivatives; Robert Rauschenberg's silk screens, Warhol's multiple-image paintings, photo-realism, Larry Rivers's erasures and pseudo-pageantry, Sherrie Levine's photographs of 'classic' photographs; Disneyland, Las Vegas, suburban strips, shopping malls, mirror-glass office building façades; William Burroughs, Tom Wolfe, Donald Barthelme, Monty Python, Don DeLillo, Isuzu 'He's lying' commercials, Philip Glass, 'Star Wars', Spalding Gray, David Hockney ('Surface is illusion, but so is depth'), Max Headroom, David Byrne, Twyla Tharp (choreographing Beach Boys and Frank Sinatra songs), Italo Calvino, 'The Gospel at Colonus', Robert Wilson, The Flying Karamazov Brothers, George Coates, the Kronos Quartet, Frederick Barthelme, MTV, 'Miami Vice', David Letterman, Laurie Anderson, Anselm Kiefer, John Ashbery, Paul Auster, the Pompidou Center, the Hyatt Regency, 'The White Hotel', E. L. Doctorow's 'Book of Daniel', 'Less than Zero', Kathy Acker, Philip Roth's 'Counterlife' (but not 'Portnoy's Complaint'), the epilogue to Rainer Werner Fassbinder's 'Berlin Alexander-platz', the 'language poets'; the French theorists Michel Foucault, Jacques Lacan, Jacques Derrida and Jean Baudrillard; television morning shows; news commentary cluing us in to the image-making and 'positioning' strategies of candidates; remote-control-equipped viewers 'grazing' around the television dial.[27]

Any such list is in principle infinitely extendable, without bound-aries and without any definite criterion of selection other than a sort of epochal intuition.[28]

The second, and related, area of incoherence concerns the problem of periodization. There are two initial aspects of this. The first is that the concept of period has a totalizing force: it 'depends upon the taxonomical privileging of one ensemble of cultural practices—identified as the distinctive or definitive one—over a plurality of others',[29] and it assumes some logical affinity between these practices. This logic is *singular*, and, in whatever terms it is identified, it functions as a *general* logic that is prior to its various

---

[27] Todd Gitlin, 'Hip-Deep in Postmodernism', *New York Times Book Review*, 6 Nov. 1988, 35.

[28] Another list: postmodernism heralds 'the end of history; the implosion of meaning; the negation of totality and coherence; "the body without organs"; the death of the referent; the end of the social; and the absence of politics'. Elspeth Probyn, 'Bodies and Anti-Bodies: Feminism and the Postmodern', *Cultural Studies*, 1: 3 (1987), 349.

[29] David Bennett, 'Wrapping up Postmodernism', *Textual Practice*, 1: 3 (1987), 256.

manifestations. This is how Edward Soja expresses it: 'The same crisis-induced rhythm that ripples through the macro-historical geography of capitalist cities and regions is seen reflected in the history of critical theoretical consciousness, creating an interlocking sequence of "regimes" of critical thought that follows in roughly the same half-century blocks that have phased the changing political economy of capitalism since the age of revolution.'[30] Further, the internal synchronic necessity of the period tends to be derived from a narrative teleology. Thus Jameson writes, in an extraordinary passage, that

In film or in rock . . . a certain historical logic can be reintroduced by the hypothesis that such newer media recapitulate the evolutionary stages or breaks between realism, modernism and postmodernism, in a compressed time span, such that the Beatles and the Stones occupy the high modernist moment embodied by the 'auteurs' of 1950s and 1960s art films.[31]

This looks in a way like an argument for uneven temporalities, for the temporal specificity of different domains; but in fact it is concerned with the ineluctable logic of historical 'stages', such that the coherence of the period is preserved despite its uneven realization.

The second aspect of the problem involves the scope and boundaries of the concept of postmodernism. Here the difficulty is that some of the most influential periodizations deal with radically incompatible objects. It is clear, I think, that for both Jean-François Lyotard and Jean Baudrillard the concept of the postmodern is set against the 'modernity' of nineteenth-century capitalism, and thus includes most *modernist* aesthetic production. Jameson, by contrast, dates the postmodern from around the 1960s, but as Mike Davis notes, Mandel's concept of 'late capitalism', with which Jameson correlates postmodernism, extends through the post-war period and *ends* with the slump of 1974–5.[32] In general, it seems true that

---

[30] Edward Soja, *Postmodern Geographies: The Reassertion of Space in Critical Social Theory* (London: Verso, 1989), 3.

[31] Fredric Jameson, 'The Politics of Theory: Ideological Positions in the Postmodernism Debate', *New German Critique*, 33 (1984), 54; cf. the corresponding passage in Jameson, *Postmodernism*, 1: in pop music postmodern status is held by 'punk and new wave rock (the Beatles and the Stones now standing as the high-modernist moment of that more recent and rapidly expanding tradition)'.

[32] Mike Davis, 'Urban Renaissance and the Spirit of Postmodernism', *New Left Review*, 151 (May–June 1985), 107.

the 'European' and the (North) 'American' versions of the post-modern refer to quite different stretches of time.

In both of these cases the problem is dependent upon the prior question of the dating of modernism, and then more broadly the rather different datings of the *modern* and of capitalist *modernity*. The classic description of the concept of the modern is perhaps Jauss's essay 'Literarische Tradition und gegenwärtiges Bewußtsein der Modernität',[33] which hinges on the paradoxical self-refutation of the concept in the history of its uses—the temporality that it seeks to foreclose. In its earliest occurrences around the fifth century AD the word *modernus* has the sense not only of newness but of actuality and immediacy: designating 'the historical Now of the present',[34] the term is nevertheless not seen as opposed to or discontinuous from the claims of the past. With the Caroline renaissance of the twelfth century, however, the Christian present is set in discontinuous opposition to heathen antiquity; rather than being a static opposition, the terms acquire a shifting content, and—as succeeding 'modernities' move backwards into a cumulative pastness—an intermediate term is inserted between antiquity and modernity. This process of succession of modernities is not—as Curtius, for example, suggests[35]—cyclical, but is rather typological: the present is understood as a renovation of the past, and has an entirely ambivalent value in relation to it—both dwarfed by the past and transcending it.

The humanistic Renaissance of the fifteenth and sixteenth centuries for the first time understands modernity in terms of radical novelty and of a non-successive discontinuity. The Christian typology of three ages is replaced by a binary opposition of antiquity to modernity, and the *media aetas* thereby comes to be perceived as a kind of temporal vacuum intercalated between the two substantive epochs of human history. Linearity is replaced by a cyclical model of rebirth.

It is with the seventeenth century *Querelle des anciens et des*

---

[33] Hans Robert Jauss, *Literaturgeschichte als Provokation* (Frankfurt am Main: Suhrkamp, 1970), 11–66; but cf. also Reinhart Koselleck, *Futures Past: On the Semantics of Historical Time*, trans. Keith Tribe (Cambridge, Mass.: MIT Press, 1985).

[34] Jauss, 'Literarische Tradition', *Literaturgeschichte als Provokation*, 16.

[35] Ernst Robert Curtius, *European Literature and the Latin Middle Ages*, trans. Willard R. Trask (New York: Harper and Row, 1953), 255.

modernes, Jauss argues, that this absolutizing typology of discontinuous correspondence starts to break down. The beginning of the Enlightenment is marked by its ambivalent inscription of the concept of modernity into an ideal of progress and into a sense of the *lateness* of the present ('C'est nous qui sommes les Anciens', as Perrault puts it).[36] At the same time antiquity and modernity come to seem radically heterogeneous: the defence of the Ancients against modern standards of taste by the relativistic application of criteria appropriate to the art of antiquity leads to a historicizing recognition of the historical plurality of norms. The consequences of this are momentous—in effect the birth of the historical consciousness that has shaped our modernity, with its postulates of the irreversibility of time, the historical specificity of different epochs, and the orientation to the future rather than the past.

From here we can isolate three key moments in the process by which the concept of the modern passes into that of aesthetic modernism (I rely here on a later essay of Jauss's, which dates the 'modern' period from the mid-eighteenth century rather than the mid-nineteenth). The first is the moment around 1800 when a fully developed historicism relegates classical antiquity to pure pastness and, freeing the modern, on the basis of an aesthetic of the sublime, the interesting and the sentimental, from the classical conception of beauty, endows it with the overriding purpose of aesthetic education. The second Jauss dates around 1830, with the development of the aesthetic of a modernity which, in the shock-experience of the new, differentiates itself internally to produce its own 'antiquity' (the constantly superseded new). This is a modernity split against itself (since every modernity including the present one slides into the past) and which registers its epochal difference in terms of a deep uncertainty about its temporal identity. This modernity which conceives of itself as pure transition transforms historicism into aestheticism and, set in opposition to no particular past, ranges freely over all of them. The final moment, around 1912, is that of a euphoric, future-directed modernism that programmatically cuts itself off from and seeks to destroy the past and the legitimacy it had previously given.[37]

---

[36] Jauss, 'Literarische Tradition', *Literaturgeschichte als Provokation*, 30.
[37] Jauss, 'Der literarische Prozeß des Modernismus von Rousseau bis Adorno', 102–3.

It should be clear from this sketch that the apparently chronological concept of the modern lacks all chronological content. This is exacerbated, however, in the case of the modernist movement by its *impossible* emphasis upon sheer, and ahistorical, actuality. Rainer Warning isolates the difficulty nicely when he writes that modernist art differs from that of all other periods in its loss of epochal unity.[38] If he is right, there is neither a singular modernism, nor a clear correlation of modernist culture with a bordered strip of time or with a coherent socioeconomic formation contained by such a strip.

For one of the driving difficulties of any attempt to think modernism and postmodernism as specific epochal structures is the temptation to *derive* the cultural from the logic of an epochal system. Jameson does this quite deliberately (postmodernism is 'the cultural logic of late capitalism'); others do it almost despite their own better intentions, as in the case of Jochen Schulte-Sasse, who, after carefully distinguishing 'social' modernity and postmodernity from 'cultural' modernism and postmodernism, then casually adds that 'postmodernity and postmodernism refer to qualitative changes in society and their cultural manifestations'.[39] 'Manifestations' gets it quite wrong because it sets up a causal relation between a primary and an epiphenomenal realm, leaving no room for discontinuity or any more complex causality.

The problem lies both with the exclusion of the cultural from the social or the socioeconomic, and with the expressive logic that then reduces it to a simple function of the more powerful pole. It is a problem in part because it then becomes an easy matter to attribute some of the effects of complex social processes to the cultural realm. The mechanism is that two-step dissociation that so completely suffuses neoliberal thinking, in which 'part one celebrates the virtues of unimpeded competition and dynamic structural change, while part two mourns the decline of the family and community "values" that were eroded precisely by the forces

---

[38] Rainer Warning, 'Surrealistische Totalität und die Partialität der Moderne', in R. Warning and W. Wehle (eds.), *Lyrik und Malerei der Avantgarde* (Munich: Fink, 1982), 481; quoted ibid. 103.

[39] Jochen Schulte-Sasse, 'Modernity and Modernism, Postmodernity and Postmodernism: Framing the Issue', *Cultural Critique*, 5 (1986–7), 6.

commended in part one'.[40] The assignment of a surrogate blame to 'cultural' forces that then follows from this shuffle[41] is matched on the left by resolute anti-modernists like Russell Berman, who suggests that aesthetic modernism is doubly functional in relation to capitalist modernity: first, in that 'the experiential models of historical modernism have generated the patterns of mass marketing and consumerist behaviour' (he instances 'the surrealist interludes in television advertising, the cruel theatre of music videos, the ubiquity of Muzak, and the proliferation of life-styles'); and second, in that the historical function of modernism has been to mount an 'attack on traditional culture', apparently in the direct service of the modernization of social relations of production.[42]

The strategy in both cases is similar to Jencks's attempt to find the essence of modernism in its participation in capitalist rationality ('Like rational schooling, rational health and rational design of women's bloomers, it has the faults of an age trying to reinvent itself totally on rational grounds').[43] The argument misses, however, both the moment of Nietzschean irrationality in modernism, and its consistent resistance to the more direct 'manifestations' of capitalist rationality. Albrecht Wellmer is surely right to speak of modern art as 'the field . . . in which the form of rationality of modernity has long been called into question, and indeed on the level of modernity'.[44] And to say that this questioning has itself been assimilated is not to posit a historical logic which would in any way be alien to modernism (the moment of institutionalization of the new is always foreseen), nor, as Stuart Hall argues, does it 'diminish

---

[40] Samuel Luttwak, 'Why Fascism is the Wave of the Future', *London Review of Books*, 7 Apr. 1994, 6, cited in Michael Bérubé, 'Cultural Criticism and the Politics of Selling Out', *Electronic Book Review*, ‹http://www.altx.com/ebr›, 1996.

[41] Cf. Jürgen Habermas, 'Modernity: An Incomplete Project', in Foster, *The Anti-Aesthetic*, 7.

[42] Russell A. Berman, 'The Routinization of Charismatic Modernism and the Problem of Post-Modernity', *Cultural Critique*, 5 (1986–7), 64.

[43] Jencks, *The Language of Post-Modern Architecture*, 10.

[44] Albrecht Wellmer, 'On the Dialectic of Modernism and Postmodernism', *Praxis International*, 5: 5 (1985), 357; cf. During, 'Postmodernism or Post-colonialism Today', 32: 'It is just as rewarding to construe literary postmodernism as an enemy of postmodernity as to consider it as its expression and helpmeet. Thus in ethico-political terms postmodernist texts do not differ from modernist texts which are simultaneously enemies of, and moments in, modernity.'

the radical break with the epistemes of the modern which modernism represented'.[45]

In order to clarify matters you might want to distinguish between three conceptual moments: those of *modernism* (an adversary aesthetic culture); of *modernization* (an economic process with social and cultural implications); and of *modernity* (which overlaps with the modernization process, but which I understand as a philosophical category performatively designating the temporality of the post-traditional world). The same distinction of ontological levels holds good, *mutatis mutandis*, for postmodernism, post-modernization, and postmodernity.

Contemporary accounts of modernization are dominated by the Weberian concept of rationality; this is as true of the modernization theory developed in the post-war period by empiricist social science as it is of Adorno and Horkheimer's concept of *Aufklärung*, Habermas's *Zweckvernunft*, Foucault's *discipline*, and Giddens's *reflexivity*. In broad terms, and allowing for significant theoretical differences, modernization is conceived as a more or less systemic process with some of the following components:

- the formation of a homogeneous economic domain through the extension and integration of commodity production and exchange;
- a shift from the closed time of feudalism to the open-ended, dynamic, and godless time of capitalism (specifically, the future-directed temporality of the return on capital and thus of capital accumulation);
- the gridding of space and time into calculable units,[46] and the restructuring of work through the agency of decentralized disciplinary systems;
- the elaboration of mediated rather than direct relations of exploitation of surplus value, and the autonomization of the ethical self as the basis of contract;

[45] Stuart Hall, 'On Postmodernism and Articulation: An Interview with Stuart Hall', ed. Lawrence Grossberg, *Journal of Communication*, 10: 2 (1986), 51.

[46] Giddens notes the key role played by the emptying and disconnection of time and space in modernity: 'The separating of time and space and their formation into standardized, "empty" dimensions cut through the connection between social activity and its "embedding" in the particularities of contexts of presence', and thus open up 'manifold possibilities of change by breaking free from the restraints of local habits and practices'. Anthony Giddens, *The Consequences of Modernity* (Stanford, Calif.: Stanford University Press, 1990), 20.

- a movement from ascriptive and localized groupings based on kinship and community to highly differentiated social and economic roles performed within functional groupings and supported by a developed education system;
- the increasingly central role of the national state and its bureaucracy in the reflexive regulation of the market, the provision of infrastructure support, and the administration of social relations;
- extensive urbanization as part of a shift from agricultural to industrial production; the extension of the communications and transportation networks;
- the development of machine technology, and the central productive role of scientific knowledge;
- the secularization and autonomization of the spheres of science, art, and morality.

Other lists might put their stress on apparently more autonomous modes of rationality (scientific, ethical, administrative, disciplinary . . .). Most such lists have in common, however, two structural features. The first is the unification of very heterogeneous processes within the concept of the modern. The second is that this unification is secured by means of binary opposition to another term, that of 'traditional' societies. Here too the apparent unity of the term disappears as soon as we recognize the great variety of social structures classed as premodern; the fact that modern and traditional social structures are by no means mutually exclusive; and the extent to which the concept of the 'modern' extrapolates from the model of industrially advanced Western societies.[47]

Dean Tipps comments on the dichotomous structure of modernization theory as follows:

Through the device of ideal-typical contrasts between the attributes of tradition and modernity, modernization theorists have done little more than to summarize, with the assistance of Parsons' pattern variables and some ethnographic updating, the earlier efforts by men such as Maine, Tönnies, Durkheim, and others in the evolutionary tradition to conceptualize the transformation of societies in terms of a transition between polar types of the status-contract, *Gemeinschaft-Gesellschaft* variety . . . Modernization then becomes a transition, or rather a series of transitions

---

[47] Cf. A. R. Desai, 'Need for Revaluation of the Concept', in Cyril E. Black (ed.), *Comparative Modernization: A Reader* (New York: Free Press, 1976), 89–103.

from primitive, subsistence economies to technology-intensive, industrial-ized economies; from subject to participant political cultures; from closed, ascriptive status systems to open, achievement-oriented systems; from extended to nuclear kinship units; from religious to secular ideologies; and so on.[48]

What is striking about this structure is that it duplicates precisely the model of binary opposition through which the ('cultural') concept of *postmodernism* is constructed: that is, the use of dichotomy as a machine for the infinite generation of quasi-historical transitions.

This returns me to my argument that the concept of the postmodern obeys a discursive rather than a descriptive necessity: its function is that of a logical operator, establishing categorical polarities which then allow—in a tautologous and self-justifying circuit—the construction of fictions of periodization and value, fictions that have no content other than the structure of binary opposition itself.

At the same time, however, we must recognize that this discursive necessity has a precise historical location. It responds to the inner contradictions of a modernism that has gone on too long. The temporality of modernism requires its own obsolescence: a modernism that failed to age, that didn't demand to be superseded, would be a contradiction in terms. Hence the necessity of a successor to modernism, but hence also its definition solely in a chronological form ('post') which refuses all indications of content. The paradoxical result of this is that, since this 'post' must be a real *alternative* to modernism, it must be based upon a different temporality: not that of novation but that of stasis. It must be the end of history (hence the postmodern preoccupation with apoca-lypse). In its determination to *succeed* modernism, however, it corresponds entirely to a modernist logic. Habermas writes that, since the nineteenth century, 'The distinguishing mark of works which count as modern is "the new" which will be overcome and made absolute through the novelty of the next style.'[49] In this sense postmodernism is precisely a moment of the modern, a 'next style'.

---

[48] Dean C. Tipps, 'Modernization Theory and the Comparative Study of Societies: A Critical Perspective', ibid. 67.

[49] Habermas, 'Modernity: An Incomplete Project', in Foster, *The Anti-Aesthetic*, 4.

Its founding gesture is a modernist destruction of the modern, a destruction which is logically entailed by the modernist programme itself.[50] As Lyotard notes, we may suspect today that this 'break' is more like a repression (that is, a repetition) of the past than it is an overcoming of it.[51]

Another way of putting this would be to say that the concept of the postmodern responds to a *narrative* necessity. This is what modernist artistic production looks like in Lyotard's heroic formulation: it is 'a sort of long, persistent, and deeply responsible labour directed towards enquiry into the presuppositions implicit in modernity': a salvational project.[52] Modernism, that is to say, is a *rigorous* programme which leads to a predetermined end; it has the pathos of a necessary trajectory. The modernist artist (Duchamp, Mies and Corbusier, Schoenberg and Webern, Mallarmé, Joyce, Artaud, Kafka) is the one who explores the given material with absolute commitment and to the point of silence or madness. But this narrative continues, not with a simple succession but with a dialectical reversal: having reached the point of absolute aporia, having taken the exploration of the material to its end, the modernist project becomes both complete and irrelevant.[53] The intervention of the discourse of postmodernism at this point thus represents a shift of ground. Although it looks as though it obeys the modernist logic of succession and overcoming, it can also be read, as Vattimo argues, 'not only as something new in relation to the modern, but also as a dissolution of the category of the new—in other words, as an experience of "the end of history"—rather than as the appearance of a different stage of history itself'.[54]

[50] Cf. Stanley Rosen, 'Post-Modernism and the End of Philosophy', *Canadian Journal of Political and Social Theory*, 9: 3 (Fall 1985), 92: 'Modernity arises as a "project".... The subsequent rejection of modernity is then simply a re-enactment of the institution of modernity.'

[51] Jean-François Lyotard, 'Note sur les sens de "post-" ', *Le Postmoderne expliqué aux enfants* (Paris: Galilée, 1986), 121.

[52] Ibid. 124–5. On modernist salvational projects, cf. Leo Bersani, *The Culture of Redemption* (Cambridge, Mass.: Harvard University Press, 1990).

[53] Connor thus speaks of postmodernism as a pressing to extremes of the 'permanent emergency' of modernism, and suggests that its appropriate model is a narrative 'in which development leads to displacement, and culmination equals catastrophe'. Steven Connor, 'The Modern and the Postmodern as History', *Essays in Criticism*, 37: 3 (July 1987), 183.

[54] Gianni Vattimo, *The End of Modernity: Nihilism and Hermeneutics in Postmodern Culture*, trans. Jon R. Snyder (Baltimore: Johns Hopkins University Press, 1988), 4.

The problem with such an account, even in the turn that Vattimo gives it, is that it continues to reduce the heterogeneity of modernism to a paradigm of epochal closure. Positing a marked break between epochs, it reinforces the ideal-typical opposition between non-contingent historical unities. Following Octavio Paz's definition of modernism as a 'tradition against itself', Matei Calinescu argues that postmodernism therefore *by definition* cannot escape this paradigm: 'Even the "post" in postmodernism appears to be an unconscious tribute to modernism and to its dialectic of transitoriness and negativity. Insofar as modernism always aspires toward its own dissolution, postmodernism should be seen as one of the most typical products of the modernist imagination.'[55] Were it to be qualitatively different, postmodernism would have to be grounded in a quite different temporality, and would thus have to be the paradoxical reversal of its own act of rupture. It would have, not to initiate but to find itself within a stasis which would perhaps be that of a neoclassicism (and in this case its most representative form would be the advertisement, the genre which is most fully reconciled to the order of things and reads it as utopia), or else that of a frenzied renewal which, in a parody of modernist *ostranenie*, occurs in such short waves that it negates itself. This is to say that the postmodern is caught between contradictory imperatives:

> to change/to be still;
> to be historical/to be the end of history.

Remarks existed in a state of permanent flotation. No one thing was either more or less plausible than any other thing. As people jolted out of reality, we were released from the need to distinguish.[56]

This jolt within the space of White Noise *corresponds to a particular narrative emergency, but the displacement it describes towards 'a state of permanent flotation' is characteristic of many of the novel's 'normal' modes of being. Think of the deliriously inaccurate conversations in the family car, or the dream-laden spaces of the supermarket and the mall; think, above all, of television, that 'primal force in the American home' (p. 51).*

---

[55] Matei Calinescu, 'Postmodernism and Some Paradoxes of Periodization', in Fokkema and Bertens, *Approaching Postmodernism*, 168.
[56] DeLillo, *White Noise*, 129.

Margaret Morse, in a closely parallel account of the derealized spaces of postmodernity, uses the concept of 'distraction' to describe this flotation between different layers of reality.[57] By distraction she means a kind of 'attenuated fiction effect' involved in the constant 'liquid' flow between different levels of attention and different ontological states in the non-space of the mall, the freeway, and television. The concept of non-space is used, not moralistically but as a way of exploring the peculiar overriding of a singular and paramount reality in these complexly and 'secondarily' constructed domains. In the case of television, she argues, the representation of 'mixed and simultaneous worlds' is closely tied to its function of

symbolically linking incommensurabilities of all sorts—the system of goods or commodities and the economic relations it orders, the sexual-matrimonial system which orders sociality, and the symbolic order of language, including images, symbols, and the spoken or written word. If television itself is a great storehouse for tokens of all these cultural systems, exchange values are created by their juxtaposition, but even more by means of passages through them, in which television programming offers many different itineraries from which to choose. (p. 207)

The very mobility of such non-space has the effect of reunifying space and time, and thus re-creating the authority of a primary or paramount reality—but precisely as a reconstruction, a 'phantom within elsewhere' (208) What is new about this is not the institutions of 'mobile privatization' themselves (since they continue earlier processes) but

the interpenetration of layer upon layer of built environment and representation, the formative and derivative, the imaginary and mundane. Embodying values as neither here nor there, both present and absent, they are ideal expressions of the zones of ontological uncertainty, expressions of both Kansas and Oz. (p. 210)

In these circumstances there can be no simple return to a pretelevisual reality; 'other' realities—and this is perhaps the central obsession of White Noise—*are always already included in representation.*

[57] Margaret Morse, 'An Ontology of Everyday Distraction: The Freeway, the Mall, the Television', in Patricia Mellencamp (ed.), *Logics of Television: Essays in Cultural Criticism* (Bloomington: Indiana University Press, 1990), 193–221.

Much of the imprecision of the concept of *post*modernism stems, then, from the difficulty of assigning temporal limits to cultural modernism, and—to complicate matters—from the different datings used in different cultural spheres. The beginnings of *literary* modernism are usually dated from around 1900 or a bit later. David Roberts puts the decisive break in 1914, and describes it in terms of the transformation of the cultural market ('High art since 1914 is no longer bourgeois but produced by and for intellectuals').[58] Certainly it seems clear that the moment of literary modernism had passed by about 1930, to be replaced by forms of writing whose relation to the modernist moment is still in need of clarification. Harry Levin's essay of 1960, 'What Was Modernism?', could speak confidently of modernism as a thing of the past, just as Lionel Trilling could speak in *Beyond Culture* of a fully accomplished and entrenched institutionalization of literary modernism.[59] In the visual arts, however, a quite different periodization obtains: here the term modernism tends in current usage to mean the period from the late 1940s to the mid-1960s, associated with the dominance of the New York School and with Clement Greenberg's 'formally reflexive' conception of modernism.[60] In architecture, finally, modernism refers to the more monolithic structure of the International Style, which has a quite different, non-oppositional relation to the culture of corporate capitalism, and which has undergone a more continuous development from the 1920s through to the 1970s. Indeed, it is in the case of architecture, which has been the privileged domain for the theorization of postmodernism, that these two problems, that of exemplification and that of periodization, most dramatically converge. The difficulty lies in the very terms of the opposition between the modern and the postmodern that is established here—that is, with the assumption of its generalizability. Does architectural Modernism have anything to do with the other modernisms, does it share a common

[58] David Roberts, 'Marxism, Modernism, Postmodernism', *Thesis 11*, 12 (1985), 54.
[59] Harry Levin, 'What Was Modernism?', repr. in *Refractions: Essays in Comparative Literature* (London: Oxford University Press, 1966), 271–95; Lionel Trilling, 'On the Teaching of Modern Literature', *Beyond Culture: Essays on Literature and Learning* (1965; repr. Harmondsworth: Penguin, 1967), 19–41.

[60] Michael Newman, 'Revising Modernism, Representing Postmodernism: Critical Discourses of the Visual Arts', *ICA Documents* 4 (Postmodernism) and 5 (London: Institute of Contemporary Arts, 1986), 32.

problematic or even a common temporality, or does it have a quite different rhythm and dynamic?

One way of establishing a correlation between architectural Modernism and other domains of aesthetic production would be in terms of a conflation of modernism with modernity. The central categories in such a model would be a certain mode of rationality and a certain complicity with the modernization process. T. W. Adorno's is perhaps the most explicit account we have of both of these features: the modernist work of art is characterized by its rigorous commitment to the inherent rationality of its material (however 'irrational' this might be in another sense) and to the progressive development of this rationality through a critique of obsolescent forms. The more or less advanced state of the material is directly correlated with the more or less advanced state of the forces of capitalist production. And the dynamic of the work of art is that of an exploration of the autonomous domain in which the material is elaborated.[61] An extrapolation of these features to architecture would describe architectural Modernism in terms of a claim to atemporal universality; a self-reflexive relation to architectonic space, including exposure of the materials and especially of the skeleton; an expressive ('functional') relation between inside and outside; and a willed autonomy with respect to the urban context. This formal separateness of the Modernist style is what Portoghesi calls a 'dam carefully built around the pure language elaborated *in vitro* on the basis of the rationalist statute'.[62] Similarly, Rosalind Krauss's description of the function of the *grid* in modernist art could be directly transposed into a description of Modernist architecture:

In the spatial sense, the grid states the autonomy of the realm of art. Flattened, geometricized, ordered, it is antinatural, antimimetic, antireal. It is what art looks like when it turns its back on nature. In the flatness that results from its coordinates, the grid is the means of crowding out the dimensions of the real and replacing them with the lateral spread of a single surface. In the overall regularity of its organization, it is the result not of

---

[61] Cf. in particular Theodor W. Adorno, *Philosophy of Modern Music*, trans. Anne Mitchell and Wesley Bloomster (London: Sheed and Ward, 1973); and Peter Bürger, 'The Decline of the Modern Age', trans. D. Parent, *Telos*, 62 (1984–5), 117–30.

[62] Paolo Portoghesi, *Postmodern: The Architecture of the Postindustrial Society*, trans. Ellen Shapiro (New York: Rizzoli, 1983), 10.

imitation, but of aesthetic decree. Insofar as its order is that of pure relationship, the grid is a way of abrogating the claims of natural objects to have any order particular to themselves; the relationships in the aesthetic field are shown by the grid to be in a world apart and, with respect to natural objects, to be both prior and final. The grid declares the space of art to be at once autonomous and autotelic.[63]

In their reliance on this principle, the organization of artistic and of architectural space display clear structural parallels. On the other hand, however, it is arguable that modernist architecture is integrated into capitalist production in a way that is not true of other domains, which remain at once complicit with and deeply antagonistic to its logic. This is in part a question of the different functional relationship of architecture to capital, but it does suggest the difficulty of imposing a universal historicity on distinct and unevenly developed domains of the social.

It is postmodern architecture that constitutes the central exemplificatory instance in Jameson's influential essay on the cultural logic of late capitalism. Portman's Bonaventure Hotel in Los Angeles doesn't exactly exemplify the populist and vernacular thrust of postmodernism, since, rather than opening itself to the 'tawdry and commercial sign-system of the surrounding city',[64] it withdraws into its own self-contained space, re-creating the outside city in miniature. In this you might think that it resembles the aloof disjunction of the High Modernist tower from its surrounding cityscape, but Jameson argues that it corresponds, instead, to a new kind of collective practice and to a new (refusal of) politics: the Bonaventure 'is content to "let the fallen city fabric continue to be in its being" (to parody Heidegger); no further effects, no larger protopolitical Utopian transformation, is either expected or desired' (pp. 41–2).

This 'peculiar and placeless dissociation of the Bonaventure from its neighbourhood' (p. 42) is emphasized both by the occlusion of entrances and by the way the building's glass skin repels its surrounds (giving back only 'distorted images' in a deliberate play of illusion). We are confronted here not just with a refusal of relationship but with a turning inwards of signification. The

---

[63] Rosalind E. Krauss, *The Originality of the Avant-Garde and Other Modernist Myths* (Cambridge, Mass.: MIT Press, 1986), 9–10.

[64] Jameson, *Postmodernism*, 39; further references will be incorporated in the text.

escalators and elevators, for example, function in the first instance as self-regarding symbols: they 'replace movement but also and above all designate themselves as new reflexive signs and emblems of movement proper'; and in this they represent 'a dialectical intensification of the autoreferentiality of all modern culture, which tends to turn upon itself and designate its own cultural production as its content' (p. 42). In the same (self-referential) movement the operation of *reference* is foiled: as the elevators rise 'the referent, Los Angeles', is spread out beneath; but once you get to the cocktail lounges at the top the city is 'now transformed into its own images by the glass windows through which you view it' (p. 43).

In all this, and in the creation of the 'hyperspace' of the atrium, the Bonaventure offers 'something like a mutation in built space itself' (p. 38), to which the human sensorium is as yet inadequate: the metaphor, which derives ultimately from the passages on the historicity of the five senses in Marx's *1844 Manuscripts* by way of Walter Benjamin's meditations on the experience of the modern city and of modern warfare, defines postmodernity as an evolution which bears strong marks of being also a fall.

Jameson's discussion assumes, however, that there *is* a general logic of 'late' capitalism, and that architectural postmodernism thus represents a definite break both with Modernist architecture and (which comes to the same thing) with the logic of an earlier phase of capitalism. This assumption is disputed by Davis (amongst others), who suggests a different periodization of the urban 'renaissance' in relation to the rise of new international circuits of speculative and rentier capital; and a different context for buildings like the Los Angeles Bonaventure in the relationship between a highly capitalized downtown and surrounding urban decay.[65]

A second problem has to do with Jameson's choice of a *signed masterpiece* (Portman's Bonaventure Hotel) as his main example— an unusual choice, given the claim that postmodernism is subversive of the signature and of authorial originality. To emblematize the monumental is as problematic a procedure when you're talking about the built environment as it is in discussing literary texts, and

---

[65] Mike Davis, 'Urban Renaissance and the Spirit of Postmodernism'. Jameson mounts a defence of the concept of totality in 'Marxism and Postmodernism', *New Left Review*, 176 (July–Aug. 1989), 31–45 (repr. from *Postmodernism/Jameson/Critique*, ed. Douglas Kellner (Washington, DC: Maisonneuve Press, 1989); cf. *Postmodernism*, 331–40 and 399–418.

it has the effect of marginalizing other kinds of built space. Now, it seems true that the aestheticization of city space, and especially decayed inner-city space, has been one key feature of 'postmodern' urban transformation (and it has to do with certain interesting transformations in the system of production and in contemporary class formations: that is, it has to do with new, 'culturalized' forms of design and marketing). But, as Sharon Zukin notes, it is already characteristic of architectural *modernism* to treat urban space in the aestheticizing terms of signature and saleable creation. It is within a modernist framework that 'the marketing of design as both a spatial and a cultural commodity' begins, and 'the production of superstar architecture derives from the same speculative building activity that generated high modernism'.[66] Indeed, if the paradigmatic shift from modernism to postmodernism is seen to consist only in certain stylistic transformations in the form of modelling of the signed monument then very little would seem to have changed.

The more meaningful shift is one of focus. The concept of postmodernism takes on life when it becomes a way of disrupting the hierarchical distinctions between important and routine architecture, between architecture and the rest of the built environment, and between spatiality and social structure. In this altered perspective (one which has particularly marked the discipline of social geography in the last decade) it becomes possible to ask questions about the urban infrastructure as a whole,[67] and perhaps especially to ask questions about the construction of architectural *series*: that is, about the intensification of the 'modernist' derealization of place through the building of non-localized environments.

[66] Sharon Zukin, 'The Postmodern Debate over Urban Form', *Theory, Culture and Society*, 5: 2–3 (1988), 440.

[67] The final two chapters of Edward Soja's *Postmodern Geographies*, for example, mention the Bonaventure as a 'concentrated representation of the restructured spatiality of the late capitalist city,' and then analyse the spatiality of Los Angeles in terms of financial and industrial agglomeration and the internationalization of the local economy; large-scale immigration and the growth of an informal economy; deindustrialization and a post-Fordist reindustrialization accompanied by a savage disciplining of labour; reliance on defence technology; the recomposition of the labour market through deskilling and an increased reliance on low-paid, non-unionized immigrant and female labour; and spatial restructuring through disagglomeration and decentralization, but also through renewed urban concentrations—the 'downtown renaissance' and the rise of the 'outer city'. Cf. also Michael Dear, 'Postmodernism and Planning', *Environment and Planning D: Society and Space*, 4 (1986), 367–84.

Much of the literature here (Relph's concept of 'placelessness', Boorstin's 'pseudo-place', Augé's 'non-place', Baudrillard's 'hyper-reality') is moralistic in tone, but you should in fact be able to use a fairly neutral vocabulary to describe the form of spatiality of serialized place: the shopping mall, the resort, the air terminal, the theme park, the motel.

(Or even to speak joyfully of them. The central spaces of White Noise *are the house, always the house; the makeshift refugee centre; the airport; the motel; the fast-food outlets; the super-market. There is the medical laboratory: 'a functional pale brick building, one story, with slab floors and bright lighting. Why would such a place be called Autumn Harvest Farms?'*[68] *And there is the Mid-Village Mall, out on the interstate, where the main structure is 'a ten story building arranged around a center court of waterfalls, promenades and gardens', with 'shops set along the tiers', 'emporiums and department stores', 'boutiques and gourmet shops', organ music rising from the great court, and a band playing live Musak.)*[69]

But once you speak of such non-localized spatial series it becomes difficult to separate the 'real' places (or the real non-places) from the representations of places that are coextensive with them: the 'locales' of film and television, for example, or the self-contained world of advertising. Equally, it becomes impossible to detach the description of place from the description of the forms of social organization that sustain postmodern spatiality: the feminization and casualization of low-paid work, the increased reliance on migrant labour, deindustrialization and the outsourcing of produc-tion to the Third World, the commodification of information and the rise of a new class of information-industry workers, the replacement of human by non-human labour . . . The force of the concept of postmodernism here lies simply in its imperative to conceptualize both a new configuration of the cultural domain (in particular the blurring of boundaries between high and low culture and between commercial and non-commercial art) and a changed relation between culture and economic production.[70]

---

[68] DeLillo, *White Noise*, 275.   [69] Ibid. 83–4.
[70] Cf. Zukin, 'The Postmodern Debate over Urban Form', 433.

The most interesting attempts to theorize the changed economic conditions which might, in one sense, be said to underpin postmodernist cultural production, but which in another sense have altogether transformed the relationship of apparent exteriority between the cultural and the economic, are the recent elaborations of a cluster of roughly overlapping concepts describing a shift in capitalist production: the 'post-Fordism' of the Regulation School (Aglietta, Billaudot and Gauron, Piore and Sabel, Boyer, Lipietz);[71] David Harvey's 'flexible accumulation';[72] Scott Lash and John Urry's 'disorganized capitalism'[73] and 'reflexive accumulation';[74] and the more dispersed concepts of postmodernization and flexible specialization. With varying degrees of assuredness these concepts attempt to construct the terms of a general shift—Harvey dates it precisely from 1972[75]—in the regime of capital accumulation and regulation. A summary of these terms would look something like this:

- with the massively increased productivity of information technologies, capital becomes 'hypermobile and hyper-flexible',[76] in the process displacing or destroying many areas of work;
- the resulting uneven geographical and sectoral development of

---

[71] Michel Aglietta, A Theory of Capitalist Regulation: The U.S. Experience, trans. David Fernbach (London: Verso, 1979); Bernard Billaudot and André Gauron, Croissance et crise: vers une nouvelle croissance, 2nd edn. (Paris: La Découverte, 1985); Michael J. Piore and Charles F. Sabel, The Second Industrial Divide: Possibilities for Prosperity (New York: Basic Books, 1984); Robert Boyer, The Regulation School: A Critical Introduction, trans. Craig Charney (New York: Columbia University Press, 1990), and Capitalismes fin de siècle (Paris: Presses Universitaires Françaises, 1986); Alain Lipietz, The Enchanted World, trans. Ian Patterson (London: Verso, 1985), Mirages and Miracles: The Crisis of Global Fordism, trans. David Macey (London: Verso, 1987), and Towards a New Economic Order: Post-Fordism, Democracy and Ecology, trans. Michael Slater (Oxford: Polity Press, 1992).

[72] David Harvey, 'Flexible Accumulation through Urbanization: Reflections on "Post-Modernism" in the American City', Antipode, 19: 3 (1987), 260.

[73] Scott Lash and John Urry, The End of Organized Capitalism (Cambridge: Polity Press, 1987).

[74] Scott Lash and John Urry, Economies of Signs and Space (London: Sage, 1994).

[75] Harvey, 'Flexible Accumulation', 260.

[76] Kevin Robins, 'Reimagined Communities? European Image Spaces beyond Fordism', Cultural Studies, 3: 2 (1989), 149.

production and of the division of labour[77] give rise to a disaggregation of large-scale industrial production and a dispersal of production units to take account of local political and market circumstances, especially the price and conditions of labour;

- none of this implies a decentralization of economic power; rather there is a paradoxical combination of dispersed production, on the one hand, and on the other of centralized control of capital accumulation and of the circulation of information.[78] A shift by firms to the raising of capital directly against equity enables the creation of extensive secondary markets in securities, the scope of which is further extended by deregulation and by electronically mediated trading;[79]
- the achievement of economies of scale is progressively abandoned in favour of the achievement of economies of scope; the diversification of demand in highly segmented and rapidly changing mass markets is met by the targeting of 'niche' markets, by increased product differentiation, and by a more rapid modification of product ranges (in contrast to the standardization of production in a Fordist regime);
- the new service classes of professionals and information workers acquire increased industrial prominence and increasing political and ideological influence;[80]
- a substantial informal sector (a black economy based on casual work performed by non-union labour, on sweatshops, on migrant workers, and on a feminization of low-paid work) develops over the last two decades; the model of welfare capitalism is in decline, and politically engineered transfers of wealth articulate an increasing gap between the poor and the rich.[81] The public sector is progressively stripped of assets and funds;

[77] Cf. Doreen Massey, *Spatial Divisions of Labour: Social Structures and the Geography of Production* (New York: Methuen, and London: Macmillan, 1984); and Neil Smith, *Uneven Development: Nature, Capital and the Production of Space* (Oxford: Blackwell, 1984).

[78] Robins, 'Reimagined Communities?', 149.

[79] Lash and Urry, *Economies of Signs and Space*, 18–21.

[80] Cf. John Frow, *Cultural Studies and Cultural Value* (Oxford: Clarendon Press, 1995), ch. 3, 'Class and Cultural Capital'.

[81] Cf. Philip Cooke, 'The Postmodern Condition and the City', in Michael Peter Smith (ed.), *Comparative Urban and Community Research*, i: *Power, Community and the City* (New Brunswick, NJ: Transaction Books, 1988), 72.

- the flexibility of international capital and the constant threat of withdrawal of capital from politically unstable or hostile regimes, together with the weakening of organized labour in its defensive reaction to international capital, impose absolute limits on socialist strategy;[82]
- inter-urban competition, developed as a response to the increased mobility of corporations, gives rise to the subsidization of corporate presence and to the renovation of the cities as centres of consumption and culture;[83] there is an upsurge in the renovation and gentrification of inner-city areas;
- the 'aestheticization of everyday life' is realized as a practice of differentiation of commodities and of places (with place now increasingly marketed as a commodity on the basis of its specific difference and/or its 'authenticity'); Zukin speaks of 'an increasing commercialization of the social category of design'.[84]

This list is problematical in its agglomeration of economic, political, and cultural aspects of postmodernization, and there are important qualifications that must be made to the generality of the model. Kevin Robins, noting that accounts of post-Fordism are 'increasingly congealing into a new orthodoxy of optimism', cautions both against the assumption of an organic epochal transition and against a disregard of the fact that 'so-called flexible specialization combines organizational and functional disintegration or disaggregation with the continued integration of control and co-ordination'.[85] Michael Rustin questions the model's adequacy to account for survivals of 'mass production' modes and indeed for regressions to apparently superseded strategies (he cites the use of unskilled labour in the hotel industry, and the return to mass formula programming in the television industry). What seems to be emerging, he argues,

is not one 'progressive' mode of information-based production, but a plethora of co-existing and competing systems, whose ultimate relative weight in the system is impossible to predict. Since socio-technical systems do not develop completely autonomously, but only in response to cultural

---

[82] Cf. Adam Przeworski, *Capitalism and Social Democracy* (Cambridge: Cambridge University Press, 1985).

[83] Harvey, 'Flexible Accumulation', 264–5.

[84] Zukin, 'The Postmodern Debate over Urban Form', 438.

[85] Robins, 'Reimagined Communities?', 147, 153.

definition, conflicts of social forces, and political decision, it is dubious in principle and possibly misleading in fact to make linear extrapolations from what might seem to be 'leading instances,' or current trends, to the shape of the whole system.[86]

For my purposes it is crucial to refuse the deduction of post-modernist cultural practice from the economic categories elaborated here,[87] while recognizing that the relation of the cultural to the economic has nevertheless significantly changed.

In these terms, the key aspect of postmodernization is the last one listed, which describes the increasing integration of the aesthetic (in the form especially of advertising and design, but also of architecture, of music and Muzak, and indeed of all the arts from the 'highest' to the 'lowest') into the marketing of commodities. Lash and Urry thus argue for a symmetrical articulation by which 'ordinary manufacturing industry is becoming more and more like the production of culture',[88] and, conversely, 'what (all) the culture industries produce becomes increasingly, not like commodities but advertisements'—for example, through the process by which a cultural text 'advertises' and sells itself as a product within a brand-name structure of cultural marketing.[89] Zukin takes as emblematic of this fusion the totalizing strategies adopted by Benetton and Macdonalds in developing 'a total "look" that merges product, production methods, a specialized consumption experience, and an advertising style'.[90] And we could perhaps suggest that it is because of this integration that the important—the really interesting—forms of postmodernist architecture are not the signed masterpieces but the relatively anonymous and highly standardized forms of the department store and the shopping mall.

'There was a life-style sale at a home-furnishing mart. Well-lighted men and women stood by the huge window looking out at us and wondering. It made us feel like fools, like tourists doing all the wrong things.[91]

[86] Michael Rustin, 'The Politics of Post-Fordism: or, The Trouble with "New Times" ', *New Left Review*, 175 (May–June, 1989), 58.

[87] Harvey, for example, speaks of (cultural) postmodernity as 'nothing more than the cultural clothing of flexible accumulation' ('Flexible Accumulation', 279).

[88] Lash and Urry, *Economies of Signs and Space*, 123.

[89] Ibid. 138.

[90] Zukin, 'The Postmodern Debate over Urban Form', 437.

[91] DeLillo, *White Noise*, 120.

Models of socioeconomic postmodernity are models of epochal change, and whatever their methodological sophistication they tend to be constructed according to the globalizing, essentializing, and spiritualizing patterns of historicism which tie the disparate and uneven temporalities of the social into a homogeneous time. Consider Harvey's synthetic modelling of 'the interpenetration of opposed tendencies in capitalist society as a whole':[92]

Fordist modernity	*Flexible postmodernity*
economies of scale/master code/ hierarchy	economies of scope/idiolect/ anarchy
homogeneity/detail division of labour	diversity/social division of labour
paranoia/alienation/symptom	schizophrenia/decentering/desire
public housing/monopoly capital	homelessness/entrepreneurialism
purpose/design/mastery/ determinacy	play/chance/exhaustion/ indeterminacy
production capital/universalism	fictitious capital/localism
state power/trade unions	financial power/individualism
state welfarism/metropolis	neo-conservatism/ counterurbanization
ethics/money commodity	aesthetics/moneys of account
God the Father/materiality	The Holy Ghost/immateriality
production/originality/authority	reproduction/pastiche/eclecticism
blue collar/avant-gardism	white collar/commercialism
interest group politics/semantics	charismatic politics/rhetoric
centralization/totalization	decentralization/deconstruction
synthesis/collective bargaining	antithesis/local contracts
operational management/master code	strategic management/idiolect
phallic/single task/origin	androgynous/multiple tasks/trace

[92] David Harvey, *The Condition of Postmodernity: An Enquiry into the Origins of Cultural Change* (Oxford: Basil Blackwell, 1989), 340–1, Table 4.1: 'Fordist modernity versus flexible postmodernity, or the interpenetration of opposed tendencies in capitalist society as a whole.' Further citations are given in the text.

Fordist modernity	Flexible postmodernity
metatheory/narrative/depth	language games/image/surface
mass production/class politics	small batch production/social
technical-scientific rationality	movements
	pluralistic otherness
utopia/redemptive art/	heterotopias/spectacle/dispersal
concentration	flexible worker/symbolic capital
specialized work/collective	
consumption	
function/representation/signified	fiction/self-reference/signifier
industry/protestant work ethic	services/temporary contract
mechanical reproduction	electronic reproduction
becoming/epistemology/regulation	being/ontology/deregulation
urban renewal/relative space	urban revitalization/place
state interventionism/	laissez-faire/deindustrialization
industrialization	geopolitics/ephemerality/space
internationalism/permanence/time	

The chart has the classic binary form of Hassan's idealist historiography (on which in part it draws), and although Harvey claims that, rather than opposing the reified categories of the modern and the postmodern, it constitutes a structural description of a totality of interpenetrating political-economic and cultural-ideological relations (p. 339), it is nevertheless clearly a model of global epochal shift, where the categories derive all their meaning (and hence all their descriptive power) from the pattern of oppositions. Crucially, it is a model in which aesthetic production is theorized as functional for the workings of post-Fordist production as a whole. The results of this theorization are ambivalent: on the one hand, because of Harvey's comprehensive grasp of the categories of Marxist political economy, he delivers a powerful account of the integration of the aesthetic in the system of flexible accumulation; the corollary to this, however, is that the aesthetic is conceived as a singular domain, moralistically understood as the analogue of the formation of fictitious capital and of the politics of simulation.

A series of metaphors relates the changing rhythms of capitalist production to those of other domains. At the most general level the 'creative destruction' of capitalism is set up as an analogue (or something stronger) to the 'creative destruction' of Nietzschean modernism. More specifically, an analysis of the speed-up in commodity turnover time is used as a basis for explaining the conditions of existence of a postmodern aesthetic:

The half-life of a typical Fordist product was, for example, from five to seven years, but flexible accumulation has more than cut that in half in certain sectors (such as textile and clothing industries), while in others— such as the so-called 'thoughtware' industries (e.g. video games and computer software programmes)—the half-life is down to less than eighteen months. Flexible accumulation has been accompanied on the consumption side, therefore, by a much greater attention to quick-changing fashions and the mobilization of all the artifices of need inducement and cultural transformation that this implies. The relatively stable aesthetic of Fordist modernism has given way to all the ferment, instability, and fleeting qualities of a postmodernist aesthetic that celebrates difference, ephemerality, spectacle, fashion, and the commodi-fication of cultural forms. (p. 156)

In so far as this refers to the integration of the aesthetic (as 'need inducement', the mobilization and channelling of desire) into industrial production, especially in the domains of fashion, design, and advertising, the argument is exact. It is surely true, moreover, that this integration does not leave other forms of cultural production untouched—that, for example, 'the deployment of advertisement as "the official art of capitalism" brings advertising strategies into art, and art into advertising strategies' (p. 63). But the argument says nothing about the ways in which texts *work* their conditions of existence, taking precisely the aporia of the integration of art into commodity production as their raw material. And if aesthetic texts are refused any reflexive or cognitive function (or if reflexivity is reduced to narcissistic self-reference), this is because of the particular political space to which the aesthetic is assigned in Harvey's schema.

Briefly, it is this: Harvey's account of postmodernity, structured initially in terms of the economics of flexible accumulation, comes at a certain stage to depend upon a supplementary framework of explanation. Transformations in the categories of space and time now constitute a deeper level of causality, and a shift in the relations between them works as the governing metaphor for the modulation to a qualitatively different regime of accumulation. The categories of space and time then split apart from each other and take on qualities of political value which are used to play off the project of modernity against the project of postmodernity. Two series of terms are chained together: on the side of *modernity* are the categories of time, of Becoming, of ethics and social theory, of Enlightenment rationality, of a 'temporal' Marxist project, and of the politicization of aesthetics; on the side of *postmodernity* are the categories of space (and of the local and nationalist politics of space, which culminate in Heidegger and Fascism), of Being, of the aesthetic and of aesthetic theory, of the 'abandonment' of rationality by post-structuralist philosophy, of a 'spatial' Hegelian project, and of the aestheticization of politics. Against the 'rational ordering and control of space as part and parcel of a modern culture founded on rationality and technique' (p. 280) (meaning, I think—although the implication is never made clear—the strategies of an exemplary *architectural* modernism) is set an eschatological vision of a postmodernity in which

the experience of time and space has changed, the confidence in the association between scientific and moral judgements has collapsed, aesthetics has triumphed over ethics as a prime focus of social and intellectual concern, images dominate narratives, ephemerality and fragmentation take precedence over eternal truths and unified politics, and explanations have shifted from the realm of material and political-economic groundings towards a consideration of autonomous cultural and political practices. (p. 328)

To be blunt: this is glib doom-saying rather than rigorous analysis. The problem is that of any totalizing vision (especially when its account of post-structuralist philosophy and postmodern art is based, as such accounts so often are, on dinner-party gossip and second-hand redactions): the construction of domains of practice as massive unities ('the aesthetic') and their expressive linkage to other unified domains. Pseudo-totalities generate pseudo-histories; the epochal sense of the concept of the postmodern depends for its existence on such historico-spiritual fictions.

The adventures of the aesthetic make up one of the great narratives of modernity: from the time of its autonomy through art for art's sake to its status as a necessary negative category, a critique of the world as it is. It is this last moment (figured brilliantly in the writings of Theodor Adorno) that it is hard to relinquish: the notion of the aesthetic as subversive, a critical interstice in an otherwise instrumental world. Now, however, we have to consider that this aesthetic space too is eclipsed—or rather, that its criticality is now largely illusory (and so instrumental).[93]

But however dubious the idea of a radical break with modernism, however incoherent and empty the concept of the postmodern, nevertheless the very existence of the concept (like the irreducibly non-disprovable concept of the unconscious in Freudian psycho-analysis) acts as a provocation to the forms of historical thinking which have accompanied or been derived from modernism. It is not just the concept of novelty or rupture (the dynamic of perpetual change) which becomes problematic, but the political force attached to it—the sense that to break with ossified formal structures is at the same time to disrupt or subvert a broader normative structure of social authority.

The extent of the problem is made clear in Meaghan Morris's careful exposition of the recuperative strategy developed in Lyotard's writings on postmodernism. She identifies two versions of the concept. The first posits a roughly consecutive relationship between modernism and postmodernism (so that the latter is paradoxically understood in terms of a model of progressive rupture derived entirely from the former). In the second version, however, Lyotard 'predicates a postmodernity which, as a recurring moment of rupture, actually *institutes* the modern: "Post-modernism . . . is not modernism at its end, but rather modernism at its very beginning—and that beginning is always recurrent." '[94] It's a brilliant move, which, in conceding the institutionalization of modernism, posits the moment of critique of (this) institutionaliza-tion as the very core of modernist practice; it is only of secondary importance, then, that the critique should occur 'afterwards', since it is structurally the *founding* moment of modernism.

The logic of this moment is what Morris calls the 'injunction to formal eventfulness (the invention of new rules)', and it is an inherently self-undermining logic because 'the very structure of the obligation to "event" (to coin a phrase), *as well as* the logic of the art market, soon drain any event of its eventfulness'. Indeed the

---

[93] Hal Foster, 'Postmodernism: A Preface', p. xv.
[94] Jean-François Lyotard, 'Answering the Question: What is Postmodernism?', *The Postmodern Condition*, 79; cited in Meaghan Morris, *The Pirate's Fiancée*, 235.

history of modernism is the history of the ever-increasing speed of this 'draining'. Lyotard's response is to insist both upon the untenability of this dynamic (there must be a moment *beyond* it) and upon its ineluctable necessity (to abandon the impulse to make it, constantly, new would be to give up on whatever critical function is possible for modernist art). But this hypothesis, says Morris, is, for all its theoretical adroitness, quite strictly banal, 'because it restores us to the paradox of a history driven by the sole, and *traditional*, imperative to break with tradition'. It seems to be driven by its *opposition* to the automatizing and deadening power of institutionalization; but

Surely an entire history of modern art institutions (including criticism, the gallery, the museum, and the relations of all three to the rest of the market) could be written precisely in terms of a strict rhythm of alternation between advance and arrest, pure event and mere innovation. The transformation of the former into the latter is vital to the art 'system'—indeed, as Lyotard's own version of the modern/postmodern relation suggests, it may actually be a rule that defines the game.[95]

Fredric Jameson has for some years now been making a similar argument about the untenability of a modernist account of aesthetic change. The paradox he identifies is that the very opposition to commodification has in fact enhanced the market value of modernist art, and has furthered the integration of high art into commodity production:

The dynamic of perpetual change is, as Marx showed in the *Manifesto*, not some alien rhythm within capital—a rhythm specific to those noninstrumental activities that are art and science—but rather is the very 'permanent revolution' of capitalist production itself: at which point the exhilaration with such revolutionary dynamism is a feature of the bonus of pleasure and the reward of the social reproduction of the system itself.[96]

The imperatives of capitalist production assign 'an increasingly essential structural function and position to aesthetic innovation and experimentation',[97] and modernism has thus become absorbed into 'an economy functionally dependent on it for its indispensable fashion changes and for the perpetual resupplying of a media

---

[95] Morris, *The Pirate's Fiancée*, 235–6.
[96] Fredric Jameson, 'Foreword' to Jean-François Lyotard, *The Post-Modern Condition*, p. xx.   [97] Jameson, *Postmodernism*, 5.

culture'.[98] One might feel that Jameson, like Harvey, reduces a complex process of aesthetic positioning too neatly to a functionalist vision of social totality, but there is surely no doubt that he is right about the extent to which modernism has been bound into the workings of the art market.

The implication of all this might be that if we are properly to understand the rhythms of contemporary aesthetic production (but can we still speak of a self-contained aesthetic domain?) we must think in terms of a quite different temporality: one in which the moment of innovation immediately gives rise to, and indeed requires, its own subsumption into the aesthetic norm (so that the notion of a norm itself becomes empty); and in which the dynamic of change is so rapid or so routinized as to resemble a vertiginous stasis. Let us follow Jameson (but also Baudelaire, who had already in 'Le Peintre de la vie moderne' identified the close connection between *mode*, the fugitive and transitory, and modernity)[99] in calling this the temporality of fashion.

Within a postmodernist paradigm time is a closed circle. It leads nowhere, it cannot be broken. The novelty that seems to puncture it is a pointless movement of change which merely reinforces its closure. This is how Iain Chambers puts it:

With electronic reproduction offering the spectacle of gestures, images, styles and cultures in a perpetual collage of disintegration and reintegration, the 'new' disappears into a permanent present. And with the end of the 'new'—a concept connected to linearity, to the serial prospects of 'progress', to 'modernism'—we move into a perpetual recycling of

---

[98] Fredric Jameson, 'The Ideology of the Text', *Salmagundi*, 31–2 (1975–6), 246. Raymond Williams speaks of modernism's forms having 'lent themselves to cultural competition and the commercial interplay of obsolescence, with its shifts of schools, styles and fashion so essential to the market. The painfully acquired techniques of significant *dis*connection are relocated, with the help of the special insensitivity of the trained and assured technicists, as the merely technical modes of advertising and the commercial cinema' ('When Was Modernism?', *New Left Review*, 175 (May–June 1989), 51). The suggestion of an elective affinity for this process ('lent themselves') seems to me to undermine the apparently historical form of the analysis: modernism is seen *always* to have been flawed, and this flaw has simply become manifest in the process of decline from an experiential to a 'merely technical' technique.

[99] Charles Baudelaire, 'Le Peintre de la vie moderne', in *Curiosités esthétiques, L'Art romantique, et autres œuvres critiques*, ed. H. Lemaitre (Paris: Garnier, 1962), 453–502.

quotations, styles and fashions; an uninterrupted montage of the 'now'.[100]

The argument takes 'fashion' and 'style' on their own terms, as the end of history—and these are terms which are thoroughly ideological in their generalization of a restricted temporality. Indeed, Chambers doesn't think through the consequences of this state of postness, which is built around a series of contradictions: such a temporality is either tensely structured on paradox or it is flat and empty—or, to push the logic of the argument further, it will be both at the same time. It seems to project a moral imperative to abandon the quest for novelty, but in so far as novelty is fully functional for the system it is never possible to dispense with it, nor even, perhaps, with the illusion that novelty is the same as genuine newness. The time of postmodernism looks something like the stability and closure of neoclassicism, but it rests on a knowing sense of the abyss that is utterly foreign to a neoclassical aesthetic. It seems to presume a cynical acceptance of the commodity status of art, at the same time as it seeks to resist the fetish of the new, the original, the unique, through a parodic imitation of fashion, of advertising, of commodified novelty which is in its turn commod-ified, and which can never break through into some politically transcendental alterity.[101] It casually junks a whole tradition of radical negativity, the gamble on an absolute and rigorous commitment to critique, that was at stake in the dynamic of modernist change. And it makes a queer virtue of the cognitive triviality implied by the word fashion (to such an extent that one might be forced to note, with Paul de Man and against our 'common-sense' reaction, that 'when it becomes fashionable to dismiss fashion, clearly something interesting is going on, and what is being discarded as *mere* fashion must also be more insistent, and more threatening, than its frivolity and transience would seem to indicate').[102]

It is in something like these terms that Nelly Richard speaks of 'the critical de-energizing of many postmodernist works that

---

[100] Iain Chambers, *Popular Culture: The Metropolitan Experience* (London: Methuen, 1986), 190.

[101] David Bennett, 'Wrapping up Postmodernism', 246.

[102] Paul de Man, Introduction to Hans Robert Jauss, *Toward an Aesthetic of Reception*, trans. Timothy Bahti, Theory and History of Literature 2 (Minneapolis: University of Minnesota Press, 1982), p. xx.

renounce, unlike those which preceded them, the contestation of the cultural institutionality (museums-galleries-markets) which welcomes them and protects them'.[103] At the same time, however, she refuses to set up the historical avant-garde as a model of good cultural-political praxis. Instead she sets out the terms of the critique which a later generation (if I may use that figure) would make of the modernist avant-garde for its 'tendency to believe, ingenuously, in the radicality of its desire for rupture and in the irreversibility of the gesture which manifests it': a stance which ignores the historical fact of recuperation, 'the ease with which history turns the meaning of the gesture of rupture *back on itself*, reintroducing this movement into the continuity of the principle which founds it as History'.[104] To formulate this critique is at the same time to be sceptical of the classic avant-gardist claim to be able to extend the moment of rupture to the realm of political practice.

What has changed is an intensification and an acceleration of the assimilative power of the art system.[105] This is the historical and institutional ground of the postmodernist dilemma: that 'the History of Art has now learned to absorb Novelty simply as a variation on Tradition, and to exercise control over the periodicity of forms that *regularizes* any alternating or rotating play between the movements, thus rendering this play predictable'.[106] And this has then meant that it has—for historical and institutional reasons—become ever more difficult to find and define 'the limit of what is unacceptable':[107] nothing is in principle 'unacceptable' any more.[108]

---

[103] Nelly Richard, 'Notes towards a (Critical) Re-evaluation of the Critique of the Avant-Garde', *Art and Text*, 16 (1984–5), 16–17.   [104] Ibid. 10.

[105] Cf. Andreas Huyssen, *After the Great Divide: Modernism, Mass Culture, Postmodernism* (Bloomington: Indiana University Press, 1986), 32: 'The earlier avant-garde was confronted with the culture industry in its stage of inception while postmodernism had to face a technologically and economically fully developed media culture which had mastered the high art of integrating, diffusing, and marketing even the most serious challenges', making the 'shock of the new' much harder to sustain.

[106] Richard, 'Notes towards a (Critical) Re-evaluation of the Critique of the Avant-Garde', 10.   [107] Ibid.

[108] Giddens argues that 'what is characteristic of modernity is not an embracing of the new for its own sake, but the presumption of wholesale reflexivity—which of course includes reflection upon the nature of reflection itself' (Giddens, *Consequences*

The smoke alarm went off in the hallway upstairs, either to let us know the battery had just died or because the house was on fire. We finished our lunch in silence. (p. 8)

When the jug-eared computer operator taps into Jack's data profile (his history—but what history? 'Where was it located exactly? Some state or federal agency, some insurance company or credit firm or medical clearinghouse?') he finds that 'We have a situation', 'It's what we call a massive data-base tally' (pp. 138–41). This tally doesn't actually mean *anything* except that Jack is 'the sum total of [his] data'. Like so many signifying structures in White Noise it offers a profound interpretability but withdraws any precise meaning, or is at best deeply ambivalent. It is nothing but data, raw and unreadable. And what constitutes data is of course not something given, as the word suggests, but a set of constructs, figures whose significance lies not in their inherent structure but in the decision that has been taken to frame them in a certain way. The word embodies all the pathos of an impoverished and institutionalized empiricism. Its faultiness is caught in a joke about the search for contamination in the girls' school; the search is carried out by men in Mylex suits, but 'because Mylex is itself a suspect material, the results tended to be ambiguous' (p. 35).

Whereas the sign causes unease, a sense that there is more to be known, the proper name is the site of a magical plenitude.[109] Proper names tend to come in cadenced triads: 'The Airport Marriott, the Downtown Travelodge, the Sheraton Inn and Conference Center'; 'Dacron, Orlon, Lycra Spandex'; 'Krylon, Rust-Oleum, Red Devil' (pp. 15, 52, 159). They appear mysteriously in the midst of the mundane world of novelistic narrative, detached, functionless, unmotivated. At the end of a paragraph on Babette's fear of death, 'the emptiness, the sense of cosmic darkness', occurs the single line: 'MasterCard, Visa, American Express' (p. 100). The sonorous, Miltonic names lack all epic content, and they are intruded into the text without any marker of a speaking source. In a

---

of Modernity, 39). If this holds equally true of both modernist and postmodernist aesthetic production, it means that their political force has to do only with their formally empty impetus to unsettlement, and that this force is therefore by definition ambivalent and unpredictable.

[109] Cf. Roland Barthes, 'Proust et les noms', *To Honour Roman Jakobson*, vol i (The Hague: Mouton, 1967), 150–8.

later episode the sleeping Steffie, speaking in 'a language not quite of this world', utters two words

that seemed to have a ritual meaning, part of a verbal spell or ecstatic chant.

Toyota Celica.

A long moment passed before I realized this was the name of an automobile. The truth only amazed me more. The utterance was beautiful and mysterious, gold-shot with looming wonder. It was like the name of an ancient power in the sky, tablet-carved in cuneiform. (p. 155)

Here there is a definite source for the utterance, but in another sense Steffie is not this source: the words are spoken through her, by her unconscious but also, as Jack recognizes, by the unconscious of her culture. Yet for all their commercial banality (the same that echoes gloriously through a phrase caught on the radio, 'It's the rainbow hologram that gives this credit card a marketing intrigue') (p. 122), the names remain charged with an opaque significance, so that Jack remarks: 'Whatever its source, the utterance struck me with the impact of a moment of splendid transcendence' (p. 155).

The question of the source of enunciation of these proper names remains an interesting one, as there seems to be a definite progression in the novel from an apparently impersonal enunciation to more localized points of origin. In a description of the supermarket, 'full of elderly people who look lost among the hedgerows', the words 'Dristan Ultra, Dristan Ultra' (p. 167) occur on a separate line but enclosed within inverted commas, which indicates a diegetic source—perhaps a public address system in the supermarket. The words have the same sort of status as the voices emanating from the television and the radio that punctuate the life of the house. At other times a psychological source seems to be indicated—when the words 'leaded, unleaded, super unleaded' intrude into Jack and Babette's desperate love-making (p. 199), or when the spelled out acronyms 'Random Access Memory, Acquired Immune Deficiency Syndrome, Mutual Assured Destruction' (p. 303) cross the text as Jack is crossing the slum districts of Iron City. At other times there seem to be verbal associations flowing between the proper names and their textual context: 'I watched light climb into the rounded summits of high-altitude clouds. Clorets, Velamints, Freedent' (p. 229). The movement is not just

the phonetic one from 'clouds' (perhaps 'cloud turrets') to 'Clorets'
but is also a circuit between the novel's imagery of sunsets and the
poetry of advertising. Another example: Jack experiences 'aural
torment' as he imagines Babette making love to the mysterious Mr
Gray; 'Then gloom moved in around the gray-sheeted bed, a circle
slowly closing.
  'Panasonic.' (p. 241)

  Like the syllables of the Proustian name, the last word is multiply
motivated. 'Pana-' is the 'circle slowly closing', 'sonic' is Jack's
'aural torment', and there are overdetermined traces of 'panoramic'
and, of course, television. But as with the name in Proust, the point
is the excess of the poetic signifier over its component parts, its
transcendental character, its plenitude. The poetic word comes
from elsewhere, and if it seems to be spoken by a character (like the
woman passing on the street who says 'a decongestant, an anti-
histamine, a cough suppressant, a pain reliever', p. 262), this is
nevertheless only a proximate source, a relay. The proper name is
its own absolute origin.

At this point, then, and without seeking to resolve these contradictions, it seems important to interrogate more closely the value
given to the concept of commodification, with its loose historical
and ethical/political overtones. The crucial caution that must be
entered is that the term 'commodity' cannot be used as a criterion
by means of which to find mass-produced works of art wanting,
because no work of art is now produced outside the system of
commodity production. A book of poetry by Ponge or by Rendra,
or my treasured Suhrkamp edition of Brecht, are as much serially
manufactured commodities as is a piece of software from Microsoft.
In the case of the visual arts the opposition between the
commodified and the non-commodified is even harder to make:
should the opposition be between an original painting or sculpture
and its reproduction on a postcard, or between a valued original
and a piece of kitsch? (And does one distinguish 'original' kitsch
from reproduced kitsch? Reproductions of 'high' art from reproductions of 'low' art?) Doesn't a Van Gogh or a Pollock now rank
as the supreme commodity in the art market, and isn't their value
reflected in, *and even constituted by*, the number of reproductions
they give rise to?
  There is a technical distinction to be made here. We tend to

assume an equivalence between the commodity and mass production, but theoretically the commodity is anything produced for
exchange and thus embodying value. 'Singular' objects, even if they
have not been industrially produced, can still be commodities. The
case of the original work of art is somewhat more complex in that
its value does not arise directly from, and is not equivalent to, the
labour expended in producing it; rather, its value relates to the
entire system of aesthetic production and to a particular fetishization
of aesthetic labour. Nevertheless, in terms of its integration into the
constitution of aesthetic desire and demand the 'singular' work of
art is clearly supportive of a system of commodity production.

But there is now a more dramatic sense in which we can say that
the singular work of art is an integral part of this system. Over the
last twenty or thirty years advanced industrial capitalism has
radically modified its techniques of manufacture and marketing in
such a way as to incorporate as a structural moment the value of
aesthetic singularity. Think of the limited edition signed print,
which mediates between the accessibility of the mass-produced
commodity (but which breaks the plate after the production run to
guarantee *limited* singularity) and the uniqueness of the signature,
the guarantee of originality and authenticity.[110] Designer clothing
and designer automobiles work in the same way: to build
originality, scarcity, and authenticity deep into mass production.
Similarly, in the case of performed rock music, Steven Connor has
spoken of a paradoxical 'inversion of the structural dependence of
copies upon originals', in so far as 'the desire for originality is a
secondary effect of various forms of reproduction', such as massive
high-fidelity amplification and the screening of multiple simultaneous images of the performance: 'The live is always in a sense the
quotation of itself—never the live, always the "live" '.[111] This
pattern is one of the ways in which we might begin to think of the
postmodernization of the relation between original and replica, and
the distinctive temporality to which it gives rise.[112]

---

[110] Cf. John Frow, 'The Signature: Three Arguments about the Commodity
Form', in Helen Grace (ed.), *Aesthesia and the Economy of the Senses* (Sydney:
University of Western Sydney, 1996), 151–200.
[111] Connor, *Postmodernist Culture*, 153. 'The Revolution will not be televised',
went the song in the 1960s, 'the Revolution will be live'—an assertion that
undermined itself by the very fact of having to be made.
[112] Cf. Jacques Attali, *Noise: The Political Economy of Music*, trans. Brian
Massumi, Theory and History of Literature 16 (Minneapolis: University of
Minnesota Press, 1985), 40–2.

This is a sketch of the conceptual machinery that runs the genre of theoretical writing which is postmodernism, and that underpins an industry now become exorbitant. As such it is, in one sense, impervious to any merely intellectual critique—or rather it absorbs critique as raw material, nourishing itself on praise and blame alike. The only criteria against which it can be judged are those of efficiency and self-preservation. As Gerald Graff says, 'it is difficult to take the concept seriously yet not easy to dismiss it', because 'once a certain number of people *believe* that a concept like the Post-Modern marks a real change in the cultural climate, the change *becomes* a reality to be reckoned with, even if the reality is not exactly what most users of the term think it is'.[113]

The industrial production of postmodernity responds, I think, to an interlocking set of genuine but inchoate theoretical problems. These have generally to do with the system of production of information, and more specifically with a set of local crises in the knowledge system ('crisis' is a charged modernist term but its sense of historical rupture is unavoidable—although you can modify with irony its apocalyptic urgency). Briefly, they take the form of the crisis of an obsolescent modernism; a crisis of political representation; a crisis of representation in general, bound up with the commodification and the proliferation of information; and a crisis of the economy of cultural values, in particular of the relations between high and low culture. The point is that these spheres of crisis are fused in a way that is, if not without precedent (think of the integration of polity, civil society, church, and war machine in the absolutist state), at least unfamiliar within the history of functional differentiation that has characterized 'modern' or 'capitalist' societies.[114] 'Postmodernism', a product of this fusion, is the self-fulfilling prophecy of its own impossible autonomy.

---

[113] Gerald Graff, Preface to Charles Newman, *The Post-Modern Aura: The Act of Fiction in an Age of Inflation* (Evanston, Ill.: Northwestern University Press, 1985), pp. i–ii.

[114] Cf. Scott Lash, *Sociology of Postmodernism* (London: Routledge, 1990), 5 ff.

2

Tourism and the Semiotics of Nostalgia

In 1689 a Japanese poet travels to the deep north. Describing a tour of the island, he is nevertheless no tourist. His journey is in part a religious pilgrimage, in part the commemoration of localities celebrated by earlier poets, and in part an allegory of a passage into death.

The Northern Province to which he travels is difficult of access, and is marked as a distinct realm by 'the barrier-gate of Shitomae which blocked the entrance . . . The gate-keepers were extremely suspicious, for very few travellers dared to pass this difficult road under normal circumstances. I was admitted after long waiting, so that darkness overtook me while I was climbing a huge mountain.' After spending the night in a filthy inn, he hires a guide to conduct him, because, 'according to the gate-keeper, there was a huge body of mountains obstructing my way to the province of Dewa, and the road was terribly uncertain'.[1]

The religious dimension of his journey is clear. Basho speaks of being constrained to silence about certain things he has seen because of the rules he must obey as a pilgrim. Before their departure, his companion Sora changes his name, takes the tonsure, and puts on the black robes of an itinerant priest. And the shrines that Basho visits are at once poetic and religious sites, and often sites of natural beauty as well. Their auratic value, and their deep linkage to the past, is made up of one or more of three elements: a name (which may encapsulate a story, or a reference to a divinity); a legend (which endows it with a history); and poetic thematization. Places are sanctified, in a way which is neither simply religious nor simply aesthetic, by the poems that have been written about them, some of which are of such antiquity that they have taken on the

---

[1] Basho, *The Narrow Road to the Deep North and Other Travel Sketches*, trans. Nobuyuki Yuasa (Harmondsworth: Penguin, 1966), 120; further references are given in the text.

anonymity of custom. Indeed, poetic theme and local tradition may have become inseparable, as at the shrine of Muro-no-yashima, where 'it was the custom . . . for poets to sing of the rising smoke, and for ordinary people not to eat *konoshiro*, a speckled fish, which has a vile smell when burnt' (p. 99). The poems that Basho writes in response are a form of homage: to the past poet, and to the place in its local particularity. They are texts to be read, but also material objects (strips of silk) left hanging in dedication at the site. Time and distance are abolished in the continuity between this gift described in the narrative and the poem that we read on the page.

Yet, in another sense, Basho's voyage is precisely a model of contemporary tourism—not in the sense of the banal anthropological analysis of tourism as sacred quest, a timeless repetition of the archetype of the voyage,[2] but in the sense that Basho sets up a relationship between the tourist sight and the form of knowledge appropriate to it which continues to hold true beyond the religious and customary framework of Basho's world.[3] Consider this passage:

My heart leaped with joy when I saw the celebrated pine tree of Takekuma, its twin trunks shaped exactly as described by the ancient poets. I was immediately reminded of the Priest Noin who had grieved to find upon his second visit this same tree cut and thrown into the River Natori as bridge-piles by the newly appointed governor of the province. This tree had been planted, cut, and replanted several times in the past, but just when I came to see it myself it was in its original shape after a lapse of perhaps a thousand years, the most beautiful shape one could possibly think of for a pine tree. The Poet Kyohaku wrote as follows at the time of my departure to express his good wishes for my journey.

> Don't forget to show my master
> The famous pine of Takekuma,
> Late cherry blossoms
> Of the far north.

[2] Cf. Nelson H. Graburn, 'Tourism: The Sacred Journey', in Valene L. Smith (ed.), *Hosts and Guests: The Anthropology of Tourism* (n.p.: University of Pennsylvania Press, 1977), 17–31; Catherine Joanne Schmidt, *Tourism: Sacred Sites, Secular Seers*, Dissertation, SUNY at Stony Brook (repr. Ann Arbor: University Microfilms International, 1985).

[3] It is therefore only partly ironic that 'Basho's tricentenary has brought a Japanese tourist boom, men, women and children following in his steps by *shinkansen* (bullet train)'. Ihab Hassan, 'Alterity? Three Japanese Examples', *Meanjin*, 49: 3 (Spring, 1990), 416.

The following poem I wrote was, therefore, a reply.

> Three months after we saw
> Cherry blossoms together
> I came to see the glorious
> Twin trunks of the pine. (p. 111)

The writings of the ancient poets establish the formal essence of the tree, and all later seeing is governed by the possibility of conformity to this pattern. Just as the tourist guidebook stipulates an ideal core of interest in the sight, so the authority of a poetic tradition which constantly refashions the essence of the tree, its normative beauty (it is necessarily in 'the most beautiful shape one could possibly think of for a pine tree' because it is nothing other than the embodied idea of the pine tree), constrains the visitor to a recognition of essence. In this case, the felicity of timing consists in the chance restoration of a conformity between the particular, more or less contingent shape of the tree and its ideal form. The poem by Kyohaku provides a second modelling of the form for Basho, and his own poem confirms (like the tourist's photograph), not an empirical act of seeing but the congruence of the sight with the idea of the sight.

The poetic record thus promulgates a form of knowledge which can be recognized in and has a greater force than the appearances of the world. What the traveller sees is what is already given by the pattern. Basho knows, for example, that the hills of Asaka are famous for a certain species of iris, although no one he speaks to there has ever heard of it. And he will travel to see 'the miraculous beauty of Kisagata' (p. 128) or 'the famous wisteria vines of Tako' (p. 132): tourist essences that precede his experience of them. At times we can see directly the process by which knowledge of place precedes and informs experience. Staying in an inn at the islands of Matsushima, and driven by excitement, 'I finally took out my notebook from my bag and read the poems given me by my friends at the time of my departure—a Chinese poem by Sodo, a *waka* by Hara Anteki, *haiku* by Sampu and Dakushi, all about the islands of Matsushima' (p. 117). At other times the relation between pattern and sight is reversed so that the former seems to derive from, rather than to generate, the latter. Weeping in front of two tombstones in a cemetery, 'I felt as if I were in the presence of the Weeping Tombstone of China' (p. 109). In a fishing village, 'the voices of the fishermen dividing the catch of the day made me even more lonely, for I was immediately reminded of an old poem which pitied them for their precarious lives on the sea' (p. 114).

It is just such a semiotic structure that Jonathan Culler describes when he argues that, for the tourist gaze, things are read as signs of themselves. A place, a gesture, a use of language are understood not as given bits of the real but as suffused with ideality, giving on to the *type* of the beautiful, or the extraordinary, or the culturally authentic. Their reality is figural rather than literal. Hence the structural role of disappointment in the tourist experience,[4] since access to the type can always be frustrated. For our time, at least, we must add that, despite the structural similarities, this ideality has a quite different force and function: lacking any transcendental anchorage, it is rather an effect of the density of representations covering our world, and of the technological conditions of this density.

Early in White Noise *Jack and Murray visit the most photographed barn in America. They pass five signs advertising it before reaching the site, and when they arrive there find forty cars and a tour bus in the car park, and a number of people taking pictures. Murray delivers a commentary: 'No one sees the barn,' he says; 'Once you've seen the signs about the barn, it becomes impossible to see the barn . . . We're not here to capture an image, we're here to maintain one. Every photograph reinforces the aura . . . We've agreed to be part of a collective perception. This literally colours our vision. A religious experience in a way, like all tourism . . . They are taking pictures of taking pictures . . . What was the barn like before it was photographed? . . . What did it look like, how was it different from other barns, how was it similar to other barns? We can't answer these questions because we've read the signs, seen the people snapping the pictures. We can't get outside the aura. We're part of the aura. We're here, we're now.'[5]*

The form of typicality characteristic of modernity has two features: it is constructed in representations which are then lived as real; and

---

[4] Schmidt, *Tourism: Sacred Sites, Secular Seers*, 59.
[5] Don DeLillo, *White Noise* (London and New York: Picador and Viking Penguin, 1985), 12–13.

it is so detailed that it is not opposed to the particular. The name often given to it is the simulacrum.

For Plato, the simulacrum is the copy of a copy. Violating an ethics of imitation, its untruth is defined by its distance from the original and by its exposure of the scandal that an imitation can in its turn function as a reality to be copied (and so on endlessly).

The most influential contemporary account of the simulacrum and the chain of simulations is that of Baudrillard. His is a melancholy vision of the emptying out of meaning (that is, of originals, of stable referents) from a world which is henceforth made up of closed and self-referring systems of semiotic exchange. In a state of what he calls hyperreality the real becomes indefinitely reproducible, an effect, merely, of the codes which continue to generate it. From the very beginning Baudrillard has been hostile to the scandalous opacity of systems of mediation. His is a historical vision: there was a referent; it has been lost; and this loss is, as in Plato, the equivalent of a moral fall.[6]

By contrast, the account that Deleuze gives of the simulacrum in *Différence et répétition*, whilst retaining the formal structure of the Platonic model, cuts it off from its ties to a lost original, and cuts it off, too, from all its Baudrillardian melancholy. The world we inhabit is one in which identity is simulated in the play of difference and repetition, but this simulation carries no sense of loss. Instead, freeing ourselves of the Platonic ontology means denying the priority of an original over the copy, of a model over the image. It means glorifying the reign of simulacra, and affirming that any original is itself already a copy, divided in its very origin. The simulacrum 'is that system in which the different is related to the different through difference itself'.[7]

The evacuation of Jack and his family is conducted by an organization called SIMUVAC, which is 'short for simulated evacuation. A new state program they're still battling for funds for.' When Jack points out to one of its employees that this is not a simulated but a real evacuation, he replies: 'We thought we could

---

[6] Jean Baudrillard, *L'Échange symbolique et la mort* (Paris: Gallimard, 1976); translated in part as *Simulations* by Paul Foss *et al.*, Foreign Agents Series (New York: Semiotext[e], 1983).

[7] Gilles Deleuze, *Différence et répétition* (Paris: Presses Universitaires Françaises, 1968), 355. My translation.

use it as a model'; it gives them 'a chance to use the real event in order to rehearse the simulation' (p. 139).

Discourse on tourism, both academic and profane, can be described in terms of a series of three more or less standard moves. The first, and least interesting, consists in the criticism of tourism as inauthentic activity.[8] Here the tourist, understood as a *faux voyageur*,[9] is contrasted with the heroic figure of the traveller and accused of a lack of interest in the culturally authentic—a category constructed both by analogy and by direct reference to high aesthetic culture. The vocabulary is that of the critique of 'mass' culture: in Daniel Boorstin's essay 'From Traveller to Tourist: The Lost Art of Travel' the key adjectives—*plastic, contrived, pre-fabricated, cheap, jerry-built, ersatz, imitation, sanitized, synthetic, artificial, antiseptic, homogeneous, factitious, pseudo*—enunciate a characteristic post-war fantasy about the masses and mass production, and express, in the process, a deep anxiety about those democratic (and 'American') values that Boorstin claims to espouse.[10] But it is possible to read the opposition of tourist to traveller outside of this cultural imaginary. In the first place, the figure of the traveller, in so far as it has a reality, is not alien to the tourism industry but functional to it, both as precursor (the hippies who opened up much of the Third World to tourism, for example; there is a close analogy here with the phenomenon of gentrification)[11] and as exemplar. And in the second place, the constant recurrence of the opposition suggests that 'these are not so much two historical categories as the terms of an opposition integral to tourism',[12] in that they carry a desire and a self-contempt which drive the industry at the most fundamental level.

The second move in the narrative of tourism is a much more complicated and ambivalent one. Associated in particular with the

---

[8] Cf. Donald L. Redfoot, 'Touristic Authenticity, Touristic Angst, and Modern Reality', *Qualitative Sociology*, 7: 4 (Winter, 1984), 292.

[9] Jean-Didier Urbain, 'Sémiotiques comparées du touriste et du voyageur', *Semiotica*, 58: 3–4 (1986), 269.

[10] Daniel J. Boorstin, *The Image: A Guide to Pseudo-Events in America* (New York: Harper and Row, 1961).

[11] Cf. John Turner and Louise Ash, *The Golden Hordes: International Tourism and the Pleasure Periphery* (London: Constable, 1975), 255.

[12] Jonathan Culler, 'Semiotics of Tourism', *American Journal of Semiotics*, 1: 1 and 2 (1981), 130.

work of Dean MacCannell, it seeks to value tourism positively by characterizing it as a quest for, rather than a turn from, that authentic experience of the world that is available to the pre-industrial traveller. In this reversal, however, the category of the authentic loses its immediacy, its unproblematic givenness; increasingly its place is taken by those semiotic mediations which, while seeming to give on to a reality other than themselves, come to defer, perhaps endlessly, the vanishing horizon of authenticity. Thus MacCannell, drawing on Goffman's distinction between the presentable 'front' and the concealed (and *therefore* more genuine) 'back' regions of a culture or a place, writes of the paradox that

it is always possible that what is taken to be entry into a back region is really entry into a front region that has been totally set up in advance for touristic visitation. In tourist settings, especially in modern society, it may be necessary to discount the importance, and even the existence, of front and back regions except as ideal poles of touristic experience.[13]

The paradox is not just that the distinction between front and back disappears, as does the slightly different one between representation and reality, but that the construction of a more 'real' reality is nevertheless entirely dependent upon it. The force of the practical distinction between front and back is to draw upon (and reinforce) that set of categories which associate truth with concealment, secrecy, and intimacy, and untruth with surfaces and visibility, in support of particular effects of truth and untruth. This has direct consequences both for the organization of everyday life and for the commercial viability of particular tourist sites. Analytically, however, the distinction is purely illusory. MacCannell thus elaborates something like Baudrillard's theory of a historical regime of simulation in which the difference between original and copy falls away, and indeed where the very existence of an 'original' is a function of the copy.[14] At the same time, MacCannell retains a

---

[13] Dean MacCannell, 'Staged Authenticity: Arrangements of Social Space in Tourist Settings', *American Journal of Sociology*, 79: 3 (1974), 597.

[14] MacCannell argues against Walter Benjamin that 'the work becomes "authentic" only after the first copy of it is produced. The reproductions *are* the aura, and ritual, far from being a point of origin, *derives* from the relationship between the original object and its socially constructed importance' (Dean MacCannell, *The Tourist: A New Theory of the Leisure Class* (London: Macmillan, 1976), 48). In fact Benjamin makes just this point in a footnote to 'The Work of Art

commitment to the categories of the authentic and the real, which, as in Baudrillard's work, are postulated historically (and nostalgically) as lost domains of experience or referentiality.

One of the ways in which this historicization works is through a reading of tourism as an allegory (or an 'ethnography')[15] of modernity—where tourism and modernity are understood as facts of experience or consciousness[16] rather than as socioeconomic institutions. MacCannell's vocabulary is at once resolutely idealist and resolutely sociologistic. Modernity is equivalent to a process of structural differentiation, and what has been lost in this process is the structural solidarity characteristic of traditional societies. Tourism reflects this differentiation, but at the same time—and paralleling 'concerns for the sacred in primitive society'[17]—it represents a quest for an authentic domain of being. It is thus a marker of the spiritual self-reflexivity of modernity, and directly parallel to the self-consciousness of intellectuals about their own alienation.[18] In these terms, *'postindustrial* or *modern society* is the coming to consciousness of industrial society, the result of industrial society's turning in on itself, searching for its own strengths and weaknesses and elaborating itself internally. The growth of tourism is the central index of modernization so defined.'[19]

---

in the Age of Mechanical Reproduction': 'Precisely because authenticity is not reproducible, the intensive penetration of certain (mechanical) processes of reproduction was instrumental in differentiating and grading authenticity. To develop such differentiations was an important function of the trade in works of art . . . [A]t the time of its origin a mediaeval picture of the Madonna could not yet be said to be "authentic." It became "authentic" only during the succeeding centuries and perhaps most strikingly so during the last one' ('The Work of Art in the Age of Mechanical Reproduction', *Illuminations*, trans. Harry Zohn (New York: Schocken, 1965), 243, n. 2). There is, however, some ambiguity in this essay about the effects of reproducibility, and we can perhaps hold against Benjamin his having failed to foresee the extent to which technologies of reproduction were used in the twentieth century to construct effects of aura. Hollywood movies are the obvious example.

[15] MacCannell, *The Tourist*, 4.

[16] 'The deep structure of modernity is a totalizing idea, a modern mentality that sets modern society in opposition both to its own past and to those societies of the present that are premodern or un(der)developed'. Ibid. 8.

[17] MacCannell, 'Staged Authenticity', 589–90.

[18] Cf. Erik Cohen, 'Authenticity and Commoditization in Tourism', *Annals of Tourism Research*, 15: 3 (1988), 376.

[19] MacCannell, *The Tourist*, 182.

The historical dimension of this vision of the modern consists in its diachronic opposition to an organicist category of the premodern or traditional. It is closely bound up with the construction of a cultural Other—a mythology of 'the primitive, the folk, the peasant, and the working class', who 'speak without self-consciousness, without criticism, and without affectation',[20] but also of the feudal and post-feudal aristocracy and its high culture. The Other of modernity—which corresponds to particular tourist objects and experiences—is defined by an absence of *design*—of calculation or of interested self-awareness. It must therefore exist outside the circuit of commodity relations and exchange values (although it is only accessible through this circuit: one form of the basic contradiction of the tourist experience). Erik Cohen cites the criteria used by curators and ethnographers to determine the authenticity of African art: an object counts as authentic only if it has not been made for acquisition by members of another culture, if it has been 'hand made' according to traditional criteria and from 'natural' materials, and if it has not been intended for sale. This is to say that ' "authenticity" is an eminently modern value, whose emergence is closely related to the impact of modernity upon the unity of social existence':[21] or, more precisely, to a definition of modernity as the converse and the historical loss of such a unity. The otherness of traditional or exotic cultures has to do with their having escaped the contamination of this fallen world: having escaped the condition of *information* (in Benjamin's sense),[22] being unaware of their own relativity, avoiding absorption into the embrace of touristic self-consciousness. The charm of displays of pre-industrial implements and artefacts in old houses and museums thus resides in their proclamation of the immediacy of use value: they are rough, differentiated, lacking the homogeneity of the commodity. This pair of black, roughly pitted scissors; this harvesting fork which still resembles the branches it is carved from;

---

[20] Susan Stewart, *On Longing: Narratives of the Miniature, the Gigantic, the Souvenir, the Collection* (Baltimore: Johns Hopkins University Press, 1984), 16.

[21] Cohen, 'Authenticity and Commoditization in Tourism', 373. On the notion of 'authentic' African art, cf. also Bennetta Jules-Rosette, *The Messages of Tourist Art: An African Semiotic System in Comparative Perspective* (New York: Plenum Press, 1984).

[22] Cf. Benjamin, 'The Storyteller: Reflections on the Works of Nikolai Leskov', *Illuminations*.

this leather harness, cut by hand from the hide, offer themselves to be read in terms of the long slow death of peasant culture of which our time is witnessing the end.

The third move in the theorization of tourism follows from the internal paradoxicality progressively revealed in the playing out of the second. On one plane this is a hermeneutic problem: how can I come to terms with that which is Other without reducing it to the terms of my own understanding? In semiotic terms, this is a problem of the constitutive role of representation for the object: 'The paradox, the dilemma of authenticity, is that to be experienced as authentic it must be marked as authentic, but when it is marked as authentic it is mediated, a sign of itself and hence not authentic in the sense of unspoiled.'[23] This paradox then gives rise to a series of others. One has to do with the inseparability of the object from its semiotic status—that is, with the fact that any valued object is, minimally, a sign of itself, and hence—as with Basho's 'famous' sites—*resembles itself*. MacCannell thus quotes a guidebook note that emphasizes the possibility of seeing objects 'as if they are pictures, maps or panoramas of themselves',[24] and John Turner and Louise Ash speak of the way every detail of a cultural monument 'is so familiar from professional and amateur photography that it seems to be a genuine, life-size reproduction of the original'.[25] From this follows the further paradox of the sheer impossibility of constructing otherness, since, as MacCannell argues, 'every nicely motivated effort to preserve nature, primitives and the past, and to represent them authentically contributes to an opposite tendency—the present is made more unified against its past, more in control of nature, less a product of history'.[26] A third moment in this series is the conclusion that in order to construct a good tourist object—one which makes 'a convincing display of honest honesty'[27]—it becomes necessary to construct it as a plausible simulation of itself. Cohen's work on 'alternative' tourism, such as hill tribe trekking in Thailand, which offers access

---

[23] Culler, 'Semiotics of Tourism', 137.
[24] MacCannell, *The Tourist*, 122.
[25] Turner and Ash, *The Golden Hordes*, 137.
[26] MacCannell, *The Tourist*, 83; cf. also the chapter 'Cannibalism Today' in MacCannell's more recent collection, *Empty Meeting Grounds: The Tourist Papers* (New York: Routledge, 1992), 17–73.
[27] MacCannell, *The Tourist*, 128.

to 'primitive and remote, authentic and unspoilt sites beyond the boundaries of the established touristic circuits'[28]—with the consequence that the traditional tribal cultures of the area are transformed by the outside forces that tourism both opens up and represents—gives some sense of the spiral of simulations to which this necessity gives rise.

This sense of paradox, it must be stressed, is generated within a conceptual framework that holds on to the distinction between the authentic and the inauthentic. Its basis in MacCannell's work is the distinction between the tourist sight and the marker that provides information about the sight. This is roughly the relation between a real object and its representation, and it therefore holds open the possibility of a sight's being either represented truly or misrepresented. The concept of the 'staging' of authenticity retains its ontological foundations. But MacCannell's work itself points to, and verges on, a different understanding of the relation between marker and sight which would resolve this particular set of aporias. This understanding would take to its logical conclusion the insight that the marker is constitutive of the sight (which cannot be 'seen' without it), and hence, as van den Abbeele puts it, 'removes or defers the sight from any undifferentiated immediacy'.[29] The sight would itself be a further marker within a chain of supplementarity.[30]

This move resolves the forms of paradox associated with the conception of the authentic, but of course opens up a different set of difficulties. It is a move, as Barbara Kirshenblatt-Gimblett and Edward M. Bruner argue, from the issue of authenticity to that of authentication,[31] and it leaves open the question of the criteria according to which authentication and differentiation might occur. This is a question about the practices by which limits and discriminations are set, and about the relativized systems of value which enable them. It is a question about postmodernism, and

---

[28] Erik Cohen, ' "Primitive and Remote": Hill Tribe Trekking in Thailand', *Annals of Tourism Research*, 16: 1 (1989), 31.

[29] Georges van den Abbeele, 'Sightseers: The Tourist as Theorist', *Diacritics*, 10: 4 (1980), 7.

[30] Ibid. 11.

[31] Barbara Kirshenblatt-Gimblett and Edward M. Bruner, 'Tourism', *International Encyclopaedia of Communications*, vol. iv (New York: Oxford University Press, 1989), 251.

perhaps, as both Maxine Feiffer and John Urry suggest,[32] about the possibilities of a post-tourism released from the touristic anxieties of modernity.

Tourist space differs from itself. Reflexively divided into a displayed authentic place and an accessory (but often overlaid) metaspace where the business of tourism is conducted, it approximates the empty non-places of the postmodern chronotope. Anthony Giddens's concept of the disembedding of social relations from local contexts of interaction and their reconstruction in more abstract and more 'stretched' space-time matrices[33] defines the conditions under which such non-places come to be characteristic forms of modernity. Marc Augé, conversely but symmetrically, defines the non-place as the opposite of the ethnographic notion of place as the localization of culture in time and space, constituting closed 'universes of recognition'.[34] Place is 'relational, historical and concerned with identity'; non-place contains such places but without integrating them; rather, they are assigned a specific position, as *lieux de mémoire*, sites of a memory which is disconnected from the present and of a history which has since been transformed into actuality and spectacle (p. 78).

Is it clear that this description is, again, a version of that critique of mass culture which has been prevalent for most of this century, and which has its roots in the writings of Carlyle, Arnold, and

---

[32] Maxine Feiffer, *Going Places: The Ways of the Tourist from Imperial Rome to the Present Day* (London: Macmillan, 1985); John Urry, *The Tourist Gaze: Leisure and Travel in Contemporary Societies* (London: Sage, 1990). Cf. Dean MacCannell, 'Introduction', *Annals of Tourism Research*, 16: 1 (1989), 1–2: 'The tourists and others no longer meet as representatives of "modernity" and "tradition", even though they may continue to *act as if* this is the basis for their interaction.' Rather, 'one finds "primitive" and "peasant" peoples exercising economic rationality alongside of "modern" peoples who live in a world seemingly shaped entirely by myth; Indian clowns, dancers and sales people gulling their white clients; and a "modern" thirst for authenticity met by a "primitive" capacity to produce dramatic representations of pseudo authenticity. In short, what one discerns here is a new set of living arrangements associated with the double displacement of the Third World which is simultaneously post-traditional and post-modern.'

[33] Anthony Giddens, *The Consequences of Modernity* (Stanford, Calif.: Stanford University Press, 1990), 21.

[34] Marc Augé, *Non-Places: Introduction to an Anthropology of Supermodernity*, trans. John Howe (London: Verso, 1995), 32–3. Further citations will be given in the text.

Ruskin? Non-places (Augé's preferred examples are taken from tourism and leisure, shopping, and transport) form a world

> where people are born in the clinic and die in hospital, where transit points and temporary abodes are proliferating under luxurious or inhuman conditions (hotel chains and squats, holiday clubs and refugee camps, shantytowns threatened with demolition or doomed to festering longevity); where a dense network of means of transport which are also inhabited spaces is developing; where the habitué of supermarkets, slot machines and credit cards communicates wordlessly, through gestures, with an abstract, unmediated commerce; a world thus surrendered to solitary individuality, to the fleeting, the temporary and ephemeral. (ibid.)

Deprived of the rich texture of social relations that characterize place, non-places enforce a 'solitary contractuality' (p. 94) which links individuals to their surroundings by means of the constant mediation of words and texts (the 'instructions for use' on maps or billboards, the textual commentary on sites of interest along the *autoroute*). Their reality is virtual, abstract, desocialized, creating 'neither singular identity nor relations; only solitude, and similitude' (p. 103). And they are organized, by way of publicity and advertising, by 'a sort of cosmology which, unlike the ones traditionally studied by ethnologists, is objectively universal, and at the same time familiar and prestigious' (p. 106).

This reference to cosmology should alert us, however, to a constant and very interesting collapse of the opposition through which Augé seeks to define the non-place. The content of the cosmology may be new, but this is, precisely, a cosmology. Whereas Augé had initially understood those 'universes which ethnology has traditionally made its own', the closed 'universes of recognition', as reflections of a kind of fantasy shared by anthropologists and their informants about cultural closure (pp. 32–3), the later argument assumes the reality of these ethnological places as sites of a plenitude of meaning. Conversely, the abstractness and virtuality of the non-place are taken to be historically new qualities, rather than having elements in common with, for example, the abstract and plural reality of the church; and textual mediation is posited as though space were once, in some more immediate world, textless. Above all, there's an assumption that non-places manifest an absence of social relations, or of the sorts of 'real' social relations that anthropologists study—an assumption which simply gives up on the job of the anthropologist, misrecognizing the uses to which tourist space (for example) is put and the ways in which virtual or highly mediated social relations nevertheless construct a familiar sociality. This collapse of the opposition between place and non-place repeats the failure played out in the theorization of tourism to hold apart the semiotic distinction between sight and marker which underpins the construction of the figure of modernity.

A similar process of paradox to that developed in theorizing tourism is played out with the concept and the practices of *tradition*—that is, with the form taken by the sacralization of the past. The concept has been extensively elaborated in Gadamer's hermeneutics, in historiography (for example, in Hobsbawm and Ranger's collection *The Invention of Tradition*), and in the disciplines that deal with customary societies, especially anthropology. The force of the argument presented by Eric Hobsbawm and others is that the ongoing reconstruction of the past is an act not only of recontextualization but of invention, and that even the most 'authentic' traditions are thus effects of a stylized simulation. Richard Handler and Jocelyn Linnekin summarize the current critique of the concept like this:

One of the major paradoxes of the ideology of tradition is that attempts at cultural preservation inevitably alter, reconstruct, or invent the traditions that they are intended to fix. Traditions are neither genuine nor spurious, for if genuine tradition refers to the pristine and immutable heritage of the past, then all genuine traditions are spurious. But if, as we have argued, tradition is always defined in the present, then all spurious traditions are genuine.[35]

This theoretical critique has been accompanied, however, by a substantial 'postmodern' growth in representations/appropriations of the past, parallel to the tourism industry's representation/appropriation of modernity's cultural Other (of which the past is of course one major form). Indeed, Patrick Wright points out that nostalgia for lost patterns of everyday life and for auratic objects which seem to be inherently meaningful 'surely forms a powerful

---

[35] Richard Handler and Jocelyn Linnekin, 'Tradition, Genuine or Spurious', *Journal of American Folklore*, 97: 385 (1984), 288. Cf. Nicholas Thomas, 'The Inversion of Tradition', *American Ethnologist*, 19: 2 (1992), 213–32, for an argument that identity and tradition are constructed as forms of negative differentiation rather than as 'positive' continuities with the past, and that they may be internally riven.

motivation even for fairly high-cultural tourism'.[36] The heritage industry, which now includes monuments not only to ruling-class power but also to those idealized patterns of everyday life and work, has become an increasingly important piece of machinery for the construction of tradition. But moralistic denunciation is as inadequate here as it is in the case of tourism. Robert Hewison exemplifies the problem when he writes: 'Postmodernism and the heritage industry are linked, in that they both conspire to create a shallow screen that intervenes between our present lives, and our history. We have no understanding of history in depth, but instead are offered a contemporary creation, more costume drama and re-enactment than critical discourse.'[37] Opposing the privilege of the written text to other forms of textuality, Hewison forgets not only that 'costume drama and re-enactment' have always been important vehicles of historical understanding, but that 'history' is always a textual construct; the question cannot at all be about the gap between representations of history and history 'itself', but only about the relative effectiveness, the relative political force, of different representations.

Patrick Wright's work offers a more complex and astute account of the heritage industry, stressing its ability both to offer a celebration of past power relations and to project a vision of unalienated rationality. On the one hand, National History involves a ritualistic staging of heroic narratives in such a way as to deny their active historicity—their usability for the present. The past is constructed as a domain of authenticity through a public process of remembrance which affirms a continuity with the dead at the same time as it continuously repositions them at the heart of a narrative of the nation.[38] On the other hand, however, the valuing of the past as it connects to a present sense of loss need not merely be an exercise in idealizing nostalgia:

If the past now includes the ordinary traces of old everyday life among its valued contents, there are different things to be said about the sense of *uniqueness* which hangs over the celebrated objects within its changing repertoire. This sense of uniqueness may indeed still characterize precious

[36] Patrick Wright, *On Living in an Old Country: The National Past in Contemporary Britain* (London: Verso, 1985), 23.

[37] Robert Hewison, *The Heritage Industry: Britain in a Climate of Decline* (London: Methuen, 1987), 135.

[38] Wright, *On Living in an Old Country*, 69, 137.

works of art, but in recent times it has drifted far from its old academic moorings and it can now be held in common by, say, a phrase of rhyming slang, an old piece of industrial machinery (preferably *in situ*), a hand-painted plate from the turn of the century and a cherished landscape or place. It is not merely official cultural policy which determines the meaning or the extent of the modern past. The uniqueness of heritage objects may indeed be pointed out in official guidebooks, but it is far more powerfully expressed in the vernacular measures of everyday life. For the perspectives of everyday life, the unique heritage object has *aura*, and in this respect the national heritage seems to have a persistent connection with earlier traditions of bourgeois culture—a connection which may even be *especially* strong as the modern past reaches out to include not masterpieces but the modest objects of bygone everyday life in its repertoire.[39]

This, I think, draws attention both to the cultural and political ambivalence of the retrieved everyday object,[40] and to the struggles that take place over its articulation with the present. The past is reworked through different economies of value, and acquires a correspondingly differential force. The concept of the everyday may in its own way be as much an idealizing and a unifying category as that of the national, but it is perhaps more workable, more flexible, more open to multiple appropriations than the modes of official history. At the same time, however, it remains crucial to guard a deep suspicion of the auratic object, whatever the uses to which it may seem to lend itself. Nostalgia for a lost authenticity is a paralysing structure of historical reflection.

In the main street of Iron City is 'a tall old Moorish movie theater, now remarkably a mosque'; it is flanked by 'blank structures called the Terminal Building, the Packer Building, the Commerce Building. How close this was to a classic photography of regret.'[41]

The 'social disease of nostalgia'[42] has a particular history within the institution of Western medicine.[43] Originally defined in the seventeenth century in terms of a set of physical symptoms

---

[39] Ibid. 253.
[40] Raphael Samuel thus seems to me to misunderstand Wright's argument when he characterizes it as an *attack* on the heritage industry. Raphael Samuel, *Theatres of Memory* i: *Past and Present in Contemporary Culture* (London: Verso, 1994), 242.
[41] DeLillo, *White Noise*, 89.   [42] Stewart, *On Longing*, 23.
[43] Cf. Jean Starobinski, 'The Idea of Nostalgia', *Diogenes*, 54 (Summer 1966), 81–103.

associated with acute homesickness, it subsequently came to be closely connected with the 'specific depression of intellectuals', melancholia.[44] By the nineteenth century it had been extended to describe a general condition of estrangement, a state of ontological homelessness which became one of the period's key metaphors for the condition of modernity (and which is also one of the central conditions of tourism, where the *Heimat* functions simultaneously as the place of safety to which we return, and as that lost origin that is sought in the alien world).[45]

A persuasive argument has been made that the development of sociology in the decades around the turn of the century was bound up with a discourse on modernity structured by nostalgia. Bryan Turner identifies four elements of the nostalgic paradigm that feeds into sociology: a sense of historical decline, giving rise to various social theologies of lost grace; a sense of the absence or loss of personal wholeness and moral certainty (the fracturing of the canopy of religious and moral value by the growth of capitalist relations and of urbanization); a sense of the loss of individual freedom and autonomy (the disappearance of genuine social relationships, and the bureaucratization of everyday life); and a sense of the loss of simplicity, personal authenticity, and emotional spontaneity.[46] Linking together the work of Tönnies, Simmel, Weber, Lukács, and Adorno is 'the notion that we constantly create life-worlds which through alienation and reification negate the spontaneity and authenticity of the will and its conscious subject, Man'.[47] Lukács's concept of the 'second nature of man-made structures'—'a complex of senses—meanings—which has become rigid and strange, and which no longer awakens interiority . . . a charnel-house of long-dead interiorities'[48]—catches precisely that

---

[44] Bryan S. Turner, 'A Note on Nostalgia', *Theory, Culture and Society*, 4: 1 (1987), 147. Cf. Wolf Lepenies, *Melancholie und Gesellschaft* (Frankfurt am Main: Suhrkamp, 1972).

[45] For a critique of the gendering of the opposition between travel and *domus*, cf. Meaghan Morris, 'At Henry Parkes Motel', *Cultural Studies*, 2: 1 (1988), 38, 43.

[46] Turner, 'A Note on Nostalgia', 150–51; cf. Roland Robertson, 'After Nostalgia? Wilful Nostalgia and the Phases of Globalization', in Bryan S. Turner (ed.), *Theories of Modernity and Postmodernity* (London: Sage, 1990), 49.

[47] Georg Stauth and Bryan S. Turner, 'Nostalgia, Postmodernism and the Critique of Mass Culture', *Theory, Culture and Society*, 5: 2–3 (1988), 514.

[48] Georg Lukács, *The Theory of the Novel: A Historico-Philosophical Essay on the Forms of Great Epic Literature*, trans. Anna Bostock (Cambridge, Mass.: MIT Press, 1971), 64.

notion of a contradiction between a will to life and the forms of human association which from the start makes sociology so ambivalent a discipline.

Within this framework, nostalgia is 'the repetition that mourns the inauthenticity of all repetition'.[49] Against a degraded present structured by those 'forms of human association' it sets a past, an otherwhere, characterized by immediacy and presence. A 'sadness without an object', nostalgia

is always ideological: the past it seeks has never existed except as narrative, and hence, always absent, that past continually threatens to reproduce itself as a felt lack. Hostile to history and its invisible origins, and yet longing for an impossibly pure context of lived experience at a place of origin, nostalgia wears a distinctly utopian face, a face that turns toward a future-past, a past which has only ideological reality. This point of desire which the nostalgic seeks is in fact the absence that is the very generating mechanism of desire . . . nostalgia is the desire for desire.[50]

Authentic and inauthentic experience; community and society; organic and mechanical solidarity; status and contract; use value and exchange value . . . the structural oppositions through which the relation between tradition and modernity is constructed (or rather, through which modernity defines itself against its mythical Other) are potentially endless but formally homologous. The relation between traveller and tourist, between the exotic and the familiar, between immediacy and the forms of human association belong to this structure, and they continue to operate as powerful experiential categories.

Consider the list of 'things' that Heidegger cites, in 'The Origin of the Work of Art', as examples of thingness: stone, clod, jug, well, milk, water, cloud, thistle, leaf, hawk. Later the list is reduced to a few essential objects: 'a stone, a clod of earth, a piece of wood . . . Lifeless beings of nature and objects of use. Natural things and utensils are the things commonly so called.'[51] All are drawn from a stable and pre-industrial rural world, the mythical time before

---

[49] Stewart, *On Longing*, 23.   [50] Ibid.
[51] Martin Heidegger, 'The Origin of the Work of Art', *Poetry, Language, Thought*, trans. Albert Hofstadter (New York: Harper and Row, 1971), 21. Further references will be incorporated in the text.

modernity. The ultimate authority for the experience of things in this world is the 'authentic experience' of thingness by the Greeks— an experience of 'the Being of beings in the sense of presence' (p. 22) which has been lost to Western philosophy in the process of translation of Greek thought into the Latin categorization of thingness as the union of substance with accidents, or as the unity of a manifold of sensations, or as formed matter.

Heidegger's choice of these *things*—auratic or 'poetic' objects—is never merely illustrative. The example of the shoes—'A piece of equipment, a pair of shoes for instance' (p. 29)—is loaded with the full force of shoeness: use value, fetish value, a 'world' that opens out from the shoe's deep interiority. 'Equipment' is *Zeug*, that which bears witness, which comes to appearance. Halfway between the brute, self-shaping thingness of a granite boulder and the craftedness of the art work, it is the embodiment of production for use. Its converse is the object produced for exchange, the commodity; but the category of exchange value is entirely and absolutely excluded from Heidegger's discourse (which is to say that it cannot be thought within it). The unstated and unspeakable opposition is that between the authentic object (since 'as a rule it is the use-objects around us that are the nearest and authentic things') (p. 29), and the inauthentic world of commodity production.

In fact, the example of the shoes happens twice, or even perhaps thrice, as Heidegger moves to 'simply describe some equipment without any philosophical theory':

We choose as example a common sort of equipment—a pair of peasant shoes. We do not even need to exhibit actual pieces of this sort of useful article in order to describe them. Everyone is acquainted with them. But since it is a matter here of direct description, it may be well to facilitate the visual realization of them. For this purpose a pictorial representation suffices. We shall choose a well-known painting by Van Gogh, who painted such shoes several times. (pp. 32–3)

The choice is first of the 'real' shoes, and then of a representation, selected purely for reasons of convenience (as a *Nachhilfe*), and as though it were transparent to the 'real' object. The distinction between reality and representation is of course a distinction between two signifieds (not between a representation and a referent), and involves a characteristically novelistic production of a reality-effect. The question of the *genre* of this writing is of crucial importance here, as Heidegger's language performs a double movement resembling that of the late nineteenth-century naturalistic novel (Zola or Dreiser or Hamsun, perhaps). The first movement is a reduction of the shoes to pure thingness, pure semiotic neutrality:

> The peasant woman wears her shoes in the field. Only here are they what they are. They are all the more genuinely so, the less the peasant woman thinks about the shoes while she is at work, or looks at them at all, or is even aware of them. She stands and walks in them. That is how shoes actually serve. It is in this process of the use of equipment that we must actually encounter the character of equipment. (p. 33)

Nothing about the shoes indicates a context or a story which would fill out this bare thingness: they are 'a pair of peasant shoes and nothing more' (p. 33). Their authenticity is directly a function of this naked being, as it is of the absence of reflection and of self-reflection on the part of the peasant woman. Woman, peasant, shoe: these are the categories of a Being that is authentic because of, and *essentially* because of, its unselfconsciousness.

The second movement is the converse of the first, a move towards semiotic fullness which is still, nevertheless, predicated on an absence of self-reflection. It begins with a tentative turn, 'And yet—' (*Und dennoch*), which then modulates into the slow unfolding of a narrative plenitude: 'From the dark opening of the worn insides of the shoes' (literally 'of the trodden-out in-turning', *des ausgetretenen Inwendigen*, a sexualized swaying between inside and outside) 'the toilsome tread of the worker stares forth'—a 'toil' which belongs to no particular system of social relations because its context is that of a generalized human condition. The image of the shoes broadens into a landscape with peasant woman ('In the stiffly rugged heaviness of the shoes there is the accumulated tenacity of her slow trudge through the far-spreading and ever-uniform furrows of the field swept by a raw wind'), and then contracts to the shoes again: 'On the leather lie the dampness and richness of the soil. Under the soles slides the loneliness of the field-path as evening falls.' The fertility of the earth, the itinerary of the path: already the scene is becoming overdetermined by categories of gender. Then again a lyrical opening out from the dark inside of the shoes to the fullness of the world:

> In the shoes vibrates the silent call of the earth, its quiet gift of the ripening grain and its unexplained self-refusal in the fallow desolation of the wintry

field. This equipment is pervaded by uncomplaining anxiety as to the certainty of bread, the wordless joy of having once more withstood want, the trembling before the impending childbed and shivering at the surrounding menace of death.

Finally, a movement of withdrawal again: this landscape, these emotions can be observed only 'in the picture', since 'the peasant woman, on the other hand, simply wears them'; 'she knows all this without noticing or reflecting' (p. 34).

We realize now that the example is not an innocent one, that 'the work did not, as it might seem at first, serve merely for a better visualizing of what a piece of equipment is. Rather, the equipment-ality of equipment first genuinely arrives at its appearance through the work and only in the work', where it discloses 'the unconcealed-ness of its being' (p. 36). But what have we been talking about? Neither the shoes in their non-representational reality, nor simply a representation of the shoes, but something which is both and neither, and which partakes both of the peasant woman's intuitive knowledge of Being and of philosophical reflection (although this is description 'without any philosophical theory'). The ambiguity of this space corresponds to the sexual ambiguity of the shoes, both inside and outside, opening and inturning; to the play between the sheltering and concealing motion of earth and the self-opening of world; and to the apparently gratuitous attribution of the shoes to a woman. In one sense, indeed, there is no ambiguity at all about this thing, this *Zeug*, this gaping hole that Heidegger and Schapiro and Derrida keep looking at, trying to go behind it to the thing-in-itself, this nameless or many-named thing, this euphemism, that opens and closes, that's laced or unlaced, that's worn by a pregnant peasant woman trudging across the furrows; this fetish. Yet the figure of the peasant woman is crucial to the problematization of the space between the inside and the outside of the painting, since, as Derrida notes in his commentary, these spaces are differently gendered:

There is something like a rule to the peasant woman's appearance on the scene. Heidegger designates in this way the (female) wearer of the shoes outside the picture, if one can put it that way, when the lace of discourse passes outside the edging of the frame, into that *hors-d'œuvre* which he claims to see presenting itself in the work itself. But each time he speaks of the exemplary product in the picture, he says, in neutral, generic fashion—

that is, according to a grammar, masculine fashion: 'ein Paar Bauern-schuhe', a pair of peasants' shoes.[52]

Derrida's 'disappointment' with the passage invoking the peasant woman has to do both with this (gendered) ambiguity, such that 'one never knows if it's busying itself around a picture, "real" shoes, or shoes that are imaginary', and with its 'consumerlike hurry toward the content of a representation', the 'massive self-assurance of the identification: "a pair of peasants' shoes", just like that!'[53] This urge to attribution, the quest to find the proper feet for the shoes (assumed to be a pair, left and right) is what Heidegger has in common with Meyer Schapiro, who claims them not for a woman and not for a peasant but for the city-dweller, and their rightful owner, Van Gogh himself.[54] Nevertheless, while continuing to insist that the shoes are 'more or less detached (in themselves, from each other and from the feet)',[55] Derrida moves, in a somewhat puzzling way, to resolve the ambiguity about the status of the shoes in the text. Everything that relates to the peasant woman and to that embarrassing intrusion of an outside into the painting, everything that relates to the ideology of peasant simplicity (in other words the genre of writing that Heidegger falls into) is, it turns out, nothing more than 'an accessory variable even if it does come massively under "projection" and answers to Heidegger's pathetic-fantasmatic-ideological-political investments'. In the presentation of philosophical truth this 'peasant' character-istic 'remains secondary', since 'the "same truth" could be "presented" by any shoe painting, or even by any experience of shoes and even of any "product" in general: the truth being that of a being-product coming back from "further away" than the matter-form couple, further away even than a "distinction between the two" '.[56] The problem of the specificity of the forms of representa-tion through which the question is posed is discarded like an old

[52] Jacques Derrida, The Truth in Painting, trans. Geoff Bennington and Ian McLeod (Chicago: University of Chicago Press, 1987), 307.

[53] Ibid. 292–3.

[54] Ibid. 283 and passim. Cf. Meyer Schapiro, 'The Still Life as a Personal Object—A Note on Heidegger and Van Gogh', in Marianne L. Simmer (ed.), The Reach of Mind: Essays in Memory of Kurt Goldstein (New York: Springer, 1968), 203–9.   [55] Derrida, The Truth in Painting, 283.

[56] Ibid. 311–12.

boot, and the example regains its innocence as a mere example, as *Nachhilfe*, regains its *supplementarity* ('accessory variable') in relation to the more important matters of philosophical origin.

But what is at stake here is more than the philosophical question. It has to do with precisely that 'pathetic-fantasmatic-ideological-political investment'. It has to do with the figure of woman and its relation to the fetish. It has to do with the impossibility of speaking exchange value. It has to do with the political implications of that construction (in 1935) of the category of 'world' as 'the self-disclosing openness of the broad paths of the simple and essential decisions in the destiny of an historical people (*im Geschick eines geschichtlichen Volkes*)'. It has to do with the politics of 'authenticity', the politics of nostalgia for a pre-modern world.

These shoes turn up again, as it happens, in Fredric Jameson's best-known essay on postmodernism—here in contrast to Warhol's *Diamond Dust Shoes*. And here, paradoxically, it is the Warhol shoes which embody the fetish, in both the Freudian and Marxist senses. It is not at all clear, however, what their sexual content (or indeed their lure as commodities) could be: they are 'a random collection of dead objects', 'as shorn of their earlier life world as the pile of shoes left over from Auschwitz', and the problem Jameson encounters with them is the impossibility of making that Heideggerian move to a 'larger lived context'. Van Gogh's shoes, by contrast, retain their Heideggerian force as an index of authenticity, although only on condition that they are restored both to their historical context of the world of peasant poverty, and to their context in the history of the sensory materiality of oil painting. Indeed, so authentic and so innocent are they that Jameson even cites Derrida as remarking—'somewhere'—that 'the Van Gogh footwear are a heterosexual pair, which allows neither for perversion nor for fetishization'.[57]

Whereas Heidegger had excluded any mention of exchange value, Warhol is all too fascinated by the commodity status of

[57] Fredric Jameson, *Postmodernism, or, The Cultural Logic of Late Capitalism* (Durham, NC: Duke University Press, 1991), 8. I have been unable to identify this particular remark in Derrida's essay on Van Gogh and Heidegger, 'Restitutions of the Truth in Painting [*pointure*]' (*Truth in Painting*, 255–382), but the essay does of course canvas every conceivable mode of sexualization of the shoe and the shoes, 'normal' and 'perverse', 'homo-' and 'heterosexual'. Derrida fundamentally questions the assumption that the shoes constitute a *pair*, and links the compulsion to pair them to a certain repression of 'perversity' (e.g. p. 333).

things. The problem posed by his work is that the images of Coca-Cola bottles or Campbell's Soup cans, 'which explicitly foreground the commodity fetishism of a transition to late capital, *ought* to be powerful and critical political statements', but refuse the certainty of such critique. Moreover, lacking the hermeneutic resonance of Van Gogh's heterosexual and unperverted shoes, they signal the emergence of 'a new kind of flatness or depthlessness, a new kind of superficiality in the most literal sense'. In this they at once resemble and draw upon photography, which 'confers its deathly quality to the Warhol image, whose glacéd X-ray elegance mortifies the reified eye of the viewer'.[58]

The shift here from locating reification in the image to locating it in the viewing subject parallels that 'more fundamental mutation both in the object world itself—now become a set of texts or simulacra—and in the disposition of the subject'[59] which constitutes the determinant condition of Warhol's work. This (Jameson acknowledges as much) is a *periodizing* shift, in which the opposition of postmodernity to modernity precisely corresponds to the construction of modernity through its nostalgic opposition to traditional society. In another essay Jameson exemplifies the transition to the commodified world of late capitalism through a familiar metaphor. With commodification, he writes,

the various forms of activity lose their immanent intrinsic satisfactions as activity and become means to an end. The objects of the commodity world of capitalism also shed their independent 'being' and intrinsic qualities and come to be so many instruments of commodity satisfaction: the familiar example is that of tourism—the American tourist no longer lets the landscape 'be in its being' as Heidegger would have said, but takes a snapshot of it, thereby graphically transforming space into its own material image.[60]

Here in a nutshell is the full nostalgic narrative of a decline from use value to commodity, from immanence to instrumentality, from the observing traveller to the possessive tourist, and from the world as being to the world as simulacrum. 'One follows step by step the moves of a "great thinker", as he returns to the origin of the work of art and of truth, traversing the whole history of the West and

---

[58] Jameson, *Postmodernism*, 9.   [59] Ibid.

[60] Fredric Jameson, 'Reification and Utopia in Mass Culture', *Social Text*, 1 (1979), 131.

then suddenly, at a bend in a corridor, here we are on a guided tour, as schoolchildren or tourists.'[61]

In a town there are houses, plants in bay windows. People notice dying better. The dead have faces, automobiles. If you don't know a name, you know a street name, a dog's name. 'He drove an orange Mazda'. You know a couple of useless things about a person that become major facts of identification and cosmic placement when he dies suddenly, after a short illness, in his own bed, with a comforter and matching pillows, on a rainy Wednesday afternoon, feverish, a little congested in the sinuses and chest, thinking about his dry cleaning.[62]

White Noise *is obsessed with one of the classical aims of the realist novel: the construction of typicality. What this used to mean was a continuous process of extrapolation from the particular to the general, a process rooted in the existence of broad social taxonomies, general structures of human and historical destiny. Social typicality precedes the literary type—which is to say that the type is laid down in the social world; it is prior to and has a different kind of reality from secondary representations of it. First there is life, and then there is art. In* White Noise, *however, it's the other way round: social taxonomies are a function not of historical necessity but of style.*

Consider this description of the parents of Jack's students:

The conscientious suntans. The well-made faces and wry looks. They feel a sense of renewal, of communal recognition. The women crisp and alert, in diet trim, knowing people's names. Their husbands content to measure out the time, distant but ungrudging, accomplished in parenthood, something about them suggesting massive insurance coverage. (p. 3)

This type is not a naïve given, an embodied universality, but a self-conscious enactment; the middle-class parents know the ideality they are supposed to represent, and are deliberately living up to it. But this means that the type loses its purity, since it can always be imitated, feigned; or rather that there is no longer a difference in kind between the social category and the life-style which brings it into everyday being: the type ceaselessly imitates itself—through the ritual assembly of station wagons, for example,

---

[61] Derrida, *The Truth in Painting*, 293.
[62] DeLillo, *White Noise*, 38–9.

which 'tells the parents they are a collection of the like-minded and the spiritually akin, a people, a nation' (p. 4).

It is thus no longer possible to distinguish meaningfully between a generality embedded in life and a generality embedded in representations of life. The 'communal recognition' that constitutes the social class is part of a more diffuse system of recognitions conveyed through an infinitely detailed network of mediations. When Jack tries to characterize the convicted murderer Heinrich plays chess with, he draws on a range of mass-cultural information, like those psychological 'profiles' that construct, above all for television, a taxonomy of criminal types, to ask: 'Did he care for his weapons obsessively? Did he have an arsenal stacked in his shabby little room off a six-story concrete car park?' (p. 44). A computer operator 'had a skinny neck and jug-handle ears to go with his starved skull—the innocent prewar look of a rural murderer' (p. 140). Those who would be affected by the airborne toxic event would be 'people who live in mobile homes out in the scrubby parts of the county, where the fish hatcheries are' (p. 117). The type of the bigot, embodied in Murray's landlord, is 'very good with all those little tools and fixtures that people in cities never know the names of', and tends to drive a panel truck 'with an extension ladder on the roof and some kind of plastic charm dangling from the rearview mirror' (p. 33). The whole of this world is covered by a fine grid of typifications, so detailed and precise that it pre-empts and contains contingency.

*If the type is susceptible of minute description, then the traditional novelistic tension between detail and generality falls away, and Lukács's account of typicality becomes unworkable. For Lukács, typicality is best embodied in the category of particularity (*Besonderheit*), which stands midway between philosophical generality (*Allgemeinheit*) and descriptive detail, or singularity (*Einzelheit*);*[63] *in a postmodern economy of mediations, however, where representations of generality suffuse every pore of the world, the opposition between the general and the singular collapses as they merge into a single, undialectical unity. The* petit fait vrai *of the realist novel, the meaningless detail whose sole function is to establish a realism-effect, is no longer meaningless. Reconstructing*

---

[63] Georg Lukács, 'Über die Besonderheit als Kategorie der Ästhetik', *Probleme der Ästhetik, Werke*, vol. x (Neuwied: Luchterhand, 1969), 539, 670–3.

the scene of his wife's adultery, Jack mentions objects like 'the fire-retardant carpet' and 'the rental car keys on the dresser' (p. 194); the definite article here marks these—as it does in much of Auden's poetry—not as concrete particulars but as generic indicators; they are not pieces of detail broken off from the contingent real but fragments of a mundane typicality.

The complexity and intricacy of the type—whether it is a character, a scene, or a landscape—is made possible by the constant repetition of its features: it is reproduced as a sort of amalgam of television and experience, the two now theoretically inseparable. At its simplest this gives us something like the image of the grandparents who 'share the Trimline phone, beamish old folks in hand-knit sweaters on fixed incomes' (p. 272)—this is of course a joke about typicality, or rather about its construction in Hollywood movies and television advertising. A somewhat more complex play with typification is this:

A woman in a yellow slicker held up traffic to let some children cross. I pictured her in a soup commercial taking off her oilskin hat as she entered the cheerful kitchen where her husband stood over a pot of smoky lobster bisque, a smallish man with six weeks to live. (p. 22)

This depends on the reader's recognition of the particular soup commercial, or at least the genre of commercials, that is being parodied by role reversal, and by the substitution of the traffic warden's yellow raincoat for the traditional and stereotyped fisherman's yellow raincoat—a substitution of the urban and feminine for the premodern world of masculine work. But part of the effect of this passage, as of that quoted at the beginning of this section, lies in its stylistic trick of pinning down the type (welcoming spouse at hearth) to an absurdly particular detail. What most of these typifications have in common, however, is their source in a chain of prior representations. Jack's dying, for example, is projected through a characterology taken from the movies, as in Murray's line to him that 'People will depend on you to be brave. What people look for in a dying friend is a stubborn kind of gravel-voiced nobility, a refusal to give in, with moments of indomitable humour' (p. 284). The cliché is a simulacrum, an ideal form that shapes and constrains both life and death.

If the tourist, with her camera, can be taken to exemplify the shifting historical relationship between the subject and the world of objects, then the specific form of this relationship—the activity of sightseeing—must also be understood historically. And, in the first place, it must be understood that this nexus between travel and vision has not always existed. Judith Adler's 'Origins of Sightseeing' gives a meticulously detailed account, which I follow here, of the birth of this 'historically new, overweaning emphasis upon the isolated exercise and systematic cultivation of the sense of sight'. The practices of contemporary sightseeing, she writes,

must ultimately be understood in relation to the historical development (and eventual popularization) of post-Baconian and Lockeian orientations toward the problem of attaining, and authoritatively representing, knowledge. They must be seen in relation to forms of subjectivity anchored in wilfully independent vision, and in the cognitive subjugation of a world of 'things'. Above all, they need to be understood in relation to that European cultural transformation which Lucien Febvre first termed 'the visualization of perception'.[64]

In the Renaissance, Adler argues, the aristocratic traveller 'went abroad for *discourse* rather than for picturesque views or scenes'. The art of travel prescribed for him (more rarely her) 'was in large measure one of discoursing with the living and the dead—learning foreign tongues, obtaining access to foreign courts, and conversing gracefully with eminent men, assimilating classical texts appropriate to particular sites, and, not least, speaking eloquently upon his return' (p. 8). The late sixteenth and the seventeenth centuries see a shift, however, away from a discursivity identified with scholasticism and traditional authority toward 'an "eye" believed to yield direct, unmediated, and personally verified experience' (p. 11). The change is clearly identifiable in Bacon's essay 'Of Travel', with its prescription both of the cultivation of and conversation with good acquaintance, and of the detailed recording of sights witnessed in the course of travel—for didactic, it should be noted, not for aesthetic ends.

What emerges at this time is, then, an investigative art of travel, governed by an ideal of objectively accurate vision. It is closely linked with the development of experimental and observational methodologies in the natural sciences,[65] and indeed one of the

[64] Judith Adler, 'Origins of Sightseeing', *Annals of Tourism Research*, 16: 1 (1989), 8. Further references will be incorporated in the text.

[65] Cf. Barbara Stafford, *Voyage into Substance: Art, Science, Nature, and the Illustrated Travel Account, 1760–1840* (Cambridge, Mass.: MIT Press, 1984), esp. ch. 1.

major motives for travelling is, in the seventeenth and eighteenth centuries, the exchange of scientific information and the establishment of intellectual networks, which are then held in place by the system of scientific correspondents. At the same time the practice of keeping a travel diary grows to become a normal way of focusing observation, as does the writing up of travel notes in the form of fictive dated letters, reinforcing the valued sense of immediacy of witness. By the second half of the eighteenth century the information-gathering focus of travel has come to include statistical enquiry and economic analysis, to such an extent, argues Adler, that 'in this new concern with what later came to be called "social indicators", as well as in the further rationalization of impersonally conducted and more easily compiled observation, the history of amateur travel merges with the history of early social science' (p. 21).

By the nineteenth century, however, the amateur collection of information had largely been displaced by professional agents, and 'a travel performance which had once been taken as a sign of seriousness and discipline was soon disdained as empty ritual, its epigone practitioners dismissed as hacks who simply ticked off a checklist of sights already exhaustively described by others' (p. 22). Its place was taken by a new discipline of connoisseurship for the eye, centring on the cultivation and display of 'taste'. In its aesthetic transformation, 'sightseeing became simultaneously a more effusively passionate activity and a more private one' (although it had some famous and highly public models in the poets of the Romantic movements in England, France, and Germany). Originating in the discriminating perusal of privately owned works of art and cabinets of curiosities, its conception of the aesthetic later broadens to take in landscape and cityscape: not just pictures but the picturesque, now integrated into a more general economy of looking.[66] It is this economy, the 'belief in the restorative effects of happily constituted scenes, and an increasingly romantic orientation to aesthetic sightseeing' (p. 23), that forms the basis of modern tourism and of what John Urry describes as a generalized tourist gaze.[67]

Photography, the descendant both of the sketch pad and of the

---

[66] Cf. Malcolm Andrews, *The Search for the Picturesque: Landscape, Aesthetics and Tourism in Britain, 1760–1800* (Stanford, Calif.: Stanford University Press, 1990).   [67] Urry, *The Tourist Gaze*, 82.

apparatus of scientific observation, unites in a dramatic way the disparate forms of knowledge—detached witnessing and aesthetic appreciation—which had made up this history. Its centrality to the industrialized tourism of the twentieth century (a 'mass' activity which may include the most 'private' and 'individual' of pursuits) is a function in the first place of its ability to make readily available those aesthetic and observational competencies which had previously been the preserve of a cultural élite; but it is a function also of its power of capturing any piece of empirically witnessed reality and transforming it into a sign of itself—of 'transforming space into its own material image' (Jameson). Photography as witness, as commemoration, as aesthetic framing partakes of just that mix of the sacred and the poetic that characterizes the testimonial poems of Basho, and like them it performs the crucial task of establishing the concordance of an empirical and personally experienced reality with an ideal pattern. The most Platonic of art forms, it describes what Urry calls 'a kind of hermeneutic circle'[68] between a set of culturally authoritative representations (brochures, advertisements, guidebooks, coffee-table books), then the experiential capture of those images for oneself, and finally the display of a further set of representations which confirm the original set and its relation to the real. It is a process of authentication, the establishment of a verified relay between origin and trace.

Two related systems of representation—the postcard and the souvenir—complement photography's function of authentication. Susan Stewart has written interestingly about each. The postcard she describes as an instrument for converting a 'public' event into a 'private' appropriation of the tourist object, in a process by which the tourist first 'recovers the object, inscribing the handwriting of the personal beneath the more uniform caption of the social', and then, 'in a gesture which recapitulates the social's articulation of the self—that is, the gesture of the *gift* by which the subject is positioned as place of production and reception of obligation'[69]— surrenders it to a third party who acts, quite involuntarily, as a witness to the simultaneous validation of the site and of the self. The souvenir similarly translates distance into proximity; it 'represents distance appropriated', and thus

---

[68] Ibid. 140.
[69] Stewart, *On Longing*, 138. Further references will be incorporated in the text.

is symptomatic of the more general cultural imperialism that is tourism's stock in trade. To have a souvenir of the exotic is to possess both a specimen and a trophy; on the one hand, the object must be marked as exterior and foreign, on the other it must be marked as arising directly out of an immediate experience of its possessor. It is thus placed within an intimate distance; space is transformed into interiority, into 'personal' space, just as time is transformed into interiority in the case of the antique object. (p. 147)

Arising not from need or use value but out of 'the necessarily insatiable demands of nostalgia' (p. 135), the souvenir has as its vocation the continual re-establishment of a bridge between origin and trace. Like the medieval relic, which operates 'by principles of sympathetic and contagious magic',[70] it works by establishing a metonymic relation with the moment of origin (and its difference from photography and the postcard lies in its metonymic rather than representational figuration of the world of past experience). Like the fetish, the souvenir is a part object, and, since it is an allusion rather than a model, 'it will not function without the supplementary narrative discourse that both attaches it to its origins and creates a myth with regard to those origins'. This narrative of origins is 'a narrative of interiority and authenticity' (p. 136), a story not of the object but of the subject who possesses it and who thus, through the souvenir, possesses the lost and recovered moment of the past.

'God, I hate tourists', said Gerald. 'They've made a mess of everything. Nothing is real anymore. They obscure anything that was there. They stand around, droves of them, clicking with their blasted cameras. Most of them don't know what they're gawking at. . . . I usually go to places where there are no tourists—places that haven't been spoilt. But it's getting to the stage now where even the size of a city or a country is no longer a defence. You know how mobs pour in and stand around taking up room, and asking the most ludicrous basic questions. They've ruined a place like Venice. It's their prerogative, but the authenticity of a culture soon becomes hard to locate. The local people themselves become altered. And of course the prices go up.'[71]

---

[70] Victor and Ethel Turner, *Image and Pilgrimage in Christian Culture: Anthropological Perspectives* (New York: Columbia University Press, 1978), 197.

[71] Murray Bail, *Homesickness* (Melbourne: Macmillan, 1980), 81–2.

The structure of the tourist experience[72] involves a paradoxical relation at once to the cultural or ontological Other and to others of the same (tourist) culture. It is tourism itself that destroys (in the very process by which it constructs) the authenticity of the tourist object; and every tourist thus at some level denies belonging to the class of tourists. Hence a certain fantasized dissociation from the others, from the rituals of tourism, is built into almost every discourse and almost every practice of tourism. This is the phenomenon of touristic shame, a 'rhetoric of moral superiority'[73] that accompanies both the most snobbish and the most politically radical critiques of tourism.[74] Hans Magnus Enzensberger was perhaps the first to define this dissociation as a structural moment of tourism, and to indicate its inherent bad faith:

> The critique of tourism . . . belongs in truth to tourism itself. Its secret ideology, the value it sets on the 'demonic', the 'elementary', 'adventure', the 'undisturbed', all this is part of its self-advertisement. The disillusionment with which the critic reacts to it corresponds to the illusions which he shares with tourism.[75]

Urry has sought to define the basis for this dissociation through the concept of the 'positional economy'—that is,

> all aspects of goods, services, work, positions, and other social relationships which are either scarce or subject to congestion or crowding. Competition is therefore zero-sum: as any one person consumes more of the good in question, so someone else is forced to consume less.[76]

The congestion and environmental destruction that accompany intensive tourist development, for example, can be explained in

---

[72] There is of course no unitary 'tourist experience', and a number of taxonomizations seek to differentiate between very diverse forms of experience (e.g. Valene Smith, 'Introduction', in Smith, *Hosts and Guests*; Erik Cohen, 'The Sociology of Tourism: Approaches, Issues, and Findings', *Annual Review of Sociology*, 10 (1984), 373–92; Donald L. Redfoot, 'Touristic Authenticity, Touristic Angst and Modern Reality', 291–309). Nevertheless, for the purposes of this essay I assume a common semiotic structure to many tourist practices. My argument is restricted to the first four of Smith's categories (ethnic, cultural, historical, and environmental tourism), and doesn't necessarily concern her fifth category, recreational tourism.   [73] MacCannell, *The Tourist*, 9.

[74] The former is embodied in the widespread distinction between the tourist and the traveller, the latter in—for example—the Marxist moralism of Turner and Ash's *The Golden Hordes*.

[75] Hans Magnus Enzensberger, 'Eine Theorie des Tourismus', *Einzelheiten I: Bewußtseins-Industrie* (Frankfurt am Main: Suhrkamp, 1962), 185.

[76] Urry, *The Tourist Gaze*, 43; further references will be incorporated in the text.

terms of the positional competition between consumers of a scarce tourist product (although this explanation, like all such rationalist economic explanations, fails to take into account the particular mode of organization of this 'competition'). The notion of 'scarcity' is itself not an absolute, however, since different kinds of consumption of limited tourist resources have different consequences. Urry distinguishes between two primary modes of tourist consumption (two modes of the tourist 'gaze'): one is the 'romantic' gaze, which is 'concerned with the élitist—and solitary— appreciation of magnificent scenery, an appreciation which requires considerable cultural capital' (p. 86), and which is therefore predominantly a middle-class form of appropriation; the other is the 'collective' gaze, which, based on popular modes of pleasure, is anti-auratic, anti-élitist, and participatory. From this distinction Urry concludes that the 'arguments about scarcity and positional competition mainly apply to those types of tourism characterized by the romantic gaze. Where the collective gaze is to be found, there is less of a problem of crowding and congestion' (p. 46). But for whom is there less of a problem? Urry's argument assumes that the two modes are alternative to and separate from each other. This is not the case: collective or convivial tourism impinges on, and may crowd out, romantic tourism, whereas the converse does not necessarily hold true. This is not to say that the romantic gaze does not itself often end up imposing a forced competition, or that it does not at times deliberately seek to control access to its preferred objects; it is to say that the category of the 'collective' here establishes a false universality.

Tourism, says John Carroll in an essay that is entirely complicit with the snobbery it denounces, 'has brought to the many an experience that they imagined to be the privilege of the few'.[77] Touristic shame is thus based not merely on the actuality of positional competition but on a *Verwerfung*, a disavowal, of the mass availability of privilege. It involves a fantasy of achieved upward mobility, and it has its favoured models of the aristocratic good life. Two letters of Wordsworth from 1844, written on the occasion of a projected extension of the railway line to Kendal and Windermere, give a sense of the contradictions to which positional

[77] John Carroll, 'The Tourist', *Sceptical Sociology* (London: Routledge, 1980), 140.

competition gives rise, and of their basis in a fantasy of class understood as cultural capital.

The attraction of the Lake District, Wordsworth writes, lies in 'its beauty and its character of seclusion and retirement', whereas the projectors of the railway have announced that their intention is 'to place the beauties of the Lake District within easier reach of those who cannot afford to pay for ordinary conveyances'.[78] But Wordsworth's argument is not directly that seclusion and accessibility are incompatible, but rather that there is no point in opening up the area to those who will not adequately appreciate it. This argument about taste is partly historical: 'the relish for choice and picturesque natural *scenery* . . . is quite of recent origin' (p. 79), and especially when the landscape is relatively wild. Wordsworth cites numerous examples of English travellers who felt only horror at the Swiss Alps, and points out that in seventeenth- and eighteenth-century travel writings, 'where precipitous rocks and mountains are mentioned at all, they are spoken of as objects of dislike and fear, and not of admiration'. The point is 'that a vivid perception of romantic scenery is neither inherent in mankind, nor a necessary consequence of even a comprehensive education' (p. 80) (the word 'romantic' here is opposed to the 'ordinary varieties of rural nature').

The question, then, is one about the appropriate means for furthering the growth in appreciation of 'romantic scenery'. But

surely that good is not to be obtained by transferring at once uneducated persons in large bodies to particular spots, where the combinations of natural objects are such as would afford the greatest pleasure to those who have been in the habit of observing and studying the peculiar character of such scenes, and how they differ one from another. Instead of tempting artisans and labourers, and the humbler classes of shopkeepers, to ramble to a distance, let us rather look with lively sympathy upon persons in that condition, when, upon a holiday, or on the Sunday, after having attended divine worship, they make little excursions with their wives and children among neighbouring fields, whither the whole of each family might stroll, or be conveyed at much less cost than would be required to take a single individual of the number to the shores of Windermere by the cheapest conveyance. It is in some such way as this only, that persons who must labour daily with their hands for bread in large towns, or are subject to

[78] William Wordsworth, *Selected Prose*, ed. John O. Hayden (Harmondsworth: Penguin, 1988), 78; further references are incorporated in the text.

confinement through the week, can be trained to a profitable intercourse with nature where she is the most distinguished by the majesty and sublimity of her forms. (pp. 81–2)

The concept of cultural capital ('taste'), which is meant to place the discussion on the level of aesthetic competencies rather than on the level of social class, transparently fails to do so, since the aesthetic is immediately a code word for class. Nature 'herself' is divided into two classes, with the lower level of 'ordinary' rural beauty—the 'neighbouring fields'—assigned to the working class. The discussion of aesthetic education is insufficient as an argument, since there is no sense of how a progression from one class of beauty to the other could take place, and in any case the economic barriers are to be retained. It seems to be a question rather of keeping these artisans and labourers and shopkeepers in their natural station—which the mobility of tourism threatens—and of protecting them (and their 'wives and children') even from their own desires: keeping them from 'temptation'.

There can be little doubt that Wordsworth's concern is indeed not for these aesthetically deprived workers but for those who enjoy a privileged and protected access to a scarce resource. Subsequent passages contrast the quiet enjoyment of natural beauty to the noisy vulgarity of those popular recreations which would inevitably accompany mass tourism (pp. 83, 84). Popular pleasures and the romantic gaze are in conflict, and it is at once a class conflict and one necessarily internal to modern tourism itself. The 'unavoidable consequence' of opening up the railways 'must be a great disturbance of the retirement, and in many places a destruction of the beauty of the country, which the parties are come in search of' (p. 84).

The irony is, however, that it is Wordsworth himself who has issued the invitation, who has already educated the vulgar crowd to the beauties of the Lake District, and whose poems (as well as, more directly, his 1822 *Guide to the Lakes*) have acted as a sort of tourist brochure.[79] This becomes a little clearer in the second

---

[79] Jonathan Raban writes: 'By 1850, when Wordsworth died, the craggy English wilderness of leech-gatherers and terrified small boys in little boats had become (largely by Wordsworth's own agency) a tourist resort. The mighty mountains were dotted with hikers. Horse-drawn carriages were transporting more sedentary holiday-makers to see Wordsworth's houses, Rydal Mount and Dove Cottage.

letter, where he writes of various manufacturers in Lancashire and Yorkshire who plan to send their workers for holidays to the banks of Windermere. The conception of nature as spiritually restorative that underlies such an initiative is in no small measure derived from Wordsworth's own writings.[80] Touristic shame and the opposition of an authentic to an inauthentic gaze work to repress an understanding of the investments (both financial and moral) that the circulation of cultural capital makes possible.

That the native does not like the tourist is not hard to explain. For every native of every place is a potential tourist. Every native everywhere lives a life of overwhelming and crushing banality and boredom and desperation and depression, and every deed, good and bad, is an attempt to forget this. Every native would like to find a way out, every native would like a rest, every native would like a tour. But some natives—most natives in the world—cannot go anywhere. They are too poor. They are too poor to go anywhere. They are too poor to escape the reality of their lives; and they are too poor to live properly in the place where they live, which is the very place you, the tourist, want to go—so when the natives see you, the tourist, they envy you, they envy your ability to turn their own banality and boredom into a source of pleasure for yourself.[81]

The infrastructure of the tourist industry is made up of

travel agents, tour operators and guides, hotels and resorts, transportation networks and information and communication systems, mass media marketing, tourist regions and attractions, travel gear and souvenirs, travel literature and films, educational institutions that train industry personnel and foster scholarly research on tourism, regulatory and policy-making bodies, government agencies, professional associations, and international travel organizations and clubs.[82]

The function of the industry is to sell a commodity to a group of consumers. Accounts of its size and turnover vary considerably, but Cohen cites a rise in the number of international tourists from 25.3

Easels and sketchbooks were pitched on every convenient rock, so that Sunday painters could catch the prettiness of Defoe's "frightful appearances". The Lake District had turned into Britain's first theme park.' Jonathan Raban, *Coasting* (1986; repr. London: Picador, 1987), 36.

[80] Cf. John Urry, 'The Making of the Lake District', *Consuming Places* (London: Routledge, 1995), 204.

[81] Jamaica Kincaid, *A Small Place* (London: Virago, 1988), 18–19.

[82] Kirshenblatt-Gimblett and Bruner, 'Tourism', 249.

million in 1950 to 291 million in 1980,[83] and Dominique Callimanopulos uses a similar figure of 285 million tourists in 1980, 85 per cent of them originating in North America and Europe, to project total export earnings of about US$79 billion annually.[84] That figure has probably doubled by today.

In some respects the commodity sold by the industry is a relatively material set of services (travel and accommodation, for example). But the more determinant aspects of this commodity (the 'hooks' that keep consumers buying) are immaterial. The product sold by the tourism industry, in its most general form, is a commodified relation to the Other. This is not precisely a relation between host and guest, because, as Cohen points out, tourism involves pressures which

transform the guest-host relationship that is based on customary, but neither precise nor obligatory, reciprocity into a commercial one that is based on remuneration. This transformation involves incorporating hospitality—an area that many societies view as founded on values that are the very opposite of economic ones—into the economic domain.[85]

One part of the relation to the Other involves, then, the commodification of hospitality. In its other major dimension, the relation involves the Other not just as a provider of services but as an object of attention. Its saleable otherness is either that of the natural or built world, or that of an alien culture.

The commodification of reciprocal bonds, of the environment, and of culture are moments of that logic of contemporary capital which extends private appropriation and ownership from material to immaterial resources, and whose paradigm case is the commodification of information. What makes the process so difficult for those affected to control is the fact that these resources have previously been more or less freely available, or at least have been restricted in non-economic ways. The effect, as Davydd Greenwood argues with respect to the commodification of culture, is that this appropriation can take place without any requirement of formal consent. Anything at all can be transformed into a commodity. This is clear when cultural services are paid for, but

[83] Cohen, 'The Sociology of Tourism', 377.
[84] Dominique Callimanopulos, 'Introduction', *Cultural Survival Quarterly*, 6: 3 (Summer 1982), 3. For a useful set of statistics on tourist visits to the Third World, cf. *New Internationalist*, 142 (Dec. 1984), 10–11.
[85] Cohen, 'The Sociology of Tourism', 380.

it is not as clear when activities of the host culture are treated as part of the 'come-on' without their consent and are invaded by tourists who do not reimburse them for their 'service'. In this case, their activities are taken advantage of for profit, but they do not profit, culturally. The onlookers often alter the meaning of the activities being carried on by local people. Under these circumstances, local culture is in effect being expropriated, and local people are being exploited.[86]

The logic of tourism is that of a relentless extension of commodity relations and the consequent inequalities of power between centre and periphery, First and Third Worlds, developed and underdeveloped regions, metropolis and countryside. Promising an explosion of modernity, it brings about structural underdevelopment, both because of its control by international capital and 'because it is precisely the *lack* of development which makes an area attractive as a tourist goal'.[87] Exalting the *non*-'modern'—the natural, the non-Western, the traditional, the exotic, the primitive, the different—it brings whatever corresponds to these imaginary terms within the sphere of their categorical opposite, a 'modernity' constructed in this relation, and destructive of the very otherness it celebrates.

[86] Davydd J. Greenwood, 'Culture by the Pound: An Anthropological Perspective on Tourism as Cultural Commoditization', in Smith, *Hosts and Guests*, 130–31.

[87] Susan Buck-Morss, 'Semiotic Boundaries and the Politics of Meaning: Modernity on Tour—A Village in Transition', in Marcus G. Raskin and Herbert J. Bernstein (eds.), *New Ways of Knowing: The Sciences, Society, and Reconstructive Knowledge* (Totowa, NJ: Rowman and Littlefield, 1987), 230.

3
Gift and Commodity

A. GIFT EXCHANGE

Who ever gives, takes libertie[1]

For much of this century one of the most powerful and most illuminating ways of thinking about the pattern of relations between persons has been through the opposition of the gift to the commodity. The apparent clarity of the contrast between two very different forms of the social life of things has made it integral to the more general logic that opposes traditional or archaic societies to industrial modernity. But just as that opposition, rather than representing a clear-cut temporal separation, turns out over and over again to be a form of mythical thinking in which the moment of rupture is endlessly repeated, so too, on closer examination, do the concepts of gift and commodity seem to partake of each other: the gift to be structured, as Marcel Mauss clearly recognized, according to forms of calculation and interest that in some sense resemble those of a market economy, and commodities in turn to be constantly endowed with non-commodity meanings as they move within the moral economy of everyday life. Indeed, it may be the case that the concept of the gift is most interesting when it is understood not as a figure of pure gratuitousness but through the very ambivalence that provokes the question of how its logic really differs from that of the commodity.

Both in its etymology[2] and in the history of its uses, this ambivalence is registered in the *Oxford English Dictionary* in the form of contradiction. The important definition is number 3: 'Something, the possession of which is transferred to another

---

[1] John Donne, 'A Hymne to Christ, at the Authors Last Going into Germany'.
[2] One of its Old English meanings was 'payment for a wife'; in Old High German it carries the notoriously twinned senses of 'gift' and 'poison'.

without the expectation or receipt of an equivalent.' This sets up two useful distinctions: first, it specifies that what is given is not the thing itself but the possession of the thing (and it thus directs us to the cultural meanings of possession); second, it calls attention to the category of equivalence (and thus the contradistinction of the gift to the commodity, where the latter is defined within the structure of abstract equivalence that constitutes exchange value). Although many of the supporting quotations sustain this sense of the gift as gratuitous offering without the reality or expectation of a counter-offering ('The prouerb is, what is so free as gift?'), others suggest precisely the opposite: 'Bounden is he that gifte takithe'; 'Giving is giving, gift claims gift's return'. It is the question of the return on and of the gift that has preoccupied anthropology since Mauss.

If I start my reading nevertheless with the simplest and purest model of the logic of the gift, it is because this model is at once culturally pervasive and an ideal type against which all more complex versions are set. Lewis Hyde's *The Gift: Imagination and the Erotic Life of Property*, for example, links together the 'erotic commerce' of gift-giving with the 'inner gift' that is the source of all aesthetic activity.[3] The 'outer gift', the carrier of social bonds, may or may not correspond to this inner gift: gifts and commodities may come to resemble each other, and any gift may be contaminated by the social interest in giving. In its pure form, however, the movement of the gift, its consumption as 'it moves from one hand to another with no assurance of anything in return' (p. 9), is free of all calculation. Hyde is thus not concerned 'with gifts given in spite or fear, nor those gifts we accept out of servility or obligation'; his concern 'is the gift we long for, the gift that, when it comes, speaks commandingly to the soul and irresistibly moves us' (p. xvii), and it is of course precisely that absence of 'assurance of anything in return' that endows the gift with this authority.

The epiphany of the gift is at the same time, however, one of the strongest forces acting for sociality, since 'any exchange, be it of ideas or of goats, will tend towards gift if it is intended to recognize, establish, and maintain community' (p. 78); conversely, 'the conversion of gifts to commodities can fragment or destroy such a

---

[3] Lewis Hyde, *The Gift: Imagination and the Erotic Life of Property* (New York: Vintage Books, 1983), p. xiv; further references are incorporated in the text.

group' (p. 80). Gift exchange is at the core of social cohesion, or rather it represents a social generosity that is absent from other, more 'contractual' or 'mechanical' forms of social solidarity. One of the main functions of the theory of the gift has accordingly been to provide an account of altruism or of non-exploitative reciprocity as a basis of community. Mauss used the concept of the gift explicitly to ground a kind of paternalistic socialism based on the 'noble expenditure' of the rich;[4] but the most developed argument for the connection between the generosity of the gift and the possible patterning of social relations is that made by Richard Titmuss in his study of the organization of public blood supplies, *The Gift Relationship: From Human Blood to Social Policy*.

Titmuss's argument, which is closely tied to an implicit defence of the post-war British welfare state, is directed against the sort of utilitarian calculus that has since become more familiar as the doctrines of neoliberal economic rationalism. Against this calculus Titmuss seeks to assert a specific domain of the social (as distinct from the economic), and to calculate the moral inputs and benefits of two strongly contrasted systems of acquisition of blood for medical purposes: the American system (at that time) of blood purchase, and the British system of donation.[5] The study has an empirical basis and finds in favour of the British system on a number of grounds, including those of economic and administrative efficiency as well as those of health standards and of social costs. My interest here is in the book's theoretical argument and in particular in the form of gift that it extrapolates from the system of donation of blood.

The question of the social, says Titmuss, is the question:

Why give to strangers?—a question provoking an even more fundamental moral issue, who is my stranger in the relatively affluent, acquisitive and divisive societies of the twentieth century? What are the connections then,

---

[4] Marcel Mauss, *The Gift: Forms and Functions of Exchange in Archaic Societies*, trans. Ian Cunnison (New York: Norton, 1967), 66. I have modified the translation where necessary; the original text, 'Essai sur le don: Forme et raison de l'échange dans les sociétés archaïques', is the second part of Marcel Mauss, *Sociologie et anthropologie* (Paris: Presses Universitaires Françaises, 1960).

[5] By 1982, the date of the next major study, the United States had largely shifted to a mix of voluntary and insurance-credit schemes, with paid donors accounting for no more than 3–4% of donations. Alvin W. Drake, Stan N. Finkelstein, and Harvey M. Sapolsky, *The American Blood Supply* (Cambridge, Mass.: MIT Press, 1982).

if obligations are extended, between the reciprocals of giving and receiving and modern welfare systems?[6]

In order to begin to answer this question, Titmuss posits the existence of a domain of transactions which stand outside economic quantification and pricing and which 'carry no explicit right, expectation or moral enforcement of a return gift' (p. 212). It is the 'creative altruism' of these social gifts that makes possible the binding together of strangers in large-scale social orders. Structures like the National Health Service—'the most unsordid act of British social policy in the twentieth century' (p. 225)—are both dependent upon and in turn foster the moral expression of altruism, reciprocity, and social duty; the act of blood donation, which is a microcosm of these structures, is perhaps not a pure altruism in so far as it depends upon some sense of social inclusion, but it goes beyond the sorts of mutually obligating transactions that Mauss describes for traditional societies. This is so because 'there is in the free gift of blood to unnamed strangers no contract of custom, no legal bond, no functional determinism, no situations of discriminatory power, domination, constraint or compulsion, no sense of shame or guilt, no gratitude imperative and no need for the penitence of a Chrysostom' (p. 239). Above all, there is no expectation of a return on the gift.[7]

Against this, Titmuss sets the atomism of a market system which puts in place some very specific *negative* freedoms: freedom from obligation to or for unnamed strangers, and freedom from a sense of inclusion in the social. At the same time, it introduces new forms of coercion by reducing the scope for moral choice and altruistic behaviour. Both donation and market systems thus entail limitations and enlargements of choice, and the role of social policy can only be that of weighing up the consequences of each. The consequences of

---

[6] Richard Titmuss, *The Gift Relationship: From Human Blood to Social Policy* (London: Allen and Unwin, 1970), 11; further citations are given in the text.

[7] In the case of the gift of body organs, however, this seems not to be the case; Renée Fox and Judith Swazey speak of a sense of onus to repay on the part of the recipient, and a sense on the part of the donor 'that part of the donor's self or personhood has been transmitted along with the organ'. This then leads to an identification with the recipient and a feeling of owning a part of their destiny. It is the very altruism of organ donation that produces this tyranny of the gift. Renée C. Fox and Judith P. Swazey, *Spare Parts: Organ Replacement in American Society* (New York: Oxford University Press, 1992), 36–43.

a market system include some very definite social costs including a redistribution of blood and blood products from the poor to the rich. But the moral externalities of such a system are also consequential, and it is on the basis of both of these dimensions that Titmuss concludes that social policy should, on the one hand, free people of the market constraint on giving to unnamed strangers, and on the other restrict their freedom to sell blood or to decide on the specific destination of the gift.

The issue of the gift of blood becomes in Titmuss's exposition something like a parable of the limits of commodification. What is crucial about blood is that it is at once a good that can be shared between strangers, and an intimate part of the person; it 'may now constitute in Western societies one of the ultimate tests of where the "social" begins and the "economic" ends' (p. 158). If it can be treated as a commodity to be traded in the marketplace, then the same status may come to be extended to other bodily organs— hearts, kidneys, eyes, and so on—with the same or even more damaging redistributional consequences. At the limit, the implications of the commodification of blood

could extend to affect our thinking over wide areas of social policy and what are conventionally called 'the social services'. Hospitals, nursing homes, clinical laboratories, schools, universities and even, perhaps, churches would no longer be protected by laws or common conventions of 'charitable' immunity; they would be exposed to the forces of economic calculation and to the laws of the marketplace. (p. 213)[8]

For both Hyde and Titmuss the gift, at least in certain exemplary forms, transcends the obligation to return that for Mauss constituted the radical ambivalence of gift exchange in archaic societies. One way of continuing to posit the gift as action unconstrained by an interest in return while still retaining Mauss's recognition of the coerciveness of gift exchange is to distinguish, as Simmel does, between the first gift and all subsequent gifts. The gift given by another, he says,

[8] Kenneth Arrow, while conceding that the price system cannot be universal because of its dependence upon a social contract, nevertheless argues against Titmuss that the critique of commodification and market structures can easily slip into a defence of privilege, and he points to the paradox that Titmuss's claims for a *generalized* and impersonal altruism 'is as far removed from the feelings of personal interaction as any marketplace'. Kenneth Arrow, 'Gifts and Exchanges', *Philosophy and Public Affairs*, 1: 4 (1972), 359–60.

because it was first, has a voluntary character which no return gift can have. For, to return the benefit we are obliged ethically; we operate under a coercion which, though neither social nor legal but moral, is still a coercion. The first gift is given in full spontaneity; it has a freedom without any duty, even without the duty of gratitude. . . . Only when we give first are we free, and this is the reason why, in the first gift, which is not occasioned by any gratitude, there lies a beauty, a spontaneous devotion to the other, an opening up and flowering from the 'virgin soil' of the soul, as it were, which cannot be matched by any subsequent gift, no matter how superior its content.[9]

And yet what sort of freedom, what sort of 'devotion to the other' can this be that exercises such coercion over its recipient? As Gasché notes, there can be no such thing as an originary gift: every gift is already a response, a counter-prestation,[10] just as for Bakhtin every utterance already includes within it the virtuality of its reception. As long as there is the expectation, or even just the structural possibility of a return, the gift is caught up within the circuits of reciprocity. In a strictly logical sense, the 'first gift' is an impossibility.

It is the widening spirals of this impossibility that Derrida explores in *Given Time*. In the Bataillean terms that frame his argument, the gift is the opposite of and interrupts economy, by which Derrida means exchange, reciprocity, the circle by means of which the gift is returned, sooner or later, along more or less devious paths, to its donor. In order for there to be a gift, 'there must be no reciprocity, return, exchange, countergift, or debt. If the other *gives* me *back* or *owes* me or has to give me back what I give him or her, there will not have been a gift, whether this restitution is immediate or whether it is programmed by a complex calculation of a long-term deferral or differance'; the gift 'is annulled each time there is restitution or countergift'.[11] Indeed, not only is it necessary that the receiver not return the gift, they must not even recognize that it is a gift. Recognition is a form of return: it gives back a 'symbolic equivalent', and 'the symbolic opens and constitutes the

[9] Georg Simmel, 'Faithfulness and Gratitude', *The Sociology of Georg Simmel*, ed. Kurt H. Wolff (New York: Free Press, 1950), 392–3.

[10] Rodolphe Gasché, 'L'Échange héliocentrique', *L'Arc*, 48 (1972), 80.

[11] Jacques Derrida, *Given Time: 1. Counterfeit Money*, trans. Peggy Kamuf (Chicago: University of Chicago Press, 1992), 12. Further references are given in the text.

order of exchange and of debt, the law or the order of circulation in which the gift gets annulled' (p. 13). At the limit, *'the gift as gift* ought *not appear as gift: either to the donee or to the donor.* It cannot be gift as gift except by not being present as gift' (p. 14). Even to refuse a gift is to recognize it as a gift and so to annul it. And even if all the conditions of non-recognition were fulfilled, there could still be an *unconscious* process of indebting at work in the act of giving:

You think there is gift, dissymmetry, generosity, expenditure, or loss, but the circle of debt, of exchange, or of symbolic equilibrium reconstitutes itself according to the laws of the unconscious; the 'generous' or 'grateful' consciousness is only the phenomenon of a calculation and the ruse of an economy. Calculation and ruse, economy in truth would be the truth of these phenomena. (p. 16)

There can be no possible 'logic of the gift', no discourse which could coherently take the gift as its object, since the gift is just whatever escapes the measure of discourse, whatever cancels itself as soon as it signifies itself as gift.

Yet what makes it possible for Derrida to conceive of the gift as impossibility is that he understands it as the purely gratuitous, non-reciprocal, and atemporal act of the 'first gift'. Its structure is the self-annihilating tension of the double-bind, of the paradox enunciated by Mauss that 'there is no gift without bond, without bind, without obligation or ligature', and yet at the same time that 'there is no gift that does not have to untie itself from obligation, from debt, contract, exchange, and thus from the bind' (p. 27). This structure has a more general, and a more familiar form: 'It so happens (but this "it so happens" does not name the fortuitous) that the structure of this impossible *gift* is also that of Being . . . and of time', because 'neither the gift nor time exist as such' (pp. 27, 28). Thought and desire are possible only on the basis of something that lies beyond thought and desire, the transcendentally impossible structure of a gift that is beyond presence; and if it then behoves us to attempt to think 'a sort of transcendental illusion of the gift', its 'groundless ground' (p. 30), this is because Derrida's move to distinguish the gift from 'the restricted economy of a differance' (p. 147), to imagine the 'first' and impossible gift, to read the gift as a figure of Being or of pure gratuitousness is what makes possible a philosophical discourse, and indeed because philosophy is finally dependent (as Derrida himself has always taught us) upon the denial of economy, of debt, of mundane temporality and the differance of exchange.

Recent literature on the gift revolves around three *topoi*, all derived from Mauss's seminal essay, which are at once exemplary and the site of small clusters of exemplary problems. They are the Maori concept of the *hau* of the gift; the potlatch; and the kula.

THE *HAU* OF THE GIFT

The central theme of Mauss's essay is the phenomenon of 'prestations which are in theory voluntary, disinterested and spontaneous, but are in fact obligatory and interested. The form usually taken is that of the gift generously offered; but the accompanying behaviour is formal pretence and social deception, while the transaction itself is based on obligation and economic self-interest [*intérêt économique*]' (p. 1). Let me briefly note that in this formulation the gift is a subset of a larger group of transactions which Mauss calls 'prestations'—a term that deliberately leaves open the question of the economic status of the operations involved; and that the ontology of the gift is said to be structured by the relation between a false appearance and a social or economic reality.

The passage on the *hau*—initially glossed by Mauss as 'the spirit of things and particularly of the forest and forest game'—is the essay's earliest example of the gift and is presented as offering the 'key' to the whole problem of the 'force . . . in the thing given which compels the recipient to make a return' (p. 1). (This notion of an inherent 'force' can of course only be read, in the Durkheimian context of Mauss's writings, as a shorthand for the social relations concentrated in and governing the object.) The text Mauss quotes had been collected from the Maori elder Tamati Ranaipiri of the Ngati-Raukawa tribe, 'one of Mr Elsdon Best's most useful informants' (p. 8), and reads as follows (this text collates Best's translation with Mauss's reinsertion of a number of key words from Ranaipiri's original text):

I shall tell you about *hau*. *Hau* is not the wind. Not at all. Suppose you have some particular object, *taonga*, and you give it to me; you give it to me without a price. We do not bargain over it. Now I give this thing to a third person who after a time decides to give me something in repayment for it (*utu*), and he makes me a present of something (*taonga*). Now this *taonga* I received from him is the spirit (*hau*) of the *taonga* I received from you and which I passed on to him. The *taonga* which I receive on account of the *taonga* that came from you, I must return to you. It would not be right on my part to keep these *taonga* whether they were desirable or not. I must give them to you since they are the *hau* of the *taonga* which you gave me. If I were to keep this second *taonga* for myself I might become ill or even die. Such is *hau*, the *hau* of personal property, the *hau* of the *taonga*, the *hau* of the forest. Enough on that subject. (pp. 8–9)

Mauss finds only one obscurity in this passage, the intervention of a third person; he clarifies it by means of a twofold interpretation: first, the gift continues to form a part of the giver even when alienated to another; second, this link is a kind of property right which persists as an obligation to return the gift, even when the gift passes through a number of hands. We are concerned here with a transaction that perhaps bears rather more resemblance to a loan than to an absolute gift or the alienation of a property right. This reading allows Mauss to infer that 'in Maori custom this bond created by things is in fact a bond between persons [*âmes*], since the thing itself is a person or pertains to a person. Hence it follows that to give something is to give a part of oneself.' And he concludes that in this system of thought

one gives away what is in reality a part of one's nature and substance, while to receive something is to receive a part of someone's spiritual essence. To keep this thing is dangerous, not only because it is illicit to do so, but also because it comes morally, physically and spiritually from a person. Whatever it is, food, possessions [*ces biens, meubles ou immeubles*], women, children or ritual, it retains a magical and religious hold over the recipient. The thing given is not inert. It is alive and often personified, and strives to bring to its original clan and homeland some equivalent to take its place. (p. 10)

Mauss's interpretation of the Ranaipiri passage is in one sense circular, in that he seeks to explain one unknown (the force of the gift) by another (the concept of *hau*). Like all good interpretations, of course, this one works by a gradual backwards-and-forwards process of mutual clarification; but the status of this interpretation, and in particular Mauss's use of an indigenous category as an independent variable, has been the object of much subsequent criticism, notably on the part of Claude Lévi-Strauss, who argued that the closeness of the indigenous category to indigenous reality ultimately prevents Mauss from conceptualizing exchange in an appropriately abstract and generalized way, as a systemic process rather than as a series of discrete operations.[12] The problem is that of the inapplicability of modern economic or legal terms to describe the 'archaic' system of prestations—a problem that Mauss explicitly recognizes (he details the impossibility of using the historically specific concept of 'interest' to understand archaic societies, for example) (pp. 73–4), whilst continuing to use these terms. Gasché thus reproaches him with being unable to think the *otherness* of other cultures, with seeking to domesticate their '*ambiguïté sauvage et originaire*', reducing what Bataille would call a general to a restricted economy.[13] But Gasché is wrong: any attempt to think cultural otherness necessarily and by definition translates it; otherwise it is unthinkable.

Among recent reinterpretations of the Ranaipiri passage, two are of particular interest. The first, by Marshall Sahlins, develops through two complementary movements: one in which the concept of *hau* is secularized, then another in which that anachronistically sharp distinction between the secular and the sacred is refused. In the first movement Sahlins—after consulting a revised translation of the passage and summarizing several later, ethnographically informed critiques of Mauss—argues that the logical reading of the text is that Ranaipiri 'was trying to explain a religious concept by an economic principle, which Mauss promptly understood the other way around and thereupon proceeded to develop the economic principle by the religious concept'.[14] The real meaning of the concept of *hau* in this context is something like 'return on' or 'product of', and what Ranaipiri is demonstrating is that the increase on the original gift—the 'interest' it accrues—should be returned to the first donor. The concept can be understood in purely secular terms: 'If the second gift is the *hau* of the first, then the *hau* of a good is its yield, just as the *hau* of a forest is its productiveness' (p. 160). The issue of the third party to the

[12] Claude Lévi-Strauss, 'Introduction à l'œuvre de Marcel Mauss', in Marcel Mauss, *Sociologie et anthropologie*, p. xxxix.
[13] Rodolphe Gasché, 'L'Échange héliocentrique', 72.
[14] Marshall Sahlins, *Stone Age Economics* (London: Tavistock Publications, 1974), 157.

transaction is directly relevant here: if it is simply a question of demonstrating the spirit of reciprocation then only two partners are needed, and the intervention of a third person is irrelevant. If the point is that 'one man's gift should not be another man's capital', however, then the introduction of a third party is necessary as a figure of the larger world of economic transactions where the gift has produced a turnover, an increase which derives from the initial investment. As Hyde independently argues, 'the increase comes to a gift as it moves from second to third party, not in the simpler passage from first to second. This increase begins when the gift has passed *through* someone, when the circle appears.'[15] Although 'the term "profit" is economically and historically inappropriate to the Maori' (pp. 160–1), it nevertheless conveys something both of the productivity of the gift and of the moral sanctions that prevail in 'a society in which freedom to gain at others' expense is not envisioned by the relations and forms of exchange' (p. 162).

It is at this point that the essay's counter-movement begins. It seems clear, Sahlins argues, that the concept of *hau* cannot be interpreted in purely secular terms, since it applies to men or to the forest in ways which seem to designate a spiritual quality; further, its use in other contexts suggests that it is not possible to separate this spiritual quality from its sense of material return or yield. What brings them together is a semantic core signifying something like 'increase' or 'productivity'. Thus 'the *hau* of the forest is its fecundity, as the *hau* of the gift is its material yield. Just as in the mundane context of exchange *hau* is the return on a good, so as a spiritual quality *hau* is the principle of fertility' (p. 168). This general principle of productiveness belongs 'neither to the domain we call "spiritual" nor that of the "material" ', and yet is applicable to either (ibid.); it is undecidable within the categorical structure of modernity. What constitutes its difficulty for us is precisely that it accords with a social formation 'in which "economic", "social", "political" and "religious" are indiscriminately organized by the same relations and intermixed in the same activities' (ibid.). If Mauss was wrong about the 'spiritual specifics' of the *hau*, yet in another sense he was profoundly right, since the logic of the *hau* is the logic that he ascribed to the gift: that of a total concept.

Annette Weiner by contrast seeks to shift attention from the

---

[15] Hyde, *The Gift*, 37.

centrality of 'the enigmatic hau' to the concept of *taonga*, 'valuables'—pointing out that in Ranaipiri's text 'the hau was not to be found in all gifts, only in those classified as taonga'.[16] So what kinds of 'valuables' are these?

In order to answer this question Weiner makes an extended argument that anthropology has systematically slighted or ignored the organization of women's wealth and prestige, noticing only those forms of wealth and power that pertain to men. Her thesis is that in a very large number of traditional societies women's specific social power is expressed in the production and, usually, the control of cloth wealth. The weaving of cloth (the term covers material made of threads and fibres of any kind) encodes a range of symbolic meanings to do with sexuality, reproduction, and nurturance, and it thereby links the human world to the world of the ancestors or gods. The specific domain of women's power in traditional societies is magical and cosmological, and it is through these powers that women play a fundamental role in social reproduction and the organization of kinship relations.

Maori culture recognizes two kinds of *taonga*, 'hard' (bones, nephrite, and precious metal) and 'soft' (cloth, cloaks, and mats). Cloaks woven by women are particularly rich in social prestige and spiritual power—a prestige and power which are summed up in the concept of *mana*. Although anthropology has tended to describe *mana* in terms of the world of male power, Weiner argues that it is in fact 'the procreative power of *women* that lies at the root of mana's metaphysical efficacy' (p. 52). *Taonga* such as famous cloaks or nephrite adzes increase in *mana* through long association with high-ranking families and acquire a particular history; in the nineteenth century wars were fought for their possession (that is, for the acquisition of the *mana* they contain). And the prestige of such *taonga* travels with them when they are given as gifts. In summary:

The authority with which taonga are imbued is authenticated through access to cosmological phenomena. Here is where we locate women's exclusive role: it is in the rituals surrounding human reproduction and cloth production where women gain control over mana which, in turn,

---

[16] Annette Weiner, *Inalienable Possessions: The Paradox of Keeping-While-Giving* (Berkeley: University of California Press, 1992), 49.

gives them a domain of authority and power in their own right. And here also, we locate the source of the 'spirit of the gift'. (p. 50)

Thus Ranaipiri's text 'is not enigmatic, nor is Mauss's interpretation of the hau mystical. The hau as a life force embedded in the person is transmitted to the person's possessions', although *hau* and *taonga* are not identical: 'the hau of each owner enters the taonga, but the taonga's value is based much less on personal identity than on the cumulative social and cosmological identities of past owners' (p. 63).

The force of the gift thus has to do with the transmission of qualities bound up with the person of the giver and the chain of previous givers. One final dimension of Weiner's argument, which I will develop more fully later, clarifies the relation between person and gift. No one has picked up, she says, the fact 'that in a few instances Mauss used the word *immeuble*, pointing out that not only Maori valuables and Trobriand kula shells, but Samoan fine mats and Northwest Coast coppers remained attached to their original owners even when they circulated among other people' (p. 46). *Immeuble* means immovable property, property closely linked to the clan or family and not, except under special circumstances, able to circulate freely (by way of trade or gift) amongst strangers; Weiner refers to it as *inalienable possessions*, and designates thereby the peculiar and partial form of alienation involved in the prestation of the gift.

POTLATCH

The concept of the gift, or more precisely of the ties of reciprocity that establish the circuits of gift exchange, is amongst the key elements of classical French structuralism. It is in part from a critique of Mauss that Lévi-Strauss developed a more 'abstract' model of the homoeostatic system of exchange, a model that could be extended to all symbolic exchanges (language, material goods, women).[17] The founding distinction here is between two modes of

---

[17] The model supposes the reciprocality of all exchanges. In the case of the exchange of women, of course, reciprocality at the level of the homosocial community of men entails a radical *non*-reciprocality between the communities of men and women, as well as 'a relation, as it were, of nonrelation between women'. Judith Butler, *Gender Trouble: Feminism and the Subversion of Identity* (New York: Routledge, 1990), 40–1.

'economy' (of the regulated circulation of values): 'Implicitly or explicitly, the double assumption is found everywhere that reciprocal gifts constitute a means—normal or privileged, depending on the group—of transferring goods, or certain goods, and that these gifts are not offered principally or essentially with the idea of receiving a profit or advantage of an economic nature.'[18] The increase that may accrue to the goods in circulation through reciprocal gift exchange thus cannot be understood as 'profit' or 'interest' in the modern sense of these words, as the calculated objective and outcome of the process; rather, 'in primitive thought there is clearly something else in what we call a "commodity" that makes it profitable to its owner or its trader. Goods are not only economic commodities, but vehicles and instruments for realities of another order, such as power, influence, sympathy, status and emotion.'[19]

This stark contrast between profit-economy and symbolic economy is problematic, both because Lévi-Strauss plays down the importance of the increase on the gift, and because, conversely, commodities circulating within a capitalist economy are always just as much 'vehicles and instruments for realities of another order'. It is thus relatively easy for Pierre Bourdieu, for example, to demonstrate that it is only by the abolition of the *interval* between giving and returning, the strategic *use* made of time and pacing in social interaction, that Lévi-Strauss is able to conceive of the return of the gift as a structural regularity rather than as a matter of the play of interests. The structuralist model of gift exchange 'has the effect of transforming into mechanical sequences of obligatory acts the at once risky and necessary improvisation of the everyday strategies which owe their infinite complexity to the fact that the giver's undeclared calculation must reckon with the receiver's undeclared calculation, and hence satisfy his expectations without appearing to know what they are', and it thereby conceals from view those mechanisms of deferral which convert calculation and interest into the socially sustaining fiction that allows gift and

---

[18] Claude Lévi-Strauss, *The Elementary Structures of Kinship*, rev. edn., trans. James Harle Bell, John Richard von Sturmer, and Rodney Needham (Boston: Beacon Press, 1969), 53.

[19] Ibid. 54.

counter-gift to be seen by participants as 'an inaugural act of generosity'.[20]

All readings of gift exchange, we might say, develop one or other of the poles of 'interest' and 'generosity' which mark what Bourdieu would call the 'objective' and the 'subjective' dimensions of gift. The major anti-structuralist reading of Maussian gift exchange at the latter pole is that of Georges Bataille (and following him, of Jean Baudrillard): a reading that challenges the very notion of a closed or 'restricted' economy directed to the accomplishment of communication or of social or economic utility. Here the privileged figure of the gift is the potlatch, the 'monster child of the gift system' (Mauss, *The Gift*, 41).

Potlatch is that form of total prestation in which the obligation to return is manifested in the negative form of rivalry. Mauss describes it as an agonistic form of gift exchange peculiar to the Indian societies of the American North-West—the Tlingit and Haida of Alaska, and the Tsimshian and Kwakiutl of British Columbia; 'essentially usurious and extravagant, it is above all a struggle among nobles to determine their position in the hierarchy to the ultimate benefit, if they are successful, of their own clans' (pp. 4–5). The system Mauss describes is that of a 'war of wealth' in which a chief will, on various ceremonial occasions, demonstrate his social and religious standing by a 'reckless consumption of everything which has been amassed with great industry from some of the richest coasts of the world' (p. 33). The point of this 'extravagant', 'exaggerated', and 'wasteful' consumption (p. 72) is the humiliation of the recipient; the gift of wealth is a challenge which must be met if one is not to lose face, but which imposes crippling burdens on the receiver, particularly since the potlatch must be repaid with interest, at rates ranging from 30 per cent to 100 per cent a year (p. 40). At its extreme, the potlatch may be a pure act of destruction: 'one destroys simply in order to give the appearance that one has no desire to receive anything back', and in this case 'whole cases of candle-fish or whale oil, houses, and blankets by the thousand are burnt; the most valuable coppers are broken and thrown into the sea to level and crush a rival' (p. 35). At this point, and despite Mauss's comments in a footnote that 'to give is to

---

[20] Pierre Bourdieu, *Outline of a Theory of Practice*, trans. Richard Nice (Cambridge: Cambridge University Press, 1977), 171.

destroy' and 'destruction seems to be a superior form of expenditure' (p. 102, n. 122), the potlatch surely reaches the very edges of the domain of the gift.

In Bataille's thought the potlatch is at once the essence of the gift and the opposite of the principle of reciprocity (understood as equilibrium or equivalence); it is the very form of the *unreturnable* gift, and as such institutes the possibility of transgression of any material or symbolic economy. Instead of reciprocity there is waste, loss, whatever breaks the closure of a system of balanced exchanges. The non-productive expenditure (*dépense*) of potlatch is the figure of an anti-economic and anti-utilitarian excess, a negation that cannot be recuperated through the dialectics of negativity since it is 'a sacrifice without return and without reserves'.[21]

The concept of *dépense* brings together a series of different activities which lie outside the utilitarian calculus, and which include 'luxury, mourning, war, cults, the construction of sumptuary monuments, games, spectacles, arts, perverse sexuality (i.e., deflected from genital finality) . . .'[22] All of these constitute a loss or 'waste' (*gaspillage*) against which there is no balance of credit; they involve the expulsion of waste matter, *la part maudite*—shit, the social surplus, the sacrificial victim, what Lacan will call the *objet petit a*, bodily waste or wealth doomed to uselessness. These are gifts in the strong sense that Bataille gives to the concept of potlatch. Distinguishing (as Mauss seems to) between donative and destructive forms of potlatch, he posits the logical (and perhaps temporal) priority of the latter. In this pure form the gift is absolute loss, consumption without profit, a sacrifice of the *part maudite* which substitutes for the sacrificial gift of the donor's own life.

Let me note two general points about the destructive potlatch as Bataille conceives it. The first is that as sacrifice it restores the primordially intimate link between the thing and its owner, a link destroyed by the instrumental rationality of the world of work. The

---

[21] Jacques Derrida, 'From Restricted to General Economy: A Hegelianism without Reserve', *Writing and Difference*, trans. Alan Bass (Chicago: University of Chicago Press, 1978), 257.

[22] Georges Bataille, 'The Notion of Expenditure', in *Visions of Excess: Selected Writings, 1927–1939*, ed. Allan Stoekl, trans. Allan Stoekl *et al.*, Theory and History of Literature 14 (Minneapolis: University of Minnesota Press, 1985), 118; hereafter cited in the text as 'Notion'.

second is that the activities of *dépense*, which 'have no end beyond themselves' ('Notion', 118), are in that Kantian sense aesthetic activities.

The ascription to them of gratuitousness encounters severe theoretical difficulties, however, within the framework of Mauss's description of potlatch. The paradox Bataille must confront is that, although giving is, in a certain sense, losing, yet 'the loss seems to profit the one who suffers it'[23]—both in the immediate sense that the gift is returned with interest, and in the indirect sense that the giver acquires power from the act of giving. Bataille's solution to this problem is to distingish between economic gain and the achievement of social prestige (*rang*), in such a way that only pursuit of the former is said to be calculating, whereas the latter involves 'an unconsidered expenditure of vital resources' ('La Part maudite', 74). But this distinction is a sleight of hand; prestige is as much a social interest as is wealth. Mauss's recognition of the coercive and calculative dimension of all gift is surely more rigorous in its theorization of the gift's constitutive ambivalence.

One further theoretical contradiction fundamentally organizes Bataille's writing. The concept of *dépense*, non-productive expenditure, belongs to a metaphorics of energy flow. At an explicit level it works as the force that disrupts the system of generalized reciprocity that, in one reading of Mauss and certainly in his structuralist succession, models the systemic equilibrium of exchange.[24] Potlatch, writes Bataille, 'is the opposite of a principle of conservation', since it makes the possession of wealth inherently unstable and always subject to the 'need for limitless loss, which exists endemically in a social group' ('Notion', 123–4). At the same time, it is clear that the system of production and instrumentality which Bataille opposes is a dynamic model of the *increase* of energy within a closed system—and that *dépense* is the release of energy that allows the system to continue functioning. Thus he speaks of blockages of energy in the global system leading to 'congestion' and either a 'festering' or an 'explosion' ('La Part maudite', 31–2); of

[23] Georges Bataille, *La Part maudite: Essai d'économie générale. I. La Consumation, Œuvres complètes*, vol. vii (Paris: Gallimard, 1976), 73. Hereafter referred to in the text as 'La Part maudite'.

[24] Cf. Julian Pefanis, *Heterology and the Postmodern* (Sydney: Allen and Unwin, 1991), 53.

the build-up of 'pressure' before unused energy is released (ibid. 37); or, in a reference to bloodletting, of the need to relieve the 'fever' caused by trade imbalances (ibid. 164). This is that metaphor of the flow of energy (or its blockage or repression) through thermodynamic systems, together with the accompanying hydraulic metaphors of reservoirs and damming, which Michel Serres has identified as a major component of nineteenth-century thought;[25] it remains in Bataille a metaphorics of the maintenance, rather than the disruption, of equilibrium.

THE KULA

Whereas for Bataille the potlatch and the kula represent opposed principles (non-reciprocal and reciprocal exchange within general and restricted economies), for Mauss the kula is in fact 'a kind of grand potlatch' (p. 20). Mauss's description closely follows Malinowski's account in an article of 1920 and in *Argonauts of the Western Pacific*.[26] The broad outlines of this account (which have been extensively modified by more recent ethnography) are as follows:[27] the kula system is located in the Massim, the islands to the east of mainland New Guinea. Two sets of valuables, shell necklaces (*veguwa*) and armshells (*mwali*) flow in (respectively) a clockwise and counter-clockwise direction round the 'ring' of islands, with armshells exchanging against necklaces and vice versa, but never armshells against armshells or necklaces against necklaces. Shells are not individually owned and there is considerable pressure for them to remain in circulation; they carry great symbolic value, derived from their age, the patina they have acquired with age, and the reputation of their previous owners; their value and fame increase with the number of transactions of which they are the object, and the most famous shells have

---

[25] Michel Serres, *Hermes: Literature, Science, Philosophy*, ed. Josué Harari and David F. Bell (Baltimore: Johns Hopkins University Press, 1982), especially the essays 'Michelet: The Soup', 'Turner Translates Carnot', and 'The Origin of Language: Biology, Information Theory, and Thermodynamics'.

[26] Bronislaw Malinowski, *Argonauts of the Western Pacific* (1922; repr. London: Routledge and Kegan Paul, 1978).

[27] I have drawn on Malinowski, Mauss, and Jerry Leach's Introduction to Jerry W. Leach and Edmund Leach (eds.), *The Kula: New Perspectives on Massim Exchange* (Cambridge: Cambridge University Press, 1983), 1–26.

individual names and histories. Famous shells bring prestige to their owners, and contact with them transmits some of the virtues of the shell to the one handling it. Exchange takes place between shells of approximately equal 'rank' and between kula partners (almost always men) who are geographically proximate in the 'ring'. Reciprocation is always delayed, and exchange is initiated by a process of solicitation with preliminary gifts (*vaga*); the great shells are the object of the most intense solicitation. Kula exchange is self-contained, but is often accompanied by a 'secular' trade in commodities. It is not barter, and haggling over value would be treated with contempt, but the exchange of kula objects is embedded in talk that 'plays up' the value of the shells being offered.[28] In the exchange, says Mauss, 'pains are taken to show one's freedom and autonomy as well as one's magnanimity, yet all the time one is actuated by the mechanisms of obligation which are resident in the gifts themselves' (p. 21). Mauss draws a number of other conclusions from the kula. He sees the shells as 'a kind of currency', and ascribes this 'money' to a stage prior to the development of abstract and 'universal' currencies (p. 94, n. 25). He argues that the kula exchange exhibits a particular form of ownership:

One might say that it includes many legal principles which we moderns have isolated from one another. It is at the same time property and a possession, a pledge and a loan, an object sold and an object bought, a deposit, a mandate, a trust [*une chose vendue et achetée et en même temps déposée, mandatée et fidéi-commise*]; for it is given only on condition that it will be used on behalf of, or transmitted to, a third person, the remote partner (*murimuri*). (p. 22)

And, noting that the kula is 'only the most solemn part of a vast system of prestations and counter-prestations which seem to embrace the whole social life of the Trobrianders', he concludes that 'in our view the whole inter-tribal *kula* is an exaggerated case, the most dignified and dramatic example, of a general system' (pp. 25–6).

The kula has become an immense ethnographic topic, and my

[28] Annette Weiner notes that 'Kula talk with partners . . . is full of bravado, expounding on the location of all one's promised and forthcoming shells and all the debts that one is owed. But as one kula player told me, all kula talk is dangerous because most of it is lies, specious rhetoric set forth to serve one's own ends.' *Inalienable Possessions*, 141.

focus on it must perforce be restricted to my immediate theoretical concerns. Many accounts of it have stressed its complexity and the difficulty of extricating it from economic exchange proper (whatever exactly that might be: the question of the difference is centrally posed in this problematic). For Edmund Leach the kula is a methodological fiction, designating nothing more than the fact that in what has come to be known as the kula area there is 'a certain general similarity about the ways in which non-utilitarian valuables . . . are "traded around" '; this trade involves a number of different types of value, but the 'value that attaches to a kula valuable at any point in its wanderings is the value of the debt relationship which it has most recently served to express'.[29] Raymond Firth criticizes Mauss for his concentration on the 'patterns of spiritual bonds between things which were to some extent parts of persons' at the expense of the question of the equivalences established in kula transfers; he himself reads the kula as a more directly economic exchange, 'a set of macro-economic relations involving price-making mechanisms'.[30] Chris Gregory, however, believes that the notion of 'equivalence' covers two quite different kinds of relation between objects: things as commodities have an 'exchange ratio', whereas things as gifts have an 'exchange order, a ranking';[31] the one creates prices, the other relations of indebtedness. In Gregory's formal definition:

Commodity exchange is an exchange of alienable objects between people who are in a state of reciprocal independence that establishes a quantitative relationship between the objects transacted, whereas gift exchange is an exchange of inalienable objects between people who are in a state of reciprocal dependence that establishes a qualitative relationship between the subjects transacting. (p. 104)

These point-for-point oppositions (alienable/inalienable objects, independence/dependence, quantitative/qualitative, equivalence between objects/between subjects) map two ideal-typical sets of social relations; the key differentiation between them is the category of alienation, since it is this (the alienability of use values)

---

[29] Edmund Leach, 'The Kula: An Alternative View', in Leach and Leach (eds.), *The Kula: New Perspectives on Massim Exchange*, 536.
[30] Raymond Firth, 'Magnitudes and Values in Kula Exchange', ibid. 89.
[31] Chris Gregory, 'Kula Gift Exchange and Capitalist Commodity Exchange: A Comparison', ibid. 109.

that, within Gregory's neo-Marxist framework, establishes the commodity form and the social structures it generates.

In this, and from a rather different perspective, he finds support from Weiner, for whom the basic paradox of the kula is the inalienability of these objects which are nevertheless in constant circulation. In Weiner's illuminating account the point of the game is not reciprocation but, on the contrary, the attempt to keep valuable shells out of circulation—against all the pressures of kinship obligations—for as long as possible. To this end, complex strategies are developed using subsidiary shells, including *kitomu*, shells which are individually owned and therefore alienable (a class of which Malinowski was apparently unaware); these shells

are used effectively by a player to forestall a partner's expectations of an anticipated shell when in fact that shell has already been promised to someone else who, at the time, is more strategically valuable. In this way, individually owned shells are like wild cards in poker, enabling a player to multiply the possibilities for success by negotiating simultaneously with several partners on different paths over the same sought-after shell. (p. 135)

Subsidiary shells thus have the function of keeping paths open in protection of the high-ranking shells that have been withdrawn. At the same time, a series of plays will be in process (involving networks of players along multiple paths) to 'woo' the high-ranking shells from their owners; these plays are set in motion by initial gifts (*vaga*) which, if accepted, must then be backed up with further shells to put pressure on for a return; transactions for famous shells may go on for a decade and involve shells of all categories. Thus 'instead of perceiving kula transactions simply as gifts and counter-gifts, it is essential to visualize the maze of players and strategies as *layers* of exchanges which one must constantly build up over time and then keep track of. There can be no dependency on one gift for one return' (p. 141). Underlying these 'layers of exchanges' is the paradox of a category that fails to accord fully with Western categories of property. Kula shells belong in some sense not to individuals but to the kula system itself, yet at any point *within* the circuit individuals are the owners *pro tempore* of their shells. Mauss's word 'prestation' is in this sense more appropriate to the status of these relations than is the word 'gift'.

These disputes are of course part of a wider debate within

anthropology about the applicability of Western categories of property to non-Western societies. Let me briefly mention two further contributions to it from anthropologists who are familiar with the Melanesian context. Nicholas Thomas has written persuasively against the possibility of isolating a particular type of transaction which would exemplify the principle of the gift: arguing against what he takes to be Malinowski's 'romantic counter-modernism in which selected features of their world serve to relativize and destabilize cherished features or cultural tenets of our own',[32] Thomas stresses the 'entanglement' of gift- and commodity-economies in the colonial and post-colonial societies where virtually all anthropological observations have been made. The effect of this entanglement is that under many circumstances (perhaps including much of the kula system) objects can be contextualized in different ways—'as commodities or gifts, as unique articles for display, as artifacts of history, or as a new category of prestige valuable' (p. 108). What is given is not necessarily the same as what is received, and the categorization of an object as gift or as commodity may be undecidable. Marilyn Strathern has objected that Thomas's privileging of the specificity of transactions over underlying, relatively stable and relatively differentiated social relations (of the 'gift economy'/'commodity economy' type) leads him to minimize the specificity of these social relations, and in particular to assume—in a 'commonsense realism of one specific cultural category, the idea of "possession" '[33]—that the appropriation of objects everywhere takes the form of private ownership. Strathern's own work is at once critical of the category of reciprocity (since the term tends to conceal unequal economic relations beneath relations of symbolic exchange) and at the same time wary of reducing 'egalitarian' gift exchanges to exploitation, since this reduction relies on the supposition 'that persons naturally own what they do, that is, they own their own capacity to labour'.[34] Gift exchange in traditional societies requires us to think the relation between persons and things in rather different ways.

[32] Nicholas Thomas, Entangled Objects: Exchange, Material Culture, and Colonialism in the Pacific (Cambridge, Mass.: Harvard University Press, 1991), 12.

[33] Marilyn Strathern, 'Entangled Objects: Detached Metaphors', Social Analysis, 34 (Dec. 1993), 97.

[34] Marilyn Strathern, The Gender of the Gift: Problems with Women and Problems with Society in Melanesia (Berkeley: University of California Press, 1988), 157.

Let me try at this point to extract some more general conclusions about the category of gift. The first follows immediately from Thomas's argument as well as from the kinds of example I have cited above: there is no single form of 'the gift', and no pure type either of the gift economy or of the commodity economy. The reasons for this are both historical and logical: on the one hand, gift and commodity economies are always intertwined in various hybrid configurations and present a range of alternative possibilities for the use of objects; on the other, gift and commodity are not mutually exclusive modes of transaction, since they tend to have in common certain forms of calculation, strategy, and motivation. The gift therefore cannot and should not be conceived as an ethical category: it embodies no general principle of creativity, of generosity, of gratuitous reciprocality, or of sacrifice or loss. At best it is an ambivalent category, oscillating between the poles of generosity and calculation; but these are still ethical terms, whereas the forms of calculation and indebtedness that are set in motion in gift economies must be understood to be structural and prior to all 'ethical' forms.

There is nothing inherent in objects that designates them as gifts; objects can almost always follow varying trajectories. Gifts are precisely not *objects* at all, but transactions and social relations. It is only in these terms that it is possible to speak of a gift economy, in the sense of an order governing transactions and the chains of debt and return that flow from them. As an order of social relations the gift economy is intimately bound up with the forms of the person as they are diversely constituted and as it constitutes them. It is a dimension of a *moral* economy: a patterning of *mores*, customary ways of behaving and being, the domain of human life that Hegel calls *Sittlichkeit*. At the core of any possible contrast between gift economy and commodity economy, then, are distinct forms of ownership governing the categories of and the relation between persons and things.

Recall the schematic opposition that Gregory sets up between two modes of exchange:

commodity exchange	gift exchange
alienable objects	inalienable objects
reciprocal independence	reciprocal dependence
quantitative relationship between objects	qualitative relationship between subjects

Here too the opposition is between two orders of social relations.[35] As Gregory argues elsewhere, a gift economy depends upon the creation of debt, where what is at stake is not the things themselves or the possibility of material profit but the personal relationships that are formed and perpetuated by ongoing indebtedness. Things in the gift economy are the vehicles, the effective mediators and generators, of social bonds: putting this in terms derived from Marx's theory of commodity fetishism, Gregory writes that 'things and people assume the social form of objects in a commodity economy while they assume the social form of persons in a gift economy'.[36]

The argument is of course already explicitly developed in Mauss, for whom gift exchange 'is first and foremost a pattern of spiritual bonds between things which are to some extent parts of persons, and persons and groups that behave in some measure as if they were things' (p. 11). In giving objects to another 'a man gives', in addition, 'himself, and he does so because he owes himself—himself and his possessions—to others' (p. 45).[37] 'Things which are . . . parts of persons': what seems most dramatically to differentiate societies predominantly structured by a gift economy and societies predominantly structured by a market economy (and the latter should be taken to include not only modern capitalist societies but all those societies, including the Rome of the classical period, where the developed legal category of the subject is grounded in its free

[35] But not two kinds of society. See the warning about substantivization of gift and commodity as forms of society in James G. Carrier, 'Maussian Occidentalism: Gift and Commodity Systems', in id. (ed.), *Occidentalism: Images of the West* (Oxford: Clarendon Press, 1995), 85–108.

[36] Chris Gregory, *Gifts and Commodities* (London: Academic Press, 1982), 41.

[37] It should be added that in the act of giving we not only acknowledge obligation to others but also acquire the power to coerce those others into a recognition of their indebtedness to us. It is in terms of this continual reinforcement of debt and obligation that reciprocity can be said to be the foundation of social order in customary societies. And it is this strand of Mauss's thinking about gift relations that has contributed most influentially to the characteristically sociological problematic of the formation and the maintenance of social cohesion. Thus David Cheal, in his study of contemporary gift economies, contrasts the short-term profits of the market economy to the long-term interest in sustaining social solidarity that drives the moral economy of interpersonal relationships. Within the latter, 'the social significance of individuals is defined by their obligations to others, with whom they maintain continuing relationships. It is the extended reproduction of these relationships that lies at the heart of a gift economy, just as it is the extended reproduction of financial capital which lies at the heart of a market economy'. David Cheal, *The Gift Economy* (London: Routledge, 1988), 40.

ownership of itself, a self-possession which in turn makes possible the freedom of ownership in general),[38] is the category of property and the forms of personification or objectification it entails. Within commodity-oriented social formations, as Marilyn Strathern argues, both the category of the person and the relation between persons and things are understood through the metaphor of the commodity. What she calls 'Western proprietism' finds expression in one of two complementary propositions: either the person is a unitary self with the power freely to alienate its possessions or to acquire possessions which become a separable component of its identity; or the person is conceived as identical with its activities and loses its unitary identity when the products of these activities are alienated from the person. In both cases the person is self-possessed and self-contained, separate from the world of social others; things have a singular value in relation to the person, and it is the external social world that gives things the plurality and diversity of their value. This assumption, however, 'runs counter to the supposition of the gift economy that persons are intrinsically plural and diverse in origin and in their acts'.[39] (We might add, too, that relations between persons within a gift economy tend to include as an intrinsic dimension relations between the living and the dead.)[40]

It is thus not possible to speak of the alienation of property in a gift economy, since 'persons simply do not have alienable items, that is, property, at their disposal; they can only dispose of items by enchaining themselves in relations with others' (p. 161).[41] With the

[38] Evgeny B. Pashukanis, *Law and Marxism: A General Theory*, ed. Chris Arthur, trans. B. Einhorn (1978; repr. London: Pluto Press, 1983), 110.

[39] Strathern, *The Gender of the Gift*, 159.

[40] Cf. Cécile Barraud, Daniel de Coppet, André Iteanu, and Raymond Jamous, *Of Relations and the Dead: Four Societies Viewed from the Angle of their Exchanges*, trans. Stephen J. Suffern (Oxford: Berg, 1994), 112: the four 'holistic' societies studied in the book all share 'the fundamental characteristic that exchanges among the living may only be understood in the framework of relations between the living, on the one hand, and the dead, the spirits or the divinity, on the other'.

[41] Jonathan Parry argues that many readings of Mauss, including Sahlins's, have been dependent on Malinowski's reduction of exchange to a dyadic relation between individuals; for Mauss, however, it is not individuals but 'groups or *moral persons*' (that is, the incumbents of status positions) who conduct exchanges, and who retain a kind of lien over the things exchanged in so far as they are not separate from their donor. As a corollary, the notion of the disinterested gift has no place in archaic societies, since it is predicated on the notion of (self-)interest, and more generally on a social process of disembedding of the 'economy' from 'society'. Jonathan Parry, '*The Gift*, the Indian Gift and the "Indian Gift" ', *Man* (NS), 21 (1986), 456–67.

concept of enchainment Strathern wishes to emphasize both the inseparability of moral persons from the stories, possessions, and social relations which define them, and the particular finality embedded in gift exchange: its productiveness of expanded social relations, within which, in turn, objects may circulate.

In Gregory's neo-Marxist framework (which Strathern here I think follows) the concept of alienation refers to the transference of privately owned property, and is thus restricted to the capitalist mode of production. But this conceptualization sets up too simple a distinction between capitalism and the totality of pre-capitalist societies. Few if any societies lack altogether the category of alienable goods and particular mechanisms for transferring them. What does seem to be almost universal, however, is the distinction between those goods that may be circulated freely and those whose circulation is restricted. It must be stressed as strongly as possible that this is a distinction not between two opposed forms of social order, temporally and ontologically distinct, but between alternative regimes of relation between moral persons and things, and between the classes of object ordered within these regimes.[42]

Again, Mauss has been here before us. Writing of the power which forces things exchanged at a potlatch to circulate, to be given away and repaid, he distinguishes between two types of property— amongst the Kwakiutl and Tsimshian as amongst the Romans, the Trobrianders and the Samoans:

They have the ordinary articles of consumption and distribution and perhaps also of sale (I have found no trace of barter). They have also the valuable family property—talismans, decorated coppers, skin blankets and embroidered fabrics. This class of articles is transmitted with that solemnity with which women are given in marriage, privileges are endowed on sons-in-law, and names and status are given to children and daughters' husbands. It is wrong to speak here of alienation, for these things are loaned rather than sold and ceded. Basically they are *sacra* which the family parts with, if at all, only with reluctance. (p. 42)

---

[42] Valerio Valeri would argue that this restriction still imposes too great a taxonomic order, since the radical opposition between gift and commodity 'is largely the result of viewing the gift as an inverted form of commodity exchange', and gift is far too heterogeneous a phenomenon to be used in this way. Valerio Valeri, 'Buying Women But Not Selling Them: Gift and Commodity Exchange in Huaulu Alliance', *Man* (NS), 29 (1994), 17–18.

How is it that objects in this set can be said to form parts of persons? Mauss has a story to explain this, and he takes it from archaic Roman law. 'Originally', he speculates, 'things had a personality and a virtue of their own. Things are not the inert objects which the laws of Justinian and ourselves imply. They are a part of the family: the Roman *familia* comprises the *res* as well as the *personae*'. Things, *res*, are further subdivided into two kinds:

Distinction was made between *familia* and *pecunia*, between the things of the house (slaves, horses, mules, donkeys) and the cattle in the fields far from the stables. There was also a distinction between *res mancipi* and *res nec mancipi* according to the manner in which they were sold. With the former, which constituted objects of value, including children and real estate [*y compris les immeubles et même les enfants*], alienation had to follow the form of *mancipatio*, 'taking into the hands'. There is still discussion whether the distinction between *familia* and *pecunia* coincided with that between *res mancipi* and *res nec mancipi*. It seems to us that there is not the slightest doubt that at least originally they did coincide. The things that escaped the *mancipatio* were precisely the cattle and *pecunia*, money, the idea, name and form of which derived from cattle. One might say that the Roman *veteres* made the same distinction as the Tsimshian and Kwakiutl do between the permanent and essential goods of the house, and the things that pass on—food, beasts in the distant grazing, and metals—in which the unemancipated son might trade. (pp. 48–9)

The distinction—which roughly corresponds to that between immovable and movable property—is between those goods that are intimately bound up with the family's local and spiritual identity, and those that are peripheral to it.

Henry Maine tells a similar fable to explain the development of secular forms of property from the originally sacred forms. Supposing that in all archaic societies (where joint ownership by the clan constitutes the primordial form of property right) goods are divided into a higher, inalienable order and a lower, alienable order, and that transfer of the former involves complex and cumbersome rituals, he then assumes a gradual assimilation of the former (the *res mancipi*) to the latter (the *res nec mancipi*), essentially for reasons of convenience, and because, 'while . . . the list of the Res Mancipi was irrevocably closed, that of the Res Nec Mancipi admitted of indefinite expansion'.[43] In the same way, at a

[43] Sir Henry Sumner Maine, *Ancient Law: Its Connection with the Early History of Society and its Relations to Modern Ideas* (1861; repr. London: John Murray, 1906), 288.

later period and in a kind of cyclical repetition, the history of property in post-medieval Europe can be read as 'the history of the subversion of the feudalized law of land by the Romanized law of movables' (ibid. 283).

It is this distinction that Annette Weiner takes up in her argument that gift economies are rooted in the category of inalienable possessions, and thus in the fundamental paradox that such economies are governed not by a law of reciprocity but by the need *not* to relinquish the things which are the object of most intense desire. Inalienable possessions like the Trobriand *mapula* and the Maori *taonga*, or like land, titles of nobility and heirlooms in the West, acquire their essential force and their scarcity-value in two ways: first, from the fact that they are heritable within a closed descent group, having an 'exclusive and cumulative identity with a particular series of owners through time' (Weiner, *Inalienable Posessions*, 33) which is authenticated by means of fictive or true genealogies; and second, from their tie to cosmological forces—the dead, the ancestors, the gods, or sacred places (for Weiner, this is essentially the realm of women's power).[44] The crucial fact about such possessions is that they cannot, under most circumstances, be freely exchanged: their authority makes them a key source of social and political prestige, and hence of social hierarchy. For the same reason, they are always the object of intense competition:

Political hierarchy arises out of the successful dual endeavours to preserve and expand one's social identity, not only through marriage and alliance, but by being bold and wealthy enough to capture someone else's inalienable possessions, embrace someone else's ancestors, magic, and power, and then transfer some parts of these identities to the next generation. The processes of cultural reproduction involve the heroic ability to reproduce more of one's self or of one's group through time by

---

[44] And she has been criticized by Marilyn Strathern for essentializing this realm and the objects that constitute it. Strathern's argument is threefold: first, that, since the world of goods is cultural, it is 'unwise to predict that objects meaningful in one context will have identical meanings in another—even when the objects are so generally defined as "women's wealth" and are to be correlated with unspecified manifestations of "women's power" '; second, and as a corollary, that it is likely to be uses of objects rather than objects in themselves which are sexed; and third, that 'womanness' is not a fixed position to which objects can be related, but is itself a variable construct which should be 'read from the data and not into them'. Marilyn Strathern, 'Culture in a Netbag: The Manufacture of a Subdiscipline in Anthropology', *Man* (NS), 16 (1981), 673–83.

asserting difference while defining an historical past that looks unchanging. (pp. 47–8)

This conception radically undermines Mauss's supposition that the agonistic play of social power through gift exchange is finally neutralized by reciprocity, since 'the motivation for reciprocity is centred not in the gift per se, but in the authority vested in keeping inalienable possessions. Ownership of these possessions makes the authentication of difference rather than the balance of equivalence the fundamental feature of exchange' (p. 40).

The distinction between alienable and inalienable possessions cuts across that between gift and commodity—there is no simple equivalence between the two pairs. Inalienable possessions can be transferred within commodity exchange, and commodities, conversely, are perhaps the most readily available and most mobile form of the gift. But the concept of inalienable possession seems to me to be of central importance in clarifying that of the gift economy. It replaces the concept of reciprocity (which always verges either on functionalism or on a myth of social altruism, but which Bataille's critique seems to me not adequately to dislodge) with that of agonistic competition; it makes it clear why the gift is more appropriately thought of as a prestation, and why it returns; and it provides a cogent explanation of the ways in which, in Mauss's words, 'everything is tied together; things have personality, and personalities are in some manner the permanent possession of the clan' (p. 44). It may tell us, finally, how it was that that 'antiquated and dangerous gift economy, encumbered by personal considerations' (ibid. 52) was left behind, or was *not* left behind, in the long historical process of commodification; and how the category of the person and of personality has again become caught up in the social form of things.

B. COMMODITY EXCHANGE

> no picture is made to endure nor to live with
> but it is made to sell and sell quickly[45]

The moral economy that governs the gift and the marketplace within which commodities are bought and sold are kinds of cultural

---

[45] Ezra Pound, *Cantos*, Canto XLV.

context for the exchange of goods. The one supposes and enacts a continuity between persons and things and thus the formation of chains of reciprocal obligation by means of the transfer of objects; the other supposes and enacts a discontinuity between persons and things and thus a reciprocal independence in relatively more abstract processes of transfer. In no real society, however, are these contexts entirely distinct; and each is present in all real societies.

Almost all things may move between these contexts, and are defined and valued accordingly. If it is possible for governments to impose a gift tax, for example, it is because almost all gifts can, in the appropriate cultural context, be measured as commodities; conversely, most commodities are capable of being gifted, and indeed the majority of gifts in modern societies with capitalist social relations *are* (purchased but not given as) commodities. The pressures tending in any society to taxonomic stability are countered by the perennial social instability of things themselves and of the uses of things. But my concern is not primarily with the wanderings and the destinies of material objects; it is rather with the struggle that is waged, perhaps particularly in advanced capitalist societies, over the line of demarcation between what can properly be bought and sold and what cannot. Every society withdraws certain domains from market relations. The domain of religion, of personal life (including personal identity, bodily integrity, sexuality, and kinship ties), the political sphere, the sphere of public services, that of art and of some kinds of writing may conform, or may be presumed to conform, to a different logic from that of strict profit maximization.[46] Exchanges in these spheres are not governed by the market: while things and services may be alienable in the sense of being transferable from one person or group to another, they are nevertheless (in Margaret Radin's useful phrase) market-inalienable.[47]

In the second part of this essay I examine how this line is drawn in contemporary capitalist societies in relation to the categories of

---

[46] This is the distinction that economists make (or should make) between things that are ends in themselves and things that are instrumental in achieving human ends. The problem, however, is that it is now increasingly possible to consider many things of final value (the human body, culture, childbirth) as being subject *also* to instrumental valuation.

[47] Margaret Jane Radin, 'Market-Inalienability', *Harvard Law Review*, 100: 8 (1987), 1849–937.

the *person* and of *information*, and I try to specify the logic (or the conflicting logics) that allow it to be drawn at a particular point. I examine some of the struggles that are taking place to commodify aspects of these categories that were previously uncommodified, and I ask whether and why it matters that they should be reserved from commodification. In trying to map these shifts in the status of the person and of information I make extensive use of changes in legal doctrine, since they offer a relatively precise way of tracing and documenting an often diffuse and generalized process of social change. It is just because the law is never a simple reflection or instrument of socioeconomic processes that it can register with such detailed exactitude the slow historical transformation of social categories.

THE COMMODITY FORM

The commodity form is a social relationship, and a commodity is anything that is governed by it. In the banal usage of neoclassical economics, however, the social texture of the commodity is erased: the word comes to designate any object produced for use or exchange, or it is given the specialized sense of an unelaborated primary product, or else it is displaced by the unspecific term 'goods'. A generalized abstraction, it loses all its historicity and its social particularity.

Without simply juxtaposing to this usage a Marxist definition of the commodity form (since that definition is part of the problem I shall be exploring), I want nevertheless to call upon certain aspects of Marxism's relational and historical theorization of the commodity. In its simplest form, the Marxist concept of the commodity refers to things produced for exchange rather than for immediate use; in this broad sense, the commodity is to be found (although episodically rather than as a dominant form) in many pre-capitalist societies.[48] In its more complex definition, the concept refers to a matrix of conditions of exchange (the capitalist market), conditions of production (capital investment and wage labour, which is itself a commodity at another level), and conditions of consumption (private rather than collective appropriation of goods). Whatever

---

[48] Cf. Georg Lukács, *History and Class Consciousness: Studies in Marxist Dialectics*, trans. Rodney Livingstone (Cambridge, Mass.: MIT Press, 1971), 84.

the problems raised by this definition,[49] it has the great virtue of enabling analytic differentiation between historical systems, and between stages or levels of particular systems.

The classic historical studies of commodification have been directed to land, labour, money, risk, and art. It is the interlocking commodification of land and labour, in particular, which, by offering an explanation for the formation of a new class of landless labourers and for the primitive accumulation that generated capital for the industrialization of farming, for petty commodity production, and finally for industrial capitalism, has provided the key narrative of the rise of the capitalist mode of production. The clean lines of this narrative are necessarily complicated by the length and complexity of the 'transition', by the role of mercantilism in the sixteenth and seventeenth centuries, and by the major importance of plantation agriculture and the slave trade (the commodification of persons) in the eighteenth century, which recent historians are now more likely to see as the decisive factor in the provision of capital for the industrial revolution.[50]

In England, the commodification of land, the demise of serfdom, and the development of a wage labour system seem all to have been in place by about 1400, and the English legal system was fully mature by the end of the thirteenth century.[51] Although feudal property is based in the legal fiction of the mutually obligating gift (the 'fee' or 'feud') from sovereign to lord and so on down the line, and although the transfer of property was, until well into the eighteenth century, hedged by the restrictions of entail, it does nevertheless seem that land could be bought and sold with relative ease from at least the thirteenth century. What is clear in the long term is a movement from one form of property right (the very limited rights of exclusion given by feudal law throughout medieval Europe, qualified as they are by communal rights of grazing, rights to collect the fruits of nature, rights of turbary, and so on) to a

---

[49] These largely concern the specification of a system: is wage labour, for example, indispensable to the concept of commodity production, and if so is it requisite in each instance or only through its generalization within an area of production?

[50] e.g., P. J. Cain and A. G. Hopkins, *British Imperialism: Innovation and Expansion, 1688–1914* (London: Longman, 1993).

[51] Alan Macfarlane, *The Culture of Capitalism* (Oxford: Basil Blackwell, 1987), 144–69.

Blackstonean conception of property as *essentially* the right to exclude all others. The enclosure movement, which in England lasts from the fifteenth to the nineteenth century, represents the practical reworking of communal and customary notions of property, and it is both reflected in and furthered by the legal transformation. E. P. Thompson writes that 'what was happening, from the time of Coke to that of Blackstone, was a hardening and concretion of the notion of property in land', and he characterizes the enclosure movement as 'a wholesale transformation of agrarian practices, in which rights are assigned away from users and in which ancient feudal title is richly compensated in its translation into capitalist property right'.[52] This commodification of real property is the model for the extension of exclusive property rights to other forms of value, and as the legal historian George Armstrong argues, 'the expansion of commodification to include ever more forms of value fosters an ideology supportive of this process so that stable ownership, the right to exclude and to alienate, are no longer the characteristics of some forms of value, they are a social expectation for all forms of value'.[53]

The history of the capitalist mode of production is, on this account, a history of the progressive extension of the commodity form to new spheres. The most succinct formulation I know of this historical logic is Wallerstein's statement that capitalism's endless drive to accumulate capital 'pushes towards the commodification of everything'.[54] Kloppenburg similarly speaks of capitalism's 'progressive generalization of the commodity form', and explains why this is a process without end:

The apparent ubiquity of commodities should not blind us to the fact that capital constantly seeks to force *all* use-values to submit to the commodity form and to convert simple commodity production to capitalist commodity production wherever and whenever it can. Indeed, primitive accumulation may be a *permanent* process, because capital systematically seeks not only

---

[52] E. P. Thompson, *Customs in Common* (London: Penguin, 1993), 135, 137.

[53] George M. Armstrong, 'The Reification of Celebrity: Persona as Property', *Louisiana Law Review*, 51 (1991), 450.

[54] Immanuel Wallerstein, 'Household Structures and Labour-Force Formation in the Capitalist World-Economy', in Étienne Balibar and Immanuel Wallerstein, *Race, Nation, Class: Ambiguous Identities* (London: Verso, 1991), 107.

to make a commodity of all use-values but also to create *new* needs whose satisfaction entails new use-values that in turn can be commodified.[55]

This is a stark narrative of a logic of historical tendency—a teleological narrative of the kind that we have come deeply to distrust. Can it be called into question by counter-examples of processes of *de*commodification?

Several such examples come to mind. Perhaps the most powerful is the abolition (in principle, if not everywhere in practice) of chattel slavery—that is, of the treatment of human beings as goods to be bought and sold. This genuine act of decommodification must, however, be understood comparatively in its historical relation to the development of wage labour and of industrial machinery. A second example is the abolition of the sale of political office and of bureaucratic appointments which characterized most political regimes before the twentieth century; what has changed is perhaps not so much the practice as its public acceptability. Other examples might include the partial decommodification of labour and of housing through state regulation of the conditions of work and of rental contracts;[56] or the 'sentimentalization' of love and of nature as a kind of paradoxical counter to the commodification of other domains.[57] It is crucial to remember, too, that every extension of the commodity form has been met with resistance and often with reversals; the struggles over enclosure, over the length of the working day, over the privatization of common resources of many kinds are central to the global development of capitalism. Yet none of this seems to me to undermine the narrative of a continual, if uneven, extension of commodification: these counter-examples qualify it, they deny it any ineluctability, but the logic of historical tendency, however uneven, however checked, and however multiply determined, retains its force. Much of the rest of this essay is devoted to charting the working out of this logic in the contemporary world. (To speak of 'logic' is not, of course, to invoke a mysterious and autonomous spirit of history; the word is a shorthand for the dynamic of a system structured around the increase of wealth in the cycle of capital investment under very

---

[55] Jack Kloppenburg, Jr., *First the Seed: The Political Economy of Plant Biotechnology, 1492–2000* (Cambridge: Cambridge University Press, 1988), 24–5.
[56] Radin, 'Market-Inalienability', 1919.
[57] Macfarlane, *The Culture of Capitalism*, 123–43.

specific historical conditions. I assume that capitalism *is* a system—rather than a contingent aggregate of circumstances—but not that its logic is either totalizing, affecting all aspects of social life in the same way, or that it is possessed of any pre-given necessity.)

The real difficulty seems to me to lie elsewhere. It has to do with questions of interpretation and value: what are we to *make* of this narrative? Is the commodity form necessarily and always less humanly beneficial than non-commodified use values, and is its historical extension necessarily and under all circumstances a change for the worse? And does this logic provide the basis for a unitary conception of 'modernity', or does it rather force us to develop more complex conceptions of the interrelation between economic, political, and cultural structures?

In one sense this is an unmanageably vast question, tantamount to asking what we are to make of the history of the modern world: of the transformation of peasant agriculture and traditional ways of life, of the organization of work as paid labour, of the creation of global markets in commodities and capital—of almost all of the conditions of developed capitalism. But the question can also be posed more narrowly. Let me do so by talking about a specific example.

In the early 1970s a 'new' mode of painting emerged among the Aboriginal people of the Australian Western Desert. It was the product of a curious syncretism: a young white schoolteacher, Geoff Bardon, introduced acrylic paints to the Papunya community, and the medium was then adopted by the older men, first for the completion of a school mural in the traditional rock-painting style, then for use on plywood and linoleum, and finally, as a market began to develop for this work, for painting on stretched canvas.[58] But this style, the acrylic dot-painting known as *Papunya Tula*—which later in the 1970s was taken up and modified by other Western Desert communities, especially at Yuendumu—is syncretistic as well in its fusion of a series of cultural functions that we would probably call 'religious' and a series of aesthetic functions which organize its value within the Western art market and endow it with author functions and values of 'authenticity' that are largely

---

[58] Christopher Anderson and Françoise Dussart, 'Dreamings in Acrylic: Western Desert Art', in Peter Sutton (ed.), *Dreamings: The Art of Aboriginal Australia* (Ringwood: Viking/Penguin, 1988), 97.

irrelevant to its initial context.[59] In a sense the market success of this style is based on an immensely productive mistake: despite its recontextualization within the Western art system, the concerns of its producers are with a communal enterprise that has to do with the 'territorial' mapping of the sacred, with the authorization and coding of the knowledges conveyed by such mapping, with iconology rather than formal pattern (or rather this opposition becomes unworkable) and with the elaboration of a form of access for outsiders which at once reveals the knowledge of the Dreaming and conceals its secrets.

At another level, however, there is no mistake: the art of the Western Desert is a major source of income for these desperately poor communities, it was called into being by the formation of markets for it (and by the marketing activities of white advisers, community art cooperatives, and specialist dealers in Alice Springs and Sydney), and it is sustained by its commodity status: as Anderson and Dussart argue, 'If non-Aborigines stopped buying the paintings, the Aborigines would stop producing them.'[60] Although this is not tourist art, there are similar stories to be told about the formation of both markets and skills for indigenous art (as well as the application of the category of 'art' itself) throughout the world.[61]

Of course it is possible to express reservations about this process. Anderson and Dussart argue that acrylic painting 'to some extent converts religious art into a commodity, thereby alienating the art from religious practice'; the result is that 'Aboriginal painters are now confronted with the alien notion of a form of personal expression that overrides ancestral heritage and obligations' and that there is thus 'an increasing identification of and association with paintings not just as depictions of Dreamings, but also as individual creations and professional achievements'.[62] But this language of alienation belongs to precisely the same metaphysics of the person as does the concept of 'individual creation' which they are here rejecting; and there is little evidence that Aboriginal people

---

[59] Cf. Eric Michaels, *Bad Aboriginal Art: Tradition, Media, and Technological Horizon* (Sydney: Allen and Unwin, 1994), especially the title essay, 143–64.

[60] Anderson and Dussart, 'Dreamings in Acrylic', 142.

[61] Cf. Benetta Jules-Rosette, *The Messages of Tourist Art: An African Semiotic System in Comparative Perspective* (New York: Plenum Press, 1984).

[62] Anderson and Dussart, 'Dreamings in Acrylic', 140, 142.

have found the tension between religious practice and the art market unmanageable. To the contrary, they seem to have managed it with remarkable grace and irony.

The conclusion I draw from this fable is that the commodity form has the potential to be enabling and productive as well as to be limiting and destructive. Historically it has almost always been both of these things at the same time, and the balance of gain and loss has rarely been easy to draw. Why is this so?

The commodity form does three things. First, it channels resources of capital into an area of production in order to expand it to its fullest capacity,[63] at the same time destroying all productive activities which are not themselves commodified. Second, it transforms the purpose of production away from the particular qualities of the thing produced and towards the generation of profit; production is the indifferent medium for capital valorization, and the qualities of the thing produced are incidental to this end. Third, it transforms previously or potentially common resources (both raw materials and final products) into private resources; the allocation of these resources normally takes place according to economic criteria (ability to pay rather than moral or civic entitlement), and it may be either restrictive or expansive in its effects. In the case of most cultural production—for example of books, perhaps the oldest of all commodities, or of movies, which would not have come into being without extensive capital investment—the effects of commodification have been massively expansive.[64]

The commodification of culture, as of any other domain, doesn't happen in a single stroke (and this is why there are such great difficulties in periodizing the process).[65] Rather, it takes place on a

---

[63] That is, to whatever capacity will generate the maximum return on investment at a given time.

[64] This account of course is schematic and ahistorical. Historically, the extension of the commodity form takes place through different strategies: through an expansion of production or of consumption, through the multiplication of productive activities or through monopolistic restriction, and so on.

[65] Cf. Dan Schiller, 'From Culture to Information and Back Again: Commodification as a Route to Knowledge', *Critical Studies in Mass Communication*, 11 (1994), 93–115, for an account of some of these difficulties. James Collins notes that 'the variation in the dates chosen for the Age of Commodification does not suggest that such transitions have not occurred, but instead undermines their alleged impact, since so much of the cultural production that has been valorized by one theorist as

number of different semiotic levels corresponding to different historical 'stages'. In the case of printed texts we could distinguish between an initial commodification of the material object ('the book'), virtually coeval with the invention of the printing press;[66] a second stage of commodification of the information contained within the material object (and conceptualized in legal doctrine as 'the work'), of which the major historical expression is the development in the eighteenth century of copyright law and the modern system of authorship;[67] and a third, contemporary moment, developed in relation to electronically stored information, which, in addition to the copyrighted information itself, commodifies access to that information. These are 'stages' in the sense that this sequence is normally progressive (although it may be condensed and is by no means uniform in its effects), and corresponds both to an application of property rights to increasingly immaterial entities and to the development of markets which are increasingly finegrained in their scope. Each of these moments is, paradoxically, at once a way of restricting the use of the commodity and of expanding its controlled use to as broad an audience as possible.

If it is true that the commodification of cultural objects is a process that extends, in a series of movements, over many centuries, then the theoretical commonplace that locates this process exclusively or largely in the twentieth century in fact refers to something rather different: on the one hand to the development of major new cultural industries in this period (radio, the movies, broadcast and narrowcast television, video games, the Internet); on the other, to the industrialization, or the more intensive industrialization, of traditional areas of cultural production (mass-market paperback books, recorded music, mechanically reproduced images . . .).

---

pre-commodified has been vilified as post-commodified by another'. James Collins, 'Postmodernism and Cultural Practice: Redefining the Parameters', *Screen*, 28: 2 (1987), 17.

[66] Cf. Lucien Febvre and Henri-Jean Martin, *The Coming of the Book: The Impact of Printing 1450–1800*, trans. David Gerard (London: Verso, 1984), esp. ch. 4.

[67] Specifically on the historical emergence of the concept of 'the work', cf. Peter Jaszi, 'Toward a Theory of Copyright: The Metamorphoses of "Authorship" ', *Duke Law Journal* (1991), 473–4. In the course of the eighteenth and nineteenth centuries 'the work' is progressively separated from its physical incarnations, to become a complex object in which limited property rights can be vested in the 'expression' but not the 'ideas'.

Industrialization is not the same thing as commodification, although the two are closely intertwined. The Romantic and post-Romantic critique of the commodity form is perhaps more properly seen as a critique of the serial and formulaic mode of industrialized mass-cultural production, to which it opposes the singularity and originality that is thought to characterize authentic art forms (a singularity and originality which, with a perverse irony, have come to be central to the system of authorship, the drive to signature as scarcity value, that organizes the second major moment of the commodification of culture).

Such an ethically and, ultimately, aesthetically grounded critique has been integral to the Marxist conceptualization of the commodity form. There are two major strands in this tradition. The first is centred on the concept of alienation (*Entfremdung*) and derives from the Schillerian category of labour in Marx's early writings, which represents an ideal of self-directed and self-realizing activity.[68] The separation of workers from the means of production and their reinsertion into a system where they have no control over either the process of work or its product have the effect, Marx argues, of constructing both the product and the capacity for work itself as something separate from the worker's human powers, their being as a subject. This separation is expressed through the recurrent metaphor of the process of *Vergegenständlichung*, 'objectification': the process by which something that belongs to me or is produced by me as subject comes to 'stand over against' me, taking on a life of its own, confronting me as an alien and threatening force.[69] In this line of argument, it is labour itself that figures crucially as a commodity, and the threat posed by commodification is its destruction of that activity which is most essentially human.

The second major strand of Marxist thinking about the

---

[68] Cf. Stephen Gaukroger, 'Romanticism and Decommodification: Marx's Conception of Socialism', *Economy and Society*, 15: 3 (1986), 305–8.

[69] Cf. Karl Marx, *The Economic and Philosophic Manuscripts of 1844*, trans. Martin Milligan (New York: International Publishers, 1964), 107: 'The *alienation* of the worker in his product means not only that his labour becomes an object, an *external* existence, but that it exists *outside him*, independently, as something alien to him, and that it becomes a power on its own confronting him. It means that the life which he has conferred on the object confronts him as something hostile and alien.'

commodity is centred on the concept of commodity fetishism, which is again a concept of objectification. The threat here is epistemological: with the advent of widespread commodification, the social relation between people which is the reality of human work and exchange comes to assume the 'fantastic' form of a relation between things. The structure of the commodity, in which local and specific use value is subordinated to the abstract universality of exchange value, effects a mystified conversion of 'the social characteristics of men's own labour' into what seem to be 'objective characteristics of the products of labour themselves'.[70] Persons and things both become thinglike, and the causal relation between work and value is inverted. This strand is clearly continuous with the first, but whereas the concept of alienation foregrounds a transcendental notion of the person, the concept of commodity fetishism turns its focus to the opposition between a simple and a complex social relation: an opposition between the immediacy of relations among direct producers of use values, and the highly mediated and abstract structure of commodity relations.

Both of these strands are taken over into Lukács's influential theorization of the commodity form in History and Class Consciousness. The concept of reification (Verdinglichung) at first follows closely Marx's account of commodity fetishism in describing the transformation of labour into an objectified, alien, and autonomous force drawn from and inverting the concrete materiality of work. But it then merges with two concepts taken from Simmel and Weber: respectively, those of abstraction and rationalization. The objectification of alienated human labour as an exchangeable commodity involves a process of abstraction that corresponds to the abstract universality of the commodity form. In one respect this is a matter of the construction of a formal equivalence between an open series of quite dissimilar use values; at the same time, however, the nature of work itself is transformed as it is subjected to 'a continuous trend towards greater rationalization, the progressive elimination of the qualitative, human and individual attributes of the worker'.[71] This trend (the shorthand

---

[70] Karl Marx, Capital: A Critique of Political Economy, vol. i, trans. Ben Fowkes (Harmondsworth: Penguin, 1976), 164–5.

[71] Lukács, History and Class Consciousness, 88; further citations are given in the text.

name for which is Taylorism) breaks the process of labour down
into 'abstract, rational, specialized operations so that the worker
loses contact with the finished product and his work is reduced to
the mechanical repetition of a specialized set of actions' (ibid.).
Calculation and specialization are the two instruments through
which the 'rationality' of the capitalist production process is
asserted; by these means the organic unity of the thing produced is
broken down into a synthetic unity of arbitrarily connected parts,
the dynamic and qualitative movement of time is frozen into 'an
exactly delimited, quantifiable continuum filled with quantifiable
"things" ' (p. 90), and the subject form itself is fragmented in the
quantification and specialization of the work process.

   Lukács's rhetoric, which flows through to the writings of the
Frankfurt School and its successors, has the nostalgic structure of
all of the great post-Romantic binarisms that oppose a state of
immediacy to a state of mediation (the authentic to the inauthentic,
the organic to the mechanical, non-reflexive experience to abstract
rationality . . .). The commodification process conceals 'the immediate—qualitative and material—character of things as things',
their 'original and authentic substantiality' (p. 92), and it replaces
'natural' and 'personal' relations (p. 91) with relations that are
'more complex and less direct' (p. 86). Complex and highly
mediated systems are taken to be inherently incompatible with
human value. In so far as the Marxist account of the commodity
form is an analysis of semiotic value, its tendency is to oppose use
value to exchange value as matter to representation, and as
immediacy to mediation.[72] More broadly: despite the force of its
historical and relational conception of the commodity form, its

---

[72] Cf. Wolfgang Haug's account of a historical process tending from the
materiality and sensuality of the use value to the abstraction of symbolic value: 'The
degree of reality, and the essence of the commodity-body as a use-value, is shifting
away from being simply "an external object, a thing which through its [physical]
qualities satisfies human needs of whatever kind" [Marx, *Capital*, vol. i], towards an
increasing emphasis on representation and symbolism in the commodity. The
balance will shift from an unmediated, materially purposeful use-value to thoughts,
feelings, and associations, which one links to the commodity or assumes that others
must associate with it.' Wolfgang F. Haug, *Critique of Commodity Aesthetics:
Appearance, Sexuality and Advertising in Capitalist Society*, trans. Robert Bock
(Minneapolis: University of Minnesota Press, 1986), 97. For a critique of the logic
according to which use value is assumed to be unmediated, 'body' rather than
'spirit', cf. Jean Baudrillard, *For a Critique of the Political Economy of the Sign*,
trans. Charles Levin (St Louis: Telos Press, 1981).

conceptual ground is a myth of presence which leads it to understand this form on the one hand as the alienation of the integrity of the person, on the other as the replacement of the simplicity, transparency, and immediacy of use value with a complex system of representations. The opposition of the commodity to the gift is a subset of this dichotomy, and the question that I now pose is whether it is possible to untie the theorization of the commodity form from these assumptions.

That question is taken up more concretely in the case studies around which the later part of this essay is organized. Before I come to them (and to a more detailed consideration of the category of the person), however, I want to broach a model of the commodity form that problematizes its stability in relation to the material things that it regulates.

Within the framework of the broadly anthropological model developed by Arjun Appadurai, Igor Kopytoff, and others in *The Social Life of Things*, the commodity form is not restricted to capitalism. It is fully distinct neither from barter nor from the gift, in so far as there is a 'calculative dimension in all these forms of exchange'.[73] If the commodity is defined in terms of a *situation*, in which 'its exchangeability (past, present, or future) for some other thing is its socially relevant feature', then all things are potentially commodities.[74] Objects can therefore move, under the appropriate circumstances, in and out of the commodity state (that is, between use value and exchange value).

---

[73] Arjun Appadurai, 'Introduction: Commodities and the Politics of Value', in Arjun Appadurai (ed.), *The Social Life of Things: Commodities in Cultural Perspective* (Cambridge: Cambridge University Press, 1986), 13.

[74] I do not, however, accept this conception in its totality. Appadurai takes over from Simmel a definition of economic value as a particular and variable effect of 'the commensuration of two intensities of demand' which takes the form of 'the exchange of sacrifice and gain' (4). It is thus the moment of exchange rather than that of production (or of the totality of moments in the cycle of production, exchange, and consumption) that governs the formation of value and 'sets the parameters of utility and scarcity, rather than the other way round' (ibid.). This subjectivization of value leads Appadurai to refuse the qualitative distinction made by Marx between use value and exchange value: commodities are a 'use value *for others*' (9; original emphasis). In this respect of course his definition of value approximates that of neoclassical economics, and involves, I think, a failure to accept the *complex* and *systemic* nature of value formation (value is rather seen as an aggregation of a series of simple transactions).

The notion of a movement *out* of the commodity state makes it necessary to posit a counter-logic to that of commodification, a logic of de- or anti-commodification that would specify which things are to be precluded from commodity status: in state societies there are restrictions on the disposal of state property (such things as 'public lands, monuments, state art collections, the paraphernalia of political power, royal residences, chiefly insignia, ritual objects . . .'); there may be a highly delimited and specialized domain of objects available to be exchanged; or there may be some form of 'terminal commoditization, in which further exchange is precluded by fiat': personalized or prescription medicines would be one example; indulgences sold by the Catholic Church would be another. In general, however, 'the fact that an object is bought or exchanged says nothing about its subsequent status and whether it will remain a commodity or not'. Thus slaves will not necessarily remain so, or necessarily do degrading work (they exist as *pure* commodities only at the moment of sale).[75]

Unless they are formally decommodified, however, 'commoditized things remain potential commodities—they continue to have an exchange value, even if they have been effectively withdrawn from their exchange sphere and deactivated, so to speak, as commodities'.[76] If, as Appadurai argues, 'it is typical that objects which represent aesthetic elaboration and objects that serve as sacra are, in many societies, not permitted to occupy the commodity state (either temporally, socially, or definitionally) for very long', this is because there is a 'perennial and universal tug-of-war between the tendency of all economies to expand the jurisdiction of commoditization and of all cultures to restrict it'.[77]

The question this raises is of the extent to which the logic of the 'cultural' is able to restrict the logic of the economic; and of the possibilities of movement out of the commodity state. To what extent, for example, can cognitive, ethical, affective, and aesthetic processes resist commodification (the commodification of knowledge in industry; of ethical decision in professional or commercial

---

[75] Igor Kopytoff, 'The Cultural Biography of Things: Commoditization as Process', in Appadurai (ed.), *The Social Life of Things*, 74–6.

[76] Kopytoff, ibid. 76.

[77] Appadurai, 'Introduction', 23, 17.

relations; of affect in service work;[78] of the aesthetic in commercially available works of art)? And what sort of value judgement should be made of these processes?

In advanced capitalist societies it has now become difficult to separate the commodification of material from that of immaterial goods, including such 'services' as knowledges and feelings. Certainly there are still firmly defined non-commodity spheres in our society (marriage, social exchanges, exchanges of personal or professional favours are all non-monetized, although this exemption is in many ways an ideology; the status of women in marriage, for example, is hardly to be thought outside of a model of property);[79] and there is certainly a culturally specific moral concern in the West 'about the commoditization of human attributes such as labour, intellect, or creativity, or, more recently, human organs, female reproductive capacity, and ova'.[80] At the same time, however, there are a number of areas of increasing uncertainty, including that of the aesthetic, especially in its growing integration into advertising and marketing. Professional sport, to take a different example, has become highly commercialized in the last twenty years and has not yet resolved many of the ethical dilemmas posed by the saleability of skills in the context of an overriding importance placed on successful performance. It is perhaps this ambivalence, or this sense of a tension between countervailing forces, that now most precisely characterizes the status, midway between the private and the publicly saleable, of that set of attributes of 'the person' and the personal which have defined in our society the protected domain of the human.

In this respect Kopytoff has pointed to cultural strategies of singularization (for example of sacred objects) or re-singulariza-tion as one of the key mechanisms for movement out of the com-modity state. One of the distinctive features of complex societies, he writes,

is that their publicly recognized commoditization operates side by side with innumerable schemes of valuation and singularization devised by indi-

---

[78] Cf. Nicky James, 'Emotional Labour: Skill and Work in the Social Regulation of Feelings', *Sociological Review*, 37: 1 (1989), 15–42.

[79] Cf. Carole Pateman, *The Sexual Contract* (Stanford, Calif.: Stanford University Press, 1988).

[80] Kopytoff, 'The Cultural Biography of Things', 84.

viduals, social categories, and groups, and these schemes stand in unresolvable conflict with public commoditization as well as with one another . . . There is clearly a yearning for singularization in complex societies. Much of it is satisfied individually, by private singularization, often on principles as mundane as the one that governs the fate of heirlooms and old slippers alike—the longevity of the relation assimilates them in some sense to the person and makes parting from them unthinkable.[81]

It is on this principle that the valorization of old objects such as cars or houses functions as a singularization that moves its objects out of their commodity status. The odd result of such moves, however, is that the process of singularization may in fact enhance the object's exchange value. It is the singularity of the signature that guarantees aesthetic value and, by direct extension, monetary value. By analogy, the gentrification of degraded housing stock can be understood through an ideology of personal, as opposed to financial, investment, and conceived as a positive aesthetic or historical project; but it tends to result in the paradox that this personal investment, a labour of love, may finally turn out to have constituted a shrewd financial speculation.[82]

Appadurai gives a number of other examples of the diversion of objects back into the trajectory of the commodity. These include economic hardship (leading to the commodification of household possessions); war and plunder (which function as the inverse of trade); and theft. A somewhat different example is that of tourist art, 'in which objects produced for aesthetic, ceremonial, or sumptuary use in small, face-to-face communities are transformed culturally, economically, and socially by the tastes, markets, and ideologies of larger economies'.[83] But perhaps the most interesting examples from contemporary culture of the diversion of commodities from their original nexus can be found

---

[81] Kopytoff, ibid. 79–80.

[82] Cf. Sharon Zukin, *Loft Living: Culture and Capital in Urban Change* (1982; repr. New Brunswick, NJ: Rutgers University Press, 1989); Neil Smith and Peter Williams (eds.), *Gentrification of the City* (Boston: Allen and Unwin, 1986); D. Rose, 'Rethinking Gentrification: Beyond the Uneven Development of Marxist Urban Theory', *Environment and Planning D: Society and Space*, 1 (1984), 47–74; Patrick Wright, *On Living in an Old Country: The National Past in Contemporary Britain* (London: Verso, 1985).

[83] Appadurai, 'Introduction', 26.

in the domain of fashion, domestic display, and collecting in the modern West. In the high-tech look inspired by the Bauhaus, the functionality of factories, warehouses, and workplaces is diverted to household aesthetics. The uniforms of various occupations are turned into the vocabulary of costume. In the logic of found art, the everyday commodity is framed and aestheticized. . . . It is the aesthetics of decontextualization (itself driven by the quest for novelty) that is at the heart of the display, in highbrow Western homes, of the tools and artifacts of the 'other': the Turkmen saddlebag, Masai spear, Dinka basket. In these objects, we see not only the equation of the authentic with the exotic everyday object, but also the aesthetics of diversion. Such diversion is not only an instrument of decommoditization of the object, but also of the (potential) intensification of commoditization by the enhancement of value attendant upon its diversion.[84]

As one of the strongest manifestations of this twist, we should note the paradox that the concept of the unique and self-determining person—precisely what seems most to resist the commodity form—lies at the basis of the values of 'singularity' and 'originality' that have come to be central to the market in industrially produced aesthetic goods, and underpins the commodification of knowledge in many areas of intellectual property law.[85]

Let me recall the distinction I made at the beginning of this section between two kinds of cultural context governing the status of things in exchange: the moral economy of the gift, and the marketplace in which commodities are bought and sold. The corollary stress laid by Appadurai and Kopytoff on the possibilities of movement between different contexts makes it difficult to continue using the notion of the commodity form as a sign of essential identity.[86] Thus, whereas the whole logic of Lukács's argument[87] is that the commodification of labour and of goods entails an ineluctable process of historical decline (which can be transformed only in the moment of revolution) and a progressive

---

[84] Appadurai, 'Introduction', 28.

[85] Cf. John Frow, 'Repetition and Limitation: Computer Software and Copyright Law', *Screen*, 29: 1 (1988), 4–21.

[86] Cf. Thomas, *Entangled Objects*, 28: 'Insistence upon the fact that objects pass through social transformations effects a deconstruction of the essentialist notion that the identity of material things is fixed in their structure and form.'

[87] But not of Marx's, since he frequently argues that capitalist production and the commodity form are historically necessary and 'progressive' moments of the evolution of human society; the same distinction can be made between Adorno (who in this respect stands close to Lukács) and Brecht and Benjamin.

contamination of all other areas of life, we might argue instead that while commodification has definite effects upon persons and goods, it does not affect them in their totality: my labour power is bought and sold on the market, but my value as a moral person is not thereby necessarily degraded; an acrylic dot-painting from the Western Desert will continue to have valid religious and aesthetic functions despite its production directly for the market (it is made 'to sell and sell quickly', but it is *also* made 'to endure [and] to live with'). Jane Gaines puts it this way, drawing an analogy from discourse theory: 'We understand, primarily from Vološinov, that although the sign may have an existence as a commodity, it may have another life and another meaning, and it may well have had a past life—a separate history which is not cancelled out by its life as a commodity'.[88] This is not to argue, however, that the social destinies of things are purely indeterminate, or that they possess an inner force that drives them to resist the limitations of context: the production of things for specific uses will tend to exercise a determinate constraint upon their destinies, and their entry into different social contexts is a matter of the multiplication and complication, rather than the absence, of determinations.

THE LIMITS OF THE MARKET

In seeking to define what it is that underlies the logic of decommodification and singularization, Appadurai and Kopytoff invoke, at various times, the categories of culture and the person. In societies characterized by a high degree of commodification, however, neither of these can be situated unproblematically as the opposite of the commodity form.

In one of the most thoughtful recent discussions of the limits of commodification, Margaret Radin proposes the concept of *market-inalienability* as a way of exploring the scope of that domain of rights or things that, like Annette Weiner's 'inalienable possessions', can be given away but not alienated by sale in the market. This domain includes personal attributes and the integrity of the body, sacred objects, and kinship relations; and the sorts of things that test its limits are, for example, the possibilities of creating a market

---

[88] Jane Gaines, *Contested Culture: The Image, the Voice, and the Law* (Chapel Hill, NC: University of North Carolina Press, 1991), 347.

in babies or in foetal gestational services, the sale of blood, of human organs, or of sexual services, or the payment of 'amateur' athletes.[89]

Radin's point of reference is the tradition of Western liberalism, with its simultaneous (and potentially contradictory) belief that the right to hold property is inalienably given, but that any particular property rights ought in principle to be able to be freely disposed of in the market. It is this potential contradiction that gives rise to neoliberal economic analysis, which implicitly challenges the distinction between inalienable and alienable rights and has thereby 'invited markets to fill the social universe' (p. 1851). Economic analysis is a vision of universal commodification: all human interactions are understood as sales and are subject to a cost-benefit analysis, and market trading represents an ideal of human freedom. Laissez-faire markets are presumptively efficient because, 'under universal commodification, voluntary transfers are presumed to maximize gains from trade, and all human interactions are characterizable as trades. Laissez-faire also presumptively expresses freedom, because freedom is defined as free choices of the person seen as trader' (p. 1861). Radin cites as an example of the workings of this model Richard Posner's application of a market rhetoric to the analysis of rape, where he writes that 'The prohibition against rape is to the marriage and sex "market" as the prohibition against theft is to explicit markets in goods and services.'[90]

Against this tradition Radin sets the vision of universal non-commodification that has largely been the province of Marxism. Covering much the same ground as I did above, she concludes that there is little scope for a concept of market-inalienability in Marxist thought, since the concept 'posits a nonmarket realm that appropriately coexists with a market realm, and this implicitly grants some legitimacy to market transactions' (p. 1875). More broadly, she argues that for both evolutionary and revolutionary (socialist and Marxist) versions of universal non-commodification the problem of transition from a market to a non-market society poses severe difficulties: a gradualist approach will need to make use of market

---

[89] Margaret Radin, 'Market-Inalienability', 1856; further citations are given in the text.

[90] Richard Posner, 'An Economic Theory of the Criminal Law', *Columbia Law Review*, 85 (1985), 1199; cited in Radin, 'Market-Inalienability', 1862–3.

structures which may undermine the eventual goal, and an approach that stakes everything on the moment of revolution can guarantee neither an instantaneous transition to non-market relations, nor that a principled decommodification during the transition process will not wreak injustice.[91]

What Radin wants to take from the argument for universal non-commodification is not a practical politics but an understanding of the effectivity of market rhetoric as a force in its own right. To do this, she sets up her own version of the relation between alienable and inalienable possessions. Distinguishing between 'fungible' forms of property (property that is readily exchangeable for money) and 'personal' forms (property that has become identified with the core of a person's identity),[92] she suggests that market rhetoric treats bodily integrity (for example) as a fungible object, replaceable with money and able to be alienated without affecting the person. But 'thinking of rape in market rhetoric implicitly conceives of as fungible something that we know to be personal, in fact conceives of as fungible property something we know to be too personal even to be personal property. Bodily integrity is an attribute and not an object, and to treat it as such is inherently degrading' (pp. 1880–1). In making it easier both to envisage and to countenance the loss of personal attributes, the rhetoric of the market represents an 'inferior conception of human flourishing' (p. 1884). In Posner's cost-benefit analysis of rape, which weighs the 'benefits' to the rapist against the 'costs' to the person raped, for example, 'the "pleasure" and "satisfaction" of maintaining one's bodily integrity is commensurate with the "pleasure" and "satisfaction" of someone who invades it. Thus, there could be circumstances in which the satisfactions or "value" to rapists would outweigh the costs or

---

[91] The example she gives is Richard Abel's proposal to decommodify tort law so as not to put a monetary value on personal qualities or on personal emotions, since to award damages for pain and suffering or for injuries to relationships has the effect of commodifying these qualities and emotions; Radin argues, however, that 'to deny money damages, inadequate though they may be, seems to compound the injury to tort victims under the present social structure, in which we have not put into practice other measures that would take care of them in better ways or prevent their injuries in the first place' (1877). Richard Abel, 'A Critique of American Tort Law', *British Journal of Law and Society*, 8 (1981), 199 ff.; cited in Radin, 'Market Inalienability', 1876.

[92] For a more detailed exposition, cf. Margaret Radin, 'Property and Person-hood', *Stanford Law Review*, 34 (1982), 957 ff.

"disvalue" to victims. In those situations rape would not be morally wrong and might instead be morally commendable' (ibid.). The idea of the fungibility of personal attributes is incompatible with the idea of human uniqueness, and in its extreme form can comprehend human freedom only in terms of the activity of 'buying and selling commodified objects in order to maximize monetizable wealth' (p. 1885).

Much of Radin's article is made up of a detailed and rigorous analysis of the philosophical infrastructure of liberal pluralism, which with its negative conception of liberty (liberty as the freedom of individuals to act as they choose as long as no others are harmed) and its constitutive notion of property (social personhood flows from a primordial self-possession, a property right in one's self) assumes both that buying and selling constitute acts of freedom or enhance freedom, and that inalienabilities (restrictions on the market) are paternalistic limitations on freedom. Within this schema there is no secure place for the fundamental inalienability that applies to the freedom of the person itself. Hence the difficulty that Mill finds in arguing against the freedom to sell oneself into slavery.

What Radin gets at nicely, in other words, is the economic core of the liberal conception of the person, as well as its complicity with some of the uglier aspects of neoliberal economics. She is able to counterpose to it, however, at most the *assertion* of a countervailing conception of 'human flourishing'. This conception, which she bases in a 'positive' notion of human liberty that includes human self-development as a central component, requires us to decide 'what market-inalienabilities are justified by the need to protect and foster personhood', and to work out 'why these inalienabilities seem to us to be freedom enhancing' (p. 1902). At its heart is an argument that both personal attributes and the contexts within which development is realized (politics, work, religion, family, love and sexuality, moral commitment, and so on) are integral to selfhood and should therefore not be treated as full commodities. To conceive either of attributes or the 'things' that are extensions of our personhood as detachable parts of our self is to assume

that persons cannot freely give of themselves to others. At best they can bestow commodities. At worst—in universal commodification—the gift is conceived of as a bargain. Conceiving of gifts as bargains not only conceives of what is personal as fungible, it also endorses the picture of persons as profit-maximizers. A better view of personhood should conceive of gifts not as disguised sales, but rather as expressions of the interrelationships between the self and others. To relinquish something to someone else by gift is to give of yourself. Such a gift takes place within a personal relationship with the recipient, or else it creates one. Commodification stresses separateness both between ourselves and our things and between ourselves and other people . . . [G]ifts diminish separateness. (pp. 1907–8)

The major weakness of Radin's argument here, it seems to me, is that in asserting the category of personhood against liberalism she is insufficiently attentive to the central role that personhood already plays there as a category of property. 'The person' is neither a real core of selfhood nor a transcendental principle that inherently resists being alienated in the market, because it is always the product of the social relations formed by the distinction between alienable and inalienable possessions. Nor is it simply on the side of the latter: what Strathern calls 'Western proprietism' is based on self-possession, a primordial property right in the self which then grounds all other property rights. 'The person' is at once the opposite of the commodity form and its condition of existence, and in some cases (which I discuss below) enters directly into its philosophical rationale. Let me now make this argument more explicit by introducing some case studies.

PROPERTY IN THE BODY

In 1991 the Human Genome Diversity Project was initiated as— amongst other things—a response to criticism of its parent, the Human Genome Project (HUGO), which is currently in the process of mapping the entirety of the human gene system, that it privileges a standardized model of European genetic material.[93] In collecting DNA samples from hundreds of indigenous populations, including genetically isolated peoples such as the !Kung, the Hadza of Tanzania, the Yamomami, the Chukchi of Siberia, and the Onge from the Andaman islands off Malaysia, the Diversity Project hoped 'to counteract in some measure the excessive standardization

---

[93] Cf. L. Roberts, 'How to Sample the World's Genetic Diversity', *Science*, 257 (1992), 1204–5. Cf. Richard Lewontin, 'The Dream of the Human Genome', *New York Review of Books*, 28 May 1992, 31–40.

and parochialism associated with HUGO, while at the same time contributing to a further debunking of racial mythologies by showing the paramount importance of individual variation'.[94]

It has, however, been a contentious project. In a sense there is already a contradiction in its deduction of genetically uniform populations from ethnic groups, since few sociocultural groups have managed rigorously to block the advent of strangers through intermarriage and migration, and in any case the project's own starting-point is the well-grounded assumption that genetic variation is much more marked at the level of the individual than at that of social and cultural demarcations: the concept of the genetic 'population', 'far from being a readily definable natural fact, is a contested and pliable concept, created to assist in the answering of specific questions and hypotheses' (ibid.). More immediately contentious, however, have been the project's focus on 'unique, historically vital populations that are in danger of dying out or being assimilated'[95]—a focus dictated by the interests of collection rather than by concern for the fate of these peoples—and the issue of how 'informed consent' could possibly be given by members of isolated tribal cultures with little knowledge either of Western scientific cosmologies or of the possibilities of commercial exploitation of their cell lines.

Commercial exploitation is, ultimately, the name of the game, and the crucial practical question is: who owns the 'immortal' cell lines developed from this sampling process, and indeed is it thinkable that the genetic commons—the common genetic material of the human race—can be privatized for commercial gain? One group strongly critical of the Human Diversity Genome Project, the Rural Advancement Fund International, found in 1992 that 'the American Type Culture Collection already contains 1,094 human cell line entries, and patent applications have been made on more than one third of them'.[96] In 1991, for example, the US government applied for a patent on the cells of an unnamed Guaymi woman.

---

[94] Margaret Lock, 'Editorial: Interrogating the Human Diversity Genome Project', *Social Science and Medicine*, 39: 5 (1994), 604.

[95] L. Roberts, 'Anthropologists Climb (Gingerly) on Board', *Science*, 258 (1992), 1300–1.

[96] RAFI Communiqué, *Patents, Indigenous Peoples, and Human Genetic Diversity*, Rural Advancement Foundation International, May 1993; cited in Lock, 'Editorial' 605.

The Panamanian Guaymi carry the Human T-Lymphotropic Virus (HTLV-II), without apparent harm to themselves, and their DNA consequently has enormous medical potential; the community had, however, placed a veto on the taking of blood samples. The patent application was withdrawn after considerable international pressure, but was replaced in 1992 by two further applications for patents on the cells of individuals from Papua New Guinea and the Solomon Islands, each of them carriers of the HTLV-I virus.[97] In March of 1995 an indigenous man of the Hagahai people from the Papua New Guinea highlands (a people which came into regular contact with the outside world only in 1984) ceded his genetic rights to the 'inventors' named in the US government patent.[98]

Behind these applications stands a 1990 California Supreme Court decision that has been of singular importance in defining the questions of property rights in the human body that are at issue in the political debate over these patent applications.[99] The decision opens up the most fundamental questions about the nature and legal status of the person and about the limits and consequences of private property.

John Moore, a Seattle businessman, was treated at the UCLA Medical Center in 1976 for a rare disease of the blood called hairy-cell leukaemia. In order to slow the progress of the disease he underwent a splenectomy, and signed a consent form for the operation; he explicitly excluded the option on the form that permitted the use of his tissue for the development of a cell line. Sections from the excised spleen were nonetheless sent to a research

---

[97] *The Gene Hunters*, ZEF Productions, Channel 4 (UK, 1994).

[98] RAFI, Internet press release, 4 Oct. 1995. A medical anthropologist associated with the patent argues that this legal mechanism is the only way to ensure that the Hagahai people receive some protection from commercial exploitation; at the same time, however, US patent law 'only allows individuals or incorporated bodies to sign a patent application, so the Hagahai are not signatories, nor is there a written document outlining the benefits they have been promised' (Mary Louise O'Callaghan, 'The Selling of Cells', *The Australian*, 14 Nov. 1995, 17). There is a comprehensive coverage of the controversy in the special issue of *Cultural Survival Quarterly*, 20: 2 (1996) devoted to it, which includes a statement from the donor and a senior member of the Hagahai.

[99] The RAFI press release thus quotes US Secretary of Commerce Ronald Brown as saying that 'under our laws . . . subject matter relating to human cells is patentable and there is no provision for considerations relating to the source of the cells that may be the subject of a patent application'.

laboratory and used to establish a cell line. During subsequent visits to the hospital between 1976 and 1983 additional samples of blood, blood serum, skin, bone marrow aspirate, and sperm were removed; on Moore's account, he was repeatedly assured by his doctor that these samples were to be used only for therapeutic purposes and had no research applications or commercial potential.

The 'Mo' cell line, which was developed some time before August 1979, did in fact have enormous commercial potential, estimated by one commentator at around 3 billion dollars by the year 1990.[100] The line was established from Moore's T-lymphocytes—a type of white blood cells that produce proteins called lymphokines that regulate the immune system; what was valuable about them in Moore's case was that his virus-infected lymphocytes overproduced lymphokines, thus drastically simplifying the needle-in-a-haystack process of locating the corresponding gene. A patent on the Mo cell line was applied for by the Regents of the University of California in 1981 and was granted in March 1984; Moore's physician, Dr David Golde, was named as the 'inventor' of the cell line, together with a researcher, Ms Shirley Quan. Commercial development of the line was then undertaken by the Genetics Institute and the Swiss-based multinational Sandoz. Moore was informed about none of this, and received no payment.

When he finally found out about the use that had been made of the tissue taken from his body,[101] Moore sued the Regents, Golde and Quan, and Genetics Institute and Sandoz, claiming in essence that they had appropriated his own property. The secondary cause of action for breach of fiduciary duty on the part of the doctors was upheld by the Supreme Court, but the cause of action for 'conversion' (interference with 'possessory and ownership interests in personal property') was not. The legal process was in fact a complex one: the lower court held against Moore, the Appeals Court supported him (with one substantial dissenting opinion), and the Californian Supreme Court then found against him on the

---

[100] Moore v. Regents of the University of California, 793 P. 2d 479 (Cal. 1990), 482; hereafter cited as 'Moore (Supreme Court)'.

[101] According to his lawyer, 'Moore became suspicious of his physician's motives only after he was offered free flights to California and paid hotel accommodations.' Rorie Sherman, 'The Selling of Body Parts', National Law Journal, 7 Dec. 1987, 33.

conversion cause of action with one partially concurring and partially dissenting opinion, and one fully dissenting opinion. More interesting than the actual outcome, perhaps, is the array of arguments marshalled around the question of whether Moore holds property rights in his own body.

At first sight the Supreme Court's decision that he does not seems counter-intuitive: it goes against both 'the strong naturalistic presumption that one owns one's own body, and . . . the ethically unattractive behaviour of Mr Moore's doctors'.[102] Indeed, one of the absurd consequences of the decision is that Sandoz, the owner of the very profitable patent in Moore's cell line, could in principle sue him were he to sell his own cells to another company.[103] But the logic of the decision has to do with the fact that there are two different property claims in play here, and that both have to do with an entity, the human body, that has traditionally been excluded from commodification (or which, in the instance of slavery, has a shameful history of commodification). It is no accident, then, that many of the opinions and commentaries on the case deploy the rhetoric of the gift, of inalienable possession.

Thus Justice Arabian, concurring with the Supreme Court majority, writes that Moore 'has asked us to recognize and enforce a right to sell one's own body tissue *for profit*. He entreats us to regard the human vessel—the single most venerated and protected subject in any civilized society—as equal with the basest commercial commodity. He urges us to commingle the sacred with the profane. He asks much.'[104] Similarly, Justice George, dissenting from the Appeals Court majority, invokes the two major pieces of federal legislation governing the transfer of human tissue, both of which (he argues) allow such transfer only as a gift.[105] What these appeals to the sanctity of the human body overlook, however, is that one way or another Moore's body tissue is already and irreversibly a commodity: to deny a property right to Moore is to concede it to the patent-holders, and—as the Appeals Court majority bitingly

---

[102] James Boyle, 'A Theory of Law and Information: Copyright, Spleens, Blackmail, and Insider Trading', *California Law Review*, 80: 6 (1992), 1519.

[103] Cf. Pat Mooney, 'John Moore's Body', *New Internationalist* (Mar. 1991), 9.

[104] Moore (Supreme Court), 497.

[105] *Moore* v. *Regents of the University of California*, 249 Cal. Rptr. 494 (Cal. App. 2 Dist. 1988), 538; hereafter cited as 'Moore (Appeals Court)'.

point out—'Defendants' position that plaintiff cannot own his tissue, but that they can, is fraught with irony'.[106]

Much of the opinion and commentary on the case stresses the unprecedented commercial value which the human body has recently acquired, and the challenge this poses to a corpus of legal doctrine predicated on the spiritual but not material value of the body. The tendency of the Supreme Court is to apply a restrictive definition of what counts as property: since Moore would be prohibited from selling his tissue, he fails to meet one of the central principles in the bundle of rights that make up the property right, and so cannot claim his excised cells as 'a species of tangible personal property capable of being converted'.[107] Justice George, dissenting from the Appeals Court decision, similarly argues that 'unlike the gizzards of domestic poultry . . . the spleens of human beings do not come within the definition of "goods" or "chattels" '; things must be able to be sold, inherited, seized in bankruptcy, and protected from invasion if they are to qualify as property.[108] Others argue, however, that the bundle of rights making up property is variable, and that alienability is not indispensable to it: I can be said to 'own' prescription drugs or a professional licence, for example, even though I cannot legally sell them. One frequently cited precedent for property rights in the body is the *Venner* case, in which a man whose faeces were examined in a hospital for evidence

---

[106] Moore (Appeals Court), 507. The point had earlier been made in an article by Hardiman: acknowledging the moral problem of putting a price on the human body, he nevertheless argued that 'the fact remains that in the context of biotechnology, the human body is extremely valuable and has an ascertainable price. While moral aversion to pricing the human body may argue against biotechnology as a whole, as long as commercial exploitation of the body continues, the argument should not deny profit participation to the patient alone.' Roy Hardiman, 'Toward the Right of Commerciality: Recognizing Property Rights in the Commercial Value of Human Tissue', *UCLA Law Review*, 34 (1986), 240. Cf. also Justice Broussard's statement (Supreme Court, 506) that 'the majority rejection of plaintiff's conversion cause of action does *not* mean that body parts may not be bought or sold for research or commercial purposes or that *no* private individual or entity may benefit economically from the fortuitous value of plaintiff's diseased cells. Far from elevating these biological materials above the marketplace, the majority's holding simply bars *plaintiff*, the source of the cells, from obtaining the benefit of the cells' value, but permits *defendants*, who allegedly obtained the cells from plaintiff by improper means, to retain and exploit the full economic value of their ill-gotten gains free of their ordinary common law liability for conversion.'

[107] Moore (Supreme Court), 489.

[108] Moore (Appeals Court), 534.

of drugs secreted in a condom successfully asserted a continuing property right in waste matter from his body.[109] A 'quasi-property' right in cadavers (sufficient to allow legitimate appropriation for the purpose of disposal) has been recognized since the nineteenth century;[110] and various other decisions and statutes recognize rights of disposal and exclusion. Jaffe gives particular weight to the right to exclude others, which has consistently been recognized as the central element in modern conceptions of property; on this view, the human body is the object of a 'rather substantial bundle of rights, while falling short of full commercial ownership due to the limited right to sell'.[111]

Bernard Edelman argues in his commentary on the Appeals Court decision that *Moore* exposes a central absence in the Western legal tradition: its consistent repression of the relation between the person and their body. Bodies are conceived 'from the outside' (as the object of assault, for example), but the legal subject—the subject of rights, of will, of legal standing—lacks any legal relation to its physical body. The one substantial precedent in Western law for property rights in the human body is the institution of slavery, and it is for this reason, Edelman argues, that the metaphor of slavery plays such a crucial role, as a kind of constitutive unease, in organizing the Court's discourse on the commodification of the body.[112] The Court writes, with a flourish of historical triumphalism, that 'the evolution of civilization from slavery to freedom, from regarding people as chattels to recognition of the individual dignity of each person, necessitates prudence in attributing the qualities of property to human tissue. There is, however, a dramatic difference between having property rights in one's own body and being the property of another. To our knowledge no public policy

---

[109] *Venner v. Maryland*, 30 Md. App. 599, 354 A. 2d 483 (Md. Ct. Spec. App. 1976), *aff'd* 279 Md. 47, 367 A. 2d 949, *cert. denied*, 431 US 932 (1977).

[110] Cf. Stephen Ashley Mortinger, 'Comment: Spleen for Sale: *Moore* v. *Regents of the University of California* and the Right to Sell Parts of Your Body', *Ohio State Law Journal*, 51 (1990), 502–3; Erik S. Jaffe, ' "She's Got Bette Davis['s] Eyes": Assessing the Nonconsensual Removal of Cadaver Organs under the Takings and Due Process Clauses', *Columbia Law Review*, 90 (1990), 543–4.

[111] Jaffe, ' "She's Got Bette Davis['s] Eyes" ', 550.

[112] Bernard Edelman, 'L'Homme aux cellules d'or', *L'Hôpital à Paris*, 116 (1990), 40.

has ever been articulated, nor is there any statutory authority, against a property interest in one's own body.'[113] Justice Mosk, writing a dissent to the Supreme Court decision, likewise derives the need for a legally protectable property interest in the body from the metaphor of slavery:

Our society acknowledges a profound ethical imperative to respect the human body as the physical and temporal expression of the unique human persona. One manifestation of that respect is our prohibition against direct abuse of the body by torture or other forms of cruel or unusual punishment. Another is our prohibition against indirect abuse of the body by its economic exploitation for the sole benefit of another person. The most abhorrent form of such exploitation, of course, was the institution of slavery. Lesser forms, such as indentured servitude or even debtors' prison, have also disappeared. Yet their spectre haunts the laboratories and boardrooms of today's biotechnological research-industrial complex. It arises wherever scientists or industrialists claim, as defendants claim here, the right to appropriate and exploit a patient's tissue for their sole economic benefit—the right, in other words, to freely mine or harvest valuable physical properties of the patient's body.[114]

Justice Mosk's reference to the economic exploitation of the body 'for the sole benefit of another person' indirectly raises (by avoiding it) the question of wage labour: that is, of the most widespread form in which the commodification of the body is expressed. The Appeals Court and Hardiman both refer explicitly to paid work as a source of value or profit,[115] and these references implicate that whole Lockian tradition that derives economic value from the fruits of human labour. To put this very simply: economic entitlement is deduced from the application of work to a raw material, where work expresses the creativity and uniqueness of the human person. Moore failed finally in his claim to the cell line derived from his

---

[113] Moore (Appeals Court), 504.

[114] Moore (Supreme Court), 515; cf. Hardiman, 'Toward the Right of Commerciality', 225: 'If an analogy to slavery is to be drawn in the context of human biologics, slavery actually argues *for* recognizing a property right in one's own body: the slave-owner profiting from ownership of the slave is analogous to the research institution profiting from the derivatives of the donor's body to the exclusion of the donor. The moral arguments raised by slavery actually favour, rather than oppose, recognition of the right of commerciality.'

[115] Moore (Appeals Court), 504; Hardiman, 'Toward the Right of Commerciality', 229.

body because his contribution failed to qualify either as unique[116] or as creative work.

Justice George gives the most lucid expression of this topos (at the same time bringing out with great clarity its aesthetic dimension): 'Although the raw material from the plaintiff's body may have been unique, it evolved into something of great value only through the unusual scientific expertise of the defendants, like unformed clay or stone transformed by the hands of a master sculptor into a valuable work of art.'[117] The argument is taken up by the Supreme Court: the Mo cell line 'is both factually and legally distinct from the cells taken from Moore's body', and the patent law that governs ownership of the cell line rewards 'inventive effort', not 'the discovery of naturally occurring raw materials'.[118] As James Boyle argues, the crucial underlying metaphor here is (as in copyright law) that of authorship. Moore's claim is that he should be recognized as the 'author' of his own body tissue; but in fact he is rather poor author material, since he plays a purely passive role in relation both to his cells and to the created cell line. In denying any uniqueness or originality to Moore's lymphokines, the Court constructs not Moore but his doctors in the figure of the romantic author, whose creative endeavours turn a passive material into a valuable product, an œuvre. 'There is something wonderful', says Boyle, 'in the way that Mr Moore becomes a "naturally occurring raw material", whose "unoriginal" genetic material is rendered unique and valuable by the "inventive effort", "ingenuity", and "artistry" of his doctors. If we look at this case through the lens of the romantic author, then Mr Moore's case is as ridiculous as if Huey Long had laid claim to ownership rights over *All the King's Men* or the baker of madeleines to *Remembrance of Things Past*.'[119]

The Moore case sets up two alternative ways in which I can

---

[116] Genetic uniqueness was the basis of an analogy made by Moore's lawyers, and supported by the Appeals Court, to right-of-publicity doctrine; the two courts differed, however, on the question of whether the genetic material coding Moore's cells was in fact unique to him. Of the analogy to the right of publicity Mortinger writes (p. 514): 'A court should not view a cause of action for appropriation of the commercial value of a person's genetic structure as too far removed from the court's current recognition of the right of a person to claim appropriation of his unique likeness or persona.'   [117] Moore (Appeals Court), 537.

[118] Moore (Supreme Court), 492–3.

[119] Boyle, 'A Theory of Law and Information', 1518–19.

formulate my relation to my body. In the first, I have a property right, which means that others cannot appropriate parts of my body without my consent, but also that I have the right to sell all or part of my body. In the second, I have no property right; I can't alienate it, but it has become a commons to which others may lay claim. In both cases one property right pushes out another. The aporia (at least in this unqualified form of the argument) stems from the central place occupied in liberal thought by the necessary link between self-possession (the form of the person) and property (the commodity form).

The classic definition of the category of self-possession, with its curious reflexivity by which the subject form is split between that which owns and that which is owned, is Locke's: 'Every Man has a *Property* in his own *Person*. This no Body has any Right to but himself.'[120] This self-possessing subject is both the foundation of all other property rights,[121] and the prototype of those things that *cannot* be alienated in the marketplace. This is to say that the system of property rights in the liberal state is paradoxically founded on the withdrawal of its founding moment from that system; but this withdrawal is always problematic. Hence one of the central cruces for liberalism has been the question of whether individuals have the freedom to sell themselves into slavery. In Mill's *On Liberty*, for example, this question—the apparent contradiction of a freedom that destroys freedom[122]—is bound up with the question of the limits of the market, and in particular the question of whether and why the human person should be considered non-commodifiable. To the extent that they take 'the person' as a point of departure rather than as the historical outcome of categories of ownership, these are questions that cannot be answered.

---

[120] John Locke, 'The Second Treatise of Government', *Two Treatises of Government*, ed. Peter Laslett (Cambridge: Cambridge University Press, 1960), 305.

[121] This free ownership of oneself (which contrasts with the slave's inability to dispose of him- or herself on the market) is the foundation of the freedom of ownership in general. Pashukanis thus accords the category of the subject logical priority over that of property, because 'property becomes the basis of the legal form only when it becomes something which can be freely disposed of in the market. The category of the subject serves precisely as the most general expression of this freedom.' Evgeny B. Pashukanis, *Law and Marxism: A General Theory*, ed. Chris Arthur, trans. B. Einhorn (1978; repr. London: Pluto Press, 1983), 110.

[122] Quoted in Radin, 'Market-Inalienability', 1902.

Two further case studies will help me to develop the complexity of the relation between the category of the person and the commodity form that it both opposes and subtends. The first is that of the trade in human organs; the second is that of the emergent right of personality in US law.

THE MARKET IN BODY PARTS

Since its development in the 1960s transplant surgery has constituted, amongst other things, a problem in gift theory: should my body accept or reject the transplanted organ, and on what terms? Who is my stranger, and why should they give me a part of their body? Should their giving receive a return payment, or should it be its own reward? These are problems in national medical policy, but they are also, now, an international problem, since the growing trade in body parts crosses national boundaries and the hierarchies of interdependency that they represent.

I should stress that my access to information about this trade is mediated largely by press reports and television documentaries which have as a part of their agenda or their effect the construction of the Third World as a site of disorderly otherness. They are organized around a relatively small number of figures—indeed, the same stories and even the same personnel tend to travel from report to report (the mysterious kidney broker Count Rainer Rene Adelman von Adelmannsfelden, for example), as do the simplifying metaphors (the 'bazaar', the 'underground network', the 'organ factory') and the ways of posing the ethical questions. What the reports construct is a domain of facticity structured around the tropes of the body resurrected and the body dispersed in pain.

The simplest way of describing the markets in organs, particularly kidneys, that have arisen in about the last decade is to distinguish between three narrative paradigms.

1. The authoritarian state

The first paradigm is that of markets run or sponsored or at least tolerated by the state, and more importantly supplied by the state from its prisons. The major instance, the Chinese market, is constructed in terms of a relationship between mainland and diasporic Chinese, particularly from Singapore and Hong Kong. Specific sites in China are nominated—the Nan Fang hospital in

Guangzhou,[123] another hospital in Guangdong[124]—and there is speculation about the source of the kidneys, hardening into a certainty in the more recent reports that they come from the cadavers of executed prisoners.[125] Prices range from $10,000 to a somewhat implausible $200,000.[126] A typical story from June of 1991 tells of a letter that has been sent to 'virtually all Hong Kong doctors' offering kidney transplants at the Eastern China Military Region Main Hospital in Nanjing for $12,880. The price covers the cost of a round-trip airfare and a kidney from a living donor. The report details rumours that the kidneys are taken from executed prisoners; this has repeatedly been denied by the Chinese Ministry of Health, which says that the kidneys are taken not from live donors at all but from Chinese who have died in hospital and whose relatives have consented to the donation of the kidneys. The article concludes by mentioning—as a way of casting some doubt on these denials—the 'traditional Chinese belief' that the body must be buried intact (*New York Times*, 3 June 1991). More recently, Amnesty has recorded a rise in the number of executions from 392 in the first half of 1993 to 696 in the first half of 1994 (although, since these are state secrets, the real figure may be many times higher), and Human Rights Watch/Asia has estimated that 2,000 to 3,000 organs, mainly kidneys and corneas, have been harvested annually from executed prisoners. Human Rights Watch warns that, although it is the increased use of capital punishment that has until now driven the organ transplant industry, that logic could be reversed as the industry becomes an increasingly lucrative source of foreign exchange earnings (*The Age*, 1 November, 1994, reprinting from *The Independent*).

The other instance of this paradigm that I know of is the

---

[123] *New York Times*, 7 Feb. 1988.

[124] James LeFanu, 'In the Kidney Bazaars, Life Comes Cheap', *The Times*, 3 Aug. 1993.

[125] Cf. Harry Wu Hongda, 'A Grim Organ Harvest in China's Prisons', *World Press Review*, 42: 6 (June 1995), 22, repr. from *Open Magazine*, Jan. 1995.

[126] In the second of their six-part series on the trade in transplant organs, Andrew Schneider and Mary Pat Flaherty draw a world map of 1985 black-market prices for kidneys (the range is from $1,000 to $4,000 in Pakistan and $1,500 to $7,000 in India, to $5,000 to $40,000 in Japan and $10,000 to $40,000 in the United States). Andrew Schneider and Mary Pat Flaherty, 'Selling the Gift (2)', *Pittsburgh Press*, 4 Nov. 1985, A1.

Philippines, where a major source of transplants is said to be the maximum-security penitentiaries. Donations are 'voluntary', but one television documentary cites Cardinal Sin as saying that a prisoner who donated a kidney to a priest was given a remission of sentence from twenty-five to five years. Peter Linebaugh has also documented recent moves in the United States to incorporate organ 'donation' into state executions.[127]

2. First World free enterprise

The second major paradigm is that of First World free enterprise. The leading case here is the United Kingdom, the most important European centre for transplants for people from many other countries lacking transplant facilities; these operations are conducted in private clinics in London. Press coverage of England is focused, however, on a single notorious case in which the trade in kidneys came to prominence. The scandal concerns the sale of his kidney by a Turkish printing worker, Ferhat Usta, aged 33, for transplantation to an Israeli citizen, Colin Benton, in a London clinic in 1988. Usta earned about £10 a week and needed money to pay for an operation for his 8-year-old daughter who was suffering from tuberculosis. After advertising in Turkish newspapers for several months, he was approached by a Turkish go-between for the London hospital and paid £2,500 for his kidney.[128]

Much of the reporting of this case is concerned with the scandal of persons rather than the scandal of structures. The figure to whom major responsibility for the 1988 case was attributed was the nephrologist, Dr Raymond Crockett, whose name had appeared in advertisements in international editions of *al-Ahram*, Egypt's leading newspaper, offering payments to kidney donors. The owner of a home overlooking the Thames at Henley worth £750,000, a villa in Sardinia, and a ski chalet in Switzerland, Crockett was struck off the register of the General Medical Council in 1989. The two renal surgeons involved, Mr Michael Bewick and Mr Michael

---

[127] Peter Linebaugh, 'Gruesome Gertie at the Buckle of the Bible Belt', *New Left Review*, 209 (Jan.–Feb. 1995), 33.

[128] A similar scandal about payment for organs had occurred in 1985; payment was not illegal in England before 1989, but following the earlier case the British Transplantation Society adopted a code of conduct forbidding it (*The Times*, 28 Jan. 1989).

Joyce, were found guilty of serious professional misconduct. The British government subsequently established a register of all transplant operations, and then introduced legislation outlawing sales of human organs. (*The Times*, 5 April 1989, summarizing a number of earlier reports.)

3. The oriental bazaar

The metaphor of the oriental bazaar organizes the third paradigm, of which India and Egypt are the major exemplars. India is described in a 1993 report as being the leading international centre for the organ trade: 'Arabs from oil-rich countries in the Gulf who have terminal renal failure and cannot obtain a kidney transplant fly to Bombay or Calcutta, where there is a lively kidney bazaar with an estimated turnover of £10 million a year. Every day, dozens of kidney brokers descend on slum villages looking for prospective donors—not difficult in places where the daily subsistence wage is 30p and the brokers can offer donors £750 in cash' (*The Times*, 3 August 1993).

The central issue in the reports from India is the role of this 'bazaar' in matching a limitless supply to an equally vast demand. There are some 80,000 cases of renal failure a year in India, and for most of these people dialysis is not a realistic option—because of the cost, because of the lack of facilities, and because of the high risk of infection. Citing a Madras transplant surgeon, Mr K. C. Reddy, the *Times* article summarizes a prevalent argument that 'modern medicine has created a valuable asset in the form of a spare kidney tradeable for a capital sum which, wisely used, can transform the lives of the very poor and their families. Banning the commercial trade in transplants would, as Mr Reddy argues, "only drive the business underground to the ultimate detriment of donor and patient".' It concludes that ' "rewarded giving" seems a much better option' (*The Times*, 3 August 1993). The complication to this rather simplified argument, however, is that it ignores the disparity of chances that structure this market; as the *New York Times* report of 17 August 1992 says, 'In India as in other countries, the donors are often poor, sometimes sick and invariably in need of money. The patients are predominantly affluent, with many coming from the Middle East and some from Europe.'

The Egyptian market is the other major journalistic instance of the oriental bazaar. A long report in the *New York Times* (23

September 1991) details the social and economic conditions that allow a major trade in kidneys to thrive here. Kidneys sell for between $10,000 and $15,000 (or for the equivalent in electronic goods or apartments). Six major centres in Cairo, performing direct transplants from live donors to recipients, service both wealthy Egyptians and other Arabs, especially from the oil-producing nations; these clients can buy replacement kidneys either here or in India. Doctors are prohibited by the physicians' union from transplanting from an Egyptian citizen to a foreigner, but this restriction doesn't apply to non-Egyptians wishing to sell their kidneys. Many of the donors are Sudanese and Somalis, but others seem to be Egyptians; the report says that 'the decision to sell organs is often a desperate act by young men who once dreamed of an education or work in Europe, but instead found themselves unable to rise above the crushing weight of third-world poverty'.

In 1992 the Egyptian government enacted legislation forbidding kidney transplants from living donors to recipients who are not relatives (*New York Times*, 23 January 1992)—although whether this would have any effect in stopping the trade, and indeed the active recruitment of donors from the slums of Cairo, seemed to be doubtful.

The trade in kidneys in these centres has arisen because of their relatively long survival time outside the body and because one of the body's two kidneys is deemed to be 'spare' (although the operation to remove it is a major one, which leaves the body vulnerable to any failure of the remaining kidney). Storage technologies now make it increasingly possible to build up stockpiles of other organs, transportable and transplantable parts taken from cadavers; but reports on trade in these other organs are relatively infrequent. The one other body tissue in which there does seem to be a major trade is the cornea.

A *Times* report on a 1993 BBC documentary, *The Body Parts Business* (*The Times*, 18 November 1993), documents a number of cases not just of sale of body parts but of forcible removal as a prelude to sale. One of these cases is that of Pedro Reggi, a patient in the Montes de Oca psychiatric clinic outside Buenos Aires, whose corneas were dug out with coffee spoons and who was then thrown into a sewer and left to die. He was rescued by friends and identified his mutilator, but is unable to do anything to bring him to trial as the testimony of psychiatric patients is not admissible in

Argentine courts. After the families of other patients had complained, 'an official investigation revealed a gruesome underground network which specialized in removing corneas from corpses in the institute's morgue for distribution to hospitals around the country where they fetched as much as $7,000'.

The documentary identifies a number of other cases of organized theft of organs from living people. Eight hundred children are said to have been kidnapped in 1992 in Tegucigalpa (Honduras), many of them for sale of their body parts. Similarly, evidence is presented of the organized kidnapping of people in Moscow for their organs, which are sold to the West at vast profit; and in Cordoba in Argentina, organs were for a period systematically removed from children who were not completely brain-dead.

Moscow seems to be one of the centres for the international trade in organs of all kinds, because of the almost complete lack of regulation of commercial activity: 'Although the sale of human tissue is illegal in Russia, the investigators found a company which in one year extracted 700 organs, including kidneys, hearts and lungs, over 1,400 liver sections, 18,000 thymus organs, 2,000 eyes and more than 3,000 pairs of testicles. Another company offered to sell 600 kidneys at $20,000 each'; and 'doctors offered to export bio-materials anywhere in the world for use in pharmaceuticals, cosmetics, or surgery' (*The Times*, 18 November 1993).

With reports like this, however, we reach the verge of mythology. Two independent accounts of widespread stories about the kidnapping and murder of Latin American children for the sake of their body parts do much to illuminate the ease with which factual evidence (or rather the journalistic construction of factual evidence) passes into and is itself perhaps partly organized by the great archaic structures of legend. In the first, an American anthropologist, Nancy Scheper-Hughes, writes of a 'terrifying rumour' which swept the shantytowns of Recife in north-east Brazil in 1987, and which continues to be prevalent. The rumour tells of vans driven through slum streets by North American or Japanese agents seeking to abduct stray children; some of their victims 'were murdered and mutilated for their organs (especially eyes, lungs, hearts, and livers) and their discarded bodies would be found by the side of the road, or tossed outside the walls of municipal cemeteries. Others were taken and sold directly to hospitals and major medical centres, and the remains of their eviscerated bodies were said to turn up in hospital dumpsters.'[129] While discounting the reality of the stories, Scheper-Hughes relates them to the realities of Brazilian slum life: the police round-ups of street children; the 'disappearance' of children into prisons and reform schools; the killings of street children by death squads; and 'an active domestic and international black market in babies' (p. 58). The urban legend of bodysnatching, she argues, has its roots in a general understanding that the bodies of the poor are worth more as sources of spare parts than as incarnate persons. In a world where symbolic and economic exchange is set up to allow the wealthy and the powerful to prey upon the bodies of the poor, the 'ring of organ exchange' is logically perceived to proceed 'from the bodies of the young, the poor, and the beautiful to the bodies of the old, the rich, and the ugly, and from the bodies of Brazilians in the south to the bodies of North Americans, Germans, and Japanese to the north' (p. 59).

In the second account Véronique Campion-Vincent explores the earlier of two cycles of a very similar rumour about children being kidnapped in Latin America and taken to the United States to be murdered for their organs.[130] Her essay is in two parts. In the first, she traces the construction of this story in the media. It first surfaces on 2 January 1987 in the Honduran daily *La Tribuna* in the course of an interview with the secretary-general of a non-governmental human rights organization; he retracts the story the next day, saying that he had only reported beliefs held by certain social workers. The story, without the retraction, is then taken up in the Latin American press. On 5 February the same story reappears in Guatemala with a different cast (this time the key figure is a middle-ranking police officer), and is likewise immediately retracted; it is now taken up by newspapers in Holland and Yugoslavia, again without the retraction. On 5 April *Pravda* reports that 'thousands' of Honduran children are being used as sources for organ transplants in the United States; this story is retransmitted by TASS and taken up around the world. Two further versions of the story,

[129] Nancy Scheper-Hughes, 'Theft of Life', *Society* (Sep.–Oct. 1990), 57.

[130] Véronique Campion-Vincent, 'Bébés en pièces détachées: Une nouvelle "légende" Latino-Américaine', *Cahiers internationaux de sociologie*, 93 (1992), 299–319. For another account of this story (I am indebted to Ken Ruthven for this reference), cf. Alvin A. Snyder, *Warriors of Disinformation: American Propaganda, Soviet Lies, and the Winning of the Cold War* (New York: Arcade Publishing, 1995), 117–20.

with the same content and narrative structure, appear during 1988, one more in Guatemala and one in Paraguay, and—despite vigorous denials by the USIA and the US State Department—the story becomes the subject of investigation by several UN committees and of a resolution of the European Parliament, on 1 September, condemning the cannibalization of children in Latin America.

In the second part of her essay, Campion-Vincent analyses the story as a legend, part of a lively oral tradition recently developed in Latin America around the theme of the traffic in children and human organs. Like Scheper-Hughes, she sees it in part as a response to the killing of street children by death squads and by militias recruited by shopkeepers; to the increasingly widespread adoption of Latin American children by foreigners;[131] and to the traffic in human organs. At the same time, noting the structural isomorphism between both the content and the narrative process of this group of stories with four distinct points of origin, she stresses its folkloric lineage. Echoing many of the themes of Western mass culture (the theme of a perverted science preying on its victims—*Frankenstein*, *Coma*; the theme of the poor having to sell their bodies to survive—Swift's *Modest Proposal*, Hugo's *Les Misérables*), it belongs more generally to the story of the Western ogre: the evil white man with supernatural qualities and a need to devour the blood or the organs of the coloured people he dominates (a story reported from many parts of Africa and from the Andean regions of South America). A contemporary Peruvian version, apparently fostered by the Maoist guerrilla organization Sendero Luminoso and given widespread credence in the suburbs of Lima, is the story of the Sacaojos: armed strangers in large black cars who gouge the eyes out of children captured in the slums (in some versions, the eyes are sold abroad to help pay the Peruvian foreign debt).

The legend of cannibalized children, says Campion-Vincent, is part of an ancient and probably universal fable about young children kidnapped and murdered by evil strangers. Its variants include medieval European stories about children killed by Jews,

---

[131] A story in the *Guardian Weekly* (22 Oct. 1995, 7) tells of a Paraguayan mother subjected to a forced Caesarean section by an adoption lawyer who needed a baby for prospective parents from abroad; the story documents numerous other cases of baby-stealing and child-trafficking in a widespread illegal trade.

contemporary North American stories about satanic sects, and innumerable stories, such as that of Gilles de Rais, about powerful and monstrous figures feeding on poor children. Its uptake by contemporary intellectuals owes much to its exemplary value as a fable of the insatiable imperialist Ogre devouring the resources and even the children of the impoverished Third World. But to emphasize its mythical charge is not to deny the reality of the traffic in human organs; and, as Campion-Vincent concludes, legends may always serve as a model for a future reality.

An important aspect of the present reality is the drastic shortage in all countries of replacement organs for people desperately in need of them[132] (although this 'need' is of course relative to a particular state of technological possibility and social expectation). It is in the fact of this demand that some of the more difficult ethical issues around transplantation arise. They are questions of means rather than ends: questions of distributive justice, and questions of the extent of the state's proper role in protecting its citizens against exploitation.

Renée Fox and Judith Swazey cite the example of a vote taken in the Oregon legislature in 1987 'to eliminate an estimated $1.1 million in discretionary Medicaid expenditures for all soft-tissue transplants except kidneys and corneas, opting instead to accept the recommendation of the state's Division of Adult and Family Services to use those funds to provide pre-natal care for an estimated 2,000 medically indigent women'.[133] One result of this decision was that a 7-year-old child who could not afford a bone-marrow transplant for acute lymphocytic leukaemia died; his death was widely publicized, and led to a retreat, in Oregon and elsewhere, from the strict application of cost-effectiveness criteria. Yet, within a context of scarce resources for expensive medical treatment, such criteria—with the consequences they entail that not everyone will have the right to unlimited treatment—are probably the only just course of action (or they are the least unjust). They

---

[132] Reynolds and Barney give precise figures for transplants of visceral organs in the United States from 1981 to 1986 and for the sharp increase in waiting lists in those years. R. Larry Reynolds and L. Dwayne Barney, 'Economics of Organ Procurement and Allocation', *Journal of Economic Issues*, 22: 2 (June 1988), 572.

[133] Fox and Swazey, *Spare Parts*, 90.

carry with them the injustice, however, that a child of wealthy parents will have greater chances of survival than a poorer child.

The other major ethical dimension concerns the privileging of gift relations over commodity relations. The Transplant Bill enacted in the United Kingdom in 1989 seems to be typical of many other such pieces of legislation in banning all transplants from living donors unless they are genetically related: that is, in privileging ties of blood over contractual ties. This is a move, however, that is at odds with almost all of the rest of the Thatcher government's market-oriented policies: its unremitting favouring of commodity relations over gift relations.[134] At the same time—and not unsurprisingly, given the drastic shortage of transplantable and potentially life-saving kidneys, on the one hand, and the biological fact of a 'spare' kidney, on the other—there has been a persistent current of argument in favour of a market solution to the problem of supply.

The *New York Times* of 1 August 1989 quotes one Joel L. Swerdlow, an analyst with the Annenberg Washington Program, as saying that ' "The altruistic 'gift relationship' may be inadequate as a motivator and an anachronism in medicine today . . . If paying seems wrong, it may nevertheless be preferable to accepting the suffering and death of patients who cannot otherwise obtain transplants".' Lloyd Cohen, a Chicago professor of law, has proposed the creation of a futures market in organs, allowing payment during life for posthumous donation—a kind of succes-sorial contract—as a way of allowing the market to reallocate resources from less to more useful ends.[135] And the *Times Higher Education Supplement* of 8 November 1991, reporting a conference organized by the Manchester University Centre for Social Ethics and Policy, asks: 'What is it that makes profiting from the body and its parts criminal when tens of thousands die each year as a result of chronic donor shortage? Is a society which allows people to die each year from want of donated organs morally preferable to one which offers incentives to others to run risks?' Professor John Harris, a member of the Centre, put the market argument in an interestingly trenchant way: ' "Nobody should be driven by

[134] Cf. Bob Brecher, 'The Kidney Trade: Or, The Customer is Always Wrong', *Journal of Medical Ethics*, 16 (1990), 120: 'There is clearly something peculiarly ironic about free marketeers, passionate advocates of "enterprise culture", objecting to people making the best use of their assets in such an enterprising way.'

[135] BBC TV, *The Great Organ Bazaar*, 1992.

poverty to do things they don't want to do", he said. "But preventing the poor from selling their body products creates a cartel from which the poor are excluded".'

More considered and more qualified cases for private property in the body and its organs have been made by other commentators. Marie-Hélène Parizeau contrasts an Anglo-Saxon 'utilitarian' tradition of ethical analysis structured around concerns for personal autonomy, for equity in the context of a disparity between demand and supply, and for balancing 'gift' relations against 'commodity' relations, with a continental neo-Kantian tradition built on the principles of the integrity of the human body as an incarnation of the person; of consent, which modifies the first principle so as to allow a contract or gift based in gratuitousness; of the gift as guarantee of the pricelessness of the person and of human solidarity; and of the rights of the human person to the dignity indissociable from respect for the body. Within the neo-Kantian tradition 'all forms of gift of organs or tissue are a priori acceptable in so far as these gifts are the expression of social solidarity and have no commercial basis'.[136] At the same time, this tradition closes the door on any commercialization of organs because of its fear that the act of giving will be instrumentalized, transformed into an 'order of cannibalism' (p. 349). The strength of the utilitarian tradition, by contrast, is its ability, within the cost constraints of existing health systems, to develop pragmatic solutions to the question of allocation of scarce resources of organs and tissue—solutions which respect both individual freedom and technological development, while leaving open the status of the human body and its parts.

For Henry Hansmann, what is at issue in the objections to the creation of markets in organs is the normative cultural distinction between market and non-market transactions, and particularly the fact that narrow calculations of personal advantage are considered inappropriate for the latter ('If one tires of one's child it is not deemed acceptable—much less praiseworthy—to stop giving it food or to sell it to the highest bidder').[137] The force of the

---

[136] Marie-Hélène Parizeau, 'Autonomie, don et partage dans les transplantations d'organes et de tissus humains', *Dialogue*, 30 (1991), 347; my translation.

[137] Henry Hansmann, 'The Economics and Ethics of Markets for Human Organs', in James F. Blumstein and Frank A. Sloan (eds.), *Organ Transplantation Policy: Issues and Prospects* (Durham, NC: Duke University Press, 1989), 75.

argument for the creation of a market, however, is that it makes it possible to economize on the use of elaborate moral codes to govern transactions, and so to 'internalize to the decisionmakers involved all of the important costs and benefits of the transactions' (p. 76): in other words, to resituate the question in a private space where only the direct participants will be involved in the decision. While cultural norms are notoriously persistent, Hansmann instances the growth of markets in a number of areas which he thinks of as culturally comparable to organ transplantation: in dating services, in the sale of sperm, and in the commercially provided care of the elderly.

Lori Andrews structures her argument negatively: *without* property rights there is no protection against certain kinds of exploitation of or harm to the body.[138] John Moore's body is the key example of the vulnerability of a commons to appropriation, but it is similarly the case that 'without characterizing the body as some form of property, theft or other harm to dead bodies or extracorporeal body parts is difficult to prosecute' (p. 29), as is harm to sperm or embryos entrusted to a hospital.

The property rights Andrews envisages would be similar to the rights that allow me to gain compensation in the courts for harm to myself or to a close relative; in the law of torts, parts of the body and mental states routinely have a value put upon them (that is, they are routinely commodified) for the purposes of assessing compensation. Likewise, Andrews argues—picking up an argument also made by Brecher[139]—creating property rights in one's own body is not dissimilar to the sale of labour power for a wage, or to the commodification of the products of my intellect in intellectual property law (p. 32).

Among the possible negative consequences of such rights would be the possibility of state coercion (the welfare system, for example, could view a person with two whole kidneys as possessing potential capital and thus disqualify them for welfare benefits, and the taxation system could similarly revalue that person's assets) and of financial coercion: 'The strongest argument against paying donors is that people in dire straits will consent to debilitating surgeries out of a desperate need for money' (p. 32). But disallowing such sales

---

[138] Lori Andrews, 'My Body, My Property', *Hastings Center Report* (Oct. 1986), 28.   [139] Brecher, 'The Kidney Trade', 121.

will equally exercise coercion upon these people, and in any case the inequities between rich and poor that a free market in organs would exacerbate are already present in other forms as long as the provision of medical care is based on ability to pay (p. 34). Many of these problems can be avoided, however, if the commodification of the body is limited: body parts would not be subject to ownership or lien by others, but would generate an entitlement to compensation. Under such an arrangement, human beings would 'have the right to treat certain physical parts of their bodies as objects for possession, gift, and trade, but they do not become objects so long as others cannot treat them as property' (p. 36).

It is through such arguments as these that the historical process of drawing boundaries between what may properly be alienated as a commodity and what should remain outside commodity transactions is continually mediated. There are several direct historical analogues to these liminal struggles.

The first is that of the life insurance industry, where the whole issue of the commodification of the body and of body parts was fought out in very similar terms in the nineteenth century. Viviana Zelizer has traced the transition from a value system that considered such things as 'death, life, human organs and other generally ritualized items or behaviour . . . sacred and therefore beyond the pale of monetary definition', to a market system of exchange which established monetary equivalents for those aspects of human life.[140]

In the United States, and in all countries of Europe apart from Britain, the early growth of the industry was hindered by a massive resistance to what was seen as a speculation on death. Indeed, as Lorraine Daston argues, 'gambling was perhaps the prototype of a formalized exchange of risk in early modern Europe',[141] and London underwriters in the eighteenth century 'issued policies on the lives of celebrities like Sir Robert Walpole, the success of

[140] Viviana A. Rotman Zelizer, *Morals and Markets: The Development of Life Insurance in the United States* (New York: Columbia University Press, 1979), pp. xi–xii, xiii.
[141] Lorraine J. Daston, 'The Domestication of Risk: Mathematical Probability and Insurance 1650–1830', Lorenz Krüger, Lorraine J. Daston, and Michael Heidelberger (eds.), *The Probabilistic Revolution*, i: *Ideas in History* (Cambridge, Mass.: MIT Press, 1987), 239.

battles, the succession of Louis XV's mistresses, the outcome of sensational trials, the fate of 800 German immigrants who arrived in 1765 without food and shelter, and in short served as bookmakers for all and sundry bets' (p. 244). The emphasis on uncertainty as the core of the aleatory contract was instrumental in retarding the adoption of probabilistic actuarial calculation with its notion of the *quantifiable* uncertainty of probabilities.

This resistance was built into the heart of Western law. The Roman legal system had always had as one of its basic principles that there could be no monetary equivalent for the life of a freeman and had proscribed successorial contracts; the French civil code ruled that 'only things belonging to commerce can be the subject of a contract' and that a man's life 'cannot be the subject of commercial speculation'—thereby outlawing life insurance, trusts, and successorial contracts. Zelizer adds, however, that 'even countries that forbade life insurance in principle allowed the insurance of slaves. Their presumed lack of human value justified economic equivalences without presenting serious moral difficulties' (p. 44). We know from other sources that slaves in the Middle Passage were at times cast overboard if it was estimated that the insurance payout on their lives would exceed their landed price.[142]

A number of factors eventually enabled the transition to market valuation of the human body to come about. It was bound up with a series of formalizations of the management of death: the professionalization of funerals; the formal drafting of wills and a highly structured system of estate management; and the growth of financial institutions specializing in the economic management of death (trust companies, in addition to life insurance). These changes represented a process of rationalization of the management of risk, such that 'strictly individualistic conceptions of self-help dwindled, replaced by more efficient cooperative risk-bearing techniques'; at the same time the imperatives of efficient risk management together with a new sense of the respectability of life insurance 'legitimized and upgraded certain speculative ventures as risk-bearing enterprises, clearly differentiated from purposeless gambling' (p. 88; cf. Daston, 'Domestication of Risk', 248).

---

[142] Cf. Philip D. Curtin, 'Chapter 10: A Postscript on Mortality', *The Atlantic Slave Trade: A Census* (Madison: University of Wisconsin Press, 1969); Daniel P. Mannix (with Malcolm Cowley), *Black Cargoes: A History of the Atlantic Slave Trade 1518–1865* (London: Longmans, 1962), 125–6.

Once established, the system of life insurance gave rise to new modes of actuarial calculation defining the capital values of working males as a function of their age, defining disease in terms of a depreciation of capital values, and allotting precise monetary sums to different forms of disablement and disability; it set in train both a commodification and a parcellization of the body, and each of these aspects anticipates the trade in human tissue.

The second historical analogue to the struggle over the demarcations at stake in the trade in organs is the existence of two different systems for the public supply of blood with directly opposed philosophical underpinnings: one based in donation, the other in sale. I discussed Titmuss's study of the two systems in the first part of this essay, but it is perhaps worth emphasizing that Titmuss considered that blood constitutes a test case as to where the dividing line between the social and the economic should be drawn: 'If blood is considered in theory, in law, and is treated in practice as a trading commodity, then ultimately human hearts, kidneys, eyes and other organs of the body may also come to be treated as commodities to be bought and sold in the marketplace'.[143] His conclusions about the workings of the market system can be applied point for point to the workings of the trade in body organs:

From our study of the private market in blood in the United States we have concluded that the commercialization of blood and donor relationships represses the expression of altruism, erodes the sense of community, lowers scientific standards, limits both personal and professional freedoms, sanctions the making of profits in hospitals and clinical laboratories, legalizes hostility between doctor and patient, subjects critical areas of medicine to the laws of the marketplace, places immense social costs on those least able to bear them—the poor, the sick and the inept—increases the danger of unethical behaviour in various sectors of medical science and practice, and results in situations in which proportionately more and more blood is supplied by the poor, the unskilled, the unemployed, Negroes and other low income groups and categories of exploited human populations of high blood yielders. Redistribution in terms of blood and blood products from the poor to the rich appears to be one of the dominant effects of the American blood banking systems. (ibid. 245–6)

Such a redistribution from the poor to the rich clearly holds true for the traffic in body organs. Indeed, it holds true at both ends of

---

[143] Titmuss, *The Gift Relationship*, 158.

the transaction: it is not just that the poor give more, but that the socially privileged receive more. Three studies done in 1988 found that white men in the United States 'are twice as likely to get a new kidney as blacks of either sex and a third more likely than white women'—even when the socioeconomic groups involved were comparable, and despite the fact that blacks in the United States have three times the rate of renal failure of whites and that the government has since 1972 paid most of the costs of a transplant operation (*New York Times*, 24 January 1989).

This is to say that even where market forces are quite strongly controlled, the practice of organ transplantation still constructs a market in which the cannibalized bodies of the poor, of women, and of blacks are used to feed the bodies of the rich, of men, and of whites.[144] At the same time, transplantation constructs a culturally very powerful myth of the social body—that is, of the limits and the powers of all our bodies. This is a myth of the restoration of wholeness and of the integrity of the body: a myth of resurrection. Yet this wholeness can be achieved only by the incorporation of the other. The restored body is prostheticized: no longer an organic unity but constructed out of a supplement, an alien part which is the condition of that originary wholeness.

This paradox of an originary state which comes into being only retrospectively and by virtue of a prosthetic addition is foregrounded in some of the key ethical issues that have been raised by transplantation: by, for example, the ban in South Africa under apartheid on the transplantation of black organs into a white body; and by the furore raised by religious groups, and many others, at the prospect of the transplantation of pigs' or baboons' hearts into human bodies. These issues of course are 'problems' only within the framework of that myth of organic integrity and self-presence.[145]

---

[144] In a different context, Carole Pateman says flatly that 'contracts about property in the person inevitably create subordination'. Pateman, *The Sexual Contract*, 153.

[145] Emiko Ohnuki-Tierney seems to me to reproduce this myth in her study of the resistance within Japanese culture to the notion of brain death. Opposing a Western, 'Cartesian' definition of human life in terms of the priority of rationality over broader cultural definitions in which the body is integral to the often prolonged process of social death, and in which its intactness may be a condition of rebirth, Ohnuki-Tierney argues that the technology of transplantation and the equation of brain death with the death of the person may lead to 'the systematic overthrow of

This is, however, the major framework that has been available as a source of critique of market forces.

A *Times* leader of 5 April 1990, commenting on the 1989 Transplant Act in the United Kingdom, rehearses some of the arguments raised by the advocates of market forces (and it must be said again that the arguments for regulation of supply and demand by the market do address real issues of market imbalance, and hence of the sufferings undergone by those who are in need of replacement parts to keep them alive). Giving the example of a father who would willingly donate a kidney to save the life of his daughter (the example closely resembles the Turk Ferhat Usta who was at the centre of the scandal that led to this legislation), the *Times* leader then makes the supposition that the daughter 'has some other medical condition, to which a kidney transplant is not relevant. What is morally wrong in his selling to a third party the kidney he would willingly have donated to her, in order to raise money to pay for her medical treatment for this other condition?' *The Times* answers this hypothetical case by saying that its logical conclusion would be that the practice of self-mutilation would become widespread, and by insisting—although this 'may seem a sentimental distinction in this no-nonsense age'—on the need to draw a line between illegitimate and legitimate motives for self-mutilation: 'Mutilation for profit falls into the former category, for charity into the latter.'

The concept of self-mutilation is I think misleading to the extent that it sets the body organic, the whole and unmutilated body, as the standard against which to judge the action of market forces. What it cannot satisfactorily explain (and this is why it stresses the arbitrariness of the drawing of moral and legislative lines) is why

almost all of our cherished cultural categories: life and death, human and nonhuman, animate and inanimate, self and other, nature and culture' (Emiko Ohnuki-Tierney, 'Brain Death and Organ Transplantation: Cultural Bases of Medical Technology', *Current Anthropology*, 35: 3 (June 1994), 239). My view is almost exactly the opposite: that the Cartesian dualism which Ohnuki-Tierney sees as triumphant will in fact reinforce these dichotomies, and that it is complicit in this with the religious myths equating bodily wholeness with the wholeness of the social person which she describes and to which she apparently also subscribes. For discussion of some of these issues of the relation between persons, whole bodies, and resurrection, cf. Paul Rabinow, 'Severing the Ties: Fragmentation and Dignity in Late Modernity', *Knowledge and Society: The Anthropology of Science and Technology*, 9 (1992), 169–87.

there *should* be a difference in kind between charitable and profitable mutilation. If we recognize that it may be right to mutilate one's body for the good of another, there is no a priori reason to exclude profit as a factor if it achieves equally desirable ends, as indeed it may. It is not mutilation as such that is the problem (and my earlier figure of a cannibalized social body must thus be seen to be too simple); rather, the problem is that of the effects on bodies of market forces in a world where market power is unequally distributed.

RIGHTS OF PERSONALITY

Ownership not of the body but of the 'person', the core of selfhood, is what is at stake in the emergent right of publicity that has developed over the last four decades in the United States. Consider the case of the fame of Elvis Presley.

During his lifetime Presley entered into a merchandising agreement with Boxcar Enterprises: in effect, Presley assigned the exclusive rights of commercial exploitation of his name and likeness (his right of publicity) to this company, which immediately after his death in 1977 sold on to Factors, Etc., Inc. the manufacture and merchandising rights to Presley souvenirs. At around the same time, however, a non-profit organization began fund-raising for the erection of a large bronze statue of Presley in downtown Memphis, and as an incentive to donors presented them with eight-inch pewter replicas. Factors attempted to prevent the distribution of the replicas, and a lawsuit ensued.[146]

In finding that a property right in Presley's fame could not survive his death, the court went against several earlier judgements involving the Presley estate which had confirmed the existence of a right of publicity that could descend to Presley's heirs.[147] The court in the later case argued that it was inappropriate to grant a private

---

[146] *Memphis Development Foundation* v. *Factors, Etc., Inc.*, 616 F. 2d 956 (6th Cir.), *cert. denied*, 449 US 953 (1980). For a commentary, cf. Barbara Singer, 'The Right of Publicity: Star Vehicle or Shooting Star?', *Cardozo Arts and Entertainment Law Journal*, 10: 1 (1992), 1–50.

[147] *Factors, Etc., Inc.* v. *Creative Card Co.*, 444 F. Supp. 279 (SDNY 1977); *Factors, Etc., Inc.* v. *Pro Arts, Inc.*, 444 F. Supp. 288 (SDNY, 1977, *aff'd & remanded*, 579 F. 2d 215 (2d Cir. 1978), *cert. denied* 440 US 908 (1979), *on remand*, 496 F. Supp. 1090 (SDNY 1980), *rev'd* 652 F. 2d 278 (2d Cir. 1981).

property right in fame because fame is transient and because the public contributes substantially to its creation:

The intangible and shifting nature of fame and celebrity status, the presence of widespread public and press participation in its creation, the unusual psychic rewards and income that often flow from it during life and the fact that it may be created by bad as well as good conduct combine to create serious reservations about making fame the permanent right of a few individuals to the exclusion of the general public. (p. 959)

Fame derives from the public domain and should return to it (although it is worth noting that what the court understands by the public domain is the freedom of anyone, without restraint, to make a profit on the replication of the Presley persona).[148] The whole trend of right-of-publicity doctrine, however, has gone in the direction of the excision of an exclusive property right from the public domain.

The right of publicity is a protection for the commercial rights that celebrities hold in aspects of their 'identity' or 'personality'. It is distinguished from the cognate right of privacy by virtue of the fact that it is a proprietary right.[149] It did, however, have its origins in that more general (but also recently developed) 'right to be left alone': paradoxically so, since in many ways the two rights are in direct opposition to each other. Privacy doctrine was first mooted late last century in an article by Warren and Brandeis[150] arguing that what the authors call the 'inviolate personality' has the right to be protected from the intrusion of the press into personal affairs. The right was fairly quickly taken up and consolidated, with the state of New York enacting a statutory 'right of privacy' in 1903.

Whereas Warren and Brandeis's concern was with seclusion from journalistic intrusion, however, the problem manifested in many cases was rather that of unauthorized commercial use; it had to do

---

[148] 'The memory, name and pictures of famous individuals should be regarded as a common asset to be shared, an economic opportunity available in the free market system' (960).

[149] As the court in one of the earlier Factors cases argued, 'When a "persona" is in effect a product, and when that product has already been marketed to good advantage, the appropriation by another of that valuable property has more to do with unfair competition than it does with the right to be left alone'. *Factors, Etc., Inc.* v. *Creative Card Co.*, 283.

[150] Samuel Warren and Louis Brandeis, 'The Right to Privacy', *Harvard Law Review*, 4 (1890), 193–216.

less with questions of intrusive misrepresentation than with the circulation of representations without consent or recompense. Despite this, as Oliver Goodenough argues, the lack of a recognized property right meant that cases dealt with within this framework had to rely upon Warren and Brandeis's rationale of personal distress and harm. The 'problems' associated with this rationale were threefold: first, that public persons, who were expected to have waived their rights to privacy because of their inurement to public exposure, were therefore denied protection; second, that there was a lifetime limit on the right to privacy, since the problem of intrusion of course disappears with the death of the person concerned; and third, that 'since privacy was only a personal right to be left alone, there was no piece of property to transfer to a third party'.[151]

The crucial shift that took place over the course of this century was the development of a property-based right in personality. This right, the right of publicity, eventually came about as a piece of judge-made law in 1953 when Judge Jerome N. Frank marked out a direct extension from the concept of privacy rights, and argued that more is at stake than the personal distress suffered by (in this case) baseball players:

For it is common knowledge that many prominent persons (especially actors and ballplayers), far from having their feelings bruised through public exposure of their likenesses, would feel sorely deprived if they no longer received money for authorizing their countenances, displayed in newspapers, magazines, buses, trains and subways. This right of publicity would usually yield them no money unless it could be made the subject of an exclusive grant which barred any other advertisers from using their pictures.[152]

This decision was actively supported in an article the following year by the copyright specialist Melville Nimmer, arguing that 'the publicity right, tied to a property approach, gave a sound theoretical basis to a market in publicity values that already existed'.[153]

---

[151] Oliver R. Goodenough, 'The Price of Fame: The Development of the Right of Publicity in the United States', Part I, *EIPR*, 14: 2 (1992), 58–9.

[152] *Haelan Laboratories, Inc.* v. *Topps Chewing Gum, Inc.*, 202 F. 2d 866 (2d Cir. 1953), *cert. denied*, 346 US 816, 74 S.Ct. 26, 98 L.Ed. 343 (1953).

[153] Melville B. Nimmer, 'The Right of Publicity', *Law and Contemporary Problems*, 19 (1954), 203. Through the late 1970s and early 1980s protection for

The core of the right of publicity, according to the commentator Thomas McCarthy, is that it recognizes 'the potential *commercial* value of every person's identity . . . and assigns that value to the person in question'.[154] Unlike the right of privacy, which is designed to shelter an individual from the outside world and introduces a subjective measure of harm, the right of publicity is formulated in such a way as to allow the exploitation of attributes of personality in the open market. The crucial difference is precisely that it is a property right, which means that ownership of the name, the image or any other commercially exploitable attribute of identity can descend to heirs and can be assigned to others. As James Boyle notes, the classic publicity rights cases pay great attention to 'the importance of commodification, alienation, and transfer of the protected interest', and very *little* attention to questions of privacy: 'To a greater or lesser extent . . . each case treats fame as a partial public good—something unique and personal that can be gainfully exploited only if it can be commodified and others excluded from its use except on pain of payment.'[155]

This development of the right of publicity out of the right of

'personality' as property was consolidated and clarified. A key case was *Zacchini* v. *Scripps-Howard Broadcasting Co.* (*Zacchini* v. *Scripps-Howard Broadcasting Co.*, 43 US 562, 97 S.Ct. 2849, 53 L.Ed. 2d 265), in which the Supreme Court confirmed the existence of a publicity right and spelled out its difference from the privacy right in two respects: first, that it gives protection to a property interest rather than reputation; second, that it is analogous in this to the goals of copyright and patent law. Two rather different traditions of what we might more generally call rights of personality have developed in the two major centres of the culture industries in the United States, New York and California. New York adopted a right of privacy early, and developed a right of publicity only within its confines. One effect of this early resolution has been a continuing problem as to whether rights exist after death. California, after a long process of development, including the seminal but ambivalent *Lugosi* case, enacted in 1985 a statutory right of publicity (Code 990 of the California Civil Code) which made rights fully assignable and descendable, and accordingly restricted the circulation of the images of celebrities through the public domain. (In the Lugosi case—*Lugosi* v. *Universal Pictures*, 25 Cal. 3d 813, 160 Cal. Rptr. 323, 603 P. 2d 425 [1979]—the court found that Bela Lugosi's right of publicity in the image of Dracula could not be inherited by his family because it had not been commercially exploited in his lifetime. Justice Rose Bird's dissent, however, which prefigured later legislation, argued for a recognition that the merchandising of identity is a business in which the celebrity acts as an investor in their own image.)

[154] J. Thomas McCarthy, *The Rights of Privacy and Publicity* (New York: Clark Boardman Co., 1991), section 1.11 (c).
[155] Boyle, 'A Theory of Law and Information', 1514–15.

privacy was historically bound up with the commercial value of reputation or celebrity in the star systems of film and sport. In her reading of Hollywood star contracts, Jane Gaines has made the case that after the Second World War actors came increasingly to be organized as independent businesses for the marketing of their images, and were thus increasingly in competition with the studios; an important aspect of these businesses was the selling of merchandising tie-ups and of product endorsements.[156] Celia Lury's analysis of the star system draws an analogy with the way a personally grounded property right is protected in copyright regimes: 'In many ways', she writes, 'the star-function can be seen as a transformation of the author-function in the later stages of corporate production for a market in that the imprint of the star acts as a means of linking the signs of creative labour with the exhibition value of the works produced.'[157]

Exercise of the right of publicity has the effect of withdrawing a public icon from the public domain. In principle there is no reason why not only 'celebrities' but any public figure whatsoever, as well as the later generations who inherit their property rights, should not seek to control the flow of representations of their person. The heirs of Al Capone sought to do so in 1965, but failed on the grounds that the pecuniary value of Capone's identity had not been exploited before his death.[158] But a different ruling in which the Georgia Supreme Court granted the heirs of Martin Luther King the right to control representations of King has opened the possibility of an extensive privatization of the persona of major historical figures.[159]

Gaines, like Boyle, has drawn attention to the contradictory nature of the relation between the rights of privacy and publicity, arguing at the same time that they are unified by their common origin in 'the rights-holding subject who has property in himself.

---

[156] Gaines, *Contested Culture*, ch. 5.
[157] Celia Lury, *Cultural Rights: Technology, Legality and Personality* (London: Routledge, 1993), 58.
[158] *Maritote* v. *Desilu Prods.*, 345 F. 2d 418 (7th Cir.), *cert. denied*, 382 US 883 (1965).
[159] *Martin Luther King, Jr. Center for Social Change* v. *American Heritage Prods.*, 250 Ga. 135, 296 SE 2d 697 (1982); cf. Timothy P. Terrell and Jane S. Smith, 'Publicity, Liberty, and Intellectual Property: A Conceptual and Economic Analysis of the Inheritability Issue', *Emory Law Journal*, 34 (1985), 12.

Whereas the one right finds its support in the human subject, the other finds its support in the self as property and in the property produced by expenditure of labour. The right of publicity is nothing more nor less than a personal monopoly reinforced.'[160] And Gaines goes on to draw an analogy with the workings of copyright law, in particular with the strategy of those English publishers 'who, faced with the expiration of their licenses after the Statute of Anne, borrowed the monopoly in perpetuity of authors' rights to extend and fortify their own rights to the literary works they published'.[161]

This is to say, I think with some cogency, that the logic by which a right initially proposed as a protection of the inviolability of the person turns into a right allowing personal identity to be considered as property and exploited either by oneself or by others is in some sense akin to the logic by which copyright law works.[162] This logic is that of a two-step process in which (1) a property right is established on the basis of the person as origin and as self-identity (hence copyright law's provisions for 'something unique', however minimal; for 'originality'); (2) this property right then forms the basis of an industrial—that is, a non-individual—regime of ownership, in which the key players are the movie, publishing, and recorded music industries, the software industry, and corporations seeking protection for information.[163]

This discussion of rights in the self is complicated, however, by the fact that what we are dealing with in all of these cases is not personal identity but rather *representations* of personal identity. Much of the interest of the major right-of-publicity cases lies

---

[160] Gaines, *Contested Culture*, 206.   [161] Ibid. 207.

[162] A still closer analogy is perhaps to be found in French *droit moral*, which is grounded in the notion 'that a work of art is, and remains, the embodiment of its creator's personality. Theoretically, any modification of the work . . . is a violation of the author's right to shape his own individuality. Not only does the modified work misrepresent the author's personality to the world, but it also detracts from his personality by frustrating his self-revelation'. Edward J. Damich, 'The Right of Personality: A Common-law Basis for the Protection of the Moral Rights of Authors', *Intellectual Property Law Review* (1990), 547–642.

[163] Cf. Lury, *Cultural Rights*, 30: 'The institutions and discourses that collectively functioned to construct the object "art" were not distinct from but allied to the determinations of the marketplace which themselves established and confirmed the commodity status of the work of art.'

precisely in the ways in which they establish a relationship between identity and particular personal attributes by which identity is signified.

Initially both the right of privacy and the right of publicity were restricted to protection of the name and the image, both of which—for particular historical reasons—are assumed in Western culture to be deeply bound up with personal identity (both operate through a kind of sympathetic magic by which a closely associated metonym—a picture, or a proper name—comes to stand for the person). In the following line of cases, however, the tokens of personal identity were extended much more widely:

In *Cohen* v. *Herbal Concepts, Inc.*,[164] a mother and daughter were photographed without permission while bathing naked in a secluded spot. The case turned on whether the rear view of the two women later used without their consent on a product label was sufficient to count as an indication of their identity. The court accepted the word of their husband and father that the image did indeed constitute what the statute calls an 'identifiable likeness'.

In *Motschenbacher* v. *R. J. Reynolds Tobacco Company*,[165] the racing driver Lothar Motschenbacher complained of an advertisement which used a car he claimed was recognizably his and with which he was closely identified. Although details of Motschenbacher's car had been modified and the face of the driver was indistinguishable, the court found both that it was clear to knowledgeable people what the car was, and that this identification constituted a metonymic link with the identity of its driver.

In *Onassis* v. *Christian Dior-New York, Inc.*,[166] a case which is discussed at some length in Jane Gaines's *Contested Culture*, Jacqueline Onassis complained about an advertisement for Dior which featured the wedding of a mythical threesome, 'the Diors', flanked by a number of minor celebrities and by what seems to be Mrs Onassis. The face is in fact that of a Washington secretary,

---

[164] *Cohen* v. *Herbal Concepts, Inc.*, 63 NY 2d 379, 482 NYS 2d 457, 472 NE 2d 307 (1984).

[165] *Motschenbacher* v. *R. J. Reynolds Tobacco Company*, 498 F. 2d 821 (9th Cir. 1974).

[166] *Onassis* v. *Christian Dior-New York, Inc.*, 122 Misc. 2d 603, 472 NYS 2d 254 (S.Ct. NY Co. 1984), aff'd 110 AD 2d 1095, 488 NYS 2d 943 (1st Dept. 1985).

Barbara Reynolds, an Onassis lookalike. The defence reasonably claimed that Onassis could not claim property rights in someone else's face and had no right to enjoin its use; lawyers for Onassis argued that the 'likeness' was recognizably that of the public figure, Jacqueline Onassis, not that of the model. Both sides depend upon what Gaines calls the 'unexamined assumption that the unauthorized use of a photograph is an appropriation of the identity of the person photographed'.[167] What the court had to decide was an issue between the actuality of the referent and the constructed fact of resemblance, and it did so by means of the notion that public fame and identity is a commercially valuable asset which is indeed carried by iconic likeness. In this ruling, privacy law comes close to the law of unfair competition.

In *Carson* v. *Johnny Portable Toilets, Inc.*[168] the late-night talk-show host Johnny Carson objected to the use by a portable toilet company of the phrase 'Here's Johnny' which, Carson claimed, was characteristically associated with the introduction to his show. The defence agreed that they were making a reference to the Carson show, but argued that the phrase was too ordinary to be withdrawn from free public circulation. What is interesting about this case, I think, is just that assumption that both sides in the case make, that a piece of language contingently associated with a celebrity can count as an aspect of that person's identity.

In *Midler* v. *Ford Motor Co.*[169] the singer Bette Midler complained of an advertisement which used a version of the Bette Midler hit 'Do You Want to Dance', sung in such a way as to resemble Midler's voice. Nancy Sinatra had previously failed in an attempt to claim property rights in her voice and style;[170] in this case the court ruled that her voice constituted 'an attribute of Midler's identity' and allowed compensation accordingly.

In all of these cases it is clear that privacy and publicity law equate representations and metonyms of identity with the substance of identity itself. So, it seems, does the law relating to the passing-off tort, which is the primary mechanism used by English and Australian courts for the protection of property rights in personal

---

[167] Gaines, *Contested Culture*, 86.
[168] *Carson* v. *Johnny Portable Toilets, Inc.*, 698 F. 2d 831 (6th Cir. 1983).
[169] *Midler* v. *Ford Motor Co.*, 849 F. 2d 460 (9th Cir. 1988).
[170] *Sinatra* v. *Goodyear Tire and Rubber Co.*, 435 F. 2d 711 (1970).

identity:[171] in two Australian cases involving the passing off of the character of Mick Dundee by other commercial interests, Paul Hogan was assumed to be identical to the character he portrayed.[172] If this is so, however, then what is alienated in commercial uses of identity would be the subject form itself, rather than the representations through which it is carried. (If, conversely, it is merely the representations that are put to commercial use, then it is not clear on what basis a property right founded in personal identity can be established in them.)

The concept of person implied by the right of publicity (based in self-possession and the alienability of representations of the self, but also in a sense in the merging of the self with its representations) is not a piece of ideology that can be demystified and then discarded. It is continuous with a millennia-long process of elaboration of the legal conception of the person, and it is intricately bound up with the workings of an entire mode of production. It corresponds in complicated ways to the imaginary forms of selfhood through which we experience the world and our relation to it. A historical effect rather than the ground of all history, formed at the intersection of the culturally specific distinction between the moral economy of the gift and the market economy of the commodity, the category of the person lacks any transcendental reality. Like the concept of 'rights', it designates not a set of inherent attributes, but a historical project and a site of intense social struggle. At the same time, however, this category is an evolving one, and its status is capable of substantial modification in the process by which new legal and political rights are formed. To describe the cultural framework within which it functions as, to use Strathern's term, 'Western proprietism', and to point to its difference from the dispersed person of the gift economy, is not to condemn it, but to recognize the constraints on its formation and on its possible historical mutations.

---

[171] Cf. W. Van Caenegem, 'Different Approaches to the Protection of Celebrities against Unauthorized Use of their Image in Advertising in Australia, the United States and the Federal Republic of Germany', *EIPR* 12: 2 (1990), 452–8; Stephen C. G. Burley, 'Passing off and Character Merchandising: Should England Lean towards Australia?', *EIPR* 13: 7 (1991), 227–30.

[172] *Hogan and Others* v. *Pacific Dunlop Ltd* 83 ALR 403; *Hogan and Other* v. *Koala Dundee Pty Ltd and Ors* 83 ALR 187.

MARKETS IN INFORMATION

The categories of the person and of information are not easily separable since 'the person' is in part an informational concept, variously designating a structure of genetic and psychic organization, the source of bodies of 'authored' practices and texts, and the object of a set of public knowledges (in a range from intimate gossip to abstract statistical data). Information is in its turn secured as property by its ties to the legal category of the person. Like the person, information has in most societies been culturally framed as an inappropriate object of private and exclusive ownership, although in the societies that we think of as constituting Western 'modernity' this ethos has coexisted with the partial monopolies granted by copyright law and other forms of intellectual property rights. In both cases, however, there has been increasing commercial pressure for the privatization of these categories and their removal from the commons.

The characteristic structure of information is that of gift exchange without monetary recompense but in contexts of calculation and strategic manœuvre. The barter of information and the estimation of who knows what condition the forms of its reciprocity but can never endow it with real scarcity, since its most important quality is its inexhaustible reproducibility: if I tell something to you I still 'possess' it myself, and so on indefinitely; unlike material goods, information is not consumed by use. This indeterminacy of positioning (the ability to exist in many places simultaneously) gives rise to a more general indeterminacy inherent in the fact that information is structured as an open system with multiple users; its 'value' can be assessed only retrospectively in relation to its contexts of use.[173] Two obstacles to commodification develop immediately from this radical indeterminacy.

The first is the problem of defining and enforcing exclusive property rights (which are the precondition for capital investment)[174] in something both intangible and diffuse.[175] The simple

[173] Cf. Benjamin J. Bates, 'Information as an Economic Good: Sources of Individual and Social Value', in Vincent Mosco and Janet Wasko (eds.), *The Political Economy of Information* (Madison: University of Wisconsin Press, 1988), 77.
[174] Cf. Gareth Locksley, 'Information Technology and Capitalist Development', *Capital and Class*, 27 (Winter 1986), 83.
[175] Cf. Raymond T. Nimmer and Patricia Ann Krauthaus, 'Information as a Commodity: New Imperatives of Commercial Law', *Law and Contemporary Problems*, 55: 3 (1992), 104–5.

solution to this problem is to treat information as a secret. (This solution builds on one of the ways in which information flow is restricted in pre-capitalist societies. The secret is the developed form of everyday uses of knowledge as advantage, and it reaches its entelechy in the public discourses of statecraft.[176]) The more complex solution, and the one that has been worked out in great detail by Western law over the last three centuries, is to restrict access to and use of information without necessarily restricting possession of it; thus copyright law restricts only the making of unauthorized copies, patent and trademark law restrict commercial exploitation, and so on.

The second obstacle is the problem of attaching exchange value to an entity which has an almost limitless use value: that is, of making an abundant good scarce. The uncertainty that flows from the indeterminacy of uses (the unpredictability of the 'take' of any information product) entails considerable risk for capital invest-ment.[177] At the same time, the relatively high costs of initial production and the relatively low costs of subsequent copying of information goods make predictability imperative.[178] The problem of the minimization of risk can be solved in part by generating 'a constant stream of unique (if often similar) products with severely limited life spans',[179] and more broadly by a combination of control of access and regulation of demand. Nicholas Garnham has detailed five strategies elaborated by the culture and information industries to this end. They are: (1) the production of scarcity by controlling the right to copy; (2) the control of distribution channels (for example by vertical integration of film production and distribution); (3) the building-in of obsolescence through the manipulation of time (for example by the creation of rapidly

---

[176] On the strategic role of secrets in creating solidarity and social division, cf. Kim Lane Scheppele, *Legal Secrets: Equality and Efficiency in the Common Law* (Chicago: University of Chicago Press, 1988); Sissela Bok, *Secrets: On the Ethics of Concealment and Revelation* (New York: Pantheon, 1978); Georg Simmel, 'The Secret and the Secret Society', *The Sociology of Georg Simmel*, 307–76.

[177] Bernard Miège, *The Capitalization of Cultural Production* (New York: International General, 1989), 43.

[178] Landes and Posner discuss this in terms of the 'public good' character of information. William M. Landes and Richard A. Posner, 'An Economic Analysis of Copyright', *Intellectual Property Law Review* (1990), 448.

[179] Paul DiMaggio, 'Classification in Art', *American Sociological Review*, 52 (1987), 446.

decaying information in journalism); (4) the sale of audiences to advertisers rather than, directly, of cultural and informational goods to consumers; (5) the socialization of production costs by means of state patronage and subsidy.[180] To these we should add the massive work of classification and certification effected by the institution of authorship, which remains the single most important channel for the creation of textual desire and the minimization of market uncertainty.

A NEW INFORMATION ORDER

The current phase of capitalist development', says Gareth Locksley, 'is one characterized by the elevation of information and its associated technology into the first division of key resources and commodities. Information is a new form of capital,'[181] and as such it undergoes a change of form: rather than being deposited primarily in an interlocking ensemble of open, 'library' systems with minimal entry requirements, it is increasingly managed within a system of private ownership where access is regulated by the payment of rent.[182] One point at which it is possible to see this change crystallizing is in the protocols relating to intellectual property in the recently concluded GATT round.[183]

An unlikely embodiment of the world-historical spirit, the GATT treaty nevertheless marks a clear historical demarcation in the global control of information. What it does, on my reading, is impose a definition of intellectual property rights directly disadvantageous to Third World countries which, holding few patents themselves, have now been brought within the scope of a regime where they will be held strictly accountable for their state of exponentially increasing indebtedness.[184] One commentator—no

---

[180] Nicholas Garnham, *Capitalism and Communication: Global Culture and the Economics of Information*, ed. Fred Inglis (London: Sage, 1990), 40.

[181] Locksley, 'Information Technology and Capitalist Development', 91.

[182] Ibid. 89.

[183] The Uruguay Round of the General Agreement on Tariffs and Trade was concluded on 15 Dec. 1993 and ratified by over 120 countries in Marrakesh on 12 Apr. 1994.

[184] Carlos Braga cites a number of analysts who have argued that 'the ultimate goal of the industrialized countries [in the GATT negotiations] would be to freeze the existing international division of labour by way of the control of technology

less convinced of the righteousness of the cause of Western property rights than the majority of Western analysts—sets up the narrative of conflicting interests in the following way:

Many L[esser] D[eveloped] C[ountrie]s have a different philosophy about the protection of intellectual property. There are some politicians and economists who assert that intellectual property protection laws simply perpetuate a system of economic imperialism which allows countries such as the United States to maintain a position of world dominance. These dissenters believe that ideas should flow freely as part of [the] common heritage of mankind. Brazil does not give drugs any patent protection within its borders because the government does not believe its people should have to pay what is to them a very high price for a basic health care commodity. Argentina takes a similar position on pharmaceuticals. One can sympathize with the plight of LDCs in their effort to make products affordable for their citizens whose per capita income is significantly lower than that of the developed countries. But an argument which does not allow for an adequate return on investment in research and development is ultimately shortsighted. Mexico is an example of a country which threatened to force pharmaceutical companies to hand over production of their drugs to local firms and accept significantly reduced royalties. But the drug companies countered with a threat to abandon the Mexican market entirely, and the government backed down. As a result of the threat, American drug firms are still leery of exposing too much of their technology in Mexico.[185]

What begins here as an argument about the ethics and the long-term inefficiencies of refusing to accept the advanced world's definition of appropriate patent rights becomes, by the end of this passage, an object lesson in *Realpolitik*: Mexico's 'shortsightedness' has nothing to do with the morality of its philosophical position, and everything to do with its miscalculation of the power of international drug companies. This shift is characteristic, I think, of the logic within which the argument has been conducted.

Much of the commentary on the GATT round is cast in terms of calculations of the losses incurred by the Western information

transfers to the Third World'. Carlos Alberto Primo Braga, 'The Economics of Intellectual Property Rights and the GATT: A View from the South', in Connie T. Brown and Eric A. Szweda (eds.), *Trade-Related Aspects of Intellectual Property* (Nashville: Vanderbilt University School of Law, 1990), 252.

[185] Kurt Stanberry, 'Piracy of Intellectual Property', *Society* (Sept.–Oct. 1990), 36.

industries as a result of 'piracy' and 'theft';[186] but these calculations rarely attempt to get to grips with the conflict of definitions of what should count as 'property' in the first place (should patents run for five years or for twenty? should pharmaceutical products be subject to special conditions such as local licensing?), and their bland assurances that subscription to an international intellectual property regime will in the long term bring about technology transfer and thus a *decreased* dependency of the 'developing' on the 'developed' nations[187] ring hollow in the light of the way the GATT regime has 'neatly and disturbingly divided developed countries, who are major net exporters of intellectual property rights, from the LDCs which are net importers'.[188] There is no 'accumulation of knowledge capital' when use of that capital is carefully controlled by monopoly rents.

One of the main objectives of the Uruguay Round of the GATT was the extension of patent enforcement to certain key industries such as pharmaceuticals and agrochemicals which in many countries were exempt from patent protection.[189] These are industries whose products—medicine and food—force in a particularly direct manner the issue of a conflict between 'social' and 'private' interests. Indira Gandhi put the *différend* starkly when she told the World Health Assembly in 1982: 'The idea of a better-ordered world is one in which medical discoveries will be free of patents and there will be no profiteering from life and death.'[190] Now, such an argument is

---

[186] Hoffman and Marcou cite an estimate by the Congressional Office of Technology Assessment that world trade in intellectual property affects 'more than 2.2% of the U.S. labour force and 5% of our gross national product' (Gary M. Hoffman and George T. Marcou, 'The Costs and Complications of Piracy', *Society*, (Sept.–Oct. 1990), 25); another study cites an International Trade Commission Report's conclusion that 'United States firms lose an estimated $43 to $61 billion annually from foreign piracy' (Mark Modak-Truran, 'Section 337 and GATT in the *Akzo* Controversy: A Pre- and Post-Omnibus Trade Competitiveness Act Analysis', *Intellectual Property Law Review* (1990), 189), although other commentators tend to be somewhat more conservative in their estimates.

[187] Cf. Hoffman and Marcou, 'Costs and Complications', 28: 'Failure to invest in "knowledge capital" fosters the same kind of dependency on the outside world as failure to accumulate other forms of productive capital.'

[188] M. M. Kostecki, 'Sharing Intellectual Property between the Rich and the Poor', *EIPR* 13: 8 (1991), 273.

[189] Cf. Carlos Correa, 'The GATT Agreement on Trade-Related Aspects of Intellectual Property Rights: New Standards for Patent Protection', *EIPR* 16: 8 (1994), 327.

[190] Cited in Braga, 'The Economics of Intellectual Property Rights and the GATT', 253.

vulnerable to attack within a framework in which research and development are primarily funded by private, profit-oriented investment. *In this context* the argument mistakes a commodity for a gift, and the consequences of this mistake are ethically dubious. But this is of course by no means the only thinkable framework. If knowledge and the information component of its products are conceived as public rather than private goods then there are at least two possible alternatives: the direct sponsorship of knowledge production by government, for public use and by means of a subsidy from the taxation system; or public subsidy for the private production of knowledge, again for public use. Historically, as Braga argues, these alternative frameworks have been propounded in international forums[191] by Third World bureaucracies, whose attitudes 'reflect the predominance of a *scientific ethos* which has at its basis the norm of complete disclosure. This "culture" . . . is hostile to the view of knowledge as a *private capital good* that is the foundation of the so-called mature intellectual property systems of the industrialized economies.'[192]

Gift and commodity: it is perhaps in this broad policy sense, and with a full recognition that this gift is in no way 'free' since it must be subsidized by the state, that it becomes possible for this opposition to regain some of its clarity. The condition for this move, however, is that 'norm of complete disclosure' which was the historical condition of possibility for scientific thought to break with a culture and a politics of the secret,[193] and which retains its power as a challenge to the increasingly pervasive ethos of private appropriation and control both of scientific and of 'cultural' knowledges.

---

[191] Which have themselves been split between those with a 'trade' orientation (the GATT, the IMF, the World Bank) and those with a 'development' orientation (the United Nations Conference on Trade and Development, the World Intellectual Property Organization, and the United Nations Economic, Scientific and Culture Organization). Cf. Bruce Lindsay, 'GATT: Development and Intellectual Property', *Arena Journal*, 3 (1994), 36.

[192] Braga, 'The Economics of Intellectual Property Rights and the GATT', 263.

[193] But the gift may of course be just as closely aligned with the secret and the sacred as with disclosure; Mauss's essay constantly returns to this conjuncture, and it is the focus as well of much of Derrida's recent work, in particular *The Gift of Death*, trans. David Wills (Chicago: University of Chicago Press, 1995). Conversely, even the most irreproachably open of scientific practices may lend itself to unjust uses.

THE OWNERSHIP OF NATURE

The norm of disclosure is of course a component of patent law, which requires a full and publicly available description of the 'invention' as the price for allowing its private appropriation for a limited term.[194] The requirement is one of those mechanisms by which Western intellectual property regimes seek to balance a component of information that resides permanently in the public domain (the 'idea' or 'method' in copyright law; the 'primary' meanings of language in trademark law; reproducible scientific inventions in patent law) and a component which is temporarily withdrawn from it (the 'expression' in copyright law; 'secondary' meanings in trademark law—at least until these become so much a part of the language as to return to their 'primary' status; and monopoly rights of exploitation of inventions for the life of the patent).[195] Patent law, to simplify drastically, is a way of locking up commercially valuable information, under rather strict conditions, for exclusive use for a limited term. I turn now to an exploration of a series of recent developments which have extended the possibility of locking up aspects of 'nature' itself.

Nature, like language, has traditionally been classified as a *res communis* which can have no human author.[196] Just as I cannot lay claim to exclusive ownership of the basic materials of the English language,[197] so I cannot patent a natural species or a particular use

[194] The 'letters patent' granting rights of exclusion in an invention which they simultaneously describe are by definition instruments of publicity (as opposed to the 'letters close' or *lettres de cachet* which fold their message within the sealed parchment); patent law requires a surrender of *secrecy* in exchange for the right to exploit the invention, and like all intellectual property it carries no exclusive rights in abstract ideas—only in the 'concrete, tangible, or physical embodiment of an abstraction' (Peter D. Rosenberg, *Patent Law Fundamentals*, vol. i, 2nd edn. (New York: Clark Boardman Callaghan, 1995), §1.01, §1.03).

[195] My examples are all taken from US law, which is in many respects the most fully developed body of doctrine relating to intellectual property law. With the signing of the Berne Convention in 1988 United States copyright law is now broadly in line with most other Western legal systems, although the integration of moral rights law has been more taken for granted than actually implemented in appropriate legislation.

[196] Cf. Bernard Edelman, 'The Law's Eye: Nature and Copyright', in Brad Sherman and Alain Strowel (eds.), *Of Authors and Origins* (Oxford: Clarendon Press, 1994), 79.

[197] 'Apart from its use in connection with a person, a title or name is the means of designating anything and everything of which one may speak, be it tangible or

of a substance found in nature. To use the cases Bernard Edelman cites, natural products like the cellulose surrounding the external fibres of coconuts cannot be patented because they exist independently of humankind; neither can the discovery of new properties of natural or patented objects (such as the recently discovered efficacy of aspirin in controlling heart disease), since these properties are contained in the structure of matter itself, and 'neither the structure of nature nor the effects which flow from it are subject to patent'.[198] Patent applies to *inventions* of industrial processes, but not to *discoveries* of the natural laws on which they are based.

The biotechnological revolution of the last twenty years has, however, brought great pressure to bear on the way in which that line between invention and discovery has been drawn. Greenfield notes that the trend in contemporary law 'is to allow patents for "products of nature" so long as the inventor has changed the product to conform to the utility, novelty, and nonobviousness requirements of the patent statute';[199] Correa elaborates:

In countries that are members of the European Patent Convention a patent can be granted when a substance found in nature can be characterized by its structure, by its process of obtention or by other criteria, if it is new in the sense that it was not previously available to the public. In the United States an isolated and purified form of a natural product can be patented if it is found in nature only in an unpurified form. As a result, a very thin line separates 'invention' from 'discovery' in those countries.[200]

---

intangible. Dissociated with the subject thereof, whatever it may be, a title or name composed of ordinary words, cannot acquire the status of property. So dissociated, it becomes merely words; and all words of our language are in the public domain. All who speak or write have an inherent right to use any and all words in the English language or any combination thereof for any legitimate purpose. Thus, it was correctly said by a learned judge that " . . . We can find no warrant in the books for considering a name, qua name, as property. No doubt 'property' is itself a conventional concept, but so are all legal concepts; this one has not as yet embraced names". Learned Hand, J., in *Mutual Life Ins. Co.* v. *Menin*, 2d Cir., 115 F. 2d 975, 979.' *Ball* v. *United Artists Corporation*, 214 NYS 2d 219, 224.

[198] Bernard Edelman, 'Vers une approche juridique du vivant', in Edelman and Marie-Angèle Hermitte (eds.), *L'Homme, la nature et le droit* (Paris: Christian Bourgois, 1988), 28–9; my translation.

[199] Michael S. Greenfield, 'Recombinant DNA Technology: A Science Struggling with the Patent Law', *Intellectual Property Law Review* (1993), 151.

[200] Correa, 'The GATT Agreement', 155. The key case in which the concept of purification is determined is *In re Bergstrom*, 427 F. 2d 1394, 166 USPQ 256 (CCPA 1970); cf. also Robert A. Armitage, 'The Emerging U.S. Patent Law for the Protection of Biotechnology Research Results', *EIPR* 11: 2 (1989), 47–57.

This is to say that patent law has been shifting towards a more expansive definition of its subject matter, and in particular towards a rather different understanding of that 'common' realm of 'nature'.

For Edelman, the move from a strict prohibition on the patenting of nature towards a range of recent decisions allowing the patenting of living matter is made possible by a fundamental split in the way Western modernity has defined nature itself (and has been constituted *as* 'modernity' in so doing). The distinction between industrial processes (which are invented) and the natural laws on which they are based (which are discovered) works to exclude from patentability whatever is independent of human intervention. Thus the model of nature that operates in Western legal systems is one that is defined with respect to human activity. The natural realm appears here not only as an object of knowledge but as a domain with its own finality distinct from and irreducible to human ends. The underlying distinction is therefore between 'human activity, which modifies the laws of nature and gives them a different meaning, and nature itself which is limited to responding to its own programme [*qui se borne à répondre à son programme*].'[201]

What this distinction in turn makes possible, however, is a further demarcation between 'natural' and 'artificial' forms of 'nature'. Edelman traces the evolution of this opposition through two key moments in US legislation. The first is the 1930 *Plant Act*, which distinguishes between 'products of nature' and 'human-made inventions'—the latter including 'invented' plant varieties. The effect of this distinction is that the category of life [*le vivant*] is split in such a way that the solidarity of the human species with other living things is lost; the human, expelled from the domain of nature, then becomes a rival to it, producing fabricated simulacra such as hybrid plant varieties which count as 'inventions'. The 1970 *Plant Variety Protection Act* further extends the category of an

---

[201] Edelman, 'Vers une approche juridique du vivant', 31. The distinction between nature and human activity is a distinction between matter and form, posited within a long cosmological tradition (rooted ultimately in Greek religious thought) which thinks form as the animation of matter; extrapolating to both copyright and patent law, Marilyn Strathern argues that ' "Form" is given value both as the unique realization or materialization of being (copyright) and as the essence of this being in the creative impetus of information or design (patent)'. Marilyn Strathern, 'Potential Property: Intellectual Rights and Property in Persons', *Social Anthropology*, 4: 1 (1996), 30.

'artificial' nature which, being humanly authored, is potentially patentable, to the *reproducibility* of plants (rather than merely single exemplars); private rights can now be held in the infinite genetic chain that is the essence of living matter. To these two moments Edelman adds the further step that is taken in the 1980 *Chakrabarty* case[202] which determined that genetically engineered organisms are either a 'manufacture' or a 'composition of matter' and are therefore patentable. From single-celled organisms the line then passes through genetically engineered plants[203] to oysters[204] to transgenic animals (the Harvard mouse, bred specifically for its susceptibility to cancer).[205] The end result of this process, he argues, is an instrumental, ultimately even an industrial conception of living matter which subordinates it to the commodity form. Edelman summarizes the stages of this historical passage as follows:

Life has been integrated into the market as easily as could be imagined because it has been a progressive process. It started with something that was symbolically far removed from mankind, the vegetable domain; from there it passed to the micro-organism, then to the most rudimentary forms of animal life like the oyster. The whole of the animal kingdom is now targeted and we are on the verge of the human, weighed down with precedents which ensure the closure of the system and make any resistance difficult. The work of man, which must be remunerated, claims repayment from the whole realm of nature which has traditionally been free of any property claims.[206]

The most spectacular theatre of patent law is currently the human genetic system itself, together with the recombinant engineering of drugs and human tissues. In 1991 the United States National Institute of Health (NIH) announced a programme of patent

---

[202] *Diamond v. Chakrabarty*, 206 USPQ 193, 447 US 303 (1980).

[203] *Ex parte Hibberd*, 227 USPQ 443 (PTO Board of Patent Appeals and Interferences, 1985).

[204] *Ex parte Allen*, 2 USPQ 2d 1425 (PTO Board of Patent Appeals and Interferences, 1987).   [205] US Patent 7 735 866.

[206] Bernard Edelman, 'Entre Personne humaine et matériau humain: le sujet de droit', in Edelman and Hermitte, *L'Homme, la nature et le droit*, 142. Edelman's description of this process as one of desacralization of the human, however, reveals again the weakness of the normative basis of any critique that takes 'the human' or 'the person' as an inviolable given.

applications on human gene fragments; early in 1992 they announced a further application on 2,375 fragments representing 5 per cent of all human genes.[207] Control of these fragments (or 'express sequence tags') would effectively block any use of the corresponding full gene, even if the identity of these genes were unknown. At first sight this move looks like an inappropriate privatization of material which ought to be openly available for scientific research. A story in the *New York Times*[208] quotes James Watson, the head of the Human Genome Project, as saying that ' "it would be a total mess for industry . . . if someone has been working on a particular gene for several years, but somebody else has patented it before they even know what they have" '; the consequence of such a pre-emptive patent would be that 'companies that uncovered the role of a particular gene could be forced to pay royalties to those that had merely isolated it' (p. A12). *The Times*'s perspective is purely industrial, of course, and doesn't really raise the question of the private ownership of the genetic commons. There is also another way of reading this story. Richard Lewontin says flatly that 'No prominent molecular biologist of my acquaintance is without a financial stake in the biotechnology business,'[209] and the director of the NIH has said that she 'wants the NIH to patent the human genome to prevent private entrepreneurs, and especially foreign capital, from controlling what has been created with American public funding'.[210] Patent rights would here be working in *defence* of the public domain (or at least that part of it that resides in the United States).

What is clear in any case is the extent of the profits at stake. 'If human DNA sequences are to be the basis of future therapy', writes Lewontin, 'then the exclusive ownership of such DNA sequences would be money in the bank.'[211] Certainly this expectation of

---

[207] Greenfield, 'Recombinant DNA Technology', 174; Wilkie notes that 'the issue was made more piquant by the fact that the sequences being patented are of genes expressed in the brain, so not only would the US Government own part of the human genome, it would also have succeeded in patenting part of the human brain'. Tom Wilkie, *Perilous Knowledge: The Human Genome Project and Its Implications* (London: Faber and Faber, 1994), 93.

[208] *New York Times*, 21 Oct. 1991.

[209] Lewontin, 'The Dream of the Human Genome', 37.

[210] Ibid. 38.

[211] Ibid. Greenfield quotes estimates that US sales of biotechnologically derived products will reach $40 billion in the year 2000, with world wide sales of $100

profit, which 'discourages open discussion of technical detail during the crucial R&D phase before patent filing',[212] has undermined that culture of shared information which the patent system supposedly fosters. Part of the problem with assessing these developments, however, is their sheer recentness, and in order to develop a clearer perspective on the patenting of living matter I want to turn now to the longer and more fully constructed history of the private appropriation of plant varieties.

The particular sort of clarity provided by this history consists in its ability to relate changes in the legal and technological frameworks of development of plant varieties to changes in farming as a global industry and a way of life. My major source here is Jack Kloppenburg's *First the Seed*, which argues that farming in the United States, as elsewhere in the advanced capitalist world, has been transformed over the last century 'from a largely self-sufficient production process into one in which purchased inputs account for the bulk of the resources employed'.[213] No longer do farmers produce most of their own means of production (such things as seed, feed, fuel, and motive power); for the most part these have moved 'off-farm and into circumstances in which fully developed capitalist relations of production can be developed' (p. 31).

A crucial factor in this process has been the transformation of seed from an infinitely reproducible public good to a scarce commodity, and at the heart of this radical transformation lay the development through systematic scientific breeding of hybrid plant varieties. The socioeconomic logic of hybridization is this: unlike open-pollinated varieties, seed from hybrid grain varieties produces

billion ('Recombinant DNA Technology', 35). The trade in genetically produced body tissue was estimated to be worth $2.2 billion in 1990 (Sean Johnston, 'Patent Protection for the Protein Products of Recombinant DNA', *Intellectual Property Law Review* (1991), 190), and as long ago as September 1988 there were between 15,000 and 16,000 biotechnology-related patents pending in the US Patent and Trademark Office.

[212] Daniel J. Kevles and Leroy Hood, 'Reflections', in Daniel J. Kevles and Leroy Hood (eds.), *The Code of Codes: Scientific and Social Issues in the Human Genome Project* (Cambridge, Mass.: Harvard University Press, 1992), 312.

[213] Kloppenburg, *First the Seed*, 10; Kloppenburg quotes Richard Lewontin to this effect ('Agricultural Research and the Penetration of Capital', *Science for the People*, 14: 1 (1982), 13): 'Farming has changed from a productive process that originated most of its own inputs and converted them into outputs, to a process that passes materials and energy through from an external supplier to an external buyer.' Further references to *First the Seed* are given in the text.

a diminished yield when it is saved and replanted. Hybridization thus 'uncouples seed as "seed" from seed as "grain" and thereby facilitates the transformation of seed from a use-value to an exchange value. The farmer choosing to use hybrid varieties must purchase a fresh supply of seed each year', with the result that seed-corn 'now accounts for about half of the $6.4 billion in annual seed sales generated by American companies' (p. 93).

If the use of scientific breeding methods, and especially, in recent years, of recombinant technologies has made seed more amenable to commodification, this process has equally been facilitated by the extension of exclusive property rights in plant germplasm in the two major pieces of US legislation this century—the 1930 *Plant Act* and the 1970 *Plant Variety Protection Act*. Critics of the latter have argued that it 'enhances economic concentration in the seed industry, facilitates noncompetitive pricing, contains the free exchange of germplasm, contributes to genetic erosion and uniformity, and encourages the deemphasis of public breeding' (p. 131). Certainly one of the major effects of the combination of new breeding technologies with extended property rights has been a complete restructuring of the industry. Public research has ceased to be the major source of new plant varieties, and in being relegated to 'basic' and thus non-profitable activities it has ceased to exercise a disciplinary effect on commercial breeders. The traditional seed companies have largely been taken over by transnational petro-chemical and pharmaceutical companies like ICI, BP, Shell, Upjohn, Ciba-Geigy, Monsanto, and Sandoz.[214] Profit in this sector is not based simply on sales of seed, but rather on the symbiosis between crops and chemicals, since most strains are now bred for their compatibility with (and thus their dependence on) chemical fertilizers and pesticides.

But the goal of bringing 'all farmers and all crops into the seed-market every year' (p. 265) has not been restricted to domestic markets—transnationals have global strategies. Jeremy Seabrook sees the new agricultural biotechnologies as in part an exacerbation

---

[214] Christie cites estimates that these companies spent around $10 billion during the 1980s on buying up seed companies or entering into joint ventures with them, and the ten biggest seed companies were reputed to have sales of more than $2.5 billion in 1987. Andrew Christie, 'Patents for Plant Innovation', *EIPR*, 11: 11 (1989), 394; the figures cited are from *The Economist*, 15 Aug. 1987, 56.

of 'the damaging technologies of the Green Revolution—the loss of the soil's productive capacity, the forfeit of genetic diversity, the spread of monocultures and the dependency of farmers on increasingly expensive inputs'.[215] With its capital-intensive reliance on high-bred and high-yielding grain varieties and on massive chemical inputs, the Green Revolution was a product of the same logic of commodification that has so dramatically restructured agriculture in the developed world. At the same time, the relation between First and Third World agricultures is asymmetrical. Apart from Japan, the regions of greatest biotic diversity (the so-called 'Havilov centres') are concentrated in the tropical and subtropical countries of the Third World, and—in Kloppenburg's summary of a complex argument—'the development of the advanced capitalist nations has been predicated on transfers of plant germplasm from the periphery' (p. 49). This is not in itself the problem, however; what is, is that the new global reach of the legal regimes governing plant varieties has made it possible for Third World plant varieties, in some cases the result of millennia of breeding, to become, with minor genetic modifications, the property of financially powerful corporations, which can then exact royalties for their use in their countries of origin.[216] Pat Mooney cites the isolation and patenting of a gene from the West African cowpea which conferred resistance to pests, where the African farmers who developed the peas to have this resistance were left without legal entitlement;[217] a similar appropriation occurred with the Indian neem tree, seeds from which are used by farming communities as an insecticide; Western scientists, drawing on traditional knowledge and local practices, extracted compounds from the tree which are now patented and marketed world-wide.[218]

---

[215] Jeremy Seabrook, 'Biotechnology and Genetic Diversity', *Race and Class*, 34: 3 (1993), 16.

[216] And which can thereby reinforce the competitive advantage of the agriculture of the developed nations. At the beginning of the Uruguay Round of GATT the then US Agriculture Secretary, John Block, said: 'The idea that developing countries should feed themselves is an anachronism from a bygone era. They could better ensure their food security by relying on U.S. agricultural products, which are available, in most cases, at lower cost.' Cited in Kevin Watkins, 'GATT and the Third World: Fixing the Rules', *Race and Class*, 34: 1 (1992), 34.

[217] Mooney, 'John Moore's Body', 8.

[218] Cameron Forbes, 'Intellectual Rights Pose Big Threat to Third World', *Weekend Australian*, 23 Oct. 1993, citing the Malaysian lawyer Gurdial Singh

The asymmetry of such transactions lies in the exchange of a gift against a non-gift:

The germplasm resources of the Third World have historically been considered a free good—the 'common heritage of mankind'. . . . Germplasm ultimately contributing billions of dollars to the economies of the core nations has been appropriated at little cost from—and with no direct remuneration to—the periphery. On the other hand, as the seed industry of the advanced industrial nations has matured, it has reached out for global markets. Plant varieties incorporating genetic material originally obtained from the Third World now appear there not as free goods but as commodities. (15)

What is involved in these transactions is in part the relation between traditional forms of peasant knowledge which have gone into the development of diverse land races over many generations, and 'expert' knowledge which has assumed the right to appropriate its products to itself: the right to rent out resources of knowledge without itself paying rent either on the biological resources or the knowledge-capital it has acquired 'for free'.

The issue is one of subsidy. The genetic uniformity that has resulted from hybridization and crop-standardization has left First World agriculture heavily dependent on importations from the Third World as a source of genetic variation. Yet this flow, which has enriched the corporate producers of hybrid varieties, has been almost entirely free of charge, since the model of knowledge as private intellectual property works to the disadvantage of the 'almost invisible, informal and collective innovation' characteristic of peasant communities.[219] Patent law, which has no hold on 'products of nature', favours innovations deriving from high-tech research rather than innovation by long-term breeding for genetic variety.[220] And as James Boyle points out, the implicit metaphor of

Nijar. Darrell Posey claims that 'the annual world market for medicines derived from medicinal plants discovered from indigenous peoples is US$43 billion. Estimated [annual] sales from three major natural products in the US alone was: digitalis, US$85 million; Resperine, US$42 million; Pilocarpine, US$28 million.' Darrell Posey, 'Intellectual Property Rights and Just Compensation for Indigenous Knowledge', *Anthropology Today*, 6: 4 (Aug. 1990), 15.

[219] Carlos Correa, 'Biological Resources and Intellectual Property Rights', *EIPR* 14: 5 (1992), 154.
[220] Cf. Pat Mooney, 'The Massacre of Apple Lincoln', *New Internationalist* (Oct. 1990), 9.

authorship plays a strongly determinant role in structuring the pattern of distribution: 'The chemical companies' scientists fit the paradigm of authorship. The [Third World] farmers are everything that authors should not be: their contribution comes from a community rather than an individual, tradition rather than an innovation, evolution rather than transformation. Guess who gets the intellectual property right?'[221]

My interest here is of course in the way this asymmetry is organized by the interplay of 'gift' and 'commodity' relations. What emerges from it is not a simple argument for a return to a gift economy, since one way of answering the question of justice for the world's poorer nations would be in terms of the exaction of a fair rent for the use of their resources.[222] Yet what is striking is the recurrent lack of commensuration between a gift relation on one side and a commodity relation on the other. Often there is an open contradiction in the arguments made on behalf of the current market order, with a demand that 'élite' commercial germplasm be a privately owned and exploited commodity, but that 'primitive' germplasm be treated as a public good—a commons open to use by

---

[221] Boyle, 'A Theory of Law and Information', 1529–30.

[222] Strong arguments have been made by indigenous organizations and their supporters for the protection of traditional knowledges by way of intellectual property rights; Tom Greaves surveys some of them in 'Intellectual Property Rights, A Current Survey', in Tom Greaves (ed.), *Intellectual Property Rights for Indigenous Peoples: A Sourcebook* (Oklahoma City: Society for Applied Anthropology, 1994), 3–16. Stephen Brush's essay in the same collection, 'A Non-Market Approach to Protecting Biological Resources', 138–43, argues, by contrast, that 'proponents of intellectual property rights for indigenous knowledge seek to expand capitalism and market relations to control the exchange of biological resources such as seeds. Overturning the historic practice of free exchange and common heritage for biological resources is a heavy cost to pay for benefits that are uncertain' (139). These costs include the possibility that 'collective endeavours might be profoundly unsettled by commoditization, since it introduces division of profits into social relations' (136); the introduction of new inequities, including divisions between the resource-rich and the resource-poor and between 'indigenous' and 'peasant' groups; and the reinforcement of the power of national bureaucracies, which has rarely been exercised in favour of indigenous groups. Brush's preferred solution is the implementation of the 'farmers' rights' which have been developed by the FAO; these are 'group rights assigned to the collective interests of those who have nurtured crop germplasm' (139), rather than monopoly rights or direct compensation. Daniela Soleri and her collaborators note that the FAO established a fund in 1987 for the support of farmers' rights, but that few contributions from industrialized countries and seed companies have been made to it (Daniela Soleri *et al.*, 'Gifts from the Creator: Intellectual Property Rights and Folk Crop Varieties', ibid. 25).

all.[223] Yet the case for an essential difference between the two is difficult to sustain. In particular, it cannot be made through an opposition of elaborated to unelaborated varieties, since the land races are not wild: they are the end result of centuries and sometimes millennia of selection.

Some plant breeders in the developed world have argued that the 'mining' of Third World plant germplasm results in no loss of the resource, since only minute samples are physically taken. But what is taken is never simply the tangible biological matter, but rather the genetic coding it contains. This argument goes to the heart of the question of property in information. Information is in principle infinitely transferable without depletion of the resource, and what can be controlled is no more than access to it. Its 'unique and subversive role' in commodity production comes from just this fact that 'it is not "consumed" or exhausted as it is used, and the more it is shared, the more it grows'.[224] Yet the argument that information is not in itself a scarce resource comes precisely from those groups that have sought to make it so. The commodification of the genetic commons has been effected by means of an investment of work, knowledge, and capital in a public good in order that it may then be treated as a scarce private good. It has been an act of enclosure rather than an opening of the public domain.

THE PUBLIC DOMAIN

The concept of a commons provides no straightforward answers, however, to the question of the equitable distribution of resources. Indeed, in the contemporary political imaginary it tends to work as a figure of the over-use of scarce resources—a figure of waste rather than equity. In a sense this meaning of the term is already prefigured in Locke's equation of the commons with the 'wast', the

---

[223] The contradiction came to a head with a resolution—the 'Undertaking on Plant Genetic Resources'—passed at the 1983 meeting of the Food and Agricultural Organization which attempted to extend the principles of common heritage and free exchange to all categories of germplasm; the developed nations have refused to comply with the resolution. Cf. Kloppenburg, *First the Seed*, 172–3; Correa, 'Biological Resources', 154.

[224] Jim Davis and Michael Stack, 'Knowledge in Production', *Race and Class*, 34: 3 (1992), 3.

area of uncultivated manorial land outside the fields.[225] Locke's notion of the commons is predicated, however, on abundance, and any encroachment on it by means of property rights developed out of productive labour (which are based in turn on the property right in one's own person) is always qualified by the caveat that there must be 'enough, and as good left in common for others'.[226] The contemporary understanding of the commons, by contrast, is largely built upon a Malthusian predicate of scarcity. The key text here is Garrett Hardin's 1968 article 'The Tragedy of the Commons'. A version of the 'prisoner's dilemma' paradox, Hardin's argument can be stated as a fable: given a piece of common pasture, each herdsman who grazes his cattle on it will, 'as a rational being', seek 'to maximize his gain'; thus 'each man is locked into a system that compels him to increase his herd without limits—in a world that is limited. Ruin is the destination toward which all men rush, pursuing his own best interest in a society that believes in the freedom of the commons. Freedom in a commons brings ruin to all.'[227] Hardin then extrapolates from this fable to a number of areas in which the commons has had to be abandoned under pressure: the gathering of food, the unregulated disposal of waste, the unlicensed use of the airwaves, and—inevitably—the uncontrolled expansion of the population.

The model is that of an unrestrained competition between individuals without common interests or the capacity to negotiate shared rights of access. Set up in these terms, however, the model misses the historically interesting questions of the social regulation of the commons (in the specific and plural use of that word): the ways in which scarce resources were allocated by means of complex manorial customs governing rights and limitations on rights.[228] In his discussion of the English enclosure movements of the seventeenth and eighteenth centuries E. P. Thompson points to the derivation of Hardin's argument from the propagandists of parliamentary enclosure; what it overlooks, he says, 'is that the commoners

---

[225] Locke, 'The Second Treatise of Government', 315; as the editor notes, however, this was often a grazing area of some value.
[226] Ibid. 306.
[227] Garrett Hardin, 'The Tragedy of the Commons', *Science*, 162 (1968), 1244.
[228] Cf. Lynda L. Butler, 'The Commons Concept: An Historical Concept with Modern Relevance', *William and Mary Law Review*, 23 (1982), 853–4.

themselves were not without commonsense. Over time and over space the users of the commons have developed a rich variety of institutions and community sanctions which have effected restraints and stints upon use.'[229] The commons were a governed space, and their destruction had to do with the pressures of capitalist agriculture upon coincident use rights, together with the sheer political power of the landholding class, rather than with competition on an equal footing between isolated individuals.

In an essay explicitly directed against Hardin's pessimism, Carole Rose similarly seeks to reclaim the logic of the public good by which the commons was governed. Reading three lines of precedent in US case law for an 'inherently public property' in such things as roadways and waterfront (the land between the low and high tides), she finds a continuance of customary rights—neither state property nor an exclusive private property right—in certain areas of modern law. 'Custom', she writes, 'is the method through which an otherwise unorganized public can order its affairs authoritatively', and the concept thus suggests a way of managing a commons 'differently from exclusive ownership by either individuals or governments. The intriguing aspect of customary rights is that they vest property rights in groups that are indefinite and informal, yet nevertheless capable of self-management'.[230] Although the enclosure of the manorial commons had by the nineteenth century largely eradicated customary claims for uses such as pasturing and woodgathering, those traditional rights nevertheless gave evidence that even in a situation of scarcity a commons need not be a chaos of conflicting property claims. In the vestigial existence of the category of customary rights in doctrine concerning roadways and waterfronts, 'the "unorganized public" begins to seem more like a civilized and self-policing group. Custom, in short, can tame and moderate the dreaded rule of capture that supposedly turns every commons into a waste' (p. 746). It has, moreover, a specifically economic rationale as well in that the expansive and open-ended use it encourages may actually enhance the value of certain kinds of property: increase of scale may produce positive rather than negative externalities. The example Rose gives is the customary

---

[229] Thompson, *Customs in Common*, 107.
[230] Carole Rose, 'The Comedy of the Commons: Custom, Commerce, and Inherently Public Property', *University of Chicago Law Review*, 53: 3 (1986), 742.

right to hold maypole dances on private land, where 'the more persons who participate in a dance, the higher its value to each participant' (p. 767): far from an increase of use having here a tragic outcome, this is the 'comedy of the commons'.

The pleasure of the dance is a kind of information—and this model of the enhancement of the value of a commons through an increase in use works particularly well in the case of shared information, which is not depleted by use. Earlier I used the notion of a 'library model' in order to set up a counterpart to the regime of commodified information. The metaphor is a useful one both logically and historically, although it does not by any means entail a straightforward dichotomy of gift and commodity forms.

A library is a collection of informational materials, traditionally but not necessarily printed matter, which have typically been bought in the market but which, in most public library systems, do not circulate as commodities. But neither do these materials circulate as gifts; they are, rather—to pick up Mauss's term— prestations, 'gifts' that return without conferring any rights of ownership or permanent use. At the same time, loaned library materials create no personal ties of obligation and lack the coerciveness of the forms of prestation that Mauss describes. In this sense, they partake of the impersonality and the abstractness of the commodity form; unlike commodities, however, they have also been largely free of the forms of coercion (the constraints on access and use) that tend to flow from the price mechanism. While the 'library model' thus tends to collapse rather than to dichotomize the categories of gift and commodity, it does nevertheless represent a genuine alternative to the privatization of the commons in information.

Public libraries as we know them came into being as part of that massive expansion of state institutions in mid-nineteenth century Europe and North America that also produced the public schooling system, post offices, railways, and public hospitals, and which set an ethos of public service against the monopolistic tendencies of the uncontrolled market.[231] Their present existence is framed by a tension between that expanded model of the state and its role in the provision of free (that is, subsidized) public services and a more

---

[231] Geoff Mulgan, 'The "Public Service Ethos" and Public Libraries', Comedia Research Working Papers, No. 6 (Brisbane: ICPS, 1993), 2.

restrictive view of the state which seeks to open the provision of information to market forces. To put it crudely, a model centred on the informing of citizens has been replaced, at least in part, by a model of choices made by consumers. The causes of this shift are many and complex, but a major one in the case of the public library system has been a change in the status of information itself, from being 'economically valueless, mainly government produced and largely public, to being value added, commercially sensitive and high cost'.[232] Thus, to take a specific example, the attempt by some governments to ensure that libraries are able to rent out computer software and to make it available for use on the premises has been bitterly fought by the software industry.[233]

Herbert and Anita Schiller identify a 1982 US government report as a turning-point in the progressive weakening of the 'library model'.[234] Announcing an end to the principle of cooperation between the public and private information sectors, the report represents 'the private industry's challenge to the right of the public sector (government, libraries, universities, etc.) to engage in *any* activities the industry regards as its own province'.[235] (Similar positions have been enunciated in recent years in relation to the Internet, seen as 'a "subsidized" threat to commercial service providers'.[236]) The screws are thenceforth on the public library system (perhaps the most genuinely popular of all cultural institutions)[237] not only to implement various local forms of

---

[232] Liz Greenhalgh, 'The Place of the Library', Comedia Research Working Papers No. 2 (Brisbane: ICPS, 1993), 5.

[233] Leslie Tilley, 'Software for the Lending', *The Times*, 25 Jan. 1990.

[234] *Public Sector/Private Sector Interaction in Providing Information Services* (Washington, DC: Government Printing Office, 1982); this document is a report of the National Commission on Libraries and Information Science, and it is discussed in Herbert I. Schiller and Anita R. Schiller, 'Libraries, Public Access to Information, and Commerce', in Mosco and Wasko, *The Political Economy of Information*, 159–60.

[235] Schiller and Schiller, 'Libraries', 160.

[236] Bruce Juddery, 'Net Threatens Private Profits', *Campus Review*, 20–26 Oct. 1994, 1; the article quotes an Australian businessman as saying that while he initially saw the university-owned research network, AARNET, as 'a threat to commercial information providers and communications companies', he now sees its 'potential to provide cost-effective distribution networks for a new range of customers on our information services and for AARNET to be a communications consumer for our network services' (ibid.).

[237] This argument is made in the Comedia Research Paper *Borrowed Time: The Future of Public Libraries in the U.K.* (Brisbane: ICPS, 1993), p. iv.

commercial practice—'charging users for information, relying on private vendors for databases, contracting out functions to private firms, and so on'[238]—but more generally to relinquish its primary role in the provision of information.

The tension between free public provision and the pressures to treat information as a commodity with a price is, I think, an aspect of the aporia that organizes all liberal and neoliberal theories of the market. In order to work efficiently and fairly, any market relies on 'perfect information' (information that is 'free, complete, instantaneous, and universally available');[239] at the same time, as Boyle argues, 'the *actual* market structure of contemporary society depends on information *itself* being a commodity—costly, partial, and deliberately restricted in its availability'.[240] The profit structure of markets directly undermines the basis of the market system itself. If structural breakdown is nevertheless avoided, it is because this tension is displaced into an endlessly deferred promise of the overcoming of information scarcity: on the one hand in the dynamic of production of new information, and, on the other, in an increasing mining of the commons in information through the ongoing privatization of the public domain.

The concept of the public domain has a precise application in modern legal systems, where it forms the cornerstone of copyright law and indeed of intellectual property doctrine generally. Yet the concept is a purely residual one: rather than being itself a set of specific rights, the public domain is that space, that possibility of access, which is left over after all other rights have been defined and distributed.[241] It has had a shadowy legal presence through common-law principles such as fair use, through administrative measures such as freedom-of-information regulations or through statutory protection of free speech, but its lack of positive doctrinal elaboration leaves it vulnerable to erosion. It is a concept which is in many ways in crisis.

Copyright law divides the 'work' between one part which can be held as private property, and another in which no property right

---

[238] Schiller and Schiller, 'Libraries', 160.
[239] Boyle, 'A Theory of Law and Information', 1437.
[240] Ibid.
[241] Cf. David Lange, 'Recognizing the Public Domain', *Law and Contemporary Problems*, 44: 4 (1981).

can inhere. This division developed, towards the end of the eighteenth century and in close proximity to the romantic paradigm of authorship, as a distinction between 'idea' and 'expression', where the 'idea' remains a common good and it is the 'expressive' dimension of texts that is able to give rise to a property claim.[242] This claim is limited in extent; although it is modelled on property rights in land, it gives no right of total exclusion (it merely restricts the making of copies) or of prohibition on use; unlike real property rights, too, the copyright expires after a certain term, and once lost cannot be appropriated (as an unowned good) by later comers.[243]

The dichotomy of idea and expression (a logically problematic distinction in so far as these are relational rather than fixed and identifiable categories)[244] corresponds, historically and theoretically, to the attempt to reconcile two contradictory interests: on the one hand the provision of a financial incentive to authors and, through them, an incentive for the production of new knowledge; on the other, the protection of public access to knowledge, including, quite crucially, protection of the raw materials on which later authors will draw.[245] It is this aspect that Litman stresses in her defence of the concept of public domain (and her argument that it provides a stronger doctrinal foundation for copyright law than the concept of 'originality'): the public domain is 'a device that permits the rest of the system to work by leaving the raw material of authorship available for authors to use',[246] whereas a rigorously

[242] Mark Rose traces a genealogy from Young's *Conjectures on Original Composition* through to Fichte's enunciation of the dichotomy of ideas and expressions (Mark Rose, *Authors and Owners: The Invention of Copyright* (Cambridge, Mass.: Harvard University Press, 1993), chs. 7 and 8); cf. also Martha Woodmansee, 'The Genius and the Copyright: Economic and Legal Conditions of the Emergence of the "Author" ', *Eighteenth-Century Studies*, 17: 4 (1984), 425–48.

[243] Wendy Gordon, 'An Inquiry into the Merits of Copyright: The Challenges of Consistency, Consent, and Encouragement Theory', *Stanford Law Review*, 41 (July 1989), 1375.

[244] Cf. John Frow, 'Repetition and Limitation', 14–16.

[245] Cf. Jaszi, 'Toward a Theory of Copyright', 464: 'Many particular doctrinal constructs . . . are simply attempts to mediate the basic contradiction between public benefit and private reward. Their instability is guaranteed because the two goals are irreconcilable.' The relation between 'first authors' and 'later authors' is discussed at some length in *Sony Corporation of America* v. *Universal City Studios, Inc.* and in my commentary on the case ('Timeshift: Technologies of Reproduction and Intellectual Property', *Economy and Society*, 23: 3 (1994), 291–304), as well as in Landes and Posner, 'An Economic Analysis of Copyright'.

[246] Jessica Litman, 'The Public Domain', *Emory Law Journal*, 39: 4 (1990), 968.

enforced notion of originality would quickly make plagiarists of all authors.

At the same time, Litman is concerned by the fact that the public domain is defined negatively and without any precise conceptual rationale. US copyright law denies protection to 'ideas, methods, systems, facts, utilitarian objects, titles, themes, plots, *scènes à faire*, words, short phrases and idioms, literary characters, style, or works of the federal government', and this 'hodgepodge of unprotectible matter' has been assembled without overarching justification.[247] Most of the doctrine defining the extent of the public domain characterizes these elements of textuality as *exceptions*, and most of the definitive cases have involved a defensive reaction on the part of the courts against far-ranging claims based on the supposition that authorial 'originality' carries with it inherent property rights.

The encroachment of property claims on to previously reserved areas of the public domain has been facilitated by the incoherence and negativity of the concept, and by the more general weakening over the past two decades of the notion of a common weal. Copyright protection now extends to 'an extraordinary variety of products that saturate our society'.[248] A later, more pessimistic article of Litman's worries that 'copyright law may be developing into the engine that drives an information policy sharply restrictive of the public's access to ideas and information',[249] as 'a tide of strong protectionism in influential commentary has encouraged the courts to view copyright as a broad property right'.[250] The landmark *Feist* case,[251] which adhered to the letter of the law in denying copyright protection to facts, caused an uproar precisely because it went so strongly against this trend.

Litman lists four areas in which the trend is evident. The first is the protection of facts by the back-door method of granting protection of the 'form' in which factual material is 'expressed'. The second is the piecemeal repeal of the first-sale doctrine, which has traditionally granted the purchaser a broad range of rights of

---

[247] Jessica Litman, 'The Public Domain', *Emory Law Journal*, 39:4 (1990), 992–3.
[248] Ibid. 995.
[249] Jessica Litman, 'Copyright and Information Policy', *Law and Contemporary Problems*, 55: 2 (1992), 187.   [250] Ibid. 188.
[251] *Feist Publications* v. *Rural Telephone Service Company*, 111 S.Ct. 1282 (1991).

use, including commercial use, of a copyrighted work. The third is the extension of protection to government-developed databases and software, as a prelude to their commercialization. And the fourth is the conflict between the fair use exemption (defending a range of rights of public access) and moral rights principles, especially as the latter have been used to prohibit use of unpublished works (Jaszi refers to moral rights doctrine in these cases as representing 'a charter for private censorship')[252] and to give, for complex technical reasons, almost unqualified protection to computer software. Litman concludes that the principle of authorial rights inherent in the idea/expression dichotomy, and the principle of a reserved commons in information embodied in the fair use exemption, are in fundamental contradiction, and that the public interests represented in each are in the process of being eroded by default.[253] Contemporary information policy, under pressure from industry groups and considerations of short-term political expediency, sets the conditions for an increasing enclosure of the commons in information under the rubric of copyright.[254]

All uses of the concept of the commons implicate in one way or another the concept of the public sphere (which in turn cuts across the gift/commodity opposition in interesting ways). Richard Sennett has documented the shift in the word 'public' from a generalized conception of the common good, *res publica*, to its modern sense, fully developed by the eighteenth century, of a special region of sociability passed outside the life of the family and intimate friends.[255] Both uses of the word conceive of the public domain as a space of association between strangers; the difference between

---

[252] Jaszi, 'Toward a Theory of Copyright', 497.

[253] To speak of public interests being 'represented' in copyright doctrine is, however, to beg some broad questions. In a fascinating account of the legislative process which led to the 1976 Act Litman details the systematic *exclusion* of representatives of 'the public' from the negotiations between the 'interested parties'—and the complete and quite deliberate abdication of Congress from this role. Jessica Litman, 'Copyright Legislation and Technological Change', *Oregon Law Review*, 68: 2 (1989), esp. 312–15.

[254] Marlin Smith makes a similar case about the erosion of the fair-use principle in recent cases involving parody of copyrighted work, where judges have privileged the test of economic harm over public rights of access to creative work. Marlin H. Smith, 'Note: The Limits of Copyright: Property, Parody, and the Public Domain', *Duke Law Journal*, 42 (1993), 1233–72.

[255] Richard Sennett, *The Fall of Public Man* (London: Faber, 1977), 16–17.

them lies in the intensity with which this sphere comes to be opposed to that of privacy, and the increasingly negative connotations that it acquires.

Western liberalism from Locke onwards is built on the logic of the opposition of a public sphere of citizenship and formal equality to the private sphere of civil society in which real differences of social status and power are operative. The dilemma that follows from this separation is that liberal theory 'must exalt the virtues of egalitarianism, of each person's voice counting equally and, at the same time, confine that egalitarianism to the public sphere'[256]—which means, by and large, to the state. The enclosure of the commons conforms to this logic of division between an egalitarian public sphere and a private and hierarchical sphere of individual power and interest.

Yet there is neither a logical nor a historical necessity for the public sphere to be equated with the state, or to figure as the opposite of civil society. In Habermas's account of the formation of *Öffentlichkeit* (the bourgeois public sphere), this category is coextensive with civil society (*bürgerliche Gesellschaft*) and embraces the *public* virtues of commerce. In the same way, the Memphis court ruling on Elvis Presley's fame defined the public domain in terms of free access to the market;[257] and Carole Rose argues that one reason why roadways and waterways were so tenaciously held in US law to be inherently public spaces is the persistent association of commerce and trade with the sorts of 'interactive' uses that actually increase the value of the commons.[258] The concept of civil society, which includes the market as a crucial component, has historically been understood both as a realm of 'private' rather than state activity (indeed as a protection against the state's incursions on personal freedom) *and* as a 'public' space of the free and open flow of information and trade. It is in this sense that it has historically been possible to equate cultural works both with a notion of the public good and with an intensification of cultural commodification;[259] and it is for

---

[256] Boyle, 'A Theory of Law and Information', 1434.
[257] *Memphis Development Foundation* v. *Factors, Etc., Inc.*, 616 F. 2d 956 (6th Cir.), *cert. denied*, 449 US 953 (1980), at 960.
[258] Rose, 'The Comedy of the Commons', 770.
[259] Cf. Lury, *Cultural Rights*, 107.

this reason that the category of the market occupies so ambivalent a position in relation to the distinction between the public and the private (it is a 'public' fact in relation to the family, but a 'private' fact *vis-à-vis* the state—although 'free' markets are of course always the product of state regulation and permission).[260]

All of this makes much more complicated Titmuss's attempt to define the state as the domain of an altruism that is in some sense gift-like. Yet the practical consequence of the way we divide the public from the private is precisely the same one that Titmuss was concerned with: the question of the extent to which social goods should be administered and allocated by public or by private means. Should it be the case—to use an example of James Boyle's— that access to medicine is a private matter dependent on my ability to pay, while the right to a lawyer is given in the (US) Constitution, and I get one whether I have the money or not? Should the opposite be the case, as it is for me in Australia? By what rationale should 'private' branches of law like torts make restitution for loss of earnings on the basis of very unequal levels of income (the wealthier I am, the more I get), while 'public' branches of law such as criminal law reject differential treatment out of hand?[261] Beyond these very general questions of principle lie a host of policy issues to do with equity, access, and efficiency, which are organized around precisely the same question of the socially contested division between 'public' and 'private' mechanisms for the administration and distribution of social goods. The anti-governmental rhetoric and the wave of privatizations of state institutions in most countries of the advanced capitalist and former-communist world over the last two decades have been the most visible outcome of these questions in the area of policy.

The 'positive' concept of the public domain that I have projected here—a reserved domain of inalienable personal and social goods and rights—is intended as a way around some of the conceptual impasses that flow from the notion of a transcendental and autonomous sphere of personhood which is prior to and essentially untouched by property relations and which exists in a 'private' rather than a 'public' space. Public domain rights are those rights

---

[260] Cf. S. Moller-Olkin, 'Gender, The Public and the Private', in David Held (ed.), *Political Theory Today* (Cambridge: Polity Press, 1991), 68–9.

[261] Boyle, 'A Theory of Law and Information', 1435.

that, rather than deriving from personhood, precede and enable it. They are rights to the raw materials of human life: language, ideas, an inherited culture, a 'common heritage' of environmental resources, bodily integrity, civil entitlement. These are not 'natural' rights, located in an originary contract or a state of nature, but customary social rights, developed and recognized as a provisional end state of the struggle for civilized conditions of life (and of course, whatever their recognition, always contested). Like all rights, they represent a balance between conflicting demands, and they carry with them a corresponding set of obligations to the common good.

Yet there are, inevitably, disadvantages and limitations attaching to such a conception of the public domain. One is that the category of *citizen*—the form of personhood most closely associated with it and currently fashionable in a number of post-leftist discourses—is in many ways a nostalgic concept, predicated on the recovery of a lost but once flourishing public sphere. The ring of officialese to the word, too (which makes it virtually equivalent to *good* citizen), covers over the fact that many of the conditions for full and active citizenship[262] are not present (not, at least, in the traditional ways) in mass-mediated societies. Margaret Morse writes eloquently of the difficulty of strengthening genuinely 'public' values in a world structured by mobile privatization and an 'attenuated fiction effect in everyday life' which slowly and pervasively undermines the 'sense of different levels of reality and of incommensurable difference between them'. The difficulty is precisely that of appealing to traditional notions of civic responsibility and the public space of the agora in the context of 'a built environment that is already evidence of dream-work in the service of particular kinds of commerce, communication, and exchange' and of a representational apparatus in which 'the public and private worlds outside are distanced ontologically under several other layers of representa-

---

[262] And even in its classical Greek and Roman forms, of course, citizenship is a category of inclusion which defines a counter-category of those excluded from civic rights. Cf. Peter Brown, *Power and Persuasion in Late Antiquity: Towards a Christian Empire* (Madison: University of Wisconsin Press, 1992); and, on the primacy of political definitions of Greek social relations, Ian Morris, 'Gift and Commodity in Archaic Greece', *Man* (NS), 21 (1986), 4–5.

tion'.[263] Imagined communities may command allegiance, but not imaginary ones.

A further limitation to the category of citizen lies in its silent genderedness. The designation of public space as masculine and of private (intimate or domestic) space as feminine has historically accompanied (as at once cause and effect) the restriction, whether by formal or informal mechanisms, of full citizenship to men.[264] This restriction is bound up in multiple ways with the association of women with the gift: on the one hand their status as themselves the gift within systems of matrimonial exchange, on the other the encoding of nurture and the gift of life as the woman's gift, a power within her gift, and thus at once beneficent and dangerous, the opposite of the enlightened abstraction of the commodity form. This opposition entails a ready-made rationale for the exclusion of women from the public sphere, and then in turn for the shaping of its rules to reflect this exclusion. 'What should be remembered', writes Rosalyn Diprose, 'is that the giving which is consistently forgotten by the law is woman's and the gift which the law consistently remembers and recognizes is man's.'[265]

More generally, a concept of the public good grounded in the category of the inalienable gift cannot be applied in any direct way to the social. The state is not a 'gift' domain because its forms of sociability do not involve the magical and dangerous ties of personal obligation; obligation at this level is an abstract matter.[266]

---

[263] Margaret Morse, 'An Ontology of Everyday Distraction: The Freeway, the Mall, the Television', in Patricia Mellencamp (ed.), *Logics of Television: Essays in Cultural Criticism* (Bloomington: Indiana University Press, 1990), 213.

[264] Cf. the discussion in Rosemary Pringle, *Secretaries Talk: Sexuality, Power and Work* (Sydney: Allen and Unwin, 1988), 227–30; Jean Bethke Elshtain, *Public Man, Private Woman: Women in Social and Political Thought* (Princeton, NJ: Princeton University Press, 1981); Moira Gatens, *Feminism and Philosophy: Perspectives on Difference and Equality* (Cambridge: Polity Press, 1991).

[265] Rosalyn Diprose, 'The Gift, Sexed Body Property and the Law', in Pheng Cheah, David Fraser, and Judith Grbich (eds.), *Thinking through the Body of the Law* (Sydney: Allen and Unwin, 1996), 133.

[266] Thomas Murray cites Michael Ignatieff's argument that 'The bureaucratized transfer of income among strangers has freed each of us from the enslavement of gift relations.' But the 'we' who are freed are the net contributors to the tax system, not the stigmatized recipients of welfare. Michael Ignatieff, *The Needs of Strangers: An Essay on Privacy, Solidarity, and the Politics of Being Human* (New York: Viking, 1984), cited in Thomas H. Murray, 'Gifts of the Body and the Needs of Strangers', *Hastings Center Report* (Apr. 1987), 30.

Nor of course is the market a domain of gift, both because it is built on the price mechanism and because, like the state, its workings are complex, impersonal, and abstract. In any strict sense, the concept of gift is irrelevant to the structural understanding of modern societies, with the exception of the micro-level of everyday life. There is no state sphere in traditional gift economies, and neither, therefore, is there a civil society (the distinction is simply not meaningful).

Yet that exception is crucial. Everyday talk is the model of all free exchange of information, and the realm of the everyday is the place where, through the constant transformation of commodity relations into gift relations, it becomes difficult to hold the two terms in their categorical purity. It is a realm permeated by the archaic patterns of gift-obligation—the dangerous, fluid, subtle generosities that bind members into crystallized orders of relation, in all dimensions of human life, from which they cannot easily be released. These patterns of obligation are, at the same time, in tension with the contractual rationality of the commodity, which produces quite different forms of the everyday. It may produce greater equalities as well as greater inequalities; it may enhance the sharing of wealth, or it may reduce it. It can be seen as a liberation from the 'antiquated and dangerous gift economy',[267] or as a destruction of human sharing; but it is never neutral in relation to the economy of gift. Gift and commodity exchange are mutually overdetermined: they merge with each other, absorb or transform each other, or clash in open contradiction. The energies, the social intensities they set in play structure and continuously transform the moral ground of everyday life—our fundamental capacity to be, to have, and to know.

[267] Mauss, *The Gift*, 52.

4
Toute la mémoire du monde:
Repetition and Forgetting

Reality favours symmetries and slight anachronisms.[1]

One way of describing the imaginary object named postmodernity is to say that it is the time of a fall from memory into history, or from history into amnesia. Fredric Jameson, for example, writes that 'what was once, in the historical novel as Lukács defines it, the organic genealogy of the bourgeois collective project ... has meanwhile itself become a vast collection of images, a multitudinous photographic simulacrum'. Our historical or post-historical situation is thus one 'in which we are condemned to seek History by way of our own pop images and simulacra of that history, which itself remains forever out of reach'.[2]

In this topos the state of loss is repeatedly linked to the lack of historical depth informing the world constructed by the mass electronic media, the world of commodity culture: at best the historical past can figure there as pastiche or as costume drama. For Jameson it is clear that the mediation of the 'pop image' does a violence to that 'organic genealogy' of class society in a way that the historical novel—more transparent to social relations, formally time-bound—does not. Writing more cautiously, but with a similar cluster of categories, Margaret Morse argues that on television the past is not so much 'remembered via narrative as it is rerun or embedded as archival images within contemporary, discursive presentation'.[3] Newsreel footage, the sound-bite, but also costume

---

[1] Jorge Luis Borges, 'The South', *Fictions* (London: John Calder, 1965), 154.
[2] Fredric Jameson, *Postmodernism, or, The Cultural Logic of Late Capitalism* (Durham, NC: Duke University Press, 1991), 18, 25.
[3] Margaret Morse, 'An Ontology of Everyday Distraction: The Freeway, the Mall, and Television', in Patricia Mellencamp (ed.), *Logics of Television: Essays in Cultural Criticism* (Bloomington: Indiana University Press, 1990), 202.

re-enactment and archive-based documentary all remove the past from its lived context to replay it within an electronic space of multiple possible worlds without ontological hierarchy or fixed relation.

One lineage for this temporal dichotomy between authentic historical memory and a debased and mediated relation to the past can perhaps be traced in the Durkheimian concept of collective memory. In Maurice Halbwachs's book of that name the key explanatory structure is the causal linkage between memory and the social group. As a direct corollary, written history is described in terms of its lack of organic connection to the group's lived memory; it comes into being only with the death of the social memory, and its claim to universality is in this sense purely abstract:

Every collective memory requires the support of a group delimited in space and time. The totality of past events can be put together in a single record only by separating them from the memory of the groups who preserved them and by severing the bonds that held them close to the psychological life of the social milieus where they occurred.[4]

Yosef Yerushalmi similarly stresses the discontinuity within Jewish culture between collective memory and history understood as a 'truly new kind of recollection' which 'challenges even those memories that have survived intact'.[5] And an organicist critique of written history is often made from within the socialist and feminist traditions of oral history, where the political guarantee of community-based memory-work is given by its relation to the 'originating constituency' that oral history serves.[6]

The most comprehensive version of this schema that I know is to be found in Pierre Nora's introduction to his seven-volume collection of materials on 'sites of memory', *Lieux de mémoire*

---

[4] Maurice Halbwachs, *The Collective Memory*, trans. Francis J. Ditter, Jr., and Vida Yazdi Ditter (New York: Harper and Row, 1980), 84.

[5] Yosef Hayim Yerushalmi, *Zakhor: Jewish History and Jewish Memory* (Seattle: University of Washington Press, 1982), 94–5.

[6] Ken Worpole, 'The Ghostly Pavement: The Political Implications of Local Working-Class History', in Samuel Raphael (ed.), *People's History and Socialist Theory* (London: Routledge and Kegan Paul, 1981), 24; the concept of memory-work is taken from Frigga Haug *et al.*, *Female Sexualization: A Collective Work of Memory*, trans. Erica Carter (London: Verso, 1987).

(1984–). 'We speak so much of memory because there is so little of it left', he begins.[7] Our world is characterized by an acceleration of history and thus by the slippage of the present into a past where it disappears from consciousness. This condition of a modernity without memory is defined by opposition to its absolute other, peasant culture, 'that quintessential repository of collective memory' (ibid.). Whereas traditional agrarian societies 'had long assured the transmission and conservation of collectively remembered values', handing them on in an unbroken continuity, we, by contrast, experience a 'mode of historical perception, which, with the help of the media, has substituted for a memory entwined in the intimacy of a collective heritage the ephemeral film of current events' (ibid.).

Thus we can speak of two kinds of memory. The effect of the acceleration of historical time is to force us to distinguish between

real memory—social and unviolated, exemplified in but also retained as the secret of so-called primitive or archaic societies—and history, which is how our hopelessly forgetful modern societies, propelled by change, organize the past. On the one hand, we find an integrated, dictatorial memory— unself-conscious, commanding, all-powerful, spontaneously actualizing, a memory without a past that ceaselessly reinvents tradition, linking the history of its ancestors to the undifferentiated time of heroes, origins, and myth—and on the other hand, our memory, nothing more in fact than sifted and sorted historical traces. (p. 8)

The disjunction, in modernity, between these two forms of memory simultaneously breaks the equation of memory with history.

Four features characterize, for Nora, the realm of memory:

1. It is a realm of immediacy and plenitude, and it is therefore different in principle from the mediating structures of writing. Within it, 'each gesture, down to the most everyday, would be experienced as the ritual repetition of a timeless practice in a primordial identification of act and meaning. With the appearance of the trace, of mediation, of distance we are not in the realm of true memory but of history' (ibid.).

2. It is a realm of presence: while history is 'the reconstruction, always problematic and incomplete, of what is no longer', memory

---

[7] Pierre Nora, 'Between Memory and History: *Les Lieux de Mémoire*', trans. Marc Roudebush, *Representations*, 26 (Spring 1989), 7; page references to further citations will be given in the text.

'is a perpetually actual phenomenon, a bond tying us to the eternal present' (ibid.).

3. It is organic and holistic, selecting and accommodating only those facts that suit it and that can be adapted to its needs; history, by contrast, works through analysis and criticism. As a corollary, memory 'installs remembrance in the sacred', whereas history is resolutely secular, and as such destructive: its 'goal and ambition is not to exalt but to annihilate what has in reality taken place' (p. 9).

4. It is plural and concrete, reflecting the diversity of actual social groups. History, on the other hand, is abstract and unitary, belonging to everyone and no one. 'Memory takes root in the concrete, in spaces, gestures, images and objects; history binds itself strictly to temporal continuities, to progressions and to relations between things. Memory is absolute, while history can only conceive the relative' (ibid.).

At this point in his argument, however, Nora transposes this series of distinctions between memory and history into an opposition internal to history itself. Again, this is a quasi-temporal dichotomy: history passes in the twentieth century from its status as a 'tradition of memory' serving the *national* community to the quite different task of interrogating tradition, and thereby serving as 'the self-knowledge of society' (pp. 10–11). In thus 'disclaiming its national identity', history at the same time 'abandoned its claim to bearing coherent meaning and consequently lost its pedagogical authority to transmit values' (p. 11). Its criticality, its reflexivity, its professionalization, in a word its *self-consciousness* marked its decline into a mere social science, while memory, severed from its public representation, becomes a purely private phenomenon.

It is at this interstitial moment, when 'an immense and intimate fund of memory disappears' (p. 12), that an alternative mode of memorialization begins to be established. It is centred on the *lieux de mémoire*—'museums, archives, cemeteries, festivals, anniversaries, treaties, depositions, monuments, sanctuaries, fraternal orders': in short, 'anything pertaining to the cult of the dead, anything relating to the patrimony, anything administering the presence of the past within the present' (pp. 12, 19)—which then begin to take on the function of devotional institutions, marking 'the rituals of a society without ritual' and embodying a form of commemoration that now has little place in the sceptical and secular discourse of professional history. These are substitutes, it should be understood, for the immediacy of an authentically collective memory: 'no longer quite life, not yet death, like shells on the shore when the sea of living memory has receded' (ibid.), the 'sites of memory', *lieux* rather than *milieux*, are the degraded aftermath of a time when memory needed no such mediation.

It is because the *lieux de mémoire* are governed by this inner duality that Nora now repeats his distinction between two modes of memory: on the one hand, 'true memory, which has taken refuge in gestures and habits, in skills passed down by unspoken traditions, in the body's inherent self-knowledge, in unstudied reflexes and ingrained memories'; on the other, 'memory transformed by its passage through history, which is nearly the opposite: voluntary and deliberate, experienced as a duty, no longer spontaneous; psychological, individual, and subjective; but never social, collective, or all-encompassing' (p. 13). What is at issue in this transformation is, above all, the role of the material mediation of memory. The latter, degraded form is 'archival' in the sense that it 'relies entirely on the materiality of the trace, the immediacy of the recording, the visibility of the image. What began as writing ends as high fidelity and tape recording'. No longer experienced 'from the inside', public memory now exists only through 'its exterior scaffolding and outward signs' (ibid.). And as archive, it covers the earth with the empty traces of a lost plenitude.

I have summarized Nora's argument at some length because it corresponds very precisely and very richly to that form of sociological thinking about modernity that Georg Stauth and Bryan Turner call 'nostalgic'. By this they mean the structuring of sociological thought by a series of contradictions between a realm of authenticity and fullness of being, and the actually existing 'forms of human association'[8]—a contradiction often projected on to a quasi-historical axis as that between modern and traditional societies.

The importance of memory within this paradigm lies not just in the privileged access it gives to this lost world, but in the immediacy with which it evokes it into presence. I mean 'immediacy' here in all of the following senses: memory is thought of as partaking of a

---

[8] Bryan S. Turner, 'A Note on Nostalgia', *Theory, Culture and Society*, 4: 1 (1987), 151; cf. Georg Stauth and Bryan Turner, 'Nostalgia, Postmodernism and the Critique of Mass Culture', *Theory, Culture and Society*, 5: 2–3 (1988), 509–26.

spirituality independent of the materiality of the sign; it is unstructured by social technologies of learning or recall; it is incapable of reflexivity (it cannot take itself as an object), and its mode of apprehension is thus rooted in the 'inherent self-knowledge' and the 'unstudied reflexes' of the body; it is organically related to its community and partakes of the continuity of tradition—a historical time without rupture or conflict, and without any but the most naturalized modes of transmission, above all that of the story, which 'embeds [an event] in the life of the storyteller in order to pass it on as experience to those listening';[9] this is to say—using Walter Benjamin's categories—that it is a function of deeply embedded experience (*Erfahrung*) rather than of more or less conscious perception (*Erlebnis*);[10] it is thus—following Benjamin's overlay of Freud's account of memory traces on to Proust's distinction—essentially *mémoire involontaire* rather than *mémoire volontaire*;[11] finally, this memory is *auratic*: it is no accident that much of the vocabulary Nora uses to describe it—that of piety, of ritual, of the relation to the ancestors—is religious, and evokes a continuity of passage between the living and the dead.[12]

This whole manner of thinking of collective memory and of its relation to autobiographical memory is surely no longer tenable. It is not a useful tool for conceptualizing the social organization of memory; it provides no mechanism for identifying its 'technological'

---

[9] Walter Benjamin, 'On Some Motifs in Baudelaire', *Illuminations*, trans. Harry Zohn (New York: Schocken, 1969), 159; cf. Benjamin, 'The Storyteller', ibid. 98, on the splitting of epic *Erinnerung* into the storyteller's *Gedächtnis* and novelistic *Eingedenken*.

[10] Benjamin, 'On Some Motifs in Baudelaire', ibid. 163; my terms are very loose renditions of the concepts by which Benjamin distinguishes between two modes of experience. The English translation of these pages, it should be noted, is somewhat inconsistent.

[11] Benjamin, ibid. 159–62; Benjamin adapts Freud's thesis in *Beyond the Pleasure Principle* that 'becoming conscious and leaving behind a memory trace (*Gedächtnisspur*) are processes incompatible with each other within one and the same system'.

[12] Jonathan Boyarin suggests that 'it is all too easy to suspect that the slogan and the multivolume project on "places of memory" work to reinvent "la France profonde" as a defense against the onslaught within France of Others making claims for their own collective rights and identities'. Jonathan Boyarin, 'Space, Time, and the Politics of Memory', in Jonathan Boyarin (ed.), *Remapping Memory: The Politics of Timespace* (Minneapolis: University of Minnesota Press, 1994), 19.

underpinnings; and it cannot account for the materiality of signs and of the representational forms by which memory is structured.

The question of an alternative conception of memory that I want to formulate is this: how can memory be thought as *tekhnè*, as mediation, as writing?

I find a clear statement of the theoretical issues involved in this formulation in Mary Carruthers's work on medieval memory systems (to which I shall return shortly in discussing archival models of memory). Writing against Walter Ong's argument that the invention of print both furthered and depended upon 'a profound reorientation within the human spirit which made it possible to think of all the possessions of the mind, that is, of knowledge and of expression, in terms more committed to space than those of earlier times',[13] and his belief that this movement is closely paralleled by the spatially diagrammed taxonomies of Agricola's and Ramus's place-logics, she refuses the qualitative distinctions he draws between pre- and post-Gutenberg, aural and visual cultures, cultures of the image and of the word, oral cultures of memory and literate cultures of spatialized information storage.[14] The salient fact she points to in medieval thought is that it draws no distinction in kind 'between writing on the memory and writing on some other surface'.[15] Rather than being an external support or implement in relation to memory, the activity of writing is a kind of memorization itself, or at least is intimately bound up with it. Thus, on the one hand, 'the symbolic representations that we call writing are no more than cues or triggers for the memorial "representations" ... upon which human cognition is based'; and, on the other, 'anything that encodes information in order to stimulate the

---

[13] Walter J. Ong, SJ, *Ramus: Method, and the Decay of Dialogue* (Cambridge, Mass.: Harvard University Press, 1958), 308.

[14] This is not, of course, to deny the profound changes in the organization of memory brought about by the advent of print; on this, cf. Lucien Febvre and Henri-Jean Martin, *The Coming of the Book: The Impact of Printing, 1450–1800*, trans. David Gerard (London: Verso, 1984); Elizabeth L. Eisenstein, *The Printing Press as an Agent of Change: Communications and Cultural Transformations in Early-Modern Europe*, 2 vols. (Cambridge: Cambridge University Press, 1979); and Paul Hirst and Penelope Woolley, *Social Relations and Human Attributes* (London: Tavistock, 1982), 37–8.

[15] Mary Carruthers, *The Book of Memory: A Study of Memory in Medieval Culture*, Cambridge Studies in Medieval Literature 10 (Cambridge: Cambridge University Press, 1990), 30; further references will be given in the text.

memory to store or retrieve information is "writing", whether it be alphabet, hieroglyph, ideogram, American Indian picture writing, or Inca knot-writing' (pp. 31–2). From the very beginning medieval educators 'had as visual and spatial an idea of *locus* as any Ramist had, which they inherited continuously from antiquity, and indeed that concern for the lay-out of memory governed much in medieval education designed to aid the mind in forming and maintaining heuristic formats that are both spatial and visualizable' (p. 32); medieval mnemotechnic systems *are* a form of writing, and—this is my extrapolation from this argument—it is only by working out the implications of 'writing' (in these senses) for memory that we can avoid the nostalgic essentialism that affirms the reality of an origin by proclaiming its loss.

Let me propose two figures through which to imagine the order and ordering of memory.

The first is a series of versions of the archive (the information storage system), which I summarize in the image of the Bibliothèque Nationale as Resnais films it in his 1957 feature *Toute la mémoire du monde* (a movie that exists for me only as I remember it across a gap of more than twenty years). The camera pans endlessly across the stacks, the storage rooms, the out-of-the-way depositories filled with an infinity of useless and forgotten print; beneath a reedy and distorted voice-over (saying what?) this waste of human memory unfolds its delirium of repetition, its 'leagues of insensate cacophony'.[16] . . . And in a dream embedded within Borges's story 'The Secret Miracle', the librarian of the Clementine library says: ' "God is in one of the letters of one of the pages of one of the 400,000 volumes of the Clementine. My fathers and the fathers of my fathers have sought after that letter. I've gone blind looking for it".'[17]

The logic of the archive is a logic of the inscription (or deposit) and the storage of information in systematically articulated space, and of ready retrieval on the basis of that articulation. The moments of inscription/deposit and of storage correspond to the two major metaphors through which European culture has conceptualized memory over the last two and a half millennia: the metaphor of the surface of inscription, traditionally a wax writing-tablet (*tabula rasa*); and that of the *thesaurus* (the storehouse, and

---

[16] Borges, 'The Library of Babel', *Fictions*, 74.   [17] Ibid. 134.

its metonyms: the aviary, the storage bin, and the box or cluster of boxes). Both metaphors suppose a direct relation between space and mental categories (Henry Roediger, mapping the history of these metaphors, writes that in each of them 'memories or memory traces are considered to be discrete objects stored in particular locations in the mind space');[18] and both suppose the physical reality of memory traces. Thus for Aristotle the metaphor of storage is a quite literal one: sense perceptions are coded as mental images (*phantasmata*) which are physically inscribed—like the imprint of a signet ring on wax—in distinct sites (*topoi*) in the brain.[19] There is an indexical linkage between the vanished past and its persistent material vestiges in the present. This model, as Mary Carruthers argues, continues to hold sway right through the Middle Ages. The metaphor of writing on wax tablets (a metaphor that captures both the stability and the instability of inscriptions)

shows that the ancients and their mediaeval heirs thought that each 'bit' of knowledge was remembered in a particular place in the memory, which it occupied as a letter occupies space on a writing surface. The words *topos*, *sedes*, and *locus*, used in writings on logic and rhetoric as well as on mnemonics, refer fundamentally to physical locations in the brain, which are made accessible by means of an ordering system that functions somewhat like a cross between the routing systems used by programs to store, retrieve, merge, and distinguish the information in a computer's 'memory', and postal addresses or library shelf-marks.[20]

---

[18] Henry L. Roediger, 'Memory Metaphors in Cognitive Psychology', *Memory and Cognition*, 8: 3 (1980), 232.

[19] Things are more complicated: to paraphrase very briefly a very difficult argument, the central problem posed for Aristotle by memory is the question of how being which has disappeared can persist in memory. The first stage of his solution to this enigma is to posit two figures of representation: the mental image (*phantasma*) inscribed 'in the soul', and the physical trace (*typos* or *graphé*) which supports it but to which it is not reducible, inscribed 'in that part of the body which contains the soul'. Since the question still remains whether what we remember is the past thing or event itself or the image that we have of it, Aristotle then proposes a second stage of his solution, which rests upon the intrinsic ambivalence of the *phantasma*: figured now as a portrait or pictorial representation (*zógraphéma*), it can be read either as an object of contemplation in its own right (*zoion*) or as a likeness or copy (*eikón*) of the thing remembered. For commentary, cf. Richard Sorabji, *Aristotle on Memory* (Providence, RI: Brown University Press, 1972); David Farrell Krell, *Of Memory, Reminiscence, and Writing: On the Verge* (Bloomington: Indiana University Press, 1990), esp. 13–23; Michael V. Wedin, *Mind and Imagination in Aristotle* (New Haven: Yale University Press, 1988).

[20] Carruthers, *The Book of Memory*, 29.

I think it is fair to say that a version of this conception is still the predominant metaphor in contemporary cognitive psychology, although it is now based more explicitly in the model of the electronic storage and random-access retrieval of coded information.[21] I identify the following problems with the model: first, its realism (its assumption that the past is accessible only because of its physical persistence as trace); second, its intentionalism (its assumption that meanings taken up are the repetition of meanings laid down); third, its inability to account for forgetting other than as a fault or as decay or as a random failure of access.[22] It is a model of memory to which forgetting is merely incidental.

Borges's story 'Funes the Memorious' tells of the remembered encounter between the narrator and a young man who, after an accident that leaves him crippled, wakens into a present which is almost intolerable in its brightness and in the vividness and detail of his memory:

He remembered the shapes of the clouds in the south at dawn on the 30th of April of 1882, and he could compare them in his recollection with the marbled grain in the design of a leather-bound book which he had seen only once, and with the lines in the spray which an oar raised in the Rio Negro on the eve of the battle of the Quebracho.[23]

His memory corresponds fully, in other words, to the infinity of his lived perceptions. But what he knows, therefore, and all he can know, is particulars. Even that impossible idiom imagined by Locke in which each individual object has its own name would be too general for Funes, since he 'not only remembered every leaf on every tree of every wood, but even every one of the times he had perceived or imagined it' (p. 103). He 'could continuously make out the tranquil advances of corruption, of caries, of fatigue. He noted the progress of death, of moisture. He was the solitary and lucid spectator of a multiform world which was instantaneously and

---

[21] The classic critique of the notion of recall as 'the re-excitement in some way of fixed and changeless "traces"' was made by Frederick Bartlett, whose experiments led him to think instead in terms of a process of schematic construction organized by a complex play of interests. Frederick C. Bartlett, *Remembering: A Study in Experimental and Social Psychology* (1932; repr. Cambridge: Cambridge University Press, 1950).

[22] Cf. C. W. Kaha, 'Memory as Conversation', *Communication*, 11: 2 (1989), 116–19.

[23] Borges, 'Funes the Memorious', *Fictions*, 102; further citations will be given in the text.

almost intolerably exact' (p. 104). But he is almost incapable of simple generalities, and—like Luria's mnemonist, who could remember at a glance extended passages of text, but, unable to sift the significant from the insignificant, had immense difficulty understanding them[24]—Funes, the narrator suspects, 'was not very capable of thought. To think is to forget a difference, to generalize, to abstract. In the overly replete world of Funes there was nothing but details, almost contiguous details' (ibid.).

'Funes'—'a long metaphor of insomnia', Borges called it[25]—is thus also a kind of allegory of the metaphor of memory as storage. But it is from Borges's stories, from the *structure* of these stories, that I take my second figure of memory.

This second figure is far less easy to cast in a visual form. It is predicated on the non-existence of the past, with the consequence that memory, rather than being the repetition of the physical traces of the past, is a construction of it under conditions and constraints determined by the present. My figure, then, is that of the logic of textuality:[26] a logic of an autonomous narrative order and necessity which takes the form of structural symmetry and the reversibility of time.[27] In Borges's stories this logic is manifested in a number of recurrent motifs: that of the *symmetry* (the reversibility) between duellists, between hero and traitor, between detective and criminal, and the spatial symmetries and mirror-images that organize the stories' *mise-en-scène*; the motif of the *labyrinth* (spatial, textual, or conceptual—the concept of infinity, or that of the *mise-en-abyme*), a structure which is at once fully determined and yet, because of its complexity, necessarily indeterminate; and the motif of *destiny*, the 'future as irrevocable as the past',[28] the textual time which is always-already written but also, because it is endlessly repeated, always reversible. Such a logic of textuality is of course in no way restricted to Borges's stories. In one way or another it is common to

[24] A. R. Luria, *The Mind of a Mnemonist* (Harmondsworth: Penguin, 1975).

[25] Jorge Luis Borges, 'Prologue' to Part Two, *Fictions*, 95.

[26] I should distinguish my use of the concept of textuality from that of Fentress and Wickham, for whom a 'textual' model of memory is a model of storage and retrieval; they contrast it with iconic memory-maps, which they take to be characteristic of pre-literate cultures. James Fentress and Chris Wickham, *Social Memory* (Oxford: Basil Blackwell, 1992), ch. 1.

[27] I equate textuality with narrative here only to the extent that any system of inscription is governed by a temporal order which can be read both sequentially and counter-sequentially.

[28] Borges, 'The Garden of Forking Paths', *Fictions*, 84.

all texts, both 'fictional' and 'non-fictional': Borges's stories merely have the merit of making it explicit, sometimes as an object of parody or critique.

Reversibility is here opposed to *retrieval*. The time of textuality is not the linear, before-and-after, cause-and-effect time embedded in the logic of the archive but the time of a continuous analeptic and proleptic shaping. Its structure is that of any dynamic but closed system, where all moments of the system are co-present, and the end is given at the same time as the beginning. In such a model the past is a function of the system: rather than having a meaning and a truth determined once and for all by its status as event, its meaning and its truth are constituted retroactively and repeatedly; if time is reversible then alternative stories are always possible. Data are not stored in already constituted places but are arranged and rearranged at every point in time. Forgetting is thus an integral principle of this model, since the activity of compulsive interpretation that organizes it involves at once selection and rejection. Like a well-censored dream, and subject perhaps to similar mechanisms, memory has the orderliness and the teleological drive of narrative. Its relation to the past is not that of truth but of desire.

Let me now extend the implications of this thesis by one more step, by extrapolating it from autobiographical memory to public memory. The relation between these two forms of 'memory' is of course problematic, based as it is on an analogy between an individual and a collective subject. Nevertheless, if we are to avoid the dichotomization of memory and history, of the individual and the group, and of the subjective and the objective—all of those overlapping pairs that both affirm these two forms of the subject and keep them apart—then it seems unavoidable to suppose that public memory, at all levels including the most 'official' ones, is governed by the logic of *Nachträglichkeit*. Žižek makes the argument in this way:

As soon as we enter the symbolic order, the past is always present in the form of historical tradition and the meaning of these traces is not given; it changes continually with the transformations of the signifier's network. Every historical rupture, every advent of a new master-signifier, changes retroactively the meaning of all tradition, restructures the narration of the past, makes it readable in another, new way.[29]

[29] Slavoj Žižek, *The Sublime Object of Ideology* (London: Verso, 1989), 56.

The question of historical truth, which I don't in any way want to discount as a crucial and legitimate issue for both autobiographical memory and the collectively organized apparatus of history, emerges as a question *within*, not outside or in opposition to, the phantasmatic economy of (personal or collective) desire.

To speak of memory as *tekhnè*, to deny that it has an unmediated relation to experience, is to say that the logic of textuality by which memory is structured has technological and institutional conditions of existence. By 'technological' I mean on the one hand storage-and-retrieval devices and sites such as books, calendars, computers, shrines, or museums; and on the other hand particular practices of recall—techniques of learning acquired in school, structured confession or reminiscence, the writing of autobiography or history, the giving of evidence in court, the telling of stories related to an artefact or a photograph, and even such apparently immediate forms of recollection as the epiphanic flash of involuntary memory or the obsessive insistence of the symptom.

Let me illustrate the enabling conditions of the 'textual' logic of memory by reference to two topics of particular intensity within current debates: the controversies over recovered memories of childhood sexual abuse; and the rapidly growing literature on remembrance of the Holocaust. Each of these areas of debate is organized around questions of truth and falsity (and around a corresponding political ordering); each, I argue, can be productively displaced, at least in part, into an examination of the apparatuses of memoration.

In the course of the 1980s, in the United States and one or two other countries, but not elsewhere in the world, there occurred a well-documented explosion of memories, recalled in therapy often after many years of oblivion, of childhood sexual assault.[30] These

[30] I have drawn in particular on: Ian Hacking, *Rewriting the Soul: Multiple Personality and the Sciences of Memory* (Princeton: Princeton University Press, 1995); Elizabeth Loftus and Katherine Ketcham, *The Myth of Repressed Memory* (New York: St Martins Press, 1994); Richard Ofshe and Ethan Watter, *Making Monsters: False Memories, Psychotherapy, and Sexual Hysteria* (New York: Scribners, 1994); Mark Pendergrast, *Victims of Memory: Incest Accusations and Shattered Lives* (Hinesburg, Vermont: Upper Access, Inc., 1995); Hollida Wakefield and Ralph Underwager, *Return of the Furies: An Investigation into Recovered Memory Therapy* (Chicago: Open Court, 1994); and Michael Yapko, *Suggestions of Abuse: True and False Memories of Childhood Sexual Trauma* (New York: Simon and Schuster, 1994).

memories were validated by other sources of information about the prevalence of sexual abuse of children, and by a feminist politics of consciousness-raising about incest.[31] Within this context, memories of abuse were largely accepted—by therapists, by courts, and by most of the people affected—as historical fact. The social consequences were widespread: families were torn apart, and a number of criminal charges were brought. Many American states amended their statutes of limitation to refer to the time of remembrance of abuse rather than the time of the event.

The typical pattern is that of a woman entering therapy to try to come to terms with either a diffuse unhappiness or more specific disorders or addictions, and then recovering a buried memory of her childhood which contradicts her 'normal' memory and reveals it to have been a screen. Recovery restores a sense of meaning to a life without order:

The more I worked on the abuse, the more I remembered. First I remembered my brother, and then my grandfather. About six months after that I remembered my father. And then about a year later, I remembered my mother. I remembered the 'easiest' first and the 'hardest' last. Even though it was traumatic for me to realize that everyone in my family abused me, there was something reassuring about it. For a long time I'd felt worse than the initial memories should have made me feel, so remembering the rest of the abuse was actually one of the most grounding things to happen. My life suddenly made sense.[32]

Increasingly, however, the status of these recovered memories became problematic: in part because of a challenge by psychologists to the working methods of many therapists, committed to believing their clients rather than to scepticism about the literal truth of recovered memories;[33] but in part too because of a pattern in which recovered memories more and more often came to refer to abuse

---

[31] e.g. Judith Lewis Herman, *Trauma and Recovery* (New York: Basic Books, 1992).
[32] Ellen Bass and Laura Davis, *The Courage to Heal: A Guide for Women Survivors of Child Sexual Abuse*, 2nd edn. (1988; repr. New York: HarperCollins, 1992), 80.
[33] Cf. Loftus and Ketcham, *The Myth of Repressed Memory*, *passim*; Carol Tavris, 'Beware the Incest-Survivor Machine', *New York Times Book Review*, 3 Jan. 1993, 1, 16–17. Judith Herman writes in *Trauma and Recovery* (177, 182) that 'it is not enough for the therapist to be "neutral" or "nonjudgmental" '. He or she must 'affirm a position of moral solidarity with the survivor'.

within satanic cults, to the ritual mutilation and murder of children, to cannibalism and the breeding of babies for sacrifice, to abduction by aliens, and to past-life abuse. These memories look like fantasies, and they seem often to have been fostered in an atmosphere of group or community hysteria.

Take, almost at random, the case of James Rud, who was charged in 1983, in Jordan, Minnesota, with sexually abusing two children in his care. Rud in turn implicated eighteen other members of the community, and the circle widened until some sixty children in the town made accusations 'against their parents, neighbours, a long-deceased resident of the town, and certain mysterious strangers'; the accusations included participation in 'two inter-connected sex rings also engaging in Satanic rites and the ritual mutilation and murder of children'.[34] The children typically made these accusations only after extended questioning by police and counsellors over several months; and the charges that were laid (of unnoticed multiple murders in a town with a population of 2,700, for example) were inherently incredible.

The case perhaps most often cited in the literature is that of Paul Ingram, who between November 1988 and April 1989 produced an astonishing series of self-incriminating 'memories' in what seems to have been a prolonged process of self-hypnosis, sustained by his own eagerness to respond appropriately to his interrogators and by a bidding war in which his two daughters made ever more bizarre accusations which Ingram then came to 'recognize' as true.[35] The importance of the Ingram case lies in the fact that his memories were the confirmatory memories of a supposed abuser rather than the originating memories of a victim; and they led police to expect hard evidence (hitherto entirely lacking) of the operations of a

[34] Denis J. Brion, 'The Hidden Persistence of Witchcraft', *Law and Critique*, 4: 2 (1993), 228–9.
[35] Extended accounts of the Ingram case can be found in Lawrence Wright, 'Remembering Satan—Parts I and II', *The New Yorker*, 17 and 24 May 1993, 60–81 and 54–76 (substantially reprinted in Wright, *Remembering Satan* (New York: Alfred Knopf, 1994)); Richard Ofshe, 'Inadvertent Hypnosis During Interrogation: False Confession Due to Dissociative State; Mis-identified Multiple Personality and the Satanic Cult Hypothesis', *International Journal of Clinical and Experimental Hypnosis*, 40: 3 (1992), 125–56; Ofshe and Watter, *Making Monsters*; Loftus and Ketcham, *The Myth of Repressed Memory*; and Lenore Terr, *Unchained Memories: True Stories of Traumatic Memories, Lost and Found* (New York: Basic Books, 1994).

satanic cult, this one (in Olympia, Washington) allegedly having sacrificed something on the order of 250 babies. What is so striking about the case, however, is the 'breathtaking readiness on the part of its major players to form lasting "memories" on very slight provocation':[36] not only Ingram and his daughters but a son, his wife, and two of his colleagues implicated in the supposed satanic cult and in ongoing abuse of the daughters either at some time remembered major and almost certainly non-existent crimes, or at least suspected their own complicity even if not remembering it; and Ingram 'remembered', and came firmly to believe in, a pseudomemory suggested to him by a sociologist working as a consultant for the prosecution.[37]

I shall talk shortly about some of the folkloric sources of these memories. For the moment, however, I want to draw attention to the problem of the belief in the literal truth of recovered memories. Lawrence Wright cites some relevant indications of how widespread this belief is:

A 1991 survey of members of the American Psychological Association found that 30% of the respondents had treated at least one client who claimed to have suffered from satanic-ritual abuse, and 93% of those who completed a second survey believed their clients' claims to be true. Another poll addressed the opinions of social workers in California. Nearly half of those interviewed accepted the idea that satanic-ritual abuse involved a national conspiracy of multi-generational abusers and baby-killers and that many of these people were prominent in their communities and appeared to live completely exemplary lives. A majority of those polled believed that victims of such abuse were likely to have repressed the memories of it and that hypnosis increased the likelihood of accurately recalling what had happened.[38]

---

[36] Frederick Crews, 'The Revenge of the Repressed', New York Review of Books, 17 Nov. 1994, 59.

[37] Ofshe, 'Inadvertent Hypnosis During Interrogation', 147.

[38] Lawrence Wright, 'Remembering Satan—Part I', 79. Wright doesn't give his sources, but the first of these polls may be the 1991 survey described in 'Profile of Ritualistic and Religion-related Abuse Allegations Reported to Clinical Psychologists in the United States', by E. L. Bottoms, P. R. Schaver, and G. S. Goodman, a paper presented at the 1993 annual meeting of the American Psychological Association in San Francisco. Michael Yapko (Suggestions of Abuse, 58) administered two questionnaires to professional therapists in 1992 and found similarly high rates of (mistaken) belief in the power of hypnosis to enhance accurate recall, and an astonishing 28% of respondents who thought that hypnosis 'can be used to recover accurate memories of past lives'.

The repressed memory of satanic abuse may stand here as a figure of the wider linkage of psychic disturbance to a *directly* causative and repressed trauma. Despite the efforts of Frederick Crews and others to link the recovered-memory movement to a discredited Freud, that movement's storage-and-retrieval model of memory corresponds rather to Freud's earliest accounts of memory, predating the fundamental break that grounds psychic reality in fantasy and desire rather than in an immediate correspondence to extra-psychic reality.[39] Ian Hacking accordingly imagines a 'reflect-ive clinician' who wonders:

Why have we been so literalist, so mechanical, and imagined that an illness produced by trauma is produced at the time of the trauma, in early childhood? Why can't we at least discuss the idea that the experience of the original event, apparently kept in memory, is not what causes distress and dysfunction; why can't we ask whether the problem comes from the possibly repressed memory itself, much later in life, and the way in which the mind has worked on and recomposed that memory?[40]

To say that memory is of the order of representation rather than a reflex of real events, and that its temporality is that of the reworking of earlier material rather than that of a causality working as a line of force from the past to the present, is not to deny the reality of traumatic experience, including childhood sexual assault, and its working through in present suffering; but it is to say that this experience is always reconstructed rather than recalled; that reconstruction takes place within the specific and formative circumstances of the present; and that causes are always attributed rather than known. Our attention should thus turn to those practices and structures within which recovered memories are produced.

Amongst the major supports of the recovered-memory movement is a large nonprofessional literature of self-help manuals, of which the most influential has been *The Courage to Heal* by Ellen Bass

---

[39] Ned Lukacher's *Primal Scenes: Literature, Philosophy, Psychoanalysis* (Ithaca, NY: Cornell University Press, 1986), performs a particularly astute reading of the implications of this break for the Freudian theory of memory, which continued to oscillate ambivalently between notions of the 'primal scene' as an ontologically undecidable event and as recollection.

[40] Hacking, *Rewriting the Soul*, 137.

and Laura Davis.[41] To the extent that these manuals are addressed to survivors of incest who remember the abuse, they are often doubtless valuable sources of help to women and men whose lives are filled with great pain. But the primary addressee of many of the manuals is a reader who has no memories of childhood sexual abuse;[42] for this reader the work performed by the manuals is that of producing a recognition through the conduct of spiritual exercises directed to the problem of disbelief. Two major epistemological tools underly this process. The first is the principle that to disbelieve is to be in a state of 'denial', and so complicit with the systematic concealment that characterizes abusive families.[43] The second, inverse principle is a 'positive' conversion of disbelief into proof of its opposite: 'The existence of profound disbelief is an indication that memories are real',[44] and the absence of memories of abuse doesn't mean none took place:

Often the knowledge that you were abused starts with a tiny feeling, an intuition. It's important to trust that inner voice and work from there. Assume your feelings are valid. So far, no one we've talked to thought she might have been abused, and then later discovered that she hadn't

---

[41] Others include Carol Poston and Karen Lison, *Reclaiming Our Lives: Hope for Adult Survivors of Incest* (New York: Bantam, 1990); Steven Farmer, *Adult Children of Abusive Parents* (New York: Ballantine, 1989); E. Sue Blume, *Secret Survivors: Uncovering Incest and its Aftereffects in Women* (New York: Ballantine, 1990); Renee Fredrickson, *Repressed Memories: A Journey to Recovery from Sexual Abuse* (New York: Simon and Schuster, 1992); John Bradshaw, *Homecoming* (New York: Bantam, 1990).

[42] Ofshe and Watters set up somewhat more forcefully the opposition between the two kinds of address: 'Unlike treatments intended to aid patients suffering from the shock of rape or grappling with lifelong memories of childhood sexual abuse, the axiom of recovered memory therapy is that the patient will have no knowledge of the sexual trauma before treatment. Patients can begin the therapy with no memories of abuse and finish with the belief that they suffered endless horrible molestations or rapes—often by their parents. Recovered memory therapists expect that patients will not only be amnesiac for the trauma in their past but that they will also disbelieve the therapist's initial suggestion that they suffered sexual assaults as children.' Ofshe and Watters, *Making Monsters*, 1.

[43] Fredrickson, *Repressed Memories*, 224: 'If you have a strong denial system, you can work on dismantling it with a skilled therapist . . . Once you recognize you are in denial, talk it out in therapy and with friends who are supportive of your recovery. Avoid talking to people who are in their own denial and therefore enable yours.'

[44] Ibid. 171.

been. The progression always goes the other way, from suspicion to confirmation.[45]

Belief itself is a matter of exercise, of practice, of imagining oneself into the truth. Thus Fredrickson recommends that the reader should 'Let yourself know what the most hopeless or shameful problem in your life is. Try saying to yourself three or four times a day for one week, "I believe this problem is about my repressed memories of abuse". After a week, write down or talk over with a friend how you see the problem now. Speculate on how it may relate to how you were abused.'[46]

Various exercises follow. One is the use of a checklist of symptoms which will 'highlight common warning signals of repressed memories' and may provide 'clues to your abuse'.[47] Typically, the symptoms are of the greatest generality, covering such things as sexual difficulties, sleep problems, phobias, eating disturbances, poor body image, compulsive behaviours, and emotional pain. They are perhaps all reducible to a condition of low self-esteem (with the range of consequences that flow from it), and, as Carol Tavris writes of the checklists scattered throughout *The Courage to Heal*, 'The same list could be used to identify oneself as someone who loves too much, someone who suffers from self-defeating personality disorder, or a mere human being in the late twentieth century. . . . Nobody doesn't fit it.'[48]

The next layer of exercises specifically addresses the generation of memories. Memory work is the practice of a discipline of

---

[45] Bass and Davis, *The Courage to Heal*, 22. Following intense criticism, a grudging qualification was added to this passage in the third edition (1994); the last two sentences became: 'It is rare that someone thinks she was sexually abused and then later discovers she wasn't. The progression usually goes the other way, from suspicion to confirmation. If you genuinely think you were abused and your life shows the symptoms, there's a strong likelihood that you were. If you're not sure, keep an open mind. Be patient with yourself. Over time, you'll become more clear, (p. 26). This edition also includes a postscript, 'Honoring the Truth: A Response to the Backlash', which describes all criticism of recovered-memory therapy as a 'backlash against survivors of child sexual abuse' (p. 477). (The concept of a 'backlash' is further elaborated in the special issue, 'Backlash against Psycho-therapy', of the *Journal of Psychohistory*, 22: 3, Winter 1995.)

[46] Fredrickson, *Repressed Memories*, 32.

[47] Ibid. 47. Sue Blume's 'Incest Survivors' Aftereffects Checklist' is similarly designed to act as 'a diagnostic device for suggesting sexual victimization when none is remembered'. Blume, *Secret Survivors*, n.p.

[48] Carol Tavris, 'Beware the Incest-Survivor Machine', 1.

rememoration, and it encompasses a range of techniques: guided visualization; hypnosis, specifically age regression; the interpretation of memories apparently stored in the body and recovered through massage or other forms of bodily manipulation; the analysis of dreams; the invocation of an 'inner child' to reveal in dreams or meditation the secrets of abuse; art therapy, usually employing an 'automatic' technique for producing images; free-associative writing; the keeping of a journal imagining or describing childhood abuse; rage and grief therapy in which repressed emotions are acted out; and group therapy.[49] Paul Ingram, a self-taught master, developed an elaborate meditation technique which he called 'praying on' and which involved four stages: first, he would pray in seclusion; then he would relax his body and reduce external stimuli; next, he would empty his mind of all thoughts, producing a sensation that he described as a 'white fog'; and finally he would dwell upon the images suggested to him by his interrogators, elaborating them into detailed and vivid narratives.[50]

This state of self-induced trance has the cumulative effect, not just of generating memories but of reinforcing belief in them.[51] The culmination of the spiritual exercises is the elaboration of a counter-hermeneutic in which the revealed past is played off against the previously accepted framework of memory. Remembering is thus 'an ongoing process of discovery' which 'involves going back and excavating the early years of your life—piecing together and reinterpreting things you already know, starting to connect feelings with images you've always had, experiencing unfamiliar body sensations.'[52] It is here that the role of survivor groups, the importance of which is emphasized in all the manuals, becomes clear: they are anti-communities to the family of origin, and—similar in this to many small religious communities—their task is to sustain a counter-reality.

[49] Fredrickson, *Repressed Memories*, 97 ff; Loftus and Ketcham, *The Myth of Repressed Memory*, 141; Bass and Davis, *The Courage to Heal, passim*.
[50] Ofshe, 'Inadvertent Hypnosis During Interrogation', 145; Wright, 'Remembering Satan—Part II', 65.
[51] Cf. Pendergrast, *Victims of Memory*, 90: 'With repeated visualization, or the verbal repetition of the stories, they become more real. Memory, then, is largely a product of rehearsal.'
[52] Laura Davis, *The Courage to Heal Workbook: For Women and Men Survivors of Child Sexual Abuse* (New York: Harper and Row, 1990), 205.

Recovered memory is a counter-memory, elaborated within a powerful therapeutic apparatus formed by the transferential relation to the therapist, the reality created and sustained by support groups, the framework of expectations that memory of childhood sexual assault is a goal to be achieved, and the systematic deployment of a set of spiritual exercises designed to produce such memories and to inculcate belief in them. Beyond this, however, this counter-reality is built upon and absorbs a broad folk-cultural reality which includes such familiar entities as satanic cults, past lives, and contact with alien civilizations. It is difficult to overestimate the influence of such books as *Satan's Underground* and *Michelle Remembers*,[53] or of such celebrity 'survivors' as Roseanne Barr Arnold. Satanism, past lives, and recovered memory are the daily stuff of tabloid journalism and of television talk shows. The day before Paul Ingram's daughter Julie wrote a letter accusing him and the circle of friends with whom he played poker of sexually abusing her—a charge which culminated in elaborate accounts of satanic worship and ritual murder—he and his family sat down and watched together a prime-time Geraldo Rivera special entitled *Devil Worship: Exposing Satan's Underground*, 'one of the most widely watched documentaries in television history'.[54] Recovered memories are recalled as much from the culture as from the archives of individual memory.

My second example, that of remembrance of the Holocaust, is similarly organized around an epistemological problematic, the question of the truth not of individual remembrances but of the historical record as an integral component of collective memory.[55] Here, however, the force of the example is completely the reverse: whereas in the case of recovered memories the weight of the evidence seems to me to lie on the side of the critics (although this is not in any way to impugn the reality of childhood sexual abuse), in

---

[53] Lauren Stratford, *Satan's Underground* (Eugene, Ore.: Harvest House, 1988); M. Smith and L. Pazder, *Michelle Remembers* (New York: Congdon and Lattes, 1980).

[54] Wright, 'Remembering Satan—Part I', 80. On satanic cults, cf. Jeffrey S. Victor, *Satanic Panic: The Creation of a Contemporary Legend* (Chicago: Open Court, 1993).

[55] My thinking about the theme of Holocaust remembrance is indebted to Mireille Juchau's 'Forgetful Memory: The Holocaust, History and Representation', *UTS Review*, 2: 2 (1996), 68–89.

the case of the Holocaust the weight of the evidence is entirely on the side of the received account (although both explanations and political uses of this narrative will of course diverge). The question of the historical record is given particular sharpness by the ethical obligation to bear true witness that is laid upon the historian by the moral enormity of the Final Solution, from which the implication is then often drawn 'that there are limits to representation which should not be but can easily be transgressed'.[56] But how are these limits to be determined? And why should they not be read simply as calls to order against alternative modes of representation and alternative protocols of validity, as in the frequent strictures directed against certain genres, such as pastoral and comedy, deemed inappropriate for representing the Holocaust (strictures which would have the effect of disqualifying books like Gunter Grass's *The Tin Drum* or Art Spiegelman's *Maus*)?[57] The dangers are neatly illustrated in the dance performed by Pierre Vidal-Naquet's argument with the revisionist historian Robert Faurisson. On the one hand Vidal-Naquet elegantly and scrupulously marshals the detailed documentary evidence needed to refute Faurisson's claims (a procedure which, *within the limits of the discursive formation of history*, succeeds in establishing something like an absolute truth—or at least so high a degree of probability as to be irrefutable), and yet on the other hand asserts that he is not *debating* (or indeed addressing) the revisionists but merely restating an incontestable truth.[58] It is only a step from this claim to Berel Lang's insistence (one which is still, by and large, the common sense of the profession) that, while historical discourse may make use of narrative and figuration, it is 'not essentially dependent on those means', because historical discourse is predicated on 'the possibility of representation that stands in direct relation to its object—in

[56] Saul Friedlander, 'Introduction', *Probing the Limits of Representation: Nazism and the 'Final Solution'* (Cambridge, Mass.: Harvard University Press, 1992), 3.
[57] Cf. Hayden White, 'Historical Emplotment and the Problem of Truth', *Probing the Limits of Representation*, 41. Often, indeed, since Adorno, these strictures are extended to aesthetic representation *tout court*.
[58] Pierre Vidal-Naquet, *Assassins of Memory: Essays on the Denial of the Holocaust*, trans. Jeffrey Mehlman (New York: Columbia University Press, 1992), p. xxiv.

effect, if not in principle, immediate and unaltered'.[59] The
Holocaust as a historical topos lends itself to this repression of the
action of the means of representation to the extent that it functions
as an index of the absolutely real.[60]

In addition to questions of the truth of representation, however,
the historiography of the Holocaust generates another, related set
of questions concerning representability itself. 'If you could lick my
heart', says Antek Zuckerman in Lanzmann's Shoah, 'it would
poison you':[61] the horror of the Holocaust lies beyond the
possibility of experience and expression.[62] Entailed in the notion of
the ontologically absolute status of the Holocaust is the notion that
it is unspeakable, incomparable, incommensurable with all other
historical experience.[63] This may be a question of the unbearable
pain of remembering, or of the impossibility of integrating so
immense an evil into a coherent narrative pattern. Geoffrey
Hartman writes that when survivors find a language in which to
speak, 'two phrases stand out in their testimony: "I was there" and

[59] Berel Lang, Art and Idea in the Nazi Genocide (Chicago: University of
Chicago Press, 1990), 156; quoted in Hayden White, 'Historical Emplotment and
the Problem of Truth', Probing the Limits of Representation, 47.

[60] To speak as I did above of the non-existence of the past is a very different thing
in relation to the writing of history than in relation to individual memory, because of
the rigorous protocols for the construction and validation of evidence that obtain in
the former. My argument is, however, that the principle holds good in both cases:
what is available to us is never the past but only representations of it, including
memories and documentary and material traces to which we impute a meaningful
connection to the past. As David Lowenthal writes, 'to name or to think of things
past seems to imply their existence, but they do not exist; we have only present
evidence for past circumstances' (David Lowenthal, The Past is a Foreign Country
(Cambridge: Cambridge University Press, 1985), 187). The real of history
corresponds precisely to the fabula of narrative theory: a projection from the present
of narration which functions as though it were its ground. I should add, however—
since these qualifications still, unfortunately, need to be made—that to speak of an
effect of reality within representation is not to deny or even to be agnostic about the
reality of the past that is referred to; it is to say only that it is inaccessible as a ground
other than through the specific reconstructive procedures of a discourse.

[61] Quoted in Saul Friedlander, 'Trauma, Memory, and Transference', in
Geoffrey H. Hartman (ed.), Holocaust Remembrance: The Shapes of Memory
(Cambridge, Mass.: Basil Blackwell, 1994), 256.

[62] The non-redemptive structure of remembrance is most powerfully argued for
in Lawrence Langer's Holocaust Testimonies: The Ruins of Memory (New Haven:
Yale University Press, 1991).

[63] This idea is expressed with great clarity in Harold Kaplan's Conscience and
Memory: Meditations in a Museum of the Holocaust (Chicago: University of
Chicago Press, 1994).

"I could not believe what my eyes had seen".[64] Shoshana Felman similarly describes the Holocaust as *invisible*: it 'unfolds as the unprecedented, inconceivable advent of *an event without a witness*, an event which consists in planning the literal erasure of its witnesses',[65] and—like the 'unconscious testimony' explored by psychoanalysis—it is made manifest in 'a truth that is, essentially, *not available* to its own speaker'.[66] For Levinas it is the immemorial, for Lyotard the unrepresentable, for Blanchot the catastrophe that erases the possibility of knowledge.

Yet in one banal but important sense none of this is true. There is a huge volume of testimonies bearing witness to the Holocaust (and Annette Wievorka suggests interestingly that the function of these testimonies is no longer to bear witness to the past but rather to assure the transmission of a collective memory to the future).[67] It is an overwhelming fact of our daily lives, constantly referred to both in scholarly and political cultures and in the mass media. There are Holocaust museums and memorials in most countries of the Western world, and it is a curricular object (if only through the reading of Anne Frank's diaries) in many education systems. Auschwitz, as Jack Kugelmass points out, 'is Poland's major tourist attraction'.[68] At a more sinister level, the fact of the Holocaust is the object of public political challenge by some anti-Zionist regimes (notably Iran) in the Arab world and by right-wing anti-Semitic politicians and intellectuals in Russia, France, Germany, the United States, and elsewhere.

Andreas Huyssen thus seems to me to be entirely correct in arguing that 'the exclusive insistence on the true representation of the Holocaust in its uniqueness, unspeakability, and incomparability may no longer be adequate in light of its multiple representations and its functioning as a ubiquitous trope in Western culture.

[64] Geoffrey H. Hartman, 'The Book of the Destruction', in *Probing the Limits of Representation*, 326.

[65] Shoshana Felman, 'Film as Witness: Claude Lanzmann's *Shoah*', in Hartman, *Holocaust Remembrance*, 96.

[66] Shoshana Felman, 'Education and Crisis, Or the Vicissitudes of Teaching', in Shoshana Felman and Dori Laub (eds.), *Testimony: Crises of Witnessing in Literature, Psychoanalysis, and History* (New York: Routledge, 1992), 15.

[67] Annette Wievorka, 'On Testimony', in Hartman, *Holocaust Remembrance*, 24.

[68] Jack Kugelmass, 'Why We Go to Poland: Holocaust Tourism as Secular Ritual', in James E. Young (ed.), *The Art of Memory: Holocaust Memorials in History* (Munich: Prestel-Verlag, 1994), 178.

Popular representations and historical comparisons are ineradicably part of a Holocaust memory which has become fractured and sedimented.'[69] In the same way, James Young argues that rather than criticizing Holocaust monuments for their reification and dehistoricization of the past, it may be more important to come to terms with their culturally variable working in the present as an apparatus of collective memory:[70] the *lieux de mémoire* are not a poor substitute for real *milieux de mémoire* but are continuous with earlier modes of commemoration.

The question thus becomes a more distanced one: something like Huyssen's 'What of the institutions and sites that organize our social memory in the age of television?'[71] And one of the things to note about the 'postmodern' organization of remembrance of the Holocaust is that it is in no way given by the continuity of experience or tradition. To the contrary: it has been the object of an intensive struggle over the forms of its representation and its collective acceptance. Nowhere, of course, has this been more evident than in post-war Germany (although in Israel, too, public acceptance and uses of the Shoah have had a complex history including, at times, strong elements of rejection).[72] Michael Geyer and Miriam Hansen speak of the difficult and contested process of creation in Germany of a collective memory, over the two decades since the mid-1970s, through a set of 'collective rituals and representations of remembering' which crucially includes the film *Hitler: A Career* in 1977, television broadcasts of the American

[69] Andreas Huyssen, 'Monument and Memory in a Postmodern Age', in Young, *The Art of Memory*, 13.

[70] James E. Young, 'The Art of Memory: Holocaust Museums in History', in Young, *The Art of Memory*, 20.

[71] Andreas Huyssen, 'Monument and Memory in the Postmodern Age', in Young *The Art of Memory*, 11.

[72] The Holocaust has of course been an instrument of legitimation of the Israeli state and the centre of a 'civil religion' (Friedlander); but Yael Zerubavel documents a 'strong tendency to deny the Holocaust' among Israelis from 1940 to the early 1960s. In those years the central focus of recollection was on the heroic narrative of the Warsaw uprising; after the 1973 Yom Kippur War, the 'tragic plot' which unites the Shoah with the Masada story became a new paradigm for binding the past to the present, and more recently a counter-narrative has been used to question the relation of Israel to the Palestinians. Saul Friedlander (in collaboration with Adam Seligman), 'Memory of the *Shoah* in Israel: Symbols, Rituals, and Ideological Polarization', in Young, *The Art of Memory*, 149; Yael Zerubavel, *Recovered Roots: Collective Memory and the Making of Israeli National Tradition* (Chicago: University of Chicago Press, 1995), 192–212.

series *Holocaust* in 1979, and the German series *Heimat* in 1984, 'each production moving Germans very deeply—and each leading them in very different directions'.[73] The Holocaust has been constructed and reconstructed as an object of public memory within the play of present interests, fears, and fascinations. If there is still a touch of condescension in Geyer and Hansen's opposition of the high culture of the intellectuals to these 'spectacular' and 'commodified' forms of cultural mass production (an opposition that perhaps fails to take seriously the way in which the academic Holocaust industry itself conforms to these industrial patterns), they are nevertheless aware that it is in *these* forms, whatever their shortcomings, that the possibility of a collective act of remembrance has been given actuality.[74]

For Western cultures, script and print have been of paramount importance in shaping memory and thought; in our world it is almost certainly the mass electronic media that play the crucial role in channelling and actively forming collective memory. The Popular Memory Group, in an important essay on oral history, cite the example of Peggy Wood's story in *Dutiful Daughters*,[75] where an act of recall within the family is triggered by a television programme about the end of the Second World War. This 'precipitating role of the public media entering right into domestic relations'[76] is, they argue, one of the central and constitutive features found in all work on popular memory, and one of the most important ways in which speakers are able to make connections between public events and private experience. But even at the more 'private' level of intensely personal affect the media play a strong organizing role: think for example of those many radio stations

---

[73] Michael Geyer and Miriam Hansen, 'German-Jewish Memory and National Consciousness', in Hartman (ed.), *Holocaust Remembrance*, 177.

[74] Cf. Miriam Hansen, '*Schindler's List* Is Not *Shoah*: The Second Commandment, Popular Modernism, and Public Memory', *Critical Inquiry*, 22: 2 (1996), 310: 'In a significant way, even before the passing of the last survivors, the remembrance of the Shoah, to the extent that it was public and collective, has always been more dependent on mass-mediated forms of memory.'

[75] Jean McCrindle and Sheila Rowbotham (eds.), *Dutiful Daughters* (Harmondsworth: Penguin, 1979), 174.

[76] Popular Memory Group, 'Popular Memory: Theory, Politics, Method', in Richard Johnson *et al.* (eds.), *Making Histories: Studies in History-Writing and Politics* (Minneapolis: University of Minnesota Press, 1982), 246.

that play 'classic rock' as a way of ritualizing the resurgence of involuntary memory.

In the remainder of this chapter I want to take up this question by exploring—briefly and schematically—an 'intermediate' domain that stands at the point of intersection of 'public' history and 'private' memory. Georges Perec's *Je me souviens* is a random set of 480 entries, each beginning 'Je me souviens' and each attempting to recover a memory which is 'almost forgotten, trivial, banal, and shared, if not by everyone, at least by many people'.[77] They are thus in no way 'personal' memories, but rather 'little bits of everyday life, things that, in one year or another, everyone of the same age saw, experienced, shared, and that then disappeared and were forgotten; they weren't worth being memorized, didn't deserve to be part of History, or to figure in the memoirs of statesmen'.[78] For the most part they date from the time between Perec's 10th and 25th birthdays, that is, between 1946 (three years after his mother's death in Auschwitz)[79] and 1961. Some of them refer to the period before the war: in this case they refer to a time that belongs to the realm of myth. Let me make a series of observations on the domain of public memory that the book constructs.

1. Most of the entries are built around proper names, either those of people (especially from film, jazz, and sport), or the brand names of commodities. Personal names and brand names circulate with a similar kind of intensity, attach to themselves a similar kind of poetic resonance. What does this mean? It may, on the one hand, indicate that persons and things here inhabit a common realm of commodity display and consumption, in which both are reduced equally to the signification of their exchange value; conversely, it may indicate the working of a kind of magic (certainly not divorced from the circulation of the commodity) that transfigures objects of desire into emblems of another and higher world, parallel to but on

---

[77] Georges Perec, 'Post-scriptum', *Je me souviens: Les choses communes I* (Paris: Hachette, 1978), 119. The translation is mine.

[78] Ibid., back cover note, signed G.P.

[79] Perec claims in W to have no childhood memories, but later in the book remembers two things: the parting from his mother at the Gare de Lyons, and a visit to an exhibition about the concentration camps on his return to Paris after the war. Georges Perec, *W: Or, The Memory of Childhood*, trans. David Bellos (London: Collins Harvill, 1988), 6.

a different plane from our own. Proust's reflections on the proper name are crucial to understanding this process of sacralization.

2. What does it mean to be a public (and publicly remembered) person—a television or sporting 'identity', for example? We now know a great deal about the creation of public persons within the star industry that was (and is) a key component of the Hollywood or the Mumbai studio systems. In the contemporary world the major star industry is perhaps centred on television and the large number of print offshoots (weeklies devoted to the soaps, for example) where the construction of a pantheon of demi-gods takes place. Perec's examples are interesting in that they mix stars from different circuits (film stars and film directors, popular musicians and more esoteric figures from the jazz world): a mix that is typical of the cultural experience of post-war intellectuals, but which thereby indicates a limit to any possible universality of the book's account of popular memory.

3. A somewhat different class of public persons is constituted by the names of those who have entered the 'public historical sphere':[80] Profumo and Keeler, Castro, Eichmann, Goldwater. They are few in number, and they enter this domain of public memory only in so far as they have become mythological. Harold Macmillan is History, Christine Keeler is a figure of collective memory; De Gaulle of course is both.

4. When the memory is of a place, it is more often than not that of a place that has disappeared or has been transformed: the metro line that had different carriages from the others, a drug-store on the Champs Élysées that burned down, various cinemas (in fact eighteen of them) that used to exist in different parts of Paris. Place is a marker and a guarantee of the continuity of personal identity; memory is a way of identifying, and perhaps repairing, loss. (It is clear that the book is shaped as much by what Perec has forgotten as by what he remembers.)

5. At a guess, I would say that I share at most about a quarter of Perec's memories. I am a generation younger than him, and I share neither his nationality nor his language. Many of the entries in the book are language-bound: there are snatches of street songs, of children's rhymes, of advertising slogans, of jokes and puns and

---

[80] I take this term from Michael Bommes and Patrick Wright, ' "Charms of Residence": The Public and the Past', in Johnson *et al.*, *Making Histories*, 266.

swear-words. The largest area of overlap is that of popular culture, especially the American popular culture that was so central to the formation of childhood in both France and Australia: I too remember some but not all of the names of the Seven Dwarfs, Davy Crockett hats, Mr Magoo, Abbott and Costello, the 'Enrich Your Vocabulary' section of the Reader's Digest, and Ephraim Zimbalist Junior. Other shared memories have to do with fashions and crazes that seem to belong to no one national culture: the yo-yo, the hula-hoop, the duffle coat. In other cases again, I share a genre but not the particular texts that Perec knows: cinema newsreels, series identifications for cars (Peugeots for Perec, Holdens and Falcons for me), and the columns in children's papers headed 'True or False?', 'Did You Know?', and 'Incredible But True'. What is amazing is perhaps not how little but how much I share with Perec—something that has to do above all with the creation of mass audiences for popular culture across both national and linguistic boundaries.

6. These memories, Perec writes in the back-cover note, may return 'years later, intact and tiny, by chance or because they have been sought out one evening amongst friends': memories can be worked at, and certainly the act of writing them down in this form (whilst not as heroic as that of the American psychologist Marigold Linton who spent six years writing down an exhaustive inventory of all her childhood memories)[81] is a disciplined exercise of recall, a 'technology' in the sense I defined above.

. . . A technology so easy to use that the effect of the book is, irresistibly, to drive the reader to produce parallel sets of memories, to construct for themselves that public domain of private memories that the book sets in play. These are the 'pop images and simulacra' (Jameson), not of a 'history . . . which itself remains forever out of reach',[82] but of a history *which they compose*. Nor—with all the obvious variations of technology and scale—was history ever constructed otherwise.

---

[81] Marigold Linton, 'Transformations of Memory in Everyday Life', in Ulric Neisser (ed.), *Memory Observed: Remembering in Natural Contexts* (San Francisco: W. H. Freeman, 1982), 77–91.

[82] Cf. n. 2 above.

Bibliography

ABEL, RICHARD, 'A Critique of American Tort Law', *British Journal of Law and Society*, 8 (1981), 199–231.

ADLER, JUDITH, 'Origins of Sightseeing', *Annals of Tourism Research*, 16: 1 (1989), 7–29.

ADORNO, THEODOR W., *Philosophy of Modern Music*, trans. Anne Mitchell and Wesley Bloomster (London: Sheed and Ward, 1973).

—— 'The Essay as Form', *Notes to Literature*, vol. i, trans. Shierry Weber Nicholsen, ed. Rolf Tiedemann (New York: Columbia University Press, 1991), 3–23.

AGLIETTA, MICHEL, *A Theory of Capitalist Regulation: The U.S. Experience*, trans. David Fernbach (London: Verso, 1979).

ALTIERI, CHARLES, 'What is Living and What is Dead in American Postmodernism: Establishing the Contemporaneity of Some American Poetry', *Critical Inquiry*, 22: 4 (1996), 764–89.

ANDERSON, CHRISTOPHER, and DUSSART, FRANÇOISE, 'Dreamings in Acrylic: Western Desert Art', in Peter Sutton (ed.), *Dreamings: The Art of Aboriginal Australia* (Ringwood: Viking/Penguin, 1988), 89–142.

ANDREWS, LORI, 'My Body, My Property', *Hastings Center Report* (Oct. 1986), 28–38.

ANDREWS, MALCOLM, *The Search for the Picturesque: Landscape, Aesthetics and Tourism in Britain, 1760–1800* (Stanford, Calif.: Stanford University Press, 1990).

APPADURAI, ARJUN, 'Introduction: Commodities and the Politics of Value', in Arjun Appadurai (ed.), *The Social Life of Things: Commodities in Cultural Perspective* (Cambridge: Cambridge University Press, 1986), 3–63.

ARMITAGE, ROBERT A., 'The Emerging U.S. Patent Law for the Protection of Biotechnology Research Results', *EIPR*, 11: 2 (1989), 47–57.

ARMSTRONG, GEORGE M., 'The Reification of Celebrity: Persona as Property', *Louisiana Law Review*, 51 (1991), 443–68.

ARONOWITZ, STANLEY, 'Postmodernism and Politics', *Social Text*, 18 (1987), 99–115.

ARROW, KENNETH, 'Gifts and Exchanges', *Philosophy and Public Affairs*, 1: 4 (1972), 343–62.

ATTALI, JACQUES, *Noise: The Political Economy of Music*, trans. Brian Massumi, Theory and History of Literature 16 (Minneapolis: University of Minnesota Press, 1985).

AUGÉ, MARC, *Non-Places: Introduction to an Anthropology of Super-modernity*, trans. John Howe (London: Verso, 1995).

BAIL, MURRAY, *Homesickness* (Melbourne: Macmillan, 1980).

BALIBAR, ÉTIENNE, and WALLERSTEIN, IMMANUEL, *Race, Nation, Class: Ambiguous Identities* (London: Verso, 1991).

BARRAUD, CÉCILE, DE COPPET, DANIEL, ITEANU, ANDRÉ, and JAMOUS, RAYMOND, *Of Relations and the Dead: Four Societies Viewed from the Angle of their Exchanges*, trans. Stephen J. Suffern (Oxford: Berg, 1994).

BARTHES, ROLAND, 'Proust et les noms', *To Honour Roman Jakobson*, vol. i (The Hague: Mouton, 1967), 150–58.

BARTLETT, FREDERICK C., *Remembering: A Study in Experimental and Social Psychology* (1932; repr. Cambridge: Cambridge University Press, 1950).

BASHO, *The Narrow Road to the Deep North and Other Travel Sketches*, trans. Nobuyuki Yuasa (Harmondsworth: Penguin, 1966).

BASS, ELLEN, and DAVIS, LAURA, *The Courage to Heal: A Guide for Women Survivors of Child Sexual Abuse*, 2nd edn. (1988; repr. New York: HarperCollins, 1992; 3rd edn. 1994).

BATAILLE, GEORGES, *La Part maudite: Essai d'économie générale. I. La Consumation, Œuvres complètes*, vol. vii (Paris: Gallimard, 1976).

—— *Visions of Excess: Selected Writings, 1927–1939*, ed. Allan Stoekl, trans. Allan Stoekl *et al.*, Theory and History of Literature 14 (Minneapolis: University of Minnesota Press, 1985).

BATES, BENJAMIN J., 'Information as an Economic Good: Sources of Individual and Social Value', in Vincent Mosco and Janet Wasko (eds.), *The Political Economy of Information* (Madison: University of Wisconsin Press, 1988), 76–94.

BAUDELAIRE, CHARLES, 'Le peintre de la vie moderne', in *Curiosités esthétiques, L'Art romantique, et autres œuvres critiques*, ed. H. Lemaitre (Paris: Garnier, 1962), 453–502.

BAUDRILLARD, JEAN, *For a Critique of the Political Economy of the Sign*, trans. Charles Levin (St Louis: Telos Press, 1981).

—— *L'Échange symbolique et la mort* (Paris: Gallimard, 1976).

—— *Simulations*, trans. Paul Foss *et al.*, Foreign Agents Series (New York: Semiotext[e], 1983).

BENJAMIN, WALTER, *Illuminations*, trans. Harry Zohn (New York: Schocken, 1969).

BENNETT, DAVID, 'Wrapping Up Postmodernism', *Textual Practice*, 1: 3 (1987), 243–61.

BERMAN, RUSSELL A., 'The Routinization of Charismatic Modernism and the Problem of Post-Modernity', *Cultural Critique*, 5 (1986–7), 49–68.

BERNSTEIN, MICHÈLE, 'The Situationist International', in Iwona Blazwick (ed.), *An Endless Adventure . . . An Endless Passion . . . An Endless Banquet: A Situationist Scrapbook* (London: ICA/Verso, n.d.), 61.

BERSANI, LEO, *The Culture of Redemption* (Cambridge, Mass.: Harvard University Press, 1990).

BÉRUBÉ, MICHAEL, 'Cultural Criticism and the Politics of Selling Out', *Electronic Book Review*, ‹http://www.altx.com/ebr›, 1996.

—— *Public Access: Literary Theory and American Cultural Politics* (London: Verso, 1994).

BHABHA, HOMI, *The Location of Culture* (London: Routledge, 1994).

BILLAUDOT, BERNARD, and GAURON, ANDRÉ, *Croissance et crise: vers une nouvelle croissance*, 2nd edn. (Paris: La Découverte, 1985).

BLOCH, ERNST, 'Ungleichzeitigkeit und Pflicht zu ihrer Dialektik', in *Erbschaft dieser Zeit* (1935; repr. Frankfurt: Suhrkamp, 1962), 104–60.

BLUME, E. SUE, *Secret Survivors: Uncovering Incest and its Aftereffects in Women* (New York: Ballantine, 1990).

BOK, SISSELA, *Secrets: On the Ethics of Concealment and Revelation* (New York: Pantheon, 1978).

BOMMES, MICHAEL, and WRIGHT, PATRICK ' "Charms of Residence": The Public and the Past', in Richard Johnson *et al.* (eds.), *Making Histories: Studies in History-Writing and Politics* (Minneapolis: University of Minnesota Press, 1982), 253–301.

BOORSTIN, DANIEL J., *The Image: A Guide to Pseudo-Events in America* (New York: Harper and Row, 1961).

BORGES, JORGE LUIS, *Fictions* (London: John Calder, 1965).

Borrowed Time: The Future of Public Libraries in the U.K. (Brisbane: ICPS, 1993).

BOTTOMS, E. L., SCHAVER, P. R., and GOODMAN, G. S., 'Profile of Ritualistic and Religion-Related Abuse Allegations Reported to Clinical Psychologists in the United States'. Paper presented to the 1993 annual meeting of the American Psychological Association in San Francisco.

BOURDIEU, PIERRE, *Outline of a Theory of Practice*, trans. Richard Nice (Cambridge: Cambridge University Press, 1977).

BOYARIN, JONATHAN, 'Space, Time, and the Politics of Memory', in Jonathan Boyarin (ed.), *Remapping Memory: The Politics of Timespace* (Minneapolis: University of Minnesota Press, 1994), 1–37.

BOYER, ROBERT, *Capitalismes fin de siècle* (Paris: Presses Universitaires Françaises, 1986).

—— *The Regulation School: A Critical Introduction*, trans. Craig Charney (New York: Columbia University Press, 1990).

BOYLE, JAMES, 'A Theory of Law and Information: Copyright, Spleens, Blackmail, and Insider Trading', *California Law Review*, 80: 6 (1992), 1413–540.

BRADSHAW, JOHN, *Homecoming* (New York: Bantam, 1990).

BRAGA, CARLOS ALBERTO PRIMO, 'The Economics of Intellectual Property Rights and the GATT: A View from the South', in Connie T. Brown and Eric A. Szweda (eds.), *Trade-Related Aspects of Intellectual Property* (Nashville: Vanderbilt University School of Law, 1990), 243–64.

BRECHER, BOB, 'The Kidney Trade: Or, The Customer is Always Wrong', *Journal of Medical Ethics*, 16 (1990), 120–23.

BRION, DENIS J., 'The Hidden Persistence of Witchcraft', *Law and Critique*, 4: 2 (1993), 227–52.

BROWN, PETER, *Power and Persuasion in Late Antiquity: Towards a Christian Empire* (Madison: University of Wisconsin Press, 1992).

BRUSH, STEPHEN, 'A Non-Market Approach to Protecting Biological Resources', in Tom Greaves (ed.), *Intellectual Property Rights for Indigenous Peoples: A Sourcebook* (Oklahoma City: Society for Applied Anthropology, 1994), 138–43.

BUCK-MORSS, SUSAN, 'Semiotic Boundaries and the Politics of Meaning: Modernity on Tour—A Village in Transition', in Marcus G. Raskin and Herbert J. Bernstein (eds.), *New Ways of Knowing: The Sciences, Society, and Reconstructive Knowledge* (Totowa, NJ: Rowman and Littlefield, 1987), 200–36.

BÜRGER, PETER, 'The Decline of the Modern Age', trans. D. Parent, *Telos*, 62 (1984–5), 117–30.

BURLEY, STEPHEN C. G., 'Passing off and Character Merchandising: Should England Lean towards Australia?', *EIPR*, 13: 7 (1991), 227–30.

BUTLER, JUDITH, 'Contingent Foundations: Feminism and the Question of "Postmodernism" ', in Judith Butler and Joan W. Scott (eds.), *Feminists Theorize the Political* (New York: Routledge, 1992), 3–21.

—— *Gender Trouble: Feminism and the Subversion of Identity* (New York: Routledge, 1990).

BUTLER, LYNDA L., 'The Commons Concept: An Historical Concept with Modern Relevance', *William and Mary Law Review*, 23 (1982), 835–935.

CAIN, P. J., and HOPKINS, A. G., *British Imperialism: Innovation and Expansion, 1688–1914* (London: Longman, 1993).

CALINESCU, MATEI, 'Postmodernism and Some Paradoxes of Periodization', in Douwe Fokkema and Hans Bertens (eds.), *Approaching Postmodernism* (Amsterdam: John Benjamins, 1986), 239–54.

CALLIMANOPULOS, DOMINIQUE, 'Introduction', *Cultural Survival Quarterly*, 6: 3 (Summer 1982), 3–5.

CALLINICOS, ALEX, *Against Postmodernism: A Marxist Critique* (Cambridge: Polity Press, 1989).

CAMPION-VINCENT, VÉRONIQUE, 'Bébés en pièces détachées: Une nouvelle "légende" Latino-Américaine', *Cahiers internationaux de sociologie*, 93 (1992), 299–319.

CARRIER, JAMES G., 'Maussian Occidentalism: Gift and Commodity Systems', in James G. Carrier (ed.), *Occidentalism: Images of the West* (Oxford: Clarendon Press, 1995), 85–108.

CARROLL, JOHN, 'The Tourist', *Sceptical Sociology* (London: Routledge, 1980), 140–49.

CARRUTHERS, MARY, *The Book of Memory: A Study of Memory in Medieval Culture*, Cambridge Studies in Medieval Literature 10 (Cambridge: Cambridge University Press, 1990).

CHAMBERS, IAIN, *Popular Culture: The Metropolitan Experience* (London: Methuen, 1986).

CHEAL, DAVID, *The Gift Economy* (London: Routledge, 1988).

CHOW, REY, *Writing Diaspora: Tactics of Intervention in Contemporary Cultural Studies* (Bloomington: Indiana University Press, 1993).

CHRISTIE, ANDREW, 'Patents for Plant Innovation', *EIPR*, 11: 11 (1989), 395–408.

COHEN, ERIK, 'Authenticity and Commoditization in Tourism', *Annals of Tourism Research*, 15: 3 (1988), 371–86.

—— ' "Primitive and Remote": Hill Tribe Trekking in Thailand', *Annals of Tourism Research*, 16: 1 (1989), 30–61.

—— 'The Sociology of Tourism: Approaches, Issues, and Findings', *Annual Review of Sociology*, 10 (1984), 373–92.

COLLINS, JAMES, 'Postmodernism and Cultural Practice: Redefining the Parameters', *Screen*, 28: 2 (1987), 11–26.

CONNOR, STEVEN, *Postmodernist Culture: An Introduction to Theories of the Contemporary* (Oxford: Basil Blackwell, 1989).

—— 'The Modern and the Postmodern as History', *Essays in Criticism*, 37: 3 (July 1987), 181–92.

CONRAD, JOSEPH, *Youth* (London: Dent, 1920).

COOKE, PHILIP, 'The Postmodern Condition and the City', in Michael Peter Smith (ed.), *Comparative Urban and Community Research*, i: *Power, Community and the City* (New Brunswick, NJ: Transaction Books, 1988), 63–80.

CORREA, CARLOS, 'Biological Resources and Intellectual Property Rights', *EIPR*, 14: 5 (1992), 154–57.

—— 'The GATT Agreement on Trade-Related Aspects of Intellectual Property Rights: New Standards for Patent Protection', *EIPR*, 16: 8 (1994), 327–35.

CREWS, FREDERICK, 'The Revenge of the Repressed', *New York Review of Books*, 17 Nov. 1994, pp. 54–60.

CULLER, JONATHAN, 'Semiotics of Tourism', *American Journal of Semiotics*, 1: 1 and 2 (1981), 127–40.

Cultural Survival Quarterly, 20: 2 (1996).

CURTIN, PHILIP D., *The Atlantic Slave Trade: A Census* (Madison: University of Wisconsin Press, 1969).

CURTIUS, ERNST ROBERT, *European Literature and the Latin Middle Ages*, trans. Willard R. Trask (New York: Harper and Row, 1953).

DAMICH, EDWARD J., 'The Right of Personality: A Common-law Basis for the Protection of the Moral Rights of Authors', *Intellectual Property Law Review* (1990), 547–642.

DASTON, LORRAINE J., 'The Domestication of Risk: Mathematical Probability and Insurance 1650–1830', in Lorenz Krüger, Lorraine J. Daston and Michael Heidelberger (eds.), *The Probabilistic Revolution*, i: *Ideas in History* (Cambridge, Mass.: MIT Press, 1987), 237–60.

DAVIS, JIM, and STACK, MICHAEL, 'Knowledge in Production', *Race and Class*, 34: 3 (1992), 1–14.

DAVIS, LAURA, *The Courage to Heal Workbook: For Women and Men Survivors of Child Sexual Abuse* (New York: Harper and Row, 1990).

DAVIS, MIKE, 'Urban Renaissance and the Spirit of Postmodernism', *New Left Review*, 151 (May–June 1985), 106–13.

DEAR, MICHAEL, 'Postmodernism and Planning', *Environment and Planning D: Society and Space*, 4 (1986), 367–84.

DEBORD, GUY, extract from *Commentaires sur la société du spectacle*, in Iwona Blazwick (ed.), *An Endless Adventure . . . An Endless Passion . . . An Endless Banquet: A Situationist Scrapbook* (London: ICA/Verso, n.d.), 95.

—— *The Society of the Spectacle*, trans. Donald Nicholson-Smith (New York: Zone Books, 1995 [1967]).

DELEUZE, GILLES, *Différence et répétition* (Paris: Presses Universitaires Françaises, 1968).

DELILLO, DON, *White Noise* (London and New York: Picador and Viking Penguin, 1985).

DE MAN, PAUL, 'Introduction' to Hans Robert Jauss, *Toward an Aesthetic of Reception*, trans. Timothy Bahti, Theory and History of Literature 2 (Minneapolis: University of Minnesota Press, 1982), pp. vii–xxv.

DERRIDA, JACQUES, *Given Time: 1. Counterfeit Money*, trans. Peggy Kamuf (Chicago: University of Chicago Press, 1992).

—— *The Gift of Death*, trans. David Wills (Chicago: University of Chicago Press, 1995).

—— *The Truth in Painting*, trans. Geoff Bennington and Ian McLeod (Chicago: University of Chicago Press, 1987).

—— *Writing and Difference*, trans. Alan Bass (Chicago: University of Chicago Press, 1978).

DESAI, A. R., 'Need for Revaluation of the Concept', in Cyril E. Black (ed.), *Comparative Modernization: A Reader* (New York: Free Press, 1976), 89–103.

DIMAGGIO, PAUL, 'Classification in Art', *American Sociological Review*, 52 (1987), 440–55.

DIPROSE, ROSALYN, 'The Gift, Sexed Body Property and the Law', in

Pheng Cheah, David Fraser, and Judith Grbich (eds.), *Thinking through the Body of the Law* (Sydney: Allen and Unwin, 1996), 120–35.

DOCHERTY, THOMAS, 'Postmodernism: An Introduction', in Thomas Docherty (ed.), *Postmodernism: A Reader* (Hemel Hempstead: Harvester Wheatsheaf, 1993), 1–31.

DRAKE, ALVIN W., FINKELSTEIN, STAN N., and SAPOLSKY, HARVEY M., *The American Blood Supply* (Cambridge, Mass.: MIT Press, 1982).

DURING, SIMON, 'Postmodernism or Post-colonialism Today', *Textual Practice*, 1: 1 (1987), 32–47.

ECO, UMBERTO, *Postscript to 'The Name of the Rose'*, trans. W. Weaver (New York: Harcourt Brace Jovanovich, 1983).

EDELMAN, BERNARD, 'L'Homme aux cellules d'or', *L'Hôpital à Paris*, 116 (1990), 38–46.

—— 'The Law's Eye: Nature and Copyright', in Brad Sherman and Alain Strowel (eds.), *Of Authors and Origins* (Oxford: Clarendon Press, 1994), 79–91.

—— 'Vers une approche juridique du vivant', in Bernard Edelman and Marie-Angèle Hermitte (eds.), *L'Homme, la nature et le droit* (Paris: Christian Bourgois, 1988), 27–37.

EISENSTEIN, ELIZABETH L., *The Printing Press as an Agent of Change: Communications and Cultural Transformations in Early-Modern Europe*, 2 vols. (Cambridge: Cambridge University Press, 1979).

ELSHTAIN, JEAN BETHKE, *Public Man, Private Woman: Women in Social and Political Thought* (Princeton, NJ: Princeton University Press, 1981).

ENZENSBERGER, HANS MAGNUS, 'Eine Theorie des Tourismus', *Einzelheiten I: Bewußtseins-Industrie* (Frankfurt am Main: Suhrkamp, 1962), 179–205.

FABIAN, JOHANNES, *Time and the Other: How Anthropology Makes its Object* (New York: Columbia University Press, 1983).

FARMER, STEVEN, *Adult Children of Abusive Parents* (New York: Ballantine, 1989).

FEBVRE, LUCIEN, and MARTIN, HENRI-JEAN, *The Coming of the Book: The Impact of Printing, 1450–1800*, trans. David Gerard (London: Verso, 1984).

FEIFFER, MAXINE, *Going Places: The Ways of the Tourist from Imperial Rome to the Present Day* (London: Macmillan, 1985).

FELMAN, SHOSHANA, 'Education and Crisis, Or the Vicissitudes of Teaching', in Shoshana Felman and Dori Laub (eds.), *Testimony: Crises of Witnessing in Literature, Psychoanalysis, and History* (New York: Routledge, 1992), 1–56.

—— 'Film as Witness: Claude Lanzmann's *Shoah*', in Geoffrey H. Hartman (ed.), *Holocaust Remembrance: The Shapes of Memory* (Cambridge, Mass., and Oxford: Basil Blackwell, 1994), 90–103.

FENTRESS, JAMES, and WICKHAM, CHRIS, *Social Memory* (Oxford: Basil Blackwell, 1992).

FINELLI, ROBERTO, 'Production of Commodities and Production of the Image: Reflections on Modernism and Postmodernism', trans. Lorenzo d'Auria, *Rethinking Marxism*, 5: 1 (1992), 44–55.

FIRTH, RAYMOND, 'Magnitudes and Values in Kula Exchange', in Jerry W. Leach and Edmund Leach (eds.), *The Kula: New Perspectives on Massim Exchange* (Cambridge: Cambridge University Press, 1983), 89–102.

FOKKEMA, DOUWE, and BERTENS, HANS, 'Introduction', in Douwe Fokkema and Hans Bertens (eds.), *Approaching Postmodernism* (Amsterdam: John Benjamins, 1986), pp. vii–x.

FORBES, CAMERON, 'Intellectual Rights Pose Big Threat to Third World', *Weekend Australian*, 23 Oct., 1993.

FOSTER, HAL, '(Post)Modern Polemics', *New German Critique*, 33 (1984), 67–78.

—— 'Postmodernism: A Preface', in Hal Foster (ed.), *The Anti-Aesthetic: Essays on Postmodern Culture* (Port Townsend, Wash.: Bay Press, 1983), pp. ix–xvi.

FOX, RENÉE C., and SWAZEY, JUDITH P., *Spare Parts: Organ Replacement in American Society* (New York: Oxford University Press, 1992).

FREDRICKSON, RENEE, *Repressed Memories: A Journey to Recovery from Sexual Abuse* (New York: Simon and Schuster, 1992).

FRIEDLANDER, SAUL, 'Introduction', in Saul Friedlander (ed.), *Probing the Limits of Representation: Nazism and the 'Final Solution'* (Cambridge, Mass.: Harvard University Press, 1992), 1–21.

—— (in collaboration with Adam Seligman), 'Memory of the *Shoah* in Israel: Symbols, Rituals, and Ideological Polarization', in James E. Young (ed.), *The Art of Memory: Holocaust Memorials in History* (Munich: Prestel-Verlag, 1994), 149–57.

—— 'Trauma, Memory, and Transference', in Geoffrey H. Hartman (ed.), *Holocaust Remembrance: The Shapes of Memory* (Cambridge, Mass.: Basil Blackwell, 1994), 252–63.

FROW, JOHN, *Cultural Studies and Cultural Value* (Oxford: Clarendon Press, 1995).

—— 'Repetition and Limitation: Computer Software and Copyright Law', *Screen*, 29: 1 (1988), 4–21.

—— 'The Signature: Three Arguments about the Commodity Form', in Helen Grace (ed.), *Aesthesia and the Economy of the Senses* (Sydney: University of Western Sydney, 1996), 151–200.

—— 'Timeshift: Technologies of Reproduction and Intellectual Property', *Economy and Society*, 23: 3 (1994), 291–304.

FUKUYAMA, FRANCIS, *The End of History and the Last Man* (New York: Avon Books, 1992).

FULLER, PETER, *Aesthetics after Modernism* (London: Writers and Readers, 1983).

GAINES, JANE, *Contested Culture: The Image, the Voice, and the Law* (Chapel Hill, NC: University of North Carolina Press, 1991).

GARNHAM, NICHOLAS, *Capitalism and Communication: Global Culture and the Economics of Information*, ed. Fred Inglis (London: Sage, 1990).

GASCHÉ, RODOLPHE, 'L'Échange héliocentrique', *L'Arc*, 48 (1972), 70–84.

GATENS, MOIRA, *Feminism and Philosophy: Perspectives on Difference and Equality* (Cambridge: Polity Press, 1991).

GAUKROGER, STEPHEN, 'Romanticism and Decommodification: Marx's Conception of Socialism', *Economy and Society*, 15: 3 (1986), 287–333.

Gene Hunters, The, ZEF Productions, Channel 4 (UK, 1994).

GEYER, MICHAEL, and HANSEN, MIRIAM, 'German-Jewish Memory and National Consciousness', in Geoffrey H. Hartman (ed.), *Holocaust Remembrance: The Shapes of Memory* (Cambridge, Mass.: Basil Blackwell, 1994), 175–90.

GIDDENS, ANTHONY, *The Consequences of Modernity* (Stanford, Calif.: Stanford University Press, 1990).

GITLIN, TODD, 'Hip-Deep in Postmodernism', *New York Times Book Review*, 6 Nov. 1988, 35.

GOODENOUGH, OLIVER R., 'The Price of Fame: The Development of the Right of Publicity in the United States', Part I, *EIPR*, 14: 2 (1992), 55–60.

GORDON, WENDY, 'An Inquiry into the Merits of Copyright: The Challenges of Consistency, Consent, and Encouragement Theory', *Stanford Law Review*, 41 (July 1989), 1343–469.

GRABURN, NELSON H., 'Tourism: The Sacred Journey', in Valene L. Smith (ed.), *Hosts and Guests: The Anthropology of Tourism* (n.p.: University of Pennsylvania Press, 1977), 17–31.

GRAFF, GERALD, Preface to Charles Newman, *The Post-Modern Aura: The Act of Fiction in an Age of Inflation* (Evanston, Ill.: Northwestern University Press, 1985), pp. i–iii.

Great Organ Bazaar, The, BBC TV, 1992.

GREAVES, TOM, 'Intellectual Property Rights, A Current Survey', in Tom Greaves (ed.), *Intellectual Property Rights for Indigenous Peoples: A Sourcebook* (Oklahoma City: Society for Applied Anthropology, 1994), 3–16.

GREENFIELD, MICHAEL S., 'Recombinant DNA Technology: A Science Struggling with the Patent Law', *Intellectual Property Law Review* (1993), 135–78.

GREENHALGH, LIZ, 'The Place of the Library', Comedia Research Working Papers No. 2 (Brisbane: ICPS, 1993).

GREENWOOD, DAVYDD J., 'Culture by the Pound: An Anthropological

Perspective on Tourism as Cultural Commoditization', in Valene Smith (ed.), *Hosts and Guests: The Anthropology of Tourism* (n.p.: University of Pennsylvania Press, 1977), 129–40.

GREGORY, CHRIS, *Gifts and Commodities* (London: Academic Press, 1982).

—— 'Kula Gift Exchange and Capitalist Commodity Exchange: A Comparison', in Jerry W. Leach and Edmund Leach (eds.), *The Kula: New Perspectives on Massim Exchange* (Cambridge: Cambridge University Press, 1983), 103–17.

HABERMAS, JÜRGEN, 'Modernity: An Incomplete Project', in Hal Foster (ed.), *The Anti-Aesthetic: Essays on Postmodern Culture* (Port Townsend: Bay Press, 1983), 3–15.

HACKING, IAN, *Rewriting the Soul: Multiple Personality and the Sciences of Memory* (Princeton: Princeton University Press, 1995).

HALBWACHS, MAURICE, *The Collective Memory*, trans. Francis J. Ditter, Jr., and Vida Yazdi Ditter (New York: Harper and Row, 1980).

HALL, STUART, 'On Postmodernism and Articulation: An Interview with Stuart Hall', ed. Lawrence Grossberg, *Journal of Communication*, 10: 2 (1986), 45–60.

HANDLER, RICHARD, and LINNEKIN, JOCELYN, 'Tradition, Genuine or Spurious', *Journal of American Folklore*, 97: 385 (1984), 273–90.

HANSEN, MIRIAM BRATU, '*Schindler's List* Is Not *Shoah*: The Second Commandment, Popular Modernism, and Public Memory', *Critical Inquiry*, 22: 2 (1996), 292–312.

HANSMANN, HENRY, 'The Economics and Ethics of Markets for Human Organs', in James F. Blumstein and Frank A. Sloan (eds.), *Organ Transplantation Policy: Issues and Prospects* (Durham, NC: Duke University Press, 1989), 57–85.

HARDIMAN, ROY, 'Toward the Right of Commerciality: Recognizing Property Rights in the Commercial Value of Human Tissue', *UCLA Law Review*, 34 (1986), 207–64.

HARDIN, GARRETT, 'The Tragedy of the Commons', *Science*, 162 (1968), 1243–8.

HARTMAN, GEOFFREY H., 'The Book of the Destruction', in Saul Friedlander (ed.), *Probing the Limits of Representation: Nazism and the 'Final Solution'* (Cambridge, Mass.: Harvard University Press, 1992), 318–34.

HARVEY, DAVID, 'Flexible Accumulation through Urbanization: Reflections on "Post-Modernism" in the American City', *Antipode*, 19: 3 (1987), 260–86.

—— *The Condition of Postmodernity: An Enquiry into the Origins of Cultural Change* (Oxford: Basil Blackwell, 1989).

HASSAN, IHAB, 'Alterity? Three Japanese Examples', *Meanjin*, 49: 3 (Spring, 1990), 410–20.

—— *The Postmodern Turn: Essays in Postmodern Theory and Culture* (n.p.: Ohio State University Press, 1987).

—— *The Right Promethean Fire: Imagination, Science, and Cultural Change* (Urbana: University of Illinois Press, 1980).

HAUG, FRIGGA, et al., *Female Sexualization: A Collective Work of Memory*, trans. Erica Carter (London: Verso, 1987).

HAUG, WOLFGANG F., *Critique of Commodity Aesthetics: Appearance, Sexuality and Advertising in Capitalist Society*, trans. Robert Bock (Minneapolis: University of Minnesota Press, 1986).

HEBDIGE, DICK, 'Postmodernism and "The Other Side" ', *Journal of Communication*, 10: 2 (1986), 78–98.

HEIDEGGER, MARTIN, 'The Origin of the Work of Art', *Poetry, Language, Thought*, trans. Albert Hofstadter (New York: Harper and Row, 1971), 15–87.

HERMAN, JUDITH LEWIS, *Trauma and Recovery* (New York: Basic Books, 1992).

HEWISON, ROBERT, *The Heritage Industry: Britain in a Climate of Decline* (London: Methuen, 1987).

HIRST, PAUL, and WOOLLEY, PENELOPE, *Social Relations and Human Attributes* (London: Tavistock, 1982).

HOFFMAN, GARY M., and MARCOU, GEORGE T., 'The Costs and Complications of Piracy', *Society* (Sept.–Oct. 1990), 25–34.

HUNTER, IAN, *Culture and Government: The Emergence of Literary Education* (London: Macmillan, 1988).

HUTCHEON, LINDA, 'The Politics of Postmodernism: Parody and History', *Cultural Critique*, 5 (1986–7), 179–207.

HUYSSEN, ANDREAS, *After the Great Divide: Modernism, Mass Culture, Postmodernism* (Bloomington: Indiana University Press, 1986).

—— 'Monument and Memory in a Postmodern Age', in James E. Young (ed.), *The Art of Memory: Holocaust Memorials in History* (Munich: Prestel-Verlag, 1994), 9–17.

—— and SCHERPE, KLAUS R., 'Einleitung', in Andreas Huyssen and Klaus R. Scherpe (eds.), *Postmoderne: Zeichen eines kulturellen Wandels*, Rowohlts Enzyklopädie (Reinbek bei Hamburg: Rowohlt, 1986), 7–11.

HYDE, LEWIS, *The Gift: Imagination and the Erotic Life of Property* (New York: Vintage Books, 1983).

IGNATIEFF, MICHAEL, *The Needs of Strangers: An Essay on Privacy, Solidarity, and the Politics of Being Human* (New York: Viking, 1984).

JAFFE, ERIK S., ' "She's Got Bette Davis['s] Eyes": Assessing the Non-consensual Removal of Cadaver Organs under the Takings and Due Process Clauses', *Columbia Law Review*, 90 (1990), 528–74.

JAMES, NICKY, 'Emotional Labour: Skill and Work in the Social Regulation of Feelings', *Sociological Review*, 37: 1 (1989), 15–42.

JAMESON, FREDRIC, 'Foreword' to Jean-François Lyotard, *The Post-*

Modern Condition: A Report on Knowledge, trans. Geoff Bennington and Brian Massumi, Theory and History of Literature 10 (Minneapolis: University of Minnesota Press, 1984), pp. vii–xxi.

JAMESON, FREDRIC, 'Marxism and Postmodernism', *New Left Review*, 176 (July–August, 1989), 31–45; repr. from *Postmodernism/Jameson/ Critique*, ed. Douglas Kellner (Washington, DC: Maisonneuve Press, 1989).

—— *Postmodernism, or, The Cultural Logic of Late Capitalism* (Durham, NC: Duke University Press, 1991).

—— 'Reification and Utopia in Mass Culture', *Social Text*, 1 (1979), 130–48.

—— 'The Ideology of the Text', *Salmagundi*, 31–2 (1975–6), 204–46.

—— 'The Politics of Theory: Ideological Positions in the Postmodernism Debate', *New German Critique*, 33 (1984), 53–65.

JANKÉLÉVITCH, VLADIMIR, *L'Irréversible et la nostalgie* (Paris: Flammarion, 1974).

JASZI, PETER, 'Toward a Theory of Copyright: The Metamorphoses of "Authorship" ', *Duke Law Journal* (1991), 455–502.

JAUSS, HANS ROBERT, 'Der literarische Prozeß des Modernismus von Rousseau bis Adorno', in Ludwig von Friedeburg and Jürgen Habermas (eds.), *Adorno-Konferenz 1983* (Frankfurt am Main: Suhrkamp, 1983), 95–130.

—— *Literaturgeschichte als Provokation* (Frankfurt am Main: Suhrkamp, 1970).

JAY, MARTIN, *Downcast Eyes: The Denigration of Vision in Twentieth-Century French Thought* (Berkeley: University of California Press, 1993).

JENCKS, CHARLES, *The Language of Post-Modern Architecture*, 4th edn. (1977; repr. London: Academy Editions, 1984).

JOHNSTON, SEAN, 'Patent Protection for the Protein Products of Recombinant DNA', *Intellectual Property Law Review* (1991), 185–211.

Journal of Psychohistory, 22: 3 (Winter 1995). Special issue, 'Backlash against Psychotherapy'.

JUCHAU, MIREILLE, 'Forgetful Memory: The Holocaust, History and Representation', *UTS Review*, 2: 2 (1996), 66–89.

JUDDERY, BRUCE, 'Net Threatens Private Profits', *Campus Review*, 20–26 Oct., 1994, 1.

JULES-ROSETTE, BENNETTA, *The Messages of Tourist Art: An African Semiotic System in Comparative Perspective* (New York: Plenum Press, 1984).

KAHA, C. W., 'Memory as Conversation', *Communication*, 11: 2 (1989), 115–22.

KAPLAN, HAROLD, *Conscience and Memory: Meditations in a Museum of the Holocaust* (Chicago: University of Chicago Press, 1994).

KEVLES, DANIEL J., and HOOD, LEROY, 'Reflections', in Daniel J. Kevles and Leroy Hood (eds.), *The Code of Codes: Scientific and Social Issues in the Human Genome Project* (Cambridge, Mass.: Harvard University Press, 1992), 300–28.

KINCAID, JAMAICA, *A Small Place* (London: Virago, 1988).

KIRSHENBLATT-GIMBLETT, BARBARA, and BRUNER, EDWARD M., 'Tourism', *International Encyclopaedia of Communications*, vol. iv (New York: Oxford University Press, 1989), 249–53.

KLOPPENBURG, JACK, Jr., *First the Seed: The Political Economy of Plant Biotechnology, 1492–2000* (Cambridge: Cambridge University Press, 1988).

KOPYTOFF, IGOR, 'The Cultural Biography of Things: Commoditization as Process', in Arjun Appadurai (ed.), *The Social Life of Things: Commodities in Cultural Perspective* (Cambridge: Cambridge University Press, 1986), 64–91.

KOSELLECK, REINHART, *Futures Past: On the Semantics of Historical Time*, trans. Keith Tribe (Cambridge, Mass.: MIT Press, 1985).

KOSTECKI, M. M., 'Sharing Intellectual Property Between the Rich and the Poor', *EIPR*, 13: 8 (1991), 271–4.

KRACAUER, SIEGFRIED, *History: The Last Things before the Last* (New York: Oxford University Press, 1969).

KRAUSS, ROSALIND E., *The Originality of the Avant-Garde and Other Modernist Myths* (Cambridge, Mass.: MIT Press, 1986).

KRELL, DAVID FARRELL, *Of Memory, Reminiscence, and Writing: On the Verge* (Bloomington: Indiana University Press, 1990).

KROKER, ARTHUR, and COOKE, DAVID, *The Postmodern Scene: Excremental Culture and Hyper-Aesthetics* (London: Macmillan, 1991).

KUBLER, GEORGE, *The Shape of Time* (New Haven: Yale University Press, 1962).

KUGELMASS, JACK, 'Why We Go to Poland: Holocaust Tourism as Secular Ritual', in James E. Young (ed.), *The Art of Memory: Holocaust Memorials in History* (Munich: Prestel-Verlag, 1994), 175–83.

LANDES, WILLIAM M., and POSNER, RICHARD A., 'An Economic Analysis of Copyright', *Intellectual Property Law Review* (1990), 447–85.

LANDOW, GEORGE P. (ed.), *Hyper/text/theory* (Baltimore: Johns Hopkins University Press, 1994).

LANG, BEREL, *Art and Idea in the Nazi Genocide* (Chicago: University of Chicago Press, 1990).

LANGE, DAVID, 'Recognizing the Public Domain', *Law and Contemporary Problems*, 44: 4 (1981), 147–78.

LANGER, LAWRENCE, *Holocaust Testimonies: The Ruins of Memory* (New Haven: Yale University Press, 1991).

LASH, SCOTT, *Sociology of Postmodernism* (London: Routledge, 1990).

—— and URRY, JOHN, *Economies of Signs and Space* (London: Sage, 1994).

LASH, SCOTT, and URRY, JOHN, *The End of Organized Capitalism* (Cambridge: Polity Press, 1987).

LATOUR, BRUNO, *We Have Never Been Modern*, trans. Catherine Porter (Hemel Hempstead: Harvester/Wheatsheaf, 1993).

LAW, JOHN, *Organizing Modernity* (Oxford: Basil Blackwell, 1994).

LEACH, EDMUND, 'The Kula: An Alternative View', in Jerry W. Leach and Edmund Leach (eds.), *The Kula: New Perspectives on Massim Exchange* (Cambridge: Cambridge University Press, 1983), 529–38.

LEACH, JERRY W., 'Introduction', in Jerry W. Leach and Edmund Leach (eds.), *The Kula: New Perspectives on Massim Exchange* (Cambridge: Cambridge University Press, 1983), 1–26.

LEFANU, JAMES, 'In the Kidney Bazaars, Life Comes Cheap', *The Times*, 3 Aug. 1993.

LEPENIES, WOLF, *Melancholie und Gesellschaft* (Frankfurt am Main: Suhrkamp, 1972).

LEVIN, HARRY, 'What Was Modernism?', repr. in *Refractions: Essays in Comparative Literature* (London: Oxford University Press, 1966), 271–95.

LÉVI-STRAUSS, CLAUDE, 'Introduction à l'œuvre de Marcel Mauss', in Marcel Mauss, *Sociologie et anthropologie* (Paris: Presses Universitaires Françaises, 1960), pp. ix–lii.

—— *The Elementary Structures of Kinship*, rev. edn., trans. James Harle Bell, John Richard von Sturmer and Rodney Needham (Boston: Beacon Press, 1969).

LEWONTIN, RICHARD, 'Agricultural Research and the Penetration of Capital', *Science for the People*, 14: 1 (1982), 12–17.

—— 'The Dream of the Human Genome', *New York Review of Books*, 28 May 1992, pp. 31–40.

LINDSAY, BRUCE, 'GATT: Development and Intellectual Property', *Arena Journal*, 3 (1994), 33–41.

LINEBAUGH, PETER, 'Gruesome Gertie at the Buckle of the Bible Belt', *New Left Review*, 209 (Jan.–Feb., 1995), 15–33.

LINTON, MARIGOLD, 'Transformations of Memory in Everyday Life', in Ulric Neisser (ed.), *Memory Observed: Remembering in Natural Contexts* (San Francisco: W. H. Freeman, 1982), 77–91.

LIPIETZ, ALAIN, *Mirages and Miracles: The Crisis of Global Fordism*, trans. David Macey (London: Verso, 1987).

—— *The Enchanted World*, trans. Ian Patterson (London: Verso, 1985).

—— *Towards a New Economic Order: Post-Fordism, Democracy and Ecology*, trans. Michael Slater (Oxford: Polity Press, 1992).

LITMAN, JESSICA, 'Copyright and Information Policy', *Law and Contemporary Problems*, 55: 2 (1992), 185–209.

—— 'Copyright Legislation and Technological Change', *Oregon Law Review*, 68: 2 (1989), 275–361.

—— 'The Public Domain', *Emory Law Journal*, 39: 4 (1990), 965–1023.

LOCK, MARGARET, 'Editorial: Interrogating the Human Diversity Genome Project', *Social Science and Medicine*, 39: 5 (1994), 603–6.

LOCKE, JOHN, 'The Second Treatise of Government', *Two Treatises of Government*, ed. Peter Laslett (Cambridge: Cambridge University Press, 1960).

LOCKSLEY, GARETH, 'Information Technology and Capitalist Development', *Capital and Class*, 27 (Winter 1986), 81–105.

LOFTUS, ELIZABETH, and KETCHAM, KATHERINE, *The Myth of Repressed Memory* (New York: St Martins Press, 1994).

LOWENTHAL, DAVID, *The Past is a Foreign Country* (Cambridge: Cambridge University Press, 1985).

LUKACHER, NED, *Primal Scenes: Literature, Philosophy, Psychoanalysis* (Ithaca, NY: Cornell University Press, 1986).

LUKÁCS, GEORG, *History and Class Consciousness: Studies in Marxist Dialectics*, trans. Rodney Livingstone (Cambridge, Mass.: MIT Press, 1971).

—— *Soul and Form*, trans. Anna Bostock (Cambridge, Mass.: MIT Press, 1974).

—— *The Theory of the Novel: A Historico-Philosophical Essay on the Forms of Great Epic Literature*, trans. Anna Bostock (Cambridge, Mass.: MIT Press, 1971).

—— 'Über die Besonderheit als Kategorie der Ästhetik', *Probleme der Ästhetik*, *Werke*, vol. x (Neuwied: Luchterhand, 1969), 539–789.

LURIA, A. R., *The Mind of a Mnemonist* (Harmondsworth: Penguin, 1975).

LURY, CELIA, *Cultural Rights: Technology, Legality and Personality* (London: Routledge, 1993).

LUTTWAK, SAMUEL, 'Why Fascism is the Wave of the Future', *London Review of Books*, 7 Apr. 1994, pp. 3, 6.

LYOTARD, JEAN-FRANÇOIS, 'Answering the Question: What is Postmodernism', trans. Régis Durand, in Lyotard, *The Post-Modern Condition: A Report on Knowledge*, trans. Geoff Bennington and Brian Massumi, Theory and History of Literature 10 (Minneapolis: University of Minnesota Press, 1984), 71–82.

—— 'Complexity and the Sublime', *ICA Documents 4 (Postmodernism) and 5* (London: Institute of Contemporary Arts, 1986), 10–12.

—— *Le Postmoderne expliqué aux enfants* (Paris: Galilée, 1986).

—— 'Rules and Paradoxes and Svelte Appendix', *Cultural Critique*, 5 (1986–7), 209–19.

MCBURNEY, BLAINE, 'The Post-Modern Transvaluation of Modernist Values', *Thesis 11*, 12 (1985), 94–109.

MACCANNELL, DEAN, *Empty Meeting Grounds: The Tourist Papers* (New York: Routledge, 1992).

MacCannell, Dean, 'Introduction', *Annals of Tourism Research*, 16: 1 (1989), 1–6.

—— 'Staged Authenticity: Arrangements of Social Space in Tourist Settings', *American Journal of Sociology*, 79: 3 (1974), 589–603.

—— *The Tourist: A New Theory of the Leisure Class* (London: Macmillan, 1976).

McCarthy, J. Thomas, *The Rights of Privacy and Publicity* (New York: Clark Boardman Co., 1991).

McCrindle, Jean, and Rowbotham, Sheila (eds.), *Dutiful Daughters* (Harmondsworth: Penguin, 1979).

Macfarlane, Alan, *The Culture of Capitalism* (Oxford: Basil Blackwell, 1987).

McHale, Brian, *Postmodernist Fiction* (London: Methuen, 1987).

Maine, Henry Sumner, *Ancient Law: Its Connection with the Early History of Society and its Relations to Modern Ideas* (1861; repr. London: John Murray, 1906).

Malinowski, Bronislaw, *Argonauts of the Western Pacific* (1922; repr. London: Routledge and Kegan Paul, 1978).

Mannix, Daniel P. (with Malcolm Cowley), *Black Cargoes: A History of the Atlantic Slave Trade 1518–1865* (London: Longmans, 1962).

Marcus, Greil, *Lipstick Traces: A Secret History of the Twentieth Century* (Cambridge, Mass.: Harvard University Press, 1989).

Marx, Karl, *Capital: A Critique of Political Economy*, vol. i, trans. Ben Fowkes (Harmondsworth: Penguin, 1976).

—— *The Economic and Philosophic Manuscripts of 1844*, trans. Martin Milligan (New York: International Publishers, 1964).

Massey, Doreen, *Spatial Divisions of Labour: Social Structures and the Geography of Production* (New York: Methuen, and London: Macmillan, 1984).

Mauss, Marcel, *Sociologie et anthropologie* (Paris: Presses Universitaires Françaises, 1960).

—— *The Gift: Forms and Functions of Exchange in Archaic Societies*, trans. Ian Cunnison (New York: Norton, 1967).

Michaels, Eric, *Bad Aboriginal Art: Tradition, Media, and Technological Horizon* (Sydney: Allen and Unwin, 1994).

Miège, Bernard, *The Capitalization of Cultural Production* (New York: International General, 1989).

Modak-Truran, Mark, 'Section 337 and GATT in the *Akzo* Controversy: A Pre- and Post-Omnibus Trade Competitiveness Act Analysis', *Intellectual Property Law Review* (1990), 189–221.

Moller-Olkin, S., 'Gender, The Public and the Private', in David Held (ed.), *Political Theory Today* (Cambridge: Polity Press, 1991), 67–90.

Mooney, Pat, 'John Moore's Body', *New Internationalist* (Mar. 1991), 8–10.

—— 'The Massacre of Apple Lincoln', *New Internationalist* (Oct. 1990), 8–9.

MORRIS, IAN, 'Gift and Commodity in Archaic Greece', *Man* (NS), 21 (1986), 1–17.

MORRIS, MEAGHAN, 'At Henry Parkes Motel', *Cultural Studies*, 2: 1 (1988), 1–47.

—— *The Pirate's Fiancée: Feminism, Reading, Postmodernism* (London: Verso, 1988).

MORSE, MARGARET, 'An Ontology of Everyday Distraction: The Freeway, the Mall, the Television', in Patricia Mellencamp (ed.), *Logics of Television: Essays in Cultural Criticism* (Bloomington: Indiana University Press, 1990), 193–221.

MORTINGER, STEPHEN ASHLEY, 'Comment: Spleen for Sale: *Moore* v. *Regents of the University of California* and the Right to Sell Parts of Your Body', *Ohio State Law Journal*, 51 (1990), 499–515.

MULGAN, GEOFF, 'The "Public Service Ethos" and Public Libraries', Comedia Research Working Papers No. 6 (Brisbane: ICPS, 1993).

MURRAY, THOMAS H., 'Gifts of the Body and the Needs of Strangers', *Hastings Center Report* (Apr. 1987), 30–8.

New Internationalist, 142 (Dec. 1984).

NEWMAN, MICHAEL, 'Revising Modernism, Representing Postmodernism: Critical Discourses of the Visual Arts', *ICA Documents 4 (Postmodernism) and 5* (London: Institute of Contemporary Arts, 1986), 32–51.

NIMMER, MELVILLE B., 'The Right of Publicity', *Law and Contemporary Problems*, 19 (1954), 203–23.

NIMMER, RAYMOND T., and KRAUTHAUS, PATRICIA ANN, 'Information as a Commodity: New Imperatives of Commercial Law', *Law and Contemporary Problems*, 55: 3 (1992), 103–30.

NORA, PIERRE, 'Between Memory and History: *Les Lieux de Mémoire*', trans. Marc Roudebush, *Representations*, 26 (Spring 1989), 7–25.

NORRIS, CHRISTOPHER, *The Truth about Postmodernism* (Oxford: Basil Blackwell, 1993).

—— *What's Wrong with Postmodernism: Critical Theory and the Ends of Philosophy* (Baltimore: Johns Hopkins University Press, 1990).

O'CALLAGHAN, MARY LOUISE, 'The Selling of Cells', *The Australian*, 14 Nov. 1995, p. 17.

OFSHE, RICHARD, 'Inadvertent Hypnosis During Interrogation: False Confession Due to Dissociative State; Mis-Identified Multiple Personality and the Satanic Cult Hypothesis', *International Journal of Clinical and Experimental Hypnosis*, 40: 3 (1992), 125–56.

—— and WATTER, ETHAN, *Making Monsters: False Memories, Psychotherapy, and Sexual Hysteria* (New York: Scribners, 1994).

OHNUKI-TIERNEY, EMIKO, 'Brain Death and Organ Transplantation: Cultural Bases of Medical Technology', *Current Anthropology*, 35: 3 (June 1994), 233–54.

O'NEILL, JOHN, *The Poverty of Postmodernism* (London: Routledge, 1995).

ONG, WALTER J., SJ, *Ramus: Method, and the Decay of Dialogue* (Cambridge, Mass.: Harvard University Press, 1958).

PARIZEAU, MARIE-HÉLÈNE, 'Autonomie, don et partage dans les transplantations d'organes et de tissus humains', *Dialogue*, 30 (1991), 343–53.

PARRY, JONATHAN, '*The Gift*, the Indian Gift and the "Indian Gift" ', *Man* (NS), 21 (1986), 456–67.

PASHUKANIS, EVGENY B., *Law and Marxism: A General Theory*, ed. Chris Arthur, trans. B. Einhorn (1978; repr. London: Pluto Press, 1983).

PATEMAN, CAROLE, *The Sexual Contract* (Stanford, Calif.: Stanford University Press, 1988).

PEFANIS, JULIAN, *Heterology and the Postmodern* (Sydney: Allen and Unwin, 1991).

PENDERGRAST, MARK, *Victims of Memory: Incest Accusations and Shattered Lives* (Hinesburg, Vt.: Upper Access, Inc., 1995).

PEREC, GEORGES, *Je me souviens: Les choses communes I* (Paris: Hachette, 1978).

—— *W: Or, The Memory of Childhood*, trans. David Bellos (London: Collins Harvill, 1988).

PIORE, MICHAEL J., and SABEL, CHARLES F., *The Second Industrial Divide: Possibilities for Prosperity* (New York: Basic Books, 1984).

POLAN, DANA, 'Postmodernism and Cultural Analysis Today,' in E. Ann Kaplan (ed.), *Postmodernism and Its Discontents: Theories, Practices* (London: Verso, 1988), 45–58.

Popular Memory Group, 'Popular Memory: Theory, Politics, Method', in Richard Johnson *et al.* (eds.), *Making Histories: Studies in History-Writing and Politics* (Minneapolis: University of Minnesota Press, 1982), 205–52.

PORTOGHESI, PAOLO, *Postmodern: The Architecture of the Postindustrial Society*, trans. Ellen Shapiro (New York: Rizzoli, 1983).

POSEY, DARRELL, 'Intellectual Property Rights and Just Compensation for Indigenous Knowledge', *Anthropology Today*, 6: 4 (Aug. 1990), 13–16.

POSNER, RICHARD, 'An Economic Theory of the Criminal Law', *Columbia Law Review*, 85 (1985), 1193–1231.

POSTON, CAROL, and LISON, KAREN, *Reclaiming Our Lives: Hope for Adult Survivors of Incest* (New York: Bantam, 1990).

PRINGLE, ROSEMARY, *Secretaries Talk: Sexuality, Power and Work* (Sydney: Allen and Unwin, 1988).

PROBYN, ELSPETH, 'Bodies and Anti-Bodies: Feminism and the Postmodern', *Cultural Studies*, 1: 3 (1987), 349–60.

PRZEWORSKI, ADAM, *Capitalism and Social Democracy* (Cambridge: Cambridge University Press, 1985).

Public Sector/Private Sector Interaction in Providing Information Services (Washington, DC: Government Printing Office, 1982).

RABAN, JONATHAN, *Coasting* (1986; repr. London: Picador, 1987).

RABINOW, PAUL, 'Severing the Ties: Fragmentation and Dignity in Late Modernity', *Knowledge and Society: The Anthropology of Science and Technology*, 9 (1992), 169–87.

RADIN, MARGARET JANE, 'Market-Inalienability', *Harvard Law Review*, 100: 8 (1987), 1849–1937.

—— 'Property and Personhood', *Stanford Law Review*, 34 (1982), 957–1015.

REDFOOT, DONALD L., 'Touristic Authenticity, Touristic Angst, and Modern Reality', *Qualitative Sociology*, 7: 4 (Winter 1984), 291–309.

REYNOLDS, R. LARRY, and BARNEY, L. DWAYNE, 'Economics of Organ Procurement and Allocation', *Journal of Economic Issues*, 22: 2 (June 1988), 571–9.

RICHARD, NELLY, 'Notes towards a (Critical) Re-evaluation of the Critique of the Avant-Garde', *Art and Text*, 16 (1984–5), 8–19.

ROBERTS, DAVID, 'Marxism, Modernism, Postmodernism', *Thesis 11*, 12 (1985), 53–63.

ROBERTS, L., 'Anthropologists Climb (Gingerly) on Board', *Science*, 258 (1992), 1300–1.

—— 'How to Sample the World's Genetic Diversity', *Science*, 257 (1992), 1204–5.

ROBERTSON, ROLAND, 'After Nostalgia? Wilful Nostalgia and the Phases of Globalization', in Bryan S. Turner (ed.), *Theories of Modernity and Postmodernity* (London: Sage, 1990), 45–61.

ROBINS, KEVIN, 'Reimagined Communities? European Image Spaces beyond Fordism', *Cultural Studies*, 3: 2 (1989), 145–65.

ROEDIGER, HENRY L., 'Memory Metaphors in Cognitive Psychology', *Memory and Cognition*, 8: 3 (1980), 231–46.

ROSE, CAROLE, 'The Comedy of the Commons: Custom, Commerce, and Inherently Public Property', *University of Chicago Law Review*, 53: 3 (1986), 711–81.

ROSE, D., 'Rethinking Gentrification: Beyond the Uneven Development of Marxist Urban Theory', *Environment and Planning D: Society and Space*, 1 (1984), 47–74.

ROSE, MARK, *Authors and Owners: The Invention of Copyright* (Cambridge, Mass.: Harvard University Press, 1993).

ROSEN, STANLEY, 'Post-Modernism and the End of Philosophy', *Canadian Journal of Political and Social Theory*, 9: 3 (Fall 1985), 90–101.

ROSENBERG, PETER D., *Patent Law Fundamentals*, vol. i, 2nd edn. (New York: Clark Boardman Callaghan, 1995).

Rural Advancement Foundation International Communiqué, *Patents, Indigenous Peoples, and Human Genetic Diversity*, Rural Advancement Foundation International, May 1993.

RUSTIN, MICHAEL, 'The Politics of Post-Fordism: or, The Trouble with "New Times" ', *New Left Review*, 175 (May–June 1989), 54–77.

SAHLINS, MARSHALL, *Stone Age Economics* (London: Tavistock Publications, 1974).

SAKAI, NAOKI, 'Modernity and its Critique: The Problem of Universalism and Particularism', *The South Atlantic Quarterly*, 87: 3 (1988), 475–504.

SAMUEL, RAPHAEL, *Theatres of Memory, i: Past and Present in Contemporary Culture* (London: Verso, 1994).

SCHAPIRO, MEYER, 'The Still Life as a Personal Object: A Note on Heidegger and Van Gogh', in Marianne L. Simmel (ed.), *The Reach of Mind: Essays in Memory of Kurt Goldstein* (New York: Springer, 1968), 203–9.

SCHEPER-HUGHES, NANCY, 'Theft of Life', *Society* (Sept.–Oct. 1990), 57–62.

SCHEPPELE, KIM LANE, *Legal Secrets: Equality and Efficiency in the Common Law* (Chicago: University of Chicago Press, 1988).

SCHILLER, DAN, 'From Culture to Information and Back Again: Commodification as a Route to Knowledge', *Critical Studies in Mass Communication*, 11 (1994), 93–115.

SCHILLER, FRIEDRICH VON, *Über Naive und Sentimentalische Dichtung, Werke in Drei Bänden* (Munich: Hanser, 1966).

—— *Naive and Sentimental Poetry*, trans. Julius A. Elias (New York: Ungar, 1966).

SCHILLER, HERBERT I., and SCHILLER, ANITA R., 'Libraries, Public Access to Information, and Commerce', in Vincent Mosco and Janet Wasko (eds.), *The Political Economy of Information* (Madison: University of Wisconsin Press, 1988), 146–66.

SCHMIDT, CATHERINE JOANNE, *Tourism: Sacred Sites, Secular Seers*, Dissertation, SUNY at Stony Brook (repr. Ann Arbor: University Microfilms International, 1985).

SCHNEIDER, ANDREW, and FLAHERTY, MARY PAT, 'Selling the Gift (2)', *Pittsburgh Press*, 4 Nov. 1985, p. A1.

SCHULTE-SASSE, JOCHEN, 'Modernity and Modernism, Postmodernity and Postmodernism: Framing the Issue', *Cultural Critique*, 5 (1986–7), 5–22.

SEABROOK, JEREMY, 'Biotechnology and Genetic Diversity', *Race and Class*, 34: 3 (1993), 15–30.

SENNETT, RICHARD, *The Fall of Public Man* (London: Faber, 1977).

SERRES, MICHEL, *Hermes: Literature, Science, Philosophy*, ed. Josué Harari and David F. Bell (Baltimore: Johns Hopkins University Press, 1982).

SHERMAN, RORIE, 'The Selling of Body Parts', *National Law Journal*, 7 Dec. 1987, pp. 32–33.

SIMMEL, GEORG, *The Sociology of Georg Simmel*, ed. Kurt H. Wolff (New York: Free Press, 1950).

SINGER, BARBARA, 'The Right of Publicity: Star Vehicle or Shooting Star?', *Cardozo Arts and Entertainment Law Journal*, 10: 1 (1992), 1–50.

SMITH, M., and PAZDER, L., *Michelle Remembers* (New York: Congdon and Lattes, 1980).

SMITH, MARLIN H., 'Note: The Limits of Copyright: Property, Parody, and the Public Domain', *Duke Law Journal*, 42 (1993), 1233–72.

SMITH, NEIL, *Uneven Development: Nature, Capital and the Production of Space* (Oxford: Basil Blackwell, 1984).

—— and WILLIAMS, PETER (ed.), *Gentrification of the City* (Boston: Allen and Unwin, 1986).

SMITH, VALENE, 'Introduction', in Valene Smith (ed.), *Hosts and Guests: The Anthropology of Tourism* (n.p.: University of Pennsylvania Press, 1977), 1–14.

SNYDER, ALVIN A., *Warriors of Disinformation: American Propaganda, Soviet Lies, and the Winning of the Cold War* (New York: Arcade Publishing, 1995).

SOJA, EDWARD, *Postmodern Geographies: The Reassertion of Space in Critical Social Theory* (London: Verso, 1989).

SOLERI, DANIELA, *et al.*, 'Gifts from the Creator: Intellectual Property Rights and Folk Crop Varieties', in Tom Greaves (ed.), *Intellectual Property Rights for Indigenous Peoples: A Sourcebook* (Oklahoma, City: Society for Applied Anthropology, 1994), 21–40.

SORABJI, RICHARD, *Aristotle on Memory* (Providence, RI: Brown University Press, 1972).

STAFFORD, BARBARA, *Voyage Into Substance: Art, Science, Nature, and the Illustrated Travel Account, 1760–1840* (Cambridge, Mass: MIT Press, 1984).

STANBERRY, KURT, 'Piracy of Intellectual Property', *Society* (Sept.–Oct. 1990), 35–40.

STAROBINSKI, JEAN, 'The Idea of Nostalgia', *Diogenes*, 54 (Summer 1966), 81–103.

STAUTH, GEORG, and TURNER, BRYAN S., 'Nostalgia, Postmodernism and the Critique of Mass Culture', *Theory, Culture and Society*, 5: 2–3 (1988), 509–26.

STEWART, SUSAN, *Crimes of Writing: Problems in the Containment of Representation* (New York: Oxford University Press, 1991).

STEWART, SUSAN, *On Longing: Narratives of the Miniature, the Gigantic, the Souvenir, the Collection* (Baltimore: Johns Hopkins University Press, 1984).

STONE, ALLUCQUÈRE ROSANNE, *The War of Desire and Technology at the Close of the Mechanical Age* (Cambridge, Mass.: MIT Press, 1995).

STRATFORD, LAUREN, *Satan's Underground* (Eugene, Ore: Harvest House, 1988).

STRATHERN, MARILYN, 'Culture in a Netbag: The Manufacture of a Subdiscipline in Anthropology', *Man* (NS), 16 (1981), 673–83.

—— 'Entangled Objects: Detached Metaphors', *Social Analysis*, 34 (Dec. 1993), 88–101.

—— 'Potential Property: Intellectual Rights and Property in Persons', *Social Anthropology*, 4: 1 (1996), 17–32.

—— *The Gender of the Gift: Problems with Women and Problems with Society in Melanesia* (Berkeley: University of California Press, 1988).

TAVRIS, CAROL, 'Beware the Incest-Survivor Machine', *New York Times Book Review*, 3 Jan. 1993, pp. 1, 16–17.

TERR, LENORE, *Unchained Memories: True Stories of Traumatic Memories, Lost and Found* (New York: Basic Books, 1994).

TERRELL, TIMOTHY P., and SMITH, JANE S., 'Publicity, Liberty, and Intellectual Property: A Conceptual and Economic Analysis of the Inheritability Issue', *Emory Law Journal*, 34 (1985), 1–64.

THOMAS, NICHOLAS, *Entangled Objects: Exchange, Material Culture, and Colonialism in the Pacific* (Cambridge, Mass.: Harvard University Press, 1991).

—— 'The Inversion of Tradition', *American Ethnologist*, 19: 2 (1992), 213–32.

THOMPSON, E. P., *Customs in Common* (London: Penguin, 1993).

TILLEY, LESLIE, 'Software for the Lending', *The Times*, 25 Jan. 1990.

TIPPS, DEAN C., 'Modernization Theory and the Comparative Study of Societies: A Critical Perspective', in Cyril E. Black (ed.), *Comparative Modernization: A Reader* (New York: Free Press, 1976), 62–88.

TITMUSS, RICHARD, *The Gift Relationship: From Human Blood to Social Policy* (London: Allen and Unwin, 1970).

TRILLING, LIONEL, 'On the Teaching of Modern Literature', *Beyond Culture: Essays on Literature and Learning* (1965; repr. Harmondsworth: Penguin, 1967), 19–41.

TURNER, BRYAN S., 'A Note on Nostalgia', *Theory, Culture and Society*, 4: 1 (1987), 147–56.

TURNER, JOHN, and ASH, LOUISE, *The Golden Hordes: International Tourism and the Pleasure Periphery* (London: Constable, 1975).

TURNER, VICTOR, and TURNER, ETHEL, *Image and Pilgrimage in Christian*

Culture: Anthropological Perspectives (New York: Columbia University Press, 1978).

URBAIN, JEAN-DIDIER, 'Sémiotiques comparées du touriste et du voyageur', *Semiotica*, 58: 3–4 (1986), 269–86.

URRY, JOHN, 'The Making of the Lake District', *Consuming Places* (London: Routledge, 1995), 193–210.

—— *The Tourist Gaze: Leisure and Travel in Contemporary Societies* (London: Sage, 1990).

VALERI, VALERIO, 'Buying Women But Not Selling Them: Gift and Commodity Exchange in Huaulu Alliance', *Man* (NS), 29 (1994), 1–26.

VAN CAENEGEM, W., 'Different Approaches to the Protection of Celebrities against Unauthorized Use of their Image in Advertising in Australia, the United States and the Federal Republic of Germany', *EIPR*, 12: 2 (1990), 452–8.

VAN DEN ABBEELE, GEORGES, 'Sightseers: The Tourist as Theorist', *Diacritics*, 10: 4 (1980), 3–14.

VATTIMO, GIANNI, *The End of Modernity: Nihilism and Hermeneutics in Postmodern Culture*, trans. Jon R. Snyder (Baltimore: Johns Hopkins University Press, 1988).

VICTOR, JEFFREY S., *Satanic Panic: The Creation of a Contemporary Legend* (Chicago: Open Court, 1993).

VIDAL-NAQUET, PIERRE, *Assassins of Memory: Essays on the Denial of the Holocaust*, trans. Jeffrey Mehlman (New York: Columbia University Press, 1992).

WAKEFIELD, HOLLIDA, and UNDERWAGER, RALPH, *Return of the Furies: An Investigation into Recovered Memory Therapy* (Chicago: Open Court, 1994).

WARNING, RAINER, 'Surrealistische Totalität und die Partialität der Moderne', in R. Warning and W. Wehle (eds.), *Lyrik und Malerei der Avantgarde* (Munich: Fink, 1982), 481–519.

WARREN, SAMUEL, and BRANDEIS, LOUIS, 'The Right to Privacy', *Harvard Law Review*, 4 (1890), 193–216.

WATKINS, KEVIN, 'GATT and the Third World: Fixing the Rules', *Race and Class*, 34: 1 (1992), 23–40.

WEDIN, MICHAEL V., *Mind and Imagination in Aristotle* (New Haven: Yale University Press, 1988).

WEINER, ANNETTE, *Inalienable Possessions: The Paradox of Keeping-While-Giving* (Berkeley: University of California Press, 1992).

WELLMER, ALBRECHT, 'On the Dialectic of Modernism and Post-modernism', *Praxis International*, 5: 5 (1985), 337–62.

WHITE, HAYDEN, 'Historical Emplotment and the Problem of Truth', in Saul Friedlander (ed.), *Probing the Limits of Representation: Nazism and the 'Final Solution'* (Cambridge, Mass.: Harvard University Press, 1992), 37–53.

WIEVORKA, ANNETTE, 'On Testimony', in Geoffrey H. Hartman (ed.) *Holocaust Remembrance: The Shapes of Memory* (Cambridge, Mass.: Basil Blackwell, 1994), 23–32.

WILKIE, TOM, *Perilous Knowledge: The Human Genome Project and Its Implications* (London: Faber and Faber, 1994).

WILLIAMS, RAYMOND, 'When Was Modernism?', *New Left Review*, 175 (May–June 1989), 48–52.

WOLLEN, PETER, 'Bitter Victory: The Situationist International', in Iwona Blazwick (ed.), *An Endless Adventure . . . An Endless Passion . . . An Endless Banquet: A Situationist Scrapbook* (London: ICA/Verso, n.d.), 9–16.

—— 'Ways of Thinking about Music Video (and Post-Modernism)', *Critical Quarterly*, 28: 1–2 (1986), 167–70.

WOODMANSEE, MARTHA, 'The Genius and the Copyright: Economic and Legal Conditions of the Emergence of the "Author" ', *Eighteenth-Century Studies*, 17: 4 (1984), 425–48.

WORDSWORTH, WILLIAM, *Selected Prose*, ed. John O. Haydon (Harmondsworth: Penguin, 1988).

WORPOLE, KEN, 'The Ghostly Pavement: The Political Implications of Local Working-Class History', in Samuel Raphael (ed.), *People's History and Socialist Theory* (London: Routledge and Kegan Paul, 1981), 22–32.

WRIGHT, LAWRENCE, 'Remembering Satan—Parts I and II', *The New Yorker*, 17 May and 24 May 1993, pp. 60–81 and 54–76.

—— *Remembering Satan* (New York: Alfred Knopf, 1994).

WRIGHT, PATRICK, *On Living in an Old Country: The National Past in Contemporary Britain* (London: Verso, 1985).

WU HONGDA, HARRY, 'A Grim Organ Harvest in China's Prisons', *World Press Review*, 42: 6 (June 1995), 22, repr. from *Open Magazine*, Jan. 1995.

YAPKO, MICHAEL, *Suggestions of Abuse: True and False Memories of Childhood Sexual Trauma* (New York: Simon and Schuster, 1994).

YERUSHALMI, YOSEF HAYIM, *Zakhor: Jewish History and Jewish Memory* (Seattle: University of Washington Press, 1982).

YOUNG, JAMES E., 'The Art of Memory: Holocaust Museums in History', in James E. Young (ed.), *The Art of Memory: Holocaust Memorials in History* (Munich: Prestel-Verlag, 1994), 19–38.

ZELIZER, VIVIANA A. ROTMAN, *Morals and Markets: The Development of Life Insurance in the United States* (New York: Columbia University Press, 1979).

ZERUBAVEL, YAEL, *Recovered Roots: Collective Memory and the Making of Israeli National Tradition* (Chicago: University of Chicago Press, 1995).

ŽIŽEK, SLAVOJ, *The Sublime Object of Ideology* (London: Verso, 1989).

ZUKIN, SHARON, *Loft Living: Culture and Capital in Urban Change* (1982; repr. New Brunswick, NJ: Rutgers University Press, 1989).

—— 'The Postmodern Debate over Urban Form', *Theory, Culture and Society*, 5: 2–3 (1988), 431–46.

Index

Abel, Richard 150
abstraction 6–8, 76, 132, 141–2, 216,
    221
Acker, Kathy 19, 28
Adler, Judith 91–2
Adorno, T. W. 12, 16, 34, 41, 53, 80,
    147, 239
advertising 5–6, 19, 23–4, 26, 33, 38,
    45, 49, 52, 56–7, 61, 76, 90, 145,
    181, 185, 190, 245
Aglietta, Michel 46
alienation 140–1, 143
Altieri, Charles 18
American Psychological Association 233
Anderson, Christopher 136–7
Anderson, Laurie 28
Andrews, Lori 173–4
Andrews, Malcolm 92
Appadurai, Arjun 143–8
Arabian, Justice 156
architecture 19, 40–4, 49, 53
archive 224–5, 229, 238
Aristotle 226
Armitage, Robert A. 195
Armstrong, George M. 134
Arnold, Matthew 75
Arnold, Roseanne Barr 238
Aronowitz, Stanley 15
Arrow, Kenneth 106
art system, art market 55–6, 58, 61,
    136–8
Artaud, Antonin 27, 37
Ashbery, John 28
Ash, Louise 69, 73, 95
Attali, Jacques 62
Auden, W. H. 90
Augé, Marc 45, 75–7
aura, auratic value 64, 67, 70–1, 77,
    79, 82, 96, 223
Auschwitz 86, 241, 244
Auster, Paul 28
authorship 139–40, 160, 183–4,
    190, 203, 210
avant-garde 4, 20, 21, 58

Bacon, Francis 91
Bail, Murray 94
Bakhtin, Mikhail 107
Bardon, Geoff 136
Barney, L. Dwayne 170
Barraud, Cécile 126
Barthelme, Donald 19, 28
Barthelme, Frederick 28
Barthes, Roland 59
Bartlett, Frederick 227
Basho 64–7, 73, 93
Bass, Ellen 231, 234–7
Bataille, Georges 27, 107, 114, 116–9,
    130
Bates, Benjamin J. 188
Baudelaire, Charles 56
Baudrillard, Jean 28, 29, 45, 68, 70,
    71, 116, 142
Beach Boys 28
Beatles 29
Beckett, Samuel 19
Benetton 49
Benjamin, Walter 43, 70–1, 72, 147,
    223
Bennett, David 29, 57
Berman, Russell 33
Bernstein, Michèle 5
Bersani, Leo 37
Bertens, Hans 17
Bérubé, Michael 19–20, 33
Best, Elsdon 109
Bhabha, Homi 10
Billaudot, Bernard 46
Bird, Justice Rose 182
Blackstone, William 134
Blake, William 27
Blanchot, Maurice 241
Bloch, Ernst 9
Block, John 201
blood supply 104–6, 149, 176
Blume, E. Sue 235–6
body organs 105, 106, 145, 162–79
    markets in 162–79
Bok, Sissela 189

Bommes, Michael 245
Boorstin, Daniel J. 45, 69
Borges, Jorge Luis 19, 218, 225, 227–9
Bottoms, E. L. 233
Bourdieu, Pierre 115–6
Boyarin, Jonathan 223
Boyer, Robert 46
Boyle, James 156, 160, 182–3, 202–3,
    209, 213–14
BP 200
Bradshaw, John 235
Braga, Carlos 190–3
Brandeis, Louis 180–1
Brecher, Bob 171, 173
Brecht, Bertolt 61, 147
Brion, Denis J. 232
Brown, Peter 215
Brown, Ronald 154
Bruner, Edward M. 74, 99
Brush, Stephen 203
Buck-Morss, Susan 101
Burley, Stephen C. G. 187
Burroughs, William 28
Butler, Judith 20–1, 114
Butler, Lynda L. 205
Byrne, David 28

Cain, P. J. 133
Calinescu, Matei 38
Callimanopulos, Dominique 100
Callinicos, Alex 23
Calvino, Italo 19, 28
Campion-Vincent, Véronique 168–70
cannibalism, cannibalization 169, 172,
    177, 179, 231
Capone, Al 183
Carlyle, Thomas 75
Carrier, James G. 125
Carroll, John 96
Carruthers, Mary 224–6
Carson, Johnny 186
Castro, Fidel 245
Chambers, Iain 56–7
Cheal, David 125
Chow, Rey 7
Christie, Andrew 200
Ciba-Geigy 200
citizen 208, 213, 215–16
civil society 213, 217
cloth wealth 113
Coates, George 28
coevalness 8–9
Cohen, Erik 71, 72–4, 95, 99–100

Cohen, Lloyd 171
Coke, Edward 134
Collins, James 138–9
commodification 4, 45, 52, 55, 61, 87,
    100, 106, 130, 132–5, 138–42,
    144–8, 149, 151–2, 156, 158–9,
    173–4, 176, 182, 188–9, 200–1,
    203–4, 213
commodity, commodity form 5–8, 10,
    25, 34, 39, 48–9, 52, 55, 57, 61–2,
    82, 86, 99–100, 102–3, 115, 120,
    121–6, 127, 132, 217, 218, 243,
    244
commodity fetishism 5, 18, 87, 125,
    141
commodity relations 72, 171–2, 217
'common heritage of mankind' 191,
    202–4, 215
common weal 211
commons 161, 173, 188, 203–7,
    212–13
  in information 4, 209, 212
communal rights 133–4
Connor, Steven 16, 37, 62
Conrad, Joseph 13
consumer 208
Cook, David 19
Cooke, Philip 47
Coppet, Daniel de 126
copyright 139, 147, 160, 181, 183–4,
    188, 189, 194, 209–12
Corbusier, Le 37
Correa, Carlos 192, 195, 202
Cortázar, Julio 19
Cowley, Malcolm 175
Crews, Frederick 233–4
Culler, Jonathan 67, 69, 73
cultural capital 96–9
cultural relativism 8
culture industry 58, 139, 182, 189
Curtin, Philip D. 175
Curtius, Ernst 30
customary rights 206

Dakushi 66
Damich, Edward J. 184
Daston, Lorraine 174–5
Davis, Jim 204
Davis, Laura 231, 235–7
Davis, Mike 29, 43
De Gaulle, Charles 245
de Man, Paul 57
Dear, Michael 44

Debord, Guy 4–8
decommodification 135, 140, 144–8, 150
Defoe, Daniel 99
Deleuze, Gilles 68
DeLillo, Don 13–15, 23–6, 28, 38–9, 45, 49, 59–61, 67, 68–9, 79, 88–90
denial 235
dépense 117–8
Derrida, Jacques 28, 84–6, 87–8, 107–9, 117, 193
Desai, A. R. 35
DiMaggio, Paul 189
Dior 185
Diprose, Rosalyn 216
distraction 39
Docherty, Thomas 15
Doctorow, E. L. 19, 28
Donne, John 102
Drake, Alvin W. 104
Dreiser, Theodore 83
Duchamp, Marcel 27, 37
Dundee, Mick 187
During, Simon 21, 33
Durkheim, Emile 35, 109, 219
Dussart, Françoise 136–7

Eco, Umberto 18
Edelman, Bernard 158, 194–7
Eichmann, Adolf 245
Eisenstein, Elizabeth L. 224
Elshtain, Jean Bethke 216
energy, energy flow 118–19
Entfremdung 140–1
Enzensberger, Hans Magnus 95
essay 11–12
everyday life 48, 78–9, 80, 102, 217
exchange value 72, 81, 82, 86, 103, 141–2, 143, 144, 189, 200, 244
exemplification 27–9, 40, 42, 84–6

Fabian, Johannes 8–9
fair use 209, 212
fame 179–80, 182
Farmer, Steven 235
farmers' rights 203–4
fashion 19, 23, 52, 55–7, 147
Fassbinder, Rainer Werner 28
Faurisson, Robert 239
Febvre, Lucien 91, 139, 224
Feiffer, Maxine 75
Felman, Shoshana 241
Fentress, James 228

fetish, fetishism 84, 86, 94
Feuerbach, Ludwig 5
Fichte, Johann Gottlieb 210
Finelli, Roberto 6
Finkelstein, Stan N. 104
first gift 106–8
Firth, Raymond 121
Flaherty, Mary Pat 163
Flying Karamazov Brothers 28
Fokkema, Douwe 17
Forbes, Cameron 201
forgetting 227, 229, 245
Foster, Hal 18, 21, 53–4
Foucault, Michel 28, 34
Fox, Renée 105, 170
Frank, Anne 241
Frank, Judge Jerome N. 181
Frankfurt School 142
Fredrickson, Renee 235–7
Freud, Sigmund 54, 86, 223, 234
Friedlander, Saul 239–40, 242
Frow, John 47, 62, 147, 210
Fukuyama, Francis 9–10
Fuller, Peter 15

Gadamer, Hans-Georg 77
Gaines, Jane 148, 183–6
gambling 174–5
Garnham, Nicholas 189–90
Gasché, Rodolphe 107, 111
Gatens, Moira 216
GATT 190–3, 201
Gaukroger, Stephen 140
Gauron, André 46
gender 83, 85, 216
general economy 111, 119
genetic commons 153, 198, 204
Genetics Institute 155
genre 11, 38, 82–3, 85, 90, 239, 246
    postmodernism 17, 21–2
    theory 26
gentrification 48, 69, 146
George, Justice 156–7, 160
Geyer, Michael 242–3
Gibson, William 19
Giddens, Anthony 34, 58–9, 75
gift 65, 93, 102–32, 133, 143, 151–2, 156, 162, 172, 174, 187–8, 193, 202–3, 207, 212, 214, 216–17
    economy 123–6, 129–30, 187, 202, 217
    relations 171–2, 217
Gilles de Rais 170

Gitlin, Todd 28
Glass, Philip 28
  Gleichzeitigkeit 9
Goffman, Erving 70
Goldwater, Barry 245
Goodenough, Oliver 181
Goodman, G. S. 233
Gordon, Wendy 210
Graburn, Nelson 65
Graff, Gerald 63
Grass, Gunter 239
Graves, Michael 28
Gray, Spalding 28
Greaves, Tom 203
Greenberg, Clement 40
Greenfield, Michael S. 195, 198–9
Greenhalgh, Liz 208
Green Revolution 201
Greenwood, Davydd J. 100
Gregory, Chris 121–2, 124–5, 127
grid 23, 41–2

Habermas, Jürgen 16, 33, 34, 36,
  213
Hacking, Ian 230, 234
Halbwachs, Maurice 219
Hall, Stuart 34
Hamsun, Knut 83
Handler, Richard 77
Hansen, Miriam 242–3
Hansmann, Henry 172–3
Hara Anteki 66
Hardiman, Roy 157, 159
Hardin, Garrett 205–6
Harris, John 171
Hartman, Geoffrey 240–1
Harvey, David 46, 48, 50–3, 56
Hassan, Ihab 16–17, 27, 51, 65
  hau of the gift 109–14
Haug, Frigga 219
Haug, Wolfgang 142
Havilov centres 201
Headroom, Max 28
Hebdige, Dick 18
Hegel, G. W. F. 7, 53, 124
Heidegger, Martin 42, 53, 81–6, 87
Heissenbüttel, Helmut 27
heritage industry 78–9
Herman, Judith Lewis 231
Hewison, Robert 78
Hirst, Paul 224
historical novel 218
historicism 10, 31

history 7–8, 19, 75,
  78–9, 81, 135, 218–22, 230,
  239–40, 246
  end of 9, 36–8, 57
  oral 219
Hobsbawm, Eric 77
Hockney, David 28
Hoffman, Gary M. 192
Hofmannsthal, Hugo von 27
Hogan, Paul 187
Holocaust 10, 230, 238–43
Hood, Leroy 199
Hopkins, A. G. 133
Horkheimer, Max 16, 34
hospitality 100
  commodification of 100
Hugo, Victor 169
human genome 197–8
Human Genome Diversity Project
  152–3
Human Genome Project 152–3, 199
Hunter, Ian 2
Hutcheon, Linda 18, 19
Huyssen, Andreas 17, 58, 241–2
hybridization 199–202
Hyde, Lewis 103–4, 106, 112
hypnosis 232–3, 237

ICI 200
Ignatieff, Michael 216–17
immovable property 114, 128
inalienable possessions 114, 122, 124,
  129–30, 148, 150–2, 156
information 4, 132, 138–9, 188–217
  industries 191–2
Ingram, Paul 232–3, 237–8
intellectuals 40, 71, 80, 170, 243, 245
International Monetary Fund 193
Internet 20, 139, 208
Iteanu, André 126

Jaffe, Erik S. 158
James, Nicky 145
Jameson, Fredric 21–2, 29, 32, 42–3,
  55–6, 86–7, 93, 218, 246
Jamous, Raymond 126
Jankélévitch, Vladimir 10–11
Jarry, Alfred 27
Jaszi, Peter 139, 210, 212
Jauss, H. R. 15, 30–1
Jay, Martin 5
Jencks, Charles 21, 33
Johnson, Philip 28

Johnston, Sean 199
Joyce, James 27, 37
Juchau, Mireille 238
Juddery, Bruce 208
Jules-Rosette, Bennetta 72, 137

Kafka, Franz 27, 37
Kaha, C. W. 227
Kant, Immanuel 118, 172
Kaplan, Harold 240
Keeler, Christine 245
Ketcham, Katherine 230–2, 237
Kevles, Daniel J. 199
Kiefer, Anselm 28
Kincaid, Jamaica 99
King, Martin Luther 183
Kirshenblatt-Gimblett, Barbara 74, 99
Kloppenburg, Jack 135, 199–204
Kopytoff, Igor 143–8
Koselleck, Reinhart 30
Kostecki, M. M. 192
Kracauer, Siegfried 9
Krauss, Rosalind 41–2
Krauthaus, Patricia Ann 188
Krell, David Farrell 226
Kroker, Arthur 19
Kronos Quartet 28
Kubler, Georg 9
Kugelmass, Jack 241
kula 119–23
Kyohaku 65–6

Lacan, Jacques 28, 117
Landes, William M. 189, 210
Landow, George P. 20
Lang, Berel 239–40
Lange, David 209
Langer, Lawrence 240
language 194–5
Lanzmann, Claude 240–1
Lash, Scott 46–7, 49, 63
Latour, Bruno 1
Lautréamont 27
Law, John 3
Leach, Edmund 121
Leach, Jerry 119
Learned Hand, Justice 195
LeFanu, James 163
Lepenies, Wolf 80
Letterman, David 28
Levin, Harry 40
Levinas, Emmanuel 241
Levine, Sherrie 28

Lévi-Strauss, Claude 16, 110–11, 114–15
Lewontin, Richard 152, 198–9
liberalism 149, 151–2, 161, 209, 213
library, library model 190, 207–9
lieux de mémoire 75, 219–22, 242
life insurance 174–6
Lindsay, Bruce 193
Linebaugh, Peter 164
Linnekin, Jocelyn 77
Linton, Marigold 246
Lipietz, Alain 46
Lison, Karen 235
list 27–8
Litman, Jessica 210–12
Lock, Margaret 153
Locke, John 91, 159, 161, 204–5, 213, 227
Locksley, Gareth 188, 190
Loftus, Elizabeth 230–2, 237
Lowenthal, David 240
Lugosi, Bela 182
Lukacher, Ned 234
Lukács, Georg 5, 11, 80, 89, 132, 141–2, 147, 218
Luria, A. R. 228
Lury, Celia 183–4, 213
Luttwak, Samuel 33
Lyotard, Jean-François 14, 16, 21, 29, 37, 54–5, 241

McBurney, Blaine 17
MacCannell, Dean 70–1, 73–4, 75, 95
McCarthy, Thomas 182
McCrindle, Jean 243
Macdonalds 49
Macfarlane, Alan 133, 135
McHale, Brian 19
mémoire involontaire 223, 230, 244
mémoire volontaire 223
Macmillan, Harold 245
Maine, Henry Sumner 35, 128–9
Malinowski, Bronislaw 119, 122, 123, 126
Mallarmé, Stéphane 37
Malthus, Thomas Robert 205
mana 113
Mandel, Ernest 29
Mannix, Daniel P. 175
Marcou, George T. 192
Marcus, Greil 5

market, market system 105–6, 125,
    130–1, 137, 139, 147, 148–52,
    161, 174, 176, 178, 179, 182, 184,
    187, 197, 203, 207–9, 213–4, 217
market-inalienability 131, 148–52
Martin, Henri-Jean 139, 224
Marx, Karl; Marxism 43, 51, 53, 55,
    86, 95, 125, 127, 132, 140–3, 146,
    147, 149–50
mass culture 6, 69, 75, 89, 140, 243
mass media 241
mass tourism 98
Massey, Doreen 47
Mauss, Marcel 102–4, 106, 108,
    109–11, 114, 116–20, 122, 125–8,
    130, 193, 207, 217
memory 7–8, 10, 78, 218–46
    autobiographical 223, 229–30
    collective 219, 223, 238, 241–3
    popular 243, 245
    public 229, 243, 244
    technologies of 223, 230, 246
memory traces 223, 226–8
memory work 219, 236
metafiction 19
Michaels, Eric 137
Middler, Bette 186
Miège, Bernard 189
Mies Van Der Rohe, Ludwig 37
Mill, John Stuart 151, 161
Milton, John 59
mobile privatization 39, 215
Modak-Truran, Mark 192
modernity, modernism 1, 3–4, 5, 6, 7,
    9, 10, 15, 29–32, 33–8, 40–2,
    71–2, 75–7, 80–2, 87, 101, 102,
    112, 136, 188, 196, 218, 222
    end of modernity 9
modernization 2, 34–6, 71
Moller-Olkin, S. 214
Monsanto 200
Monty Python 28
Mooney, Pat 156, 201–2
Moore, John 154–61, 173
moral economy 124, 130, 147, 187
moral person 126–7, 148
moral rights (droit moral) 184, 194,
    212
Morris, Ian 215
Morris, Meaghan 27, 54–5, 80
Morse, Margaret 39, 215–16, 218–19
Mortinger, Stephen Ashley 158, 160
Mosk, Justice 159

Motschenbacher, Lothar 185
Mulgan, Geoff 207
Murray, Thomas 216–7
Muzak 33, 45, 49
    Nachträglichkeit 229

nature 194–204
neoclassicism 38, 57
neoliberalism 32, 104, 149, 151, 209
Newman, Michael 40
Nietzsche, Friedrich 33, 52
Nijar, Gurdial Singh 201
Nimmer, Melville 181
Nimmer, Raymond T. 188
Noin 65
non-space (non-place) 39, 45, 75–7
Nora, Pierre 219–23
Norris, Christopher 22–3
nostalgia 2, 11, 71, 77–81, 86, 87, 94,
    142, 215, 222, 225
    nostalgic paradigm 80

objectification 140–10
O'Callaghan, Mary Louise 154
Ofshe, Richard 230, 232–3, 235, 237
Ohnuki-Tierney, Emiko 177–8
Olson, Charles 27
Onassis, Jacqueline 185–6
O'Neill, John 23
Ong, Walter 224
    ostranenie 38
ownership 126, 161
    Papunya Tula 136

Parizeau, Marie-Hélène 172
Parry, Jonathan 126
Parsons, Talcott 35
Pashukanis, Evgeny B. 126, 161
passing-off tort 186–7
Pateman, Carole 145, 177
patent 153–6, 160, 189, 190–2,
    194–202
Paz, Octavio 38
Pazder, L. 238
Pefanis, Julian 118
Pendergrast, Mark 230, 237
Perec, Georges 244–6
periodization 3, 8, 27, 28–32, 36–8,
    40–42, 43, 87, 138–9
Perrault, Charles 31
person 4, 110, 114, 123–7, 130,
    131–2, 137, 141, 143, 145, 147,
    148–52, 154–62, 172, 177–8, 182,
    184–8, 196, 197, 205, 214–15

photography 67, 73, 87, 92–4, 186, 218, 230
picturesque 92, 97
Piore, Michael J. 46
plant varieties 199–204
Plato 68, 93
Polan, Dana 16
Pollock, Jackson 61
Ponge, Francis 61
Popular Memory Group 243
Portman, John 42–3
Portoghesi, Paolo 41
Posey, Darrell 202
positional competition 95–7
Posner, Richard 149–51, 189, 210
possession 103, 120, 123, 126–7, 174,, 189
postcard 93–4
Post-Fordism 6, 46–9, 51
postmodern, postmodernity, postmodernism 1, 3–4, 7–8, 13–63, 74, 78, 86–7, 89, 242
postmodernization 34
Poston, Carol 235
post-tourism 75
potlatch 114–19, 127
   donative and destructive forms 117
Pound, Ezra 27, 130
Powers, Richard 19
Presley, Elvis 179–80, 213
prestation 109, 111, 114, 116, 120, 122, 130, 207
price mechanism 207, 217
price system 106
primal scene 234
Pringle, Rosemary 216
prisoner's dilemma 205
Probyn, Elspeth 28
Profumo, John 245
proper name 20, 26, 59–61, 64, 185, 244–5
property, property right 120, 122, 126–9, 133–4, 139, 145, 149–52, 154–61, 173–4, 180, 182–4, 186–8, 191–2, 195, 200, 203, 205–6, 209–11
Proust, Marcel 59, 61, 223, 245
Przeworski, Adam 48
public domain 180, 183, 194–5, 198, 204, 209–15, 246
public historical sphere 245
public sphere 11, 212–13, 215–16
Pynchon, Thomas 19, 27

Queneau, Raymond 27

Raban, Jonathan 98–9
Rabinow, Paul 178
Radin, Margaret 131, 135, 148–52, 161
Ranaipiri, Tamati 109–12, 114
Ranger, Terence 77
rape 149–52
rationality 16, 33, 34, 35, 41, 51, 53, 78, 117, 142, 177, 217
rationalization 141–2, 175
Rauschenberg, Robert 28
Readers Digest 246
reciprocity 104–5, 107–8, 112, 114–15, 117–20, 122–4, 129–31, 188
recovered memories 230–8
Redfoot, Donald L. 69, 95
reference, referentiality 20, 22, 27, 43, 68, 71, 186
Regulation School 46
reification 141–2
Relph, E. 45
Rendra, W. S. 61
repetition 37, 65, 81, 90, 129, 142, 220, 225, 227
repressed memory 234, 236
   res mancipi 128
   res nec mancipi 128
Resnais, Alain 225
restricted economy 108, 111, 116, 119
resurrection 177–8
Reynolds, Barbara 186
Reynolds, R. Larry 170
Richard, Nelly 57–8
right of privacy 180–3, 185–6
right of publicity 160, 179–87
rights of personality 162, 179–87
Rimbaud, Arthur 27
Rivera, Geraldo 238
Rivers, Larry 28
Roberts, David 40
Roberts, L. 152–3
Robertson, Roland 80
Robins, Kevin 46–8
Roediger, Henry 226
Rolling Stones 29
Rose, Carole 206, 213
Rose, D. 146
Rose, Mark 210
Rosen, Stanley 37
Rosenberg, Peter D. 194

Roth, Philip 28
Roussel, Raymond 27
Rowbotham, Sheila 243
Rud, James 232
Rural Advancement Fund International 153–4
Rushdie, Salman 19
Ruskin, John 76
Rustin, Michael 48–9

Sabel, Charles F. 46
sacrifice 117, 124, 143
Sade, D. A. F. de 27
Sahlins, Marshall 111–2, 126
Sakai, Naoki 1–2
Sampu 66
Samuel, Raphael 79
Sandoz 155–6, 200
Sapolsky, Harvey M. 104
Satanism, satanic rites 232–4, 238
Schapiro, Meyer 84–5
Schaver, P. R. 233
Scheper-Hughes, Nancy 167–9
Scheppele, Kim Lane 189
Scherpe, Klaus 17
Schiller, Anita 208–9
Schiller, Dan 138
Schiller, Friedrich von 2, 140
Schiller, Herbert 208–9
Schmidt, Catherine Joanne 65, 67
Schneider, Andrew 163
Schoenberg, Arnold 37
Schulte-Sasse, Jochen 32
scientific ethos 193
Seabrook, Jeremy 200–1
secret 189, 193–4
Sendero Luminoso 169
Sennett, Richard 212
Serres, Michel 119
Sex Pistols 5
Shell 200
Sherman, Rorie 155
signature 43, 62, 140, 146
Simmel, Georg 80, 106–7, 141, 143, 189
simulacrum, simulation 7, 27, 51, 68–70, 73–4, 87, 90, 196, 218, 246
Sin, Cardinal 163
Sittlichkeit 124
Sinatra, Frank 28
Sinatra, Nancy 186
Singer, Barbara 179
Situationist International 4–5

slavery 133, 135, 144, 156, 158–9, 161, 175
Smith, Jane S. 183
Smith, Marlin 212
Smith, M. 238
Smith, Neil 47, 146
Smith, Valene 95
Snyder, Alvin A. 168
Sodo 66
Soja, Edward 29, 44
Soleri, Daniela 203
Sorabji, Richard 226
souvenir 93–4, 99
space/time 7, 8–9, 11, 34, 52–3, 75, 94, 142, 189, 224–6
spectacle 5–7
Spiegelman, Art 239
spiritual exercises 235, 237–8
sport 145, 149
Stack, Michael 204
Stafford, Barbara 91
Stanberry, Kurt 191
star system 20, 183, 245
Starobinsky, Jean 79
Stauth, Georg 80, 222
Stein, Gertrude 27
Sterne, Lawrence 27
Stewart, Susan 8, 72, 79, 81, 93–4
Stone, Allucquère Rosanne 20
stranger 104–6, 153, 162, 212
Stratford, Lauren 238
Strathern, Marilyn 123, 126–7, 129, 152, 187, 196
sublime 14, 31
subsidy 202, 207–8
successorial contracts 171, 175
supplement 86
Swazey, Judith 105, 170
Swerdlow, Joel L. 171
Swift, Jonathan 169
    tabula rasa 225
    taonga 109–10, 113–14, 129

Tavris, Carol 231, 236
Taylorism 142
television 5, 14, 18, 19, 20, 23–6, 33, 39, 45, 61–3, 89–90, 139, 218, 238, 242, 245
Terr, Lenore 232
Terrell, Timothy P. 183
Tharp, Twyla 28
Thatcher, Margaret 171
    thesaurus 225–6

Thomas, Nicholas 77, 123–4, 147
Thompson, E. P. 134, 205
Tilley, Leslie 208
Tipps, Dean 35–6
Titmuss, Richard 104–6, 176, 214
Tönnies, Ferdinand 35, 80
tort law 150, 173, 214
tourism, tourists 49, 64–101
  tourist art 137, 146
  tourist gaze 67, 92, 96
  tourist industry 99–100
  tourist sight 65–6, 77
  tourist site 70, 73–4
  tourist space 75, 77
  touristic shame 95–6, 99
trademark 189, 194
tradition 21, 33, 35, 72, 75, 77–9, 81, 136
  traditional knowledge 203
  traditional societies 8, 33–6, 71, 87, 102, 105, 113, 220, 222
traveller 69–70, 81, 87, 95
Trilling, Lionel 38
Turner, Brian 80, 222
Turner, Ethel 94
Turner, J.M.W. 14
Turner, John 69, 73, 95
Turner, Victor 94
typicality 67–8, 88–9

UNCTAD 193
Underwager, Ralph 230
UNESCO 193
  Ungleichzeitigkeit 9
Upjohn 200
Urbain, Jean-Didier 69
urban legend 168–70
Urry, John 46–7, 49, 75, 92, 95–6, 99
use value 81, 87, 134, 141–3, 189, 200
Usta, Ferhat 164, 178

Valeri, Valerio 127
Van Caenegem, W. 187
van den Abbeele, Georges 74
Van Gogh, Vincent 61, 82, 85, 86–7
Vattimo, Gianni 37–8
  Verdinglichung 141–2
  Vergegenständlichung 140–1
Victor, Jeffrey S. 238
Vidal-Naquet, Pierre 239
video clips 19

Volosinov, V.N. 148

wage labour 133, 135–6, 159, 173
Wakefield, Hollida 230
Wallerstein, Immanuel 134
Walpole, Robert 174
Warhol, Andy 26, 86–7
Warning, Rainer 32
Warren, Samuel 180–1
Watkins, Kevin 201
Watson, James 198
Watter, Ethan 230, 232, 235
Weber, Max 34, 80, 141
Webern, Anton von 37
Wedin, Michael V. 226
Weiner, Annette 112–14, 120, 122, 129–30, 148
Wellmer, Albrecht 33
White, Hayden 239–40
Wickham, Chris 228
Wievorka, Annette 241
Wilkie, Tom 198
Williams, Peter 146
Williams, Raymond 56
Wilson, Robert 28
WIPO 193
Wolfe, Tom 28
Wollen, Peter 4, 10, 19
women's wealth 113, 129
Woodmansee, Martha 210
Woods, Peggy 243
Woolley, Penelope 224
Wordsworth, William 96–9
World Bank 193
Worpole, Ken 219
Wright, Lawrence 232–4, 237–8
Wright, Patrick 77–9, 146, 245
writing 223–6
Wu Hongda, Harry 163

Yapko, Michael 230, 233
Yerushalmi, Yosef 219
Young, Edward 210
Young, James 242

Zelizer, Viviana A. 174–5
Zerubavel, Yael 242
Zizek, Slavoj 229
Zola, Émile 83
Zuckerman, Antek 243
Zukin, Sharon 44, 45, 48, 49, 146